The Writer's World
Essays
With Enhanced Reading Strategies

Fourth Edition

Lynne gaetz
Lionel Groulx College

Suneeti phadke
St. Jerome College

Pearson 330 Hudson Street, NY NY 10013

VP & Portfolio Manager: Eric Stano
Development Consulting: V. Tomaiuolo
Project Marketer: Fiona Murray
Program Manager: Erin Bosco
Project Coordination, Text Design, and Electronic Page Makeup: SPi Global
Cover: Pentagram
Cover illustration: Anju Shrestha
Senior Manufacturing Buyer: Roy L. Pickering, Jr.
Printer/Binder: LSC Communications/Crawfordsville
Cover Printer: Pheonix Color/Hagerstown

Library of Congress Cataloging-in-Publication Data

Gaetz, Lynne, 1960– author. | Phadke, Suneeti, 1961– author.
The writer's world: essays; with enhanced reading strategies / Lynne
   Gaetz, Suneeti Phadke.
Fourth edition. | Boston : Pearson, 2017.
LCCN 2017002011 | ISBN 9780134195414 (student edition) |
   ISBN 9780134277943 (annotated instructor edition) |
   ISBN 9780134277981 (loose leaf)
LCSH: English language—Rhetoric—Problems, exercises, etc. |
   Report writing—Problems, exercises, etc.
LCC PE1413 .G34 2017 | DDC 808.4—dc23
LC record available at https://lccn.loc.gov/2017002011

3 17

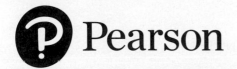

Student Edition ISBN-13:   978-0-13-419541-4
Student Edition ISBN-10:   0-13-419541-8
A la Carte Edition ISBN-13:   978-0-13-427798-1
A la Carte Edition ISBN-10:   0-13-427798-8

Brief Contents

Contents

APPENDICES

Inside Back Cover

Editing Checklist
Revising and Editing Symbols

Readings Listed by Rhetorical Mode

Preface

Thank you for making *The Writer's World* series a resounding success. We are delighted that *Essays* has been able to help so many students produce writing that is technically correct and richly detailed, whether students have varying skill levels, are native or nonnative speakers of English, or learn more effectively using visuals.

When we started writing the first edition, we set out to develop practical and pedagogically sound approaches to these challenges. We began with the idea that collaboration is crucial. So we met with more than forty-five instructors from around the country, asking for their opinions and insights regarding (1) the challenges posed by the course, (2) the needs of today's ever-changing student population, and (3) the ideas and features we were proposing in order to provide a more effective teaching and learning tool. For that first edition and every edition since, Pearson also commissioned dozens of detailed manuscript reviews from instructors, asking them to analyze and evaluate each draft of the manuscript. These reviewers identified numerous ways in which we could refine and enhance our key features. Their invaluable feedback has been incorporated throughout *The Writer's World*. This text is truly the product of a successful partnership between the authors, publisher, and more than one hundred developmental writing instructors.

What's New in the Fourth Edition?

Revel™

Educational Technology Designed for the Way Today's Students Read, Think, and Learn

When students are engaged deeply, they learn more effectively and perform better in their courses. This simple fact inspired the creation of Revel: an interactive learning environment designed for the way today's students read, think, and learn.

Revel enlivens course content with media interactives and assessments—integrated directly within the authors' narrative—that provide opportunities for students to read, practice, and study in one continuous experience. This immersive educational technology replaces the textbook and is designed to measurably boost students' understanding, retention, and preparedness.

Learn more about Revel at http://www.pearsonhighered.com/revel/.

Enhanced Reading Support

Brimming with insightful readings and vocabulary tips, *The Writer's World* series has always drawn attention to the strong connection between reading and writing. This edition goes a step further by offering **extra reading strategies** in a new Chapter 40, such as previewing, determining meaning, making inferences, and interpreting visuals. Students build their reading skills as they work on dozens of sample paragraphs, essays, and practices. By enhancing their reading skills, students are also better equipped to do research for essay writing.

2016 Modern Language Association (MLA) Updates

In Spring 2016, the Modern Language Association (MLA) published updates to their writing and documentation guidelines. We've updated

Chapter 17, "The Research Essay," and related content to reflect the new in-text citation and Works Cited formats.

New Grammar Practices

One-third of the practices in Part IV: The Editing Handbook are new, providing updated grammar and style instruction through the lens of topical and culturally relevant content. All of the themes—from Travel and Survival to Inventions and Discoveries—were chosen to appeal to Developmental Writing students of any background.

New Readings

In Chapter 41, six new thought-provoking essays discuss timely topics, including public shaming online, the paradoxes of technology, fake online reviews, and the power of "nudges" by schools, marketers, and governments to encourage certain life choices. As with all *The Writer's World* readings, students can respond to engaging prompts that test comprehension, applied knowledge, and writing skills.

New and Updated Media Writing Prompts

Like many of us, students rely heavily on mobile devices. In a single day, a student may listen to a podcast while commuting, stream music while studying, scroll through or post to social media while waiting for a food order, or watch videos before turning in for the night. In *The Writer's World*, the end-of-chapter writing prompts in Chapters 6–14 have been updated to include more forms of media, including **podcasts**, **film**, **music**, and **online video**. The Media Writing prompts suggest titles and episodes to help ignite ideas about each writing topic. For example, podcast suggestions include highly rated,

Millennial-friendly TED Radio Hour, Planet Money, Serial, and Marc Maron's WTF. And film selections, such as *Ex-Machina* and *The Revenant*, range from independent to mainstream movies.

New "At Work" Paragraphs

Chapters 6–14 feature examples of the nine writing modes applied to real-world contexts. In this edition, new "At Work" paragraphs include an early childhood educator's summary about a young client's social development and some customer-care how-to's from a hospitality management training manual. All are annotated to highlight the individual elements of each paragraph (topic sentence, supporting ideas, and concluding statement).

A Fresh Look

An updated, clean, and modern design streamlines instruction and increases usability, allowing students to more effectively find and retain the information covered. And, of course, our signature "sunglasses" are back on the cover by popular demand!

How *The Writer's World* Meets Students' Diverse Needs

We created *The Writer's World* to meet your students' diverse needs. To accomplish this, we asked both the instructors in our focus groups and the reviewers at every stage not only to critique our ideas but also to offer their suggestions and recommendations for features that would enhance the learning process of their students. The result has been the integration of many elements that are not found in other textbooks, including our **visual program, coverage of nonnative speaker material, and strategies for addressing the varying skill levels students bring to the course**.

The Visual Program

A stimulating, full-color book with more than 160 photos, *The Writer's World* recognizes that today's world is a visual one, and it encourages students to become better communicators by responding to images. Chapter-opening visuals in Parts I, II, and III help students to think about the chapter's key concept in a new way.

The visuals in Part II provide students with another set of opportunities to write in response to images, with Media Writing activities that encourage them to respond using particular paragraph and essay patterns.

Throughout *The Writer's World*, words and images work together to encourage students to explore, develop, and revise their writing.

Seamless Coverage for Nonnative Speakers

Instructors in our focus groups consistently note the number of nonnative/ESL/ELL students enrolling in writing courses. Although some of these students have special needs related to the writing process, many native speakers in your courses have more traditional needs that must be met. In order to address this rapidly changing dynamic, we have carefully implemented and integrated content throughout to assist these students.

The Writer's World does not have separate ESL boxes, ESL chapters, or tacked-on ESL appendices. Instead, information that traditionally poses a challenge to nonnative speakers is woven seamlessly throughout the book. In our extensive experience teaching writing to both native and nonnative speakers of English, we have learned that both groups learn best when they are not distracted by ESL labels. With the seamless approach, nonnative speakers do not feel self-conscious and segregated, and native speakers do not tune out detailed explanations that may also benefit them. Many of these traditional problem areas receive more coverage than you would find in other textbooks, arming the instructor with the material to effectively meet the needs of nonnative speakers. Moreover, the *Annotated Instructor's Edition* provides more than seventy-five ESL Teaching Tips designed specifically to help instructors better meet the needs of their nonnative-speaking students.

Issue-Focused Thematic Grammar

In surveys, many of you indicated that one of the primary challenges in teaching your course is finding materials that are engaging to students in a contemporary context. This is especially true in grammar instruction. **Students come to the course with varying skill levels**, and many students are simply not interested in grammar. To address this challenge, we introduced **issue-focused thematic grammar** into *The Writer's World*.

Each chapter centers on a theme that is carried out in examples and activities. These themes include topics related to conflict, urban development, travel and survival, inventions and discoveries, our natural world, and human development. The thematic approach enables students to broaden their awareness of subjects important to American life, such as understanding how to manage relationships or finances. The thematic approach makes reading about grammar more engaging. And the more engaging grammar is, the more likely students are to retain key concepts—raising their skill level in these important building blocks of writing.

We also think that it is important to teach grammar in the context of the writing process. Students should not think that grammar is an isolated exercise. Therefore, each grammar chapter concludes with writing activities.

What Tools Can Help Students Get the Most from *The Writer's World*?

Overwhelmingly, focus group participants and reviewers asked that both a larger number and a greater diversity of exercises and activities be incorporated into *The Writer's World*. In response, we have developed and tested the following learning aids in *The Writer's World*. We are confident they will help your students become better writers.

Hints

In each chapter, **Hint** boxes highlight important writing and grammar points. Hints are useful for all students, but many will be particularly helpful for nonnative speakers. For example, in Chapter 14, one Hint encourages students to state an argument directly and a second Hint explains how research can strengthen an essay. In Chapter 22, a Hint discusses word order in embedded questions. Hints include brief discussions and examples so that students will see both concept and application.

Vocabulary Boosts

Throughout Part II of *The Writer's World*, Vocabulary Boost boxes give students tips to improve their use of language and to revise and edit their word choices. For example, a Vocabulary Boost in Chapter 6 asks students to replace repeated words with synonyms, and the one in Chapter 8 explains how to use vivid language. These lessons give students concrete strategies and specific advice for improving their diction.

The Writer's Desk

Parts I, II, and III include **The Writer's Desk** exercises, which help students get used to practicing all stages and steps of the writing process. As the chapter progresses, students warm up with a prewriting activity and then use specific methods for developing, organizing (using paragraph and essay plans), drafting, and finally, revising and editing to create a final draft.

The Writer's Room

The Writer's Room contains writing activities that correspond to general, college, and workplace topics. Some prompts are brief to allow students to freely form ideas while others are expanded to give students more direction.

There is something for every student writer in this end-of-chapter feature. Students who respond well to visual or auditory cues will appreciate the television, film, music, podcast, and online media writing prompts in The Writer's Room in Part II: Essay Patterns. To help students see how grammar is not isolated from the writing process, there are also The Writer's Room activities at the ends of sections 1–6 in Part IV: The Editing Handbook.

How We Organized *The Writer's World*

The Writer's World: Essays is separated into five parts for ease of use, convenience, and ultimate flexibility.

Part I: The Writing Process Part I teaches students (1) how to formulate ideas (Exploring); (2) how to expand, organize, and present those ideas in a piece of writing (Developing); and (3) how to polish writing so that they convey their message as clearly as possible (Revising and

Editing). The result is that writing a paragraph or an essay becomes far less daunting because students have specific steps to follow.

Part II: Essay Patterns Part II gives students a solid overview of the patterns of development. Using the same easy-to-understand process (Exploring, Developing, and Revising and Editing), each chapter in this section explains how to convey ideas using one or more writing patterns. As they work through the practices and write their own essays, students begin to see how using a writing pattern can help them fulfill their purpose for writing.

Part III: More College and Workplace Writing Part III covers topics ranging from the letter and résumé to the research essay. This section also explains how to respond to films and literary works and how to prepare for essay exams.

Part IV: The Editing Handbook Part IV is a thematic grammar handbook. In each chapter, the examples correspond to a theme, such as conflict, inventions and discoveries, and human development. As students work through the chapters, they hone their grammar and editing skills while gaining knowledge about a variety of topics. In addition to helping build interest in the grammar practices, the thematic material provides a spark that ignites new ideas that students can apply to their writing.

Part V: Reading Strategies and Selections Part V offers tips, readings, and follow-up questions. Students learn how to write by observing and dissecting what they read. The readings relate to the themes found in Part IV: The Editing Handbook, providing more fodder for generating writing ideas.

Pearson Writing Resources for Instructors and Students

Book-Specific Ancillary Material

Annotated Instructor's Edition for *The Writer's World: Essays*, 4/e

The AIE offers in-text answers, and marginal annotations for teaching each chapter. It is a valuable resource for experienced and first-time instructors alike.

Instructor's Resource Manual for *The Writer's World: Essays*, 4/e

The material in the IRM is designed to save instructors time and provide them with effective options for teaching their writing classes. It offers suggestions for setting up their course; provides lots of extra practice for students who need it; offers quizzes and grammar tests, including unit tests; furnishes grading rubrics for each rhetorical mode; and supplies answers in case instructors want to print them out and have students grade their own work. This valuable resource is exceptionally useful for adjuncts who might need advice in setting up their initial classes or who might be teaching a variety of writing classes with too many students and not enough time.

PowerPoint Presentation for *The Writer's World: Essays, 4/e*

PowerPoint presentations to accompany each chapter consist of classroom-ready lecture outline slides, lecture tips and classroom activities, and review questions. Available for download from the Instructor Resource Center.

Answer Key for *The Writer's World: Essays, 4/e*

The Answer Key contains the solutions to the exercises in the student edition of the text. Available for download from the Instructor Resource Center.

MyWritingLab

MyWritingLab, a complete online learning resource, provides additional practice exercises and engaging animations for developing writers. It accelerates learning through layered assessment and a personalized learning path using the Knewton Adaptive Learning Platform™, which customizes standardized educational content. Each student receives the perfect personalized bundle of content. With over eight thousand exercises and immediate feedback to answers, the integrated learning aids of MyWritingLab reinforce learning throughout the semester.

Additional Resources

Pearson is pleased to offer a variety of support materials to help make writing instruction easier for teachers and to help students excel in their coursework. Many of our student supplements are available for free or at a greatly reduced price when packaged with *The Writer's World: Essays, 4/e*. Visit www.pearsonhighereducation.com, contact your local Pearson sales representative, or review a detailed listing of the full supplements package in the *Instructor's Resource Manual* for more information.

Acknowledgments

Many people have helped us produce *The Writer's World*. First and foremost, we would like to thank our students for inspiring us and providing us with extraordinary feedback. Their words and insights pervade this book.

We also benefited greatly from the insightful comments and suggestions from more than one hundred instructors across the nation, all of whom are listed in the opening pages of the *Annotated Instructor's Edition*. Our colleagues' feedback was invaluable and helped shape *The Writer's World* series content, focus, and organization.

Reviewers

The following reviewers provided insight and assistance in the latest revision of *The Writer's World* series:

Tia Adger, Piedmont Technical College; Phillip Bannowsky, University of Delaware; Betty Benns, Orangeburg-Calhoun Technical College; Justin Bonnett, Saint Paul College; Cheryl Borman, Hillsborough CC, Ybor City Campus; Adam Carlberg, Tallahessee CC; Judith L. Carter, Amarillo College; Connie Caskey, Jefferson State CC; Zoe Ann Cerny, Horry-Georgetown Technical College; Cathy J. Clements, State Fair CC; Michael F. Courteau, St. Paul College; Cynthia Dawes, Edgecombe CC; Mary F. Di Stefano Diaz, Broward College; Claudia Edwards, Piedmont CC; Stephanie Fischer, Southern Connecticut State University; Paul Gallagher, Red Rocks CC; Kim Allen Gleed, Harrisburg Area CC; Ellen Hernandez, Camden CC; Karen Hindhede, Central Arizona College; Schahara Hudelson, South Plains College; Nikkina Hughes, Tarrant CC; Dianna W. Hydem, Jefferson State CC; Stacy Janicki, Ridgewater College; Patrice Johnson, Dallas County CC District; Jennifer Johnston, Hillsborough CC; Julie Keenan, Harrisburg Area CC; Patricia A. Lacey, Harper College; Nicole Lacroix, Red Rock

CC; Ruth K. MacDonald, Lincoln College of New England; Joy McClain, Ivy Technical CC, Evansville; Heather Moulton, Central Arizona College; Ellen Olmstead, Montgomery College; Deborah Peterson, Blinn College; Rebecca Portis, Montgomery College; Sharon Race, South Plains College; Lisa M. Russell, Georgia Northwestern Technical College; Stephanie Sabourin, Montgomery College; Sharisse Turner, Tallahassee CC; Samantha Vance, Chattahoochee Valley CC; Jody Wheeler, Saint Paul College; Julie Yankanich, Camden County College

We are indebted to the team of dedicated professionals who have helped make this project a reality. They have boosted our spirits and have believed in us every step of the way. Special thanks to Veronica Tomaiuolo for developing this series and to Matthew Wright for trusting our instincts and enthusiastically propelling us forward and to Diego Pelaez-Gaetz for writing contemporary and thought provoking grammar practices. We would also like to thank Kathleen Reynolds for her help finding relevant readings. We owe a deep debt of gratitude to Yolanda de Rooy, whose encouraging words helped ignite *The Writer's World* project. Ohlinger Publishing Services helped keep us motivated and on task during the production process. Thanks to everyone's efforts, *The Writer's World* is a much better resource for both instructors and students.

Finally, we would like to dedicate this book to our families who supported us and who patiently put up with our long hours on the computer. Manu and Murray continually encouraged us, as did Diego, Rebeka, Kiran, and Meghana.

A Note to Students

Your knowledge, ideas, and opinions are important. The ability to clearly communicate those ideas is invaluable in your personal, academic, and professional life. When your writing is error-free, readers will focus on your message, and you will be able to persuade, inform, entertain, or inspire them. *The Writer's World* includes strategies that will help you improve your reading skills and written communication. Quite simply, when you become a better reader and writer, you become a better communicator. It is our greatest wish for *The Writer's World* to make you excited about learning. Enjoy!

Lynne Gaetz and Suneeti Phadke

Lynne Gaetz in Morocco

Suneeti Phadke in India

Part I
The Writing Process

CHAPTER 1 EXPLORING
- Think about your topic.
- Think about your audience.
- Think about your purpose.
- Try exploring strategies.

CHAPTER 2, 3, 4 DEVELOPING
- Express your main idea.
- Develop your supporting ideas.
- Make a plan or an outline.
- Write your first draft.

CHAPTER 5 REVISING AND EDITING
- Revise for unity.
- Revise for adequate support.
- Revise for style.
- Edit for technical errors.

Model Paragraph

A sentence is a group of words (at least one subject and one verb) that expresses an idea. A paragraph is a series of sentences that are about one central idea. Paragraphs can stand alone, or they can be part of a longer work such as an essay or report. The topic sentence expresses the main idea, and body sentences develop that idea. Most paragraphs end with a concluding sentence that brings the paragraph to a satisfactory close.

Many people protest that their vote doesn't matter, but each vote can make a difference. For instance, in Vermont's 1997 election, representative Sydney Nixon lost by one vote. In the 1974 senate election in New Hampshire, there was a two-vote difference between Louis Wyman and John A. Durkin. Also, large enough groups of like-minded people can change policies and laws, so voting can lead to concrete results. Everyone should remember that each and every vote counts!

The **topic sentence** expresses the main point of the paragraph.

The **supporting ideas** contain details and examples.

The **concluding sentence** brings the paragraph to a close.

Model Essay

An essay consists of an introduction, several body paragraphs, and a conclusion. Observe the parts of the sample essay.

The Importance of Voting

Most people get involved in politics for the right reasons. For instance, they say they want to make a difference. Each person in the country can also make a difference. Every time there is an election, there is an action that everyone should take. Everyone should vote for three reasons.

First, it is easy to vote. During each election, students and workers are given enough hours to present themselves to polling stations. There are a lot of volunteers who ensure that the voting process is smooth. Those with limited mobility can get a ride to the polling station, usually by a team from the party that they are supporting. College student Luc Robitaille says, "It only took twenty minutes of my time to vote."

Furthermore, many people protest that their vote doesn't matter, but each vote can make a difference. For instance, in Vermont's 1997 election, representative Sydney Nixon lost by one vote. In the 1974 senate election in New Hampshire, there was a two-vote difference between Louis Wyman and John A. Durkin. Also, large enough groups of like-minded people can change policies and laws, so voting can lead to concrete results. Everyone should remember that each and every vote counts.

Finally, North Americans should value their right to vote, remembering that people in other nations suffer horribly just because they want democracy. In many nations, pro-democracy supporters are sent to prison. Myanmar politician Aung San Suu Kyi spent almost fifteen years under house arrest because she wanted free and open elections. In 2011, Iranian officials arrested and jailed the leader of the reform movement, Mir-Hossein Mousavi. Also, during the past few years, protesters in Egypt, Tunisia, and Libya have been killed during their fight to have free and open elections. When people live in a nation that has a thriving democracy, it is their duty to support it.

Unfortunately, many people are cynical about politics. But each vote is important, and the right to vote is a historical right that everyone should respect. As critic and editor George Jean Nathan said, "Bad officials are elected by good citizens who do not vote."

The **introduction** generates interest in the topic. The **thesis statement** expresses the essay's topic and controlling idea.

Each **body paragraph** begins with a **topic sentence** that supports the thesis and contains details and examples.

The **concluding paragraph** briefly restates the main points and ends with a suggestion, prediction, or quotation.

1 Exploring

LEARNING OBJECTIVES

1.1 Follow the key steps in exploring.

1.2 Define topic.

1.3 Define audience.

1.4 Define purpose.

1.5 Use exploring strategies.

1.6 Keep a journal and writing portfolio.

Before planting seeds or shrubs, a gardener might look for ideas in magazines, online, or in nurseries. Similarly, a writer uses various prewriting strategies to explore topics for writing.

Key Steps in Exploring

1.1 Follow the key steps in exploring.

Essay-length prose is the backbone of written communication in and out of college. Throughout your life, you will use principles of essay writing in various written communications, including research papers, emails, reports, formal letters, newsletters, and Web pages. Essays help you explore ideas and share those thoughts with others. By reading through this text and completing the many helpful writing practices in it, you will significantly improve your chances of getting more out of your courses and jobs. Enjoy the journey!

Perhaps you recently received a writing assignment and have been staring at the blank page, thinking, "I don't know what to write." Well, it is not necessary to write a good essay immediately. There are certain things that you can do to focus on your topic.

Understand Your Assignment

As soon as you receive an assignment, make sure that you understand the task. Answer the following questions about the assignment.

- How many words or pages does the assignment require?
- What is the due date for the assignment?
- Are there any special qualities it should include? For example, should it be double-spaced? Should it include a list of references or works cited?

After you have thought about your assignment, consider the following four key steps in the exploring stage of the writing process.

Exploring

STEP 1 **Think about your topic.** Determine what you will write about.

STEP 2 **Think about your audience.** Consider your intended readers and what interests them.

STEP 3 **Think about your purpose.** Ask yourself what your goal is.

STEP 4 **Try exploring strategies.** Experiment with different ways to generate ideas.

Topic

1.2   Define topic.

Your **topic**, or **subject**, is what you are writing about. When an instructor gives you a writing topic, narrow the topic and find an angle that interests you. When you think about your topic, ask yourself the following questions.

- What special knowledge do I have about the topic?
- What subtopics are most relevant to me?
- What aspect of the topic do I care deeply about?

Audience

1.3   Define audience.

In your personal, academic, and professional life, you will often write for a specific **audience**—the people who will read what you write. You can keep your readers interested by adapting your tone and vocabulary to suit them.

Tone shows your general attitude or feeling toward a topic. You might write in a tone that is humorous, sarcastic, or serious. For example, before writing invitations to an event, you would probably consider how well you know the guests as well as their ages, lifestyles, gender, and even communication styles (snail mail or online).

Knowing your reader is especially important when you are preparing academic or workplace documents. When you consider your audience, ask yourself the following questions.

- Who will read my essay? Will my instructor be my only reader, or will others also read it?
- What does my audience already know about the topic?
- What information will my readers expect?
- Should I use formal or informal language?
- How should I adjust my vocabulary and tone to appeal to my readers?

HINT: Instructor as the Audience

Your instructor represents a general audience. Such an audience of educated readers will expect you to use correct grammar and to reveal what you have learned or understood about the topic. Do not leave out information because you assume that your instructor is an expert in the field. Your ideas should be presented in a clear and organized manner.

Purpose

1.4   Define purpose.

Your **purpose** is your reason for writing. Sometimes you may have more than one purpose. When you consider your purpose, ask yourself the following questions.

- Is my goal to **entertain**? Do I want to tell a personal story or anecdote?
- Is my goal to **persuade**? Do I want to convince readers that my point of view is the correct one?
- Is my goal to **inform**? Do I want to explain something or present information?

HINT: General and Specific Purpose

Your **general purpose** is to entertain, inform, or persuade. Your **specific purpose** is your more precise reason for writing. For example, imagine that you are writing about music. You can have the following general and specific purposes.

> **General purpose:** to inform
> **Specific purpose:** to explain how to become a better musician

Practice 1

As you read the following messages, consider the differences in both the tone and the vocabulary the writer uses. Then answer the questions that follow.

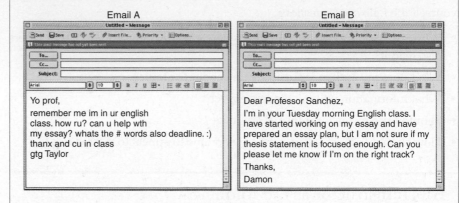

Email A

Yo prof,
remember me im in ur english
class. how ru? can u help wth
my essay? whats the # words also deadline. :)
thanx and cu in class
gtg Taylor

Email B

Dear Professor Sanchez,
I'm in your Tuesday morning English class. I
have started working on my essay and have
prepared an essay plan, but I am not sure if my
thesis statement is focused enough. Can you
please let me know if I'm on the right track?
Thanks,
Damon

1. Why is the language inappropriate in the first instant message?

_____

_____

2. What judgments, based on the messages, might the instructor make about the two students?

_____

_____

Practice 2

The following selections are all about food; however, each excerpt has a different purpose, has been written for a different audience, and has been taken from a different source. Read each selection carefully. Then underline any language clues (words or phrases) that help you identify the selection's source, audience, and purpose. Finally, answer the questions that follow each selection.

EXAMPLE:

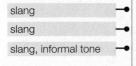

slang

slang

slang, informal tone

I just made my very first dessert. It looks awesome. I hope it tastes alright. I almost freaked out when I realized I forgot to turn the oven on. My instructor is super, and he's got a great sense of humor with me and the other students. Next, I am going to try to make a more complicated dessert.

What is the most likely source of this paragraph?

a. website article   b. ⟨personal journal⟩   c. textbook   d. memoir

What is its primary purpose? <u>to inform</u>

Who is the audience? <u>friend or family member</u>

1.   I never mastered the art of the thump. Whether the melon is ripe or not, the thump sounds the same to me. Each one I cut, however, seems to be at its pinnacle—toothy crispness, audacious sweetness. . . . Sitting on the stone wall, sun on my face, big slice of watermelon—I'm seven again, totally engrossed in shooting seeds between my fingers and spooning out circles from the dripping quarter moon of fruit.

What is the most likely source of this paragraph?

a. website article   b. personal journal   c. textbook   d. memoir

What is its primary purpose? _____

Who is the audience? _____

_____

2.   Eat regularly. Eating is one of life's great pleasures, and it is important to take time to stop, relax, and enjoy mealtimes and snacks. By scheduling eating times, people do not miss meals. People may not get adequate nutrients if they miss a meal, and they might not be able to compensate for a lack of nutrients by eating a subsequent meal. So eating meals regularly is especially important for school-age children, adolescents, and older adults.

What is the most likely source of this paragraph?

a. website article   b. personal journal   c. textbook   d. memoir

What is its primary purpose? _____

Who is the audience? _____

_____

3.   About 5,000 years ago, another revolution in technology was taking place in the Middle East, one that would end up changing the entire world. This was the discovery of agriculture, large-scale cultivation using plows harnessed to animals or more powerful energy sources. So important was the invention of the animal-drawn plow, along with other breakthroughs of the period—including irrigation, the wheel, writing, numbers, and the use of various metals—that this moment in history is often called "the dawn of civilization."

What is the most likely source of this paragraph?

a. website article   b. personal journal   c. textbook   d. memoir

What is its purpose? _____

Who is the audience? _____

_____

Exploring Strategies

1.5   Use exploring strategies.

After you determine your topic, audience, and purpose, try some **exploring strategies**—also known as **prewriting strategies**—to help get ideas flowing. Four common strategies are *freewriting*, *brainstorming*, *questioning*, and *clustering*. It is not necessary to do all of the strategies explained in this chapter. Find the strategy that works best for you.

You can do both general and focused prewriting. If you have writer's block and do not know what to write about, use **general prewriting** to come up with possible writing topics. Then, after you have chosen a topic, use **focused prewriting** to find an aspect of the topic that is interesting and that could be developed in your essay.

HINT: When to Use Exploring Strategies

You can use the exploring strategies at any stage of the writing process:

- To find a topic
- To narrow a broad topic
- To generate ideas about your topic
- To generate supporting details

Narrow Your Topic

An essay has one main idea. If your topic is too broad, you might find it difficult to write a focused essay about the subject. For example, imagine that you are given the broad topic "music." To narrow it, think about more specific topics, such as *the best types of music*, *the value of music education*, or *censorship of lyrics*. Find one aspect of the topic that you know a lot about and that you personally find interesting. If you have a lot to say and you think the topic is compelling, chances are that your reader will also like your topic.

Review the following examples of general and narrowed topics.

Topic	Narrowed Topic
jobs	preparing for a job interview
music	protest songs from the past and present

To help narrow and develop your topic, you can use the following exploring strategies: freewriting, brainstorming, questioning, and clustering.

Freewriting

Freewriting gives writers the freedom to write without stopping for a set period of time. The goal of this exercise is to record the first thoughts that come to mind. If you run out of ideas, don't stop writing. Simply fill in the pause with phrases such as "blah blah blah" or "What else can I write?" As you write, do not be concerned with word choice, grammar, or spelling. If you use a computer, let your ideas flow and do not worry about typing mistakes. You could try typing without looking at the screen.

CASSIE'S FREEWRITING

College student Cassie Harding thought about important decisions college students must make. During her freewriting, she wrote down everything that came to mind.

> Important decisions about college. Which college? Two-year. four-year. What major to study. Last year, I had no idea what I wanted to do. Still kind of confused. I like math but I also like music. What kind of a career will I have in math or music. Nursing. commerce? Teaching? not sure. What about working part time? Will it cut into my study time? Friends and activities. Should I join the choir? Join other clubs? Will I have enough time to do everything I want to do? I don't know what to do.

Brainstorming

Brainstorming is like freewriting, except that you create a list of ideas and you can take the time to stop and think when you create your list. As you think about the topic, write down words or phrases that come to mind. Do not worry about grammar or spelling; the point is to generate ideas.

CASSIE'S BRAINSTORMING

Topic: Important decisions that college students make

— choosing a major
— find the right college

— working while studying

— make a budget

— balancing party time with studying

— exercise and a healthy lifestyle

— extracurricular activities

Questioning

Another way to generate ideas about a topic is to ask yourself a series of questions and write responses to them. The questions can help you define and narrow your topic. One common way to do this is to ask yourself *who, what, when, where, why,* and *how* questions.

CASSIE'S QUESTIONING

Why should someone go to college?	— better jobs, more money, more satisfaction
What can people study?	— music, teaching, math, nursing
Who can provide advice?	— parents, school counselor, friends, boss
Which type of college is best?	— two year? four year? career college?
Where should students study?	— local college? state college? out of state?
How can students pay for college?	— part-time job, scholarship, loans, borrow from parents
What extracurricular or volunteer activities should students do?	— public speaking club, writing center, peer mentor

Clustering

Clustering is like drawing a word map; ideas are arranged in a visual image. To begin, write your topic in the middle of the page and draw a box or a circle around it. That idea will lead to another, so write the second idea and draw a line connecting it to your topic. Keep writing, circling, and connecting ideas until you have groups, or "clusters," of them on your page.

CASSIE'S CLUSTERING

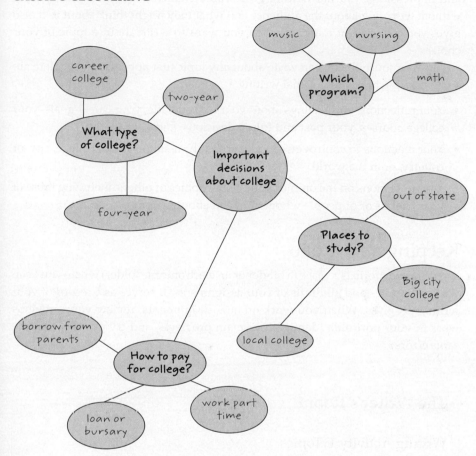

The Writer's Desk: Exploring

Explore the next three topics. Use a different exploring strategy for each topic. You can choose to do freewriting, brainstorming, questioning, or clustering.

       health   overconsumption   volunteer work

Journal and Portfolio Writing

1.6   Keep a journal and writing portfolio.

Keeping a Journal

You may write for work or school, but you can also practice writing for pleasure. One way to practice your writing is to keep a journal. A **journal** can be a book, computer file, or even a blog where you record your thoughts, opinions, ideas, and impressions. Journal writing gives you a chance to practice your writing without worrying about the audience and what they might think about it. It also gives you a source of material when you want to write about a topic of your choice.

In your journal, you can write about any topic that appeals to you. Here are some possible topics for journal writing.

- Your reflections and feelings about your personal life, your career goals, your college courses, your past and future decisions, and your work
- Your reactions to controversies in your family, neighborhood, college, city, or country, or in the world
- Your reflections on the opinions and philosophies of others, including those of your friends or of people whom you read about in your courses

Keeping a Portfolio

A **writing portfolio** is a place (a binder or an electronic file folder) where you keep writing samples and all drafts of your assignments. It serves as a record of your writing progress. When you work on new assignments, review your previous work in your portfolio. Identify your main problems, and try not to repeat the same errors.

The Writer's Room

Writing Activity 1: Topics

Choose one of the following topics, or choose your own topic. Then generate ideas about the topic. You may want to try the suggested exploring strategy.

General Topics

1. Try freewriting about people who have helped you succeed.
2. Brainstorm a list of thoughts about online shopping.
3. Create a cluster diagram about problems with social networking.
4. Ask and answer questions about family traditions.

College- and Work-Related Topics

5. Try freewriting about a mistake you made at work or at college. Include any emotions or details that come to mind.
6. Brainstorm a list of ideas about noisy work environments.
7. Ask and answer questions about bosses.
8. Create a cluster diagram about different types of students.

Writing Activity 2: Photo Writing

Use questioning to generate ideas about the following image. Ask and answer *who, what, when, where, why,* and *how* questions.

Checklist: Exploring

When you explore a topic, ask yourself these questions.

- ❏ What is my **topic**? Consider what you will write about.
- ❏ Who is my **audience**? Think about your intended reader.
- ❏ What is my **purpose**? Determine your reason for writing.
- ❏ Which exploring strategy will I use? You could try one strategy or a combination of strategies.
  Freewriting is writing without stopping for a limited period of time.
  Brainstorming is making a list.
  Questioning is asking and answering a series of questions.
  Clustering is drawing a word map.

2 Developing the Main Idea

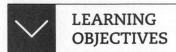

LEARNING OBJECTIVES

2.1 Follow key steps in developing the main idea.

2.2 Write a thesis statement.

2.3 Develop the supporting ideas.

Faced with so many plant and flower varieties, a gardener narrows down which ones are most appropriate for his or her garden. Similarly, a writer considers many ideas before choosing a main idea for an essay.

Key Steps in Developing the Main Idea

2.1   Follow key steps in developing the main idea.

In Chapter 1, you learned how to consider your reading audience and your purposes for writing. You also practiced using exploring strategies to formulate ideas. In this chapter, you focus on developing a main idea that can be expanded into a complete essay. There are two key steps in this process.

Developing the Main Idea

STEP 1   Write a thesis statement. Write a statement that expresses the main idea of the piece of writing.

STEP 2   Develop your supporting ideas. Find facts, examples, or anecdotes that best support your main idea.

Writing a Thesis Statement

2.2   Write a thesis statement.

Your **thesis** is the main idea that you want to express. A clear thesis statement presents the topic of the essay, and it includes a **controlling idea** that expresses the writer's opinion, attitude, or feeling about the topic. The controlling idea can appear at the beginning or end of the thesis statement.

topic   controlling idea
Volunteer work should be compulsory for all high school students.

controlling idea   topic
Extra credit should be given to **high school students who do volunteer work**.

Practice 1

Circle the topic and underline the controlling idea in each thesis statement.

EXAMPLE: Discipline your children more effectively by practicing the next three steps.

1. Startups can fail for many reasons.

2. Parents should be held responsible for crimes committed by their children.

3. My bedroom is a pleasant state of chaos.

4. There are three types of common cyber scams.

5. Good teachers do not intimidate their students; they act as sincere mentors.

6. My sister and I became closer when we took a road trip together.

Writing an Effective Thesis Statement

When you develop your thesis statement, ask yourself the following questions to help you avoid thesis statement errors.

1. **Is my thesis a complete statement?**

   Make sure that your thesis does not express an incomplete idea or more than one idea. A thesis statement should reveal one complete thought.

Incomplete	Allergies: so annoying.
	(This is not a complete statement.)
More than one idea	There are many types of allergens, and allergies affect people in different ways.
	(This statement contains two distinct ideas. Each idea could become an essay.)

Thesis statement	Doctors suggest several steps people can take to relieve symptoms related to pet allergies.

2. **Does my thesis statement have a controlling idea?**

   Rather than announcing the topic, your thesis statement should make a point about the topic. It should have a controlling idea that expresses your attitude or feeling about the topic. Avoid phrases such as *My topic is* or *I will write about*.

Announces	I will write about computers. (This sentence says nothing relevant about the topic. The reader does not know what the point of the essay is.)
Thesis statement	When Microsoft develops a new operating system, there are political, financial, and environmental consequences.

3. **Can I support my thesis statement in an essay?**

   Your thesis statement should express an idea that you can support in an essay. If it is too narrow, you will find yourself with nothing to say. If it is too broad, you will have an endless composition.

Too broad	There are many childless couples in our world. (This topic needs a more specific and narrow focus.)
Too narrow	The average age of first-time mothers is approximately twenty-six years old. (It would be difficult to write an entire essay about this fact.)
Thesis statement	Many couples are choosing to remain childless for several reasons.

4. **Does my thesis statement make a valid and interesting point?**

   Your thesis statement should make a valid point. It should not be a vaguely worded statement or an obvious and uninteresting comment.

Vague	Censorship is a big problem. (For whom is it a big problem?)
Obvious	The Internet is important. (So what? Everyone knows this.)
Invalid	The Internet controls our lives. (This statement is difficult to believe or prove.)
Thesis statement	The Internet has become a powerful presence in our personal, social, and working lives.

Practice 2

Examine each statement.

- Write **TS** if it is an effective thesis statement.
- Write **I** if it is an incomplete idea.
- Write **M** if it contains more than one complete idea.
- Write **A** if it is an announcement.

EXAMPLE: In my opinion, new parents should take
parenting classes.   _____A_____

1. I think that colleges should make physical education
   classes compulsory for students.   _____

2. Our government should encourage citizens to reduce
   their waste.   _____

3. Young students benefit by using technology, but
   teachers should be trained to use classroom technology
   effectively.   _____

4. Successful environmental activism.   _____

5. Students should avoid getting student loans, and
   they should minimize credit card debt.   _____

6. Pet owners should be discouraged from keeping exotic
   animals.   _____

Practice 3

Examine each statement.

- Write **TS** if it is a complete thesis statement.
- Write **V** if it is too vague.
- Write **O** if it is too obvious.

EXAMPLE: Americans are more nationalistic.   _____V_____

1. New York has a large population.   _____

2. We had a major problem.   _____

3. Some adult children have legitimate reasons for
   moving back into their parents' homes.   _____

4. The roads are very crowded during holiday periods.   _____

5. There are several ways to do this.   _____

6. Children in our culture are changing.   _____

Practice 4

Examine each pair of sentences.

- Write **B** if the sentence is too broad.
- Write **TS** if the sentence is an effective thesis statement.

EXAMPLE: ___B___ Plants can help people.

___TS___ Learning to care for plants gave me unexpected pleasure.

1. _____ Music is important around the world.

_____ Some simple steps can help you successfully promote your music.

2. _____ My neighborhood is being altered by youth gangs.

_____ Violence is a big problem everywhere.

3. _____ My life has been filled with mistakes.

_____ My jealousy, insecurity, and anger ruined my first marriage.

4. _____ Surprisingly, the car accident transformed my life in positive ways.

_____ Everybody's career path has dramatic moments.

Practice 5

Examine each pair of sentences.

- Write **N** if the sentence is too narrow.
- Write **TS** if the sentence is an effective thesis statement.

EXAMPLE: ___N___ I grow coriander in my garden.

___TS___ Learning to care for my hedgehog gave me a tiny taste of parenthood.

1. _____ Our roads are very icy.

_____ Driving in the winter requires particular skills.

2. _____ Carjacking rates have increased by 20 percent in our city.

_____ You can avoid being a carjacking victim by taking the next steps.

3. _____ I hurt myself in various ways during my three days on the beach.

_____ There are many sharp pieces of shell on the local beach.

4. _____ Identical twins who are raised together have distinct personalities.

_____ My twin sisters have similar birthmarks on their necks.

Revising Your Thesis Statement

A thesis statement is like the foundation that holds up a house. If the thesis statement is weak, it is difficult to construct a solid and compelling essay. Most writers must revise their thesis statements to make them strong, interesting, and supportable.

When you plan your thesis, ask yourself whether you can support it with at least three ideas. If not, modify your thesis statement. To enliven a dead-end statement, ensure that your thesis can answer the _why, what,_ or _how_ questions. Sometimes, just by adding a few words, you can turn a dead-end statement into a supportable thesis.

Weak Thesis: At college, many students think about their future careers.

(This thesis statement lacks a controlling idea.)

Better Thesis: College students can make good career choices by following the next steps.

(You could support this thesis with at least three ideas. This thesis statement answers the question "How?")

HINT: Writing a Guided Thesis Statement

You can write a thesis statement that guides the reader through the main points. To do this, mention your main and supporting ideas in the thesis statement. In other words, your thesis statement provides a map for the readers to follow.

Weak	My first job taught me many things.
Better	My first job taught me about the importance of responsibility, organization, and teamwork.

Practice 6

The next thesis statements are weak. First, identify the problem with the statement (write _vague, obvious, incomplete, announces,_ and so on) and ask yourself questions to determine how you might be able to revise it. Then revise each statement to make it more forceful and focused.

EXAMPLE: Many diseases have impacted society.

Comments: <u>Broad / Vague</u>

Revised: <u>The stigma from AIDS still has devastating effects on patients.</u>

1. I will write about cheating on exams.

   Comments: _____

   Revision: _____

2. Bella wakes up every morning at 6:15 A.M.

   Comments: _____

   Revision: _____

3. Teenagers are disrespectful to adults.

   Comments: _____

   Revision: _____

4. New technology causes social problems.

   Comments: _____

   Revision: _____

5. Overpaid athletes.

   Comments: _____

   Revision: _____

Overview: Writing a Thesis Statement

To create a forceful thesis statement, you should follow the next steps.

Step 1

Find your topic. You can use exploring strategies to get ideas.

General topic: Traditions

Brainstorming:

♦ Commercialization of holidays

♦ My family traditions

♦ Important ceremonies

♦ Why do we celebrate?

♦ Benefits of traditions

♦ Initiation ceremonies

Step 2

Narrow your topic. Decide what point you want to make.

Narrowed topic: Initiation ceremonies

Point I want to make: Initiation ceremonies can help people make the transition from childhood to adulthood.

Step 3

Develop a thesis statement that you can support with specific evidence. You may need to revise your statement several times.

Initial thesis statement: Initiation ceremonies serve a valuable function.

Revised thesis statement: Meaningful initiation ceremonies benefit individuals, families, and communities.

The Writer's Desk: Write Thesis Statements

Write a thesis statement for each of the next topics. If you explored these topics in Chapter 1, use those ideas to help write your thesis statement. If you have not explored these topics yet, then spend a few minutes exploring them. Brainstorm some ideas for each topic to help you define and narrow it. Then develop a thesis statement that makes a point and is not too broad or too narrow.

health   overconsumption   volunteer work

EXAMPLE: Topic: Important decisions college students make

Thesis statement: To ensure a successful career path, students should discuss choices with friends and family, take advantage of career resources, and volunteer in their chosen field.

1. _____

   _____

2. _____

   _____

3. _____

   _____

Developing the Supporting Ideas

2.3   Develop the supporting ideas.

Just as the legs support a table, in an essay, the topic sentences must support the thesis.

The next step in essay writing is to plan your supporting ideas. Support is not simply a restatement of the thesis. The body paragraphs must develop and prove the validity of the thesis statement.

Each body paragraph has a **topic sentence** that expresses the main idea of the paragraph. Like a thesis statement, a topic sentence must have a controlling idea. Details and examples support the topic sentence. In the following illustration, you can see how the ideas flow in an essay. Topic sentences support the thesis statement, and details bolster the topic sentences. Every idea in the essay is unified and helps to strengthen the essay's thesis.

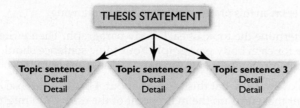

Practice 7

Write a thesis statement for each group of supporting ideas. Make sure that your thesis statement is clear, makes a point, and is not too broad or too narrow.

EXAMPLE: Thesis: <u>When you buy a car, make an informed decision</u>.

    a. Ask family members what type of car they would prefer.
    b. Research online or in car guides to find information about specific models that interest you.
    c. Keeping your budget in mind, compare new and used cars.

1. Thesis: _____

_____

    a. First, keeping teens off the street at night will ensure that they do not become victims of crime.
    b. Next, requiring adolescents to remain at home will prevent them from committing delinquent acts.
    c. Finally, parents won't need to worry about the whereabouts of their children after dark.

2. Thesis: _____

_____

    a. Standardized tests cause extra stress for students and teachers.
    b. Standardized tests measure mostly hard skills like math; they do not measure some soft skills like creativity.
    c. The test questions often discriminate against students who do not have sufficient background knowledge to give complete answers.

3. Thesis: _____

_____

    a. First, internalize and believe in your sales pitch.
    b. Speak softly, and do not scare the customer with a commanding voice or aggressive mannerisms.
    c. Finally, involve the customer in your sales presentation.

Practice 8

Read the full essay in this practice and then do the following.

1. First, determine the topic of each body paragraph. Then write a topic sentence for each body paragraph. Your topic sentence should have a controlling idea and express the main point of the paragraph.

2. Next, ask yourself what this essay is about. Finally, compose a thesis statement that sums up the main point of the essay. You might look in the concluding paragraph to get some ideas.

(Introduction) Paparazzi are photographers who take pictures of celebrities. For a shocking photograph of a well-known person, a tabloid photographer can earn more than $100,000. Thus, such photographers hunt for unusual and possibly embarrassing images of well-known people.

Thesis statement: _____

_____

(Body 1) Topic Sentence: _____

_____

When people discover gossip in magazines, online, or on TV, they always see paparazzi surrounding the stars. They also see celebrities jumping into cars and trying to get away from the photographers. This type of behavior can cause serious accidents. The most famous case was the death of Princess Diana. Trying to escape from paparazzi, she died in a car crash in 1997. Other celebrities have been injured while trying to escape photographers.

(Body 2) Topic Sentence: _____

_____

Some paparazzi stalk celebrities and take photos from trees, rooftops, helicopters, or boats. For instance, Jennifer Hudson, a former *American Idol* contestant, lived through a great personal tragedy. Her mother, brother, and nephew were murdered. Photographers and reporters were seen hounding Hudson with questions and taking photographs of her during this misfortune.

(Body 3) Topic Sentence: _____

_____

Magazine covers regularly display photographs of celebrities' spouses and children. The family members may not want or appreciate the attention. For example, the children of Brad Pitt and Angelina Jolie are exposed to scrutiny, criticized for their clothing choices, and occasionally ridiculed. Several years ago, Pierce Brosnan's wife was mocked for gaining weight.

(Conclusion) Paparazzi hurt people rather than help them. It is almost sickening to think of what a photographer is willing to do to get a story. The public should stop buying gossip magazines so photographers will not be able to earn a living by committing gross invasions of privacy.

Generating Supporting Ideas

When you plan your supporting ideas, make certain that they develop and provide evidence for the central point that you are making in the thesis statement. To generate ideas for body paragraphs, you could use the exploring strategies (brainstorming, freewriting, questioning, or clustering) that you learned in Chapter 1.

Review the process that student Cassie Washington went through. First, she created a list to support her thesis statement. Then she reread her supporting ideas and removed ideas that she did not want to develop in her essay. She also grouped together related ideas.

INITIAL IDEAS

Draft Thesis Statement: College students can make good career choices by following the next steps.

Supporting ideas:

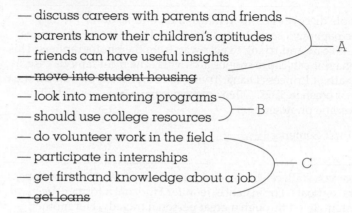

— discuss careers with parents and friends
— parents know their children's aptitudes
— friends can have useful insights
— ~~move into student housing~~
— look into mentoring programs
— should use college resources
— do volunteer work in the field
— participate in internships
— get firsthand knowledge about a job
— ~~get loans~~

A

B

C

After critically examining her supporting ideas, Cassie chose three that could become body paragraphs. She evaluated each set of linked ideas and summarized the connections between ideas in the set. These sentence summaries then became her topic sentences.

REVISED THESIS AND SUPPORTING POINTS

Thesis Statement: To ensure a successful career pathway, students should discuss choices with friends and family, take advantage of career resources, and volunteer in their chosen field.

Topic Sentence: College students should discuss their career goals with friends and family.

Topic Sentence: Students should take advantage of career resources.

Topic Sentence: Students should participate in internship programs or volunteer in areas that are related to their career field.

HINT: Look Critically at Your Supporting Ideas

After you have made a list of supporting ideas, look at it carefully and ask yourself the next questions.

- **Which ideas could I develop into complete paragraphs?** Look for connections between supporting ideas. Group together ideas that have a common thread. Then create a topic sentence for each group of related ideas. In Cassie's example, three of her ideas became topic sentences.

- **Does each idea support my thesis?** Choose ideas that directly support the thesis statement, and drop any ideas that might go off topic. In Cassie's example, two ideas, "move into student housing" and "get loans," do not support her thesis, so she crossed them out.

Practice 9

Brainstorm three supporting ideas for the next thesis statements. Find ideas that do not overlap, and ensure that your ideas support the thesis. (You can brainstorm a list of ideas on a separate sheet of paper, and then add the three best ideas here.)

EXAMPLE: Sex education classes should be mandatory in middle schools.

_____

_____

_____

_____

_____

1. There are three main causes for insomnia.

   —students will receive the correct information about their bodies

   —students will be able to make more informed decisions about

   becoming sexually active

   —students will be more comfortable with their own sexuality as they grow

   into adults

2. Sibling rivalry can be caused by many factors.

   _____

   _____

   _____

   _____

3. It is easy to look fashionable on a limited budget if you follow the next steps.

   _____

   _____

   _____

   _____

The Writer's Desk: Generate Supporting Ideas

Brainstorm supporting ideas for two or three of your thesis statements from the previous Writer's Desk on page 21. Look critically at your lists of supporting ideas. Ask yourself which supporting ideas you could expand into body paragraphs, and then drop any unrelated ideas.

The Writer's Room

Writing Activity 1

Choose one of the Writer's Room topics from Chapter 1 and write a thesis statement. Using an exploring strategy, develop supporting ideas for your thesis.

Writing Activity 2

Narrow one of the following topics. Then develop a thesis statement and some supporting ideas.

General Topics	College- and Work-Related Topics
1. social networking	5. pressures students face
2. an interesting hobby	6. salary for college athletes
3. online shopping	7. compulsory attendance for college students
4. traditions	8. benefits of activities outside of work and school

Checklist: Thesis Statement and Topic Sentences

When you write a thesis statement and topic sentences, ask yourself these questions.

❑ Is my thesis a complete sentence?

❑ Does it contain a narrowed topic and a controlling idea?

❑ Is my main point clear and interesting?

❑ Can the thesis be supported with several body paragraphs? (Verify that the topic is not too narrow, or you will hit a dead-end with it. Also check that the topic is not too broad. Your essay requires a clear focus.)

❑ Is my thesis forceful and direct, and not too vague or obvious?

❑ Does my thesis make a valid point?

❑ Do I have good supporting ideas?

❑ Does each topic sentence have a controlling idea and support the thesis statement?

3 Developing the Essay Plan

Organizing Supporting Ideas

3.1 Follow key steps in developing the essay plan.

3.2 Organize supporting ideas.

3.3 Develop an essay plan.

Like gardens, essays require careful planning. Some ideas thrive while others do not. Writers develop essay plans to help them decide which ideas support the main idea most effectively and where to place those ideas so that readers can understand them.

Key Steps in Developing the Essay Plan

3.1 Follow key steps in developing the essay plan.

In the previous chapters, you learned how to use exploring strategies to formulate ideas and narrow topics. You also learned to develop main ideas for essays. In this chapter, you will focus on the third stage of the essay writing process: developing the essay plan. There are two key steps in this process.

Developing the Essay Plan

STEP 1   **Organize your supporting ideas.** Choose an appropriate method of organization.

STEP 2   **Write an essay plan.** Place your main and supporting ideas in an essay plan.

Organizing Supporting Ideas

3.2   Organize supporting ideas.

Once you have a list of main ideas that will make up the body paragraphs in an essay, you need to organize those ideas in a logical manner using time, space, or emphatic order.

Time Order

To organize an essay using **time order (chronological order)**, arrange the details according to the sequence in which they occurred. Time order can be effective for narrating a story, explaining how to do something, or describing an event.

When writing essays using time order, include the following transitional expressions to help your readers understand when certain events happened. (There is a more extensive list of transitions on page 60 in Chapter 5.)

after that	first	later	next
eventually	in the beginning	meanwhile	suddenly
finally	last	months after	then

Practice 1

The writer uses time order to organize supporting ideas for the following thesis statement.

Thesis Statement: Organizing a play for charity was hard work but worthwhile.

1. In the spring, the Little Theatre committee had to find an appropriate play to produce.
2. For six weeks, the group planned the production meticulously.
3. Last Saturday evening, the Little Theatre committee staged the play successfully.

One paragraph from the essay uses time order. Underline any words or phrases that help show time order.

> Last Saturday evening, the Little Theatre productions staged the play successfully. A couple hours before the show got under way, the cast and crew arrived. The technicians made equipment checks, and the actors put on their makeup and costumes. About fifteen minutes before curtain call, the audience started to arrive. Meanwhile, the actors took their places on stage behind the curtain. Then, the show began. During the performance, the audience laughed enthusiastically. At the end of the show, the cast received a standing ovation, and the theatregoers smiled and chatted as they left the auditorium.

Space Order

Organizing ideas using **space order** helps the reader to visualize what you are describing in a specific space. For example, you can describe someone or something from top to bottom or bottom to top, from left to right or right to left, or from far to near or near to far.

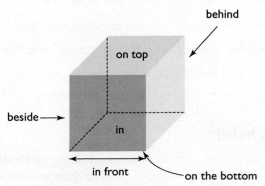

Help readers find their way through your essay by using the following transitional expressions.

above	beneath	nearby	on top
behind	closer in	on the bottom	toward
below	farther out	on the left	under

Practice 2

The writer uses space order to organize supporting ideas for the following thesis statement.

Thesis statement: The first day of my internship made an impression on me that I have never forgotten.

1. From the sidewalk, I gazed at the shining glass and steel design of the building.
2. The interior space was simply beautiful.
3. Each work station had a creative layout.

One paragraph from the essay uses space order. Underline any words or phrases that indicate space order.

> The interior space was simply beautiful. Artwork created by design students hung on the wall at the front of the room. There were abstract images of many colors and shapes. From the right-hand side of the room, the sun filtered in through three huge, arched windows, and the rays shone on the artwork. On the left-hand side, the wall was covered with a massive screen. Images were projected on it, but I couldn't see it clearly because a pillar in front of the screen obstructed my view. The computer work stations were arranged in small groupings of four in the center of the room. My mentor, who was standing near the door, noticed me, smiled, and welcomed me inside.

Emphatic Order

To organize the supporting details of an essay using **emphatic order**, arrange them in a logical sequence. For example, you can arrange details from the least to the most important, from general to specific, from the least appealing to the most appealing, and so on.

Here are some transitional expressions that help readers understand which ideas you want to emphasize the most or the least in the body paragraphs of an essay.

above all	first	moreover	principally
clearly	in particular	most importantly	the least important
especially	last	of course	the most important

HINT: Using Emphatic Order

When you organize details using emphatic order, use your own values and opinions to determine what is the most or the least important, upsetting, remarkable, and so on. Another writer may organize the same ideas in a different way.

Practice 3

The writer uses emphatic order to organize supporting ideas for the following thesis statement.

Thesis Statement: Chronic stress creates immense costs for society.

1. First, businesses lose millions of dollars because of employee stress.
2. In addition, psychological stress can take a toll on interpersonal relationships.
3. Above all, untreated stress may shorten the lives of many.

One paragraph from the essay also uses emphatic order. Underline any words or phrases that help show emphatic order.

Businesses lose millions of dollars because of employee stress. First, work-related stress often causes absences from work. Employers must deal with lost productivity and replacement costs of absent employees. Next, highly stressed workers may develop grievances, and may even sue companies for failing to recognize and prevent worker stress. Most importantly, overly stressed workers might not be able to perform at their peak. Stress can negatively influence a person's intellectual and emotional ability. An employee might not be able to react creatively and logically in a crisis because stress diminishes a person's ability to think through a problem. Clearly, businesses must look at ways to reduce employee stress.

HINT: Combining Time, Space, and Emphatic Order

You will probably use more than one type of organizational method in an essay. For example, in a time order essay about a journey, one paragraph might be devoted to a particular place that you visited, and in that paragraph, you might use space order to describe the scene.

Practice 4

Read each list of supporting ideas, and number the items in a logical order. Then write *time*, *space*, or *emphatic* to indicate the organization method.

EXAMPLE: Thesis Statement: Painting a picture can be a rewarding experience.

   _1_ Choose a location that you find particularly peaceful.

   _3_ Add colors to your sketch that best represent the mood you are feeling.

   _2_ Settle in and make a preliminary sketch of the place.

Order: _____time_____

1. Thesis Statement: As I sat in my back garden, I pinpointed the locations of various loud sounds.

   ____ Two cardinals were fluttering above their nest in the tree top and squawking desperately.

   ____ Pierce, my sister's cocker spaniel, sat at the foot of a spindly tree, barking angrily at the cat.

___ A cat, perched precariously on the branch, was hissing at the birds.

Order: _____

2. Thesis Statement: Julius faced a series of problems as he rushed to his job interview.

___ On his way to the interview a half an hour later, he was stuck in a traffic jam.

___ Right after breakfast, Julius started his car but panicked when it made funny noises.

___ After advancing only one block in twenty minutes, he decided to park the car and walk to his interview.

Order: _____

3. Thesis Statement: Top college athletes should get paid to play on sports teams.

___ Coaches and colleges receive millions of dollars in revenues when college sports teams win.

___ Top athletes raise a school's profile and help attract more students to the college.

___ Many college athletes don't receive enough scholarship money to cover the costs of going to college.

Order: _____

Developing an Essay Plan

3.3   Develop an essay plan.

A contractor would never build a house without making a drawing or plan of it first. In the same way, an essay plan can help you organize ideas before you write the first draft. Planning an essay actually saves time because you have already figured out your supporting ideas and how to organize them so readers can easily follow them. To create an essay plan, follow the next steps.

- Looking at the list of ideas that you created while prewriting, identify the ones that most effectively support your thesis statement.
- Next, write topic sentences that express these main supporting ideas.
- Finally, add details under each topic sentence.

A formal essay plan uses Roman numerals and letters of the alphabet to identify main and supporting ideas. A formal plan also contains complete sentences. The basic structure is shown below.

Thesis Statement: _____

    I. _____

        A. _____

        B. _____

    II. _____

        A. _____

        B. _____

Concluding Idea: _____

In the planning stage, you do not have to develop your introduction and conclusion. It is sufficient to simply write your thesis statement and an idea for your conclusion. Later, when you write your essay, you can develop the introduction and conclusion.

Cassie's Essay Plan

Notice that in her essay plan, Cassie organizes her main ideas using emphatic order. She begins with her thesis statement, adds topic sentences with clear controlling ideas, and indents her supporting examples.

Thesis Statement: To ensure a successful career pathway, students should discuss choices with friends and family, take advantages of career resources on their college campus, and participate in internships or volunteer in their career field.

    I. Students should discuss their career goals with friends and family.

        A. Parents have a vested interest in ensuring that their children make informed choices.

        B. They are in a unique position to assess their children's skills and abilities.

        C. Friends and other family members may have useful insight as well.

    II. Students should take advantage of career resources.

        A. Most educational facilities have career centers with resources.

        B. Many colleges have mentoring programs where parents, professors, and alumni offer advice.

III. Students should participate in internship programs or volunteer in areas that are related to their career field.

    A. Internships and volunteering give students valuable information and skills about their career choice.

    B. By working in their preferred career area, students can learn what they like or dislike about that profession.

    C. Internships and volunteering can lead to networking connections.

Practice 5

Read the following essay plan. Brainstorm and develop three supporting ideas for each topic sentence.

THESIS STATEMENT: Each generation has produced influential musical icons.

    Topic Sentence: In the 1960s, some amazing singers and bands influenced their generation.

_____

_____

_____

    Topic Sentence: During the 1980s, certain musical stars made lasting impressions.

_____

_____

_____

    Topic Sentence: From 2000 to 2010, a wide variety of music styles became popular.

_____

_____

_____

_____

Practice 6

Read the following essay plan. Brainstorm and develop three supporting ideas for each topic. Include specific anecdotes.

THESIS STATEMENT: I learned valuable life lessons in primary and secondary school.

> **Topic Sentence:** Through various activities, I learned to get along with others.
>
> _____
>
> _____
>
> _____
>
> _____
>
> **Topic Sentence:** I learned about the importance of knowledge.
>
> _____
>
> _____
>
> _____
>
> _____
>
> **Topic Sentence:** Finally, I learned self-discipline.
>
> _____
>
> _____
>
> _____
>
> _____

The Writer's Desk: Write an Essay Plan

Brainstorm ideas for an essay. You can choose ideas that you developed in Chapter 2. Then do the following.

1. Highlight at least three ideas from your list that you think are the most compelling and most clearly illustrate the point you are making in your thesis statement. These three ideas will make up your body paragraphs.

2. Group together any related ideas with the three supporting ideas.

3. Organize your ideas for the body paragraphs using time, space, or emphatic order.

4. Create a complete essay plan.

The Writer's Room

Writing Activity 1

Choose one of the Writer's Room topics from Chapter 2, and create an essay plan. Using an exploring strategy, develop supporting ideas for your thesis.

Writing Activity 2

Create a list of supporting ideas for one of the next thesis statements. Then develop an essay plan.

General Topics

1. Single people should (or should not) have the right to adopt children.
2. The three talents I would most like to have are. . . .
3. Driver education classes should (or should not) be compulsory.
4. There are good reasons to live near (or move away from) family members.

College- and Work-Related Topics

5. New employees make three types of common mistakes.
6. An elected official should have the following characteristics.
7. College tuition should be free for three reasons.
8. (Choose a story, novel, or film) has important lessons for all of us.

Checklist: Essay Plan

When you develop an essay plan, ask yourself these questions.

❑ Does my thesis statement express the main idea of the essay?

❑ In my plan, does each body paragraph contain a topic sentence?

❑ Does each topic sentence support the thesis statement?

❑ In each body paragraph, do the ideas support the topic sentence?

❑ Are my ideas well organized?

4 Developing the First Draft

LEARNING OBJECTIVES

4.1 Follow key steps in developing the first draft.

4.2 Write an introduction.

4.3 Write complete body paragraphs.

4.4 Write a conclusion.

4.5 Choose an essay title.

4.6 Write the first draft.

By preparing the soil and planting seeds and shrubs, a gardener creates a landscape's basic foundation. In the same way, a writer plans the main idea, develops the plan, and then prepares the first draft of a writing assignment.

Key Steps in Developing the First Draft

4.1 Follow key steps in developing the first draft.

In previous chapters, you learned how to develop a thesis statement, support it with ideas, and create an essay plan. To develop a first draft, follow the next five steps.

Developing the First Draft

STEP 1 Write an introduction. Try to attract the reader's attention in the first paragraph of your essay.

STEP 2 Write complete body paragraphs. Expand each supporting idea with specific details.

STEP 3 **Write a conclusion.** Bring your essay to a satisfactory close.

STEP 4 **Title your essay.** Sum up your essay topic in a few words.

STEP 5 **Write the first draft.** Tie the introduction, body paragraphs, and conclusion into a cohesive essay.

Writing an Introduction

4.2   Write an introduction.

The **introductory paragraph** establishes the subject of your essay and contains the thesis statement. A strong introduction will capture readers' attention and make them want to read on. Introductions can be developed in several different ways.

The Lead-In

The point of writing an essay is to have people read it. Your essay should entertain, inform, or persuade readers. So, you can try to grab your readers' attention in the first sentence. There are three common lead-ins:

- a quotation
- a surprising or provocative statement
- a question

Introduction Styles

You can develop the introduction in several ways. Experiment with any of the following introduction styles.

- **Give general or historical background information** that gradually leads to your thesis. In an essay about gender stereotypes in movies, you might begin by discussing some classic films.

- **Tell an interesting anecdote** or a story that leads to your thesis statement. You might begin your essay about film violence by describing how agitated your younger brother and his friends became after they watched the movie *The Revenant*.

- **Describe something in vivid detail**, and then state your thesis. You might begin your essay about the beauty myth by describing a cosmetic surgery procedure.

- **Define a term**, and then state your thesis. For example, in an essay about ways to avoid marital conflicts, begin by defining a happy marriage.

- **Present a contrasting or opposite position**. Your readers will not expect you to present one side first and then to argue for the other side later. For example, in an essay about abortion, begin by presenting the arguments of those who would not agree with your particular point of view on the debate.

- **Pose several questions**, and end with a thesis statement. The purpose may be to engage your readers by inviting them to think about the topic. You might also ask questions that you will answer in your essay. In an essay about lotteries, you might ask, *Have you ever bought a lottery ticket? Why do so many people play lotteries?*

The next example presents the structure of a typical introduction.

Lead-in ➞

Have good manners disappeared? In past centuries, a gentleman would spread his cloak over a muddy road so that his lady wouldn't dirty her feet. Twenty years ago, an elderly man

Historical background information ➞

or woman would never have to stand in a bus because other passengers would offer up their seats. Times have certainly changed. Today, many people lack consideration for others. **Parents and**

Thesis statement ➞

schools should teach children basic good manners.

Practice 1

Read the following introductions. Underline each thesis statement, and determine what introduction style the writer used.

1.   The year 1929 was not the best time to be a movie mogul. By the end of the year, 8,700 theatres had been wired for sound, at great expense. Many silent stars made the transition to sound; some didn't. But the new stars, the ones who were created by talkies, would never have been so successful in silent films as they were in sound. Dialogue made actors real, and the kind of dialogue that audiences fell in love with was tough, slangy, and above all, colloquial. For the first time, the life depicted on the screen was as feisty as American movie audiences had always been. Sound made the movies democratic.

—adapted from *Flashback* by Louis Giannetti and Scott Eyman

a. Underline the thesis statement.

b. What is the introduction style? Indicate the best answer.

_____ historical background   _____ anecdote

_____ definition   _____ contrasting position

2.   Adolescent males are dangerous. They join gangs, and they are responsible for most of the crime in our society. They drive too fast, causing accidents on our highways. They all experiment with drugs, and they annoy others with their loud music. But is such a portrayal of our nation's young men really fair? In fact, most stereotypes about adolescent males are incorrect and misleading.

—Abeer Hamad, student

a. Underline the thesis statement.

b. What type of lead-in did the writer use?

_____ quotation   _____ question   _____ surprising statement

    c. What is the introduction style? Indicate the best answer.

      _____ historical background   _____ anecdote

      _____ definition   _____ contrasting position

3.   Where did you buy that blouse? I heard the question every time I wore it. It was a truly lovely designer model that had been marked down to $40. It was pale blue with swirling tiny flower buds running down each front panel. The little buttons were topped with imitation pearls. Unfortunately, the middle button kept coming undone. People at a certain angle to my left could peek in and view the lace eyelets on my brassiere. When I wore the blouse, my head kept bobbing down, looking to see if I was exposing myself. Over the years, I have had several humorous and embarrassing wardrobe and makeup malfunctions.

                                            —Catalina Ortega, student

    a. Underline the thesis statement.

    b. What type of lead-in was used?

      _____ quotation   _____ question   _____ surprising statement

    c. What is the introduction style? Indicate the best answer.

      _____ general background   _____ contrasting position

      _____ definition   _____ description

4.   The term *cool jazz* refers to modern jazz that tends to be softer and easier than the bebop of Charlie Parker and Dizzy Gillespie. Cool jazz avoids roughness and brassiness. The term *cool jazz* has been applied to the music of saxophonist Lester Young and some of the musicians whom he and Count Basie influenced. Though musicians inspired by Basie and Young were found in almost all regions of America, many of them were based in California during the 1950s. The West Coast became one center of innovation in cool jazz.

                        —Mark C. Gridley, *Concise Guide to Jazz*

    a. Underline the thesis statement.

    b. What is the introduction style? Indicate the best answer.

      _____ general background   _____ anecdote

      _____ definition   _____ contrasting position

5.   "All the men were frightened," Julius Matthews said. On June 6, 1944, he, along with other young men, landed on the French beach. German bullets were flying all around him. He ran as fast as he could towards the cliffs, but his heavy boots sank into the sand, slowing him down. He saw men around him fall to the ground as bullets penetrated their bodies. On that day, many of the best-laid military plans went awry.

                                  —Niles Logan, journalist

    a. Underline the thesis statement.

    b. What type of lead-in was used?

      _____ quotation   _____ question   _____ surprising statement

c. What is the introduction style? Indicate the best answer.

_____ general background   _____ anecdote

_____ definition   _____ questions

6.   Why do some hip-hop artists embed jewels and gold in their teeth? Are the grills meant to impress others, or do the grills fit some deep need on the part of the artists to show that they matter? Is the hip-hop artist who shows off his "bling" any different from the accountant who buys a BMW to show that she has succeeded, or the corporate executive who marries a beautiful trophy wife? Showing off one's wealth is not new. In fact, throughout history, people have found extravagant ways to flaunt their wealth.

—Jamal Evans, student

a. Underline the thesis statement.

b. What type of lead-in was used?

_____ quotation   _____ question   _____ surprising statement

c. What is the introduction style? Indicate the best answer.

_____ general background   _____ anecdote

_____ definition   _____ questions

Practice 2

Write interesting lead-ins (opening sentences) for the next topics. Use the type of lead-in that is indicated in parentheses.

EXAMPLE: College tuition (question)

How much student debt do you have?

1. Crowd funding (a provocative statement)

_____

_____

2. Climate change (a quotation)

_____

_____

3. Curfews (a question)

_____

_____

Practice 3

Choose *one* of the next thesis statements or write your own thesis statement. Then write three introductions using three different introduction styles. Use the same thesis statement in each introduction.

1. Athletes caught using drugs should be banned from their sport for life.
2. American films and television shows do not reflect the cultural diversity of the nation.
3. Beauty pageants are sexist.

You can choose any three of the following introduction styles:

- general or historical background
- anecdote
- description

- definition
- contrasting position
- series of questions

The Writer's Desk: Write Two Introductions

In Chapter 3, you prepared an essay plan. Now write two different styles of introductions for your essay. Use the same thesis statement in both introductions. Later, you can choose the best introduction for your essay.

Writing Complete Body Paragraphs

4.3   Write complete body paragraphs.

In your essay plan, you developed supporting ideas for your topic. When you prepare the first draft, you must expand or elaborate on those ideas. As you write each body paragraph, make sure that it is complete. Do not offer vague generalizations, and do not simply repeat your ideas. Provide evidence for each topic sentence by inserting specific details. You might include examples, facts, statistics, anecdotes, or quotations.

Examples are people, places, things, or events that illustrate your point. To support the view that some local spots are eyesores, the writer could give the following examples.

The bowling alley on Kennedy Street needs to be renovated.

The children's park in our neighborhood looks shabby.

The Allen Drive mini-mall has tacky signs and cracked store windows.

Facts are objective details that can be verified by others. **Statistics** are facts that are expressed in numbers. (Make sure that your statistics are from reliable sources.) To support the view that transportation costs are too high for students, you could give the following facts and statistics as evidence.

A one-way bus ticket now costs $3.50 for students.

The monthly subway pass just increased to $160 for students.

In a college survey of four hundred students, 70 percent expressed concern about the recent rate increases in public transportation.

Anecdotes are true experiences that you or someone else went through. An anecdote tells the story of what happened. **Quotations** are somebody's exact words, and they are set off in quotation marks. To support the view that lack of sleep can have dangerous consequences, you could include the following anecdote and quotation as evidence.

When Allen Turner finished his night shift, he got into his car and headed home. On Forest Drive, he started to nod off. Luckily, a truck driver in another lane noticed that Turner's car was weaving, and the trucker honked. Turner said, "My eyes snapped open, and I saw a wall growing larger in front of me. I slammed on my brakes just before smashing into it."

Essay with Sample Body Paragraphs

Read the next body paragraphs. Notice how they are fleshed out with specific evidence.

Thesis Statement: For personal and financial reasons, a growing number of adult children are choosing to live with their parents.

Body Paragraphs

The cost of education and housing is very high, so it is more economical to live at home. First, rents have increased dramatically
`fact` → since the 1990s. In *The Daily Journal*, Anna Reinhold states that rents tripled in the past ten years. During the same period, student wages
`fact` → have not risen as much as the rents. In fact, the minimum wage is only $7.25 an hour. Also, college fees are increasing each year. Tuition and
`statistic` → fees at four-year public colleges rose $265, or 2.9 percent this year, to an average of $9,410 according to the College Board's annual "Trends in College Pricing" report.

Many young people want to build a nest egg before moving out of the family home. If they remain at home, they can save income from
`quotation` → part-time jobs. "I've saved $14,000 by staying in my parents' place," says Kyle Nehme, a twenty-four-year-old student at the University of Texas. Such students do not need to worry about student loans. According to
`quotation` → financial analyst Raul Gomez, "Students who stay in the family home reap significant financial benefits."

   Students who remain in their parents' home have a much more
relaxed and comfortable lifestyle. Often, the parents do the shopping and
housework. For example, Liz Allen, a twenty-six-year-old marketing
student, moved back in with her parents last May. She discovered how   •— anecdote
much more convenient it was when someone else did the vacuuming,
laundry, and cooking. Moreover, such students feel more secure and safe
in the cocoon of their parents' home. In a *Daily Journal* survey of ninety
adults who live at home, 64 percent cited "comfort" as their major reason. •— statistic

---

HINT: Using Research to Support Your Point

Your instructor might ask you to back up your ideas with research. You can investigate
several resources, including books, magazines, and the Internet, for relevant quotations,
statistics, and factual evidence. For more information about doing research, see
Chapter 17, "The Research Essay."

Practice 4

Make the next body paragraphs more complete by adding very specific
examples. You can include the following:

• examples

• anecdotes from your own life or from the lives of others

• quotations (for this exercise, you can make up punchy quotations)

• facts, statistics, or descriptions of events that you have read about or seen

THESIS STATEMENT: Prospective pet owners should become informed
                     before buying an animal.

   Body Paragraph 1 First, when families choose a dog, they should

   consider the inconvenience and possible dangers. Some breeds of dogs

   can become extremely aggressive. _____

   _____

   _____

   _____

   _____ Moreover,

   dog owners must accept that dogs require a lot of time and attention.

_____

_____

_____

_____ Furthermore, it is very expensive to

own a dog. _____

_____

Body Paragraph 2 Some new pet owners decide to buy exotic

pets. However, such pets come with very specific problems and require

particular environments. _____

_____

_____ Also, some exotic pets seem

interesting when they are young, but they can become distinctly

annoying or dangerous when they reach maturity. _____

_____

_____

_____

HINT: Making Detailed Essay Plans

You can shorten the time you spend developing the first draft if you make a very detailed essay plan. In addition to your main ideas, your plan can include details for each supporting idea. Notice the detailed evidence in the following excerpt from an essay plan.

Thesis Statement: For personal and financial reasons, a growing number of adult children are choosing to live with their parents.

I. **Topic Sentence:** The cost of education and housing is very high.
   A. Rents have increased dramatically in the past ten years.
      Evidence: _The Daily Journal_ states that rents have tripled in the past ten years.
   B. Student wages have not risen as much as the rents.
      Evidence: The minimum wage is only $7.25 an hour.
   C. Tuition fees are very high.
      Evidence: Tuition and fees at four-year public colleges rose $265, or 2.9 percent this year, to an average of $9,410, according to the College Board's annual "Trends in College Pricing" report.

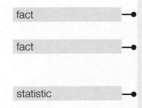

fact

fact

statistic

The Writer's Desk: Make Complete Body Paragraphs

In Chapter 3, you prepared an essay plan. Now write complete body paragraphs for your essay. Make certain that each body paragraph contains specific details.

Writing a Conclusion

4.4 Write a conclusion.

The **concluding paragraph** gives you one last chance to impress the reader and to make your point clear. A good conclusion makes the essay seem complete. One common and effective way to conclude a composition is to summarize the main ideas. The essay then comes full circle, and you remind the reader of your strongest points.

To make your conclusion more interesting and original, you could also close with a prediction, a suggestion, a quotation, or a call to action.

HINT: Linking the Conclusion to the Introduction

One effective way to conclude an essay is to continue an idea that was introduced in the introduction.

- If you began an anecdote in the introduction, you can finish it in the conclusion.
- If you posed some questions in the introduction, you can answer them in the conclusion.
- If you highlighted a problem in the introduction, you might suggest a solution in the conclusion.

Look at the concluding paragraph to an essay about etiquette in our technological age.

> Do not hide behind technology as your excuse for displaying rude or annoying behavior. Avoid posting insulting comments on social networking sites. If someone is writing an email, do not read over his or her shoulder. Also, never text or fumble with your phone while driving.

The last sentence in the essay could be one of the following.

Prediction	If you follow the basic rules of etiquette, you will ensure that your friends and colleagues maintain their respect for you.
Suggestion	The next time you go out with friends, turn off your smartphone.

Quotation	As the French author Colette once said, "It is wise to apply the oils of refined politeness to the mechanism of friendship."
Call to Action	To help the next generation learn good manners, offer to teach a class to local high school students about etiquette in the technological age.

Practice 5

Read the following conclusions and answer the questions.

A.   Recent events in the Chesapeake have given reason for hope for the recovery of the Chesapeake Bay system. The EPA agreed in 2010 to hold bay states to strict pollutant "budgets" that aim to substantially reduce inputs of nitrogen and phosphorus into the bay by 2015. If these initiatives can begin to restore the bay to health, Deal Island and other communities may again enjoy the prosperity they once did on the scenic shores of the Chesapeake.

—Jay Withgott and Matthew Laposta, *Environment*

1. What method does the author use to end the conclusion? _____

B.   Mary Jane Hiebert says that instead of being the death knell of the industry, the Internet has propelled it forward, allowing agents to maintain closer relationships with clients and arming them with a richer network of travel options for those clients. "People have become more savvy, confident and independent," she says. "People are doing research, but they still want security."

—Maryam Siddiqi, "Travel Agents Haven't Been Replaced by the Internet"

2. What method does the author use to end the conclusion? _____

C.   In this new millennium, let's put the concept of IQ to rest, once and for all. Stop giving IQ tests. Stop all the studies on IQ and birth order, IQ and nutrition, or IQ and Mozart. Let's find newer, more fluid, and more fair ways to debate and enable human potential. Let's use our heads for a change.

—Dorothy Nixon, "Let's Stop Being Stupid About IQ"

3. What method does the author use to end the conclusion? _____

HINT: Avoiding Conclusion Problems

In your conclusion, do not contradict your main point, and do not introduce new or irrelevant information. Also, avoid ending your essay with a rhetorical question, which is a question that cannot be answered, such as "When will humans stop having wars?"

The Writer's Desk: Write a Conclusion

Write a conclusion for the essay you've been preparing in the previous Writer's Desk exercises.

Choosing an Essay Title

4.5   Choose an essay title.

Think of a title *after* you have written your essay because you will have a more complete impression of your essay's main point. The most effective titles are brief, depict the topic and purpose of the essay, and attract the reader's attention.

GRAMMAR HINT: Capitalizing Titles

Place your title at the top center of your page. Capitalize the first and last words of your title. Also capitalize the main words except for prepositions (*in, at, for, to,* etc.) and articles (*a, an, the*). Leave about an inch of space between the title and the introductory paragraph.

Descriptive Titles

Descriptive titles are the most common titles in academic essays. They depict the topic of the essay clearly and concisely. Sometimes, the writer takes key words from the thesis statement and uses them in the title. Here are two examples of descriptive titles.

> Etiquette in the Technological Age
>
> Avoiding Mistakes in the First Year of College

Titles Related to the Writing Pattern

You can also relate your title directly to the writing pattern of your essay. Here are examples of titles for different writing patterns.

Illustration:	Problems with Internet Dating
Narration:	My Worst Nightmare
Description:	The Anniversary Party
Process:	How to Handle a Workplace Bully
Definition:	The Meaning of Tolerance
Classification:	Three Types of Fathers

Comparison and Contrast: Fads Versus Timeless Fashions

Cause and Effect: The Reasons People Pollute

Argument: Why Writing Matters

HINT: Avoiding Title Pitfalls

When you write your title, watch out for problems.

- Do not view your title as a substitute for a thesis statement.
- Do not write a really long title because it can confuse readers.
- Do not write flashy or provocative titles because academic essays are not the same as works of fiction or news headlines.
- Do not put quotation marks around the title of your essay.

Practice 6

Read the next introductions, and underline the thesis statements. Then write titles for each essay.

1.   Some people fear mistakes more than others fear snakes. Perfectionism refers to self-defeating thoughts and behaviors aimed at reaching excessively high, unrealistic goals. Unfortunately, nobody is perfect. In fact, there are many problems associated with the desire to be perfect.

Title: _____

2.   Gang life, once associated with large urban centers in the United States, has become a common part of adolescent experience in towns and rural areas. Many of the gang members have no strong role models at home, and their gang affiliation makes them feel like part of a powerful group. To combat the problems associated with youth gangs, adults need to give adolescents more responsibilities.

Title: _____

3.   "A person who is not initiated is still a child," says Malidoma Somé. Somé is from the Dagara tribe in West Africa, and he underwent a six-week initiation ceremony. Left alone in the bush with no food or clothing, he developed a profound appreciation of nature and of magic. When he returned to his village, everyone welcomed him and other initiates with food and dancing. Somé had passed from childhood into adulthood and was expected to assume adult responsibilities. The ceremony helped Somé and the other initiates feel that they were valued participants in village life. Our culture should have formal initiation ceremonies for adolescents.

Title: _____

Practice 7

Read the next body paragraphs of a short essay. First, underline the topic sentence in each body paragraph. Then, on a separate sheet of paper, develop a title, a compelling introduction with a thesis statement, and a conclusion.

ADD A TITLE

ADD AN INTRODUCTION

Body Paragraph 1

Celebrity psychologists offer superficial suggestions on quick-fix counseling shows. For example, Dr. Phil asks guests so-called probing questions and then offers simplistic solutions. Other shows such as *Intervention* or *Hoarders* give audiences a view into the private lives of vulnerable people. Addicts undergo rehabilitation treatments that are not always successful, and viewers do not see the complexity of an addiction. They believe that the celebrity psychologist has found a solution for the guests' complicated troubles.

Body Paragraph 2

Furthermore, celebrity doctors deliberately create controversy, confusion, and drama about medical treatments. For instance, Dr. Oz advertises upcoming segments of his show by using headlines such as "What Your Doctor Won't Tell You!" The theme of the show revolves around doctors debating alternative medicine that has not been scientifically tested or proven to be effective. Audiences may conclude that unproven alternative medicines are the key to improving their health. Other medical shows are theatrical. On *The Doctors*, the panelists resort to many visual images as well as jokes when discussing a medical topic. The important information gets lost in all the theatrics.

Body Paragraph 3

Most importantly, audiences must be very wary about accepting health information from celebrities. Generally, celebrities who offer opinions or advice on health are not health-care professionals. Tom Cruise has publicly stated that depression does not exist and that psychiatry is a pseudoscience. Suzanne Somers encourages people to use bioidentical hormone replacement therapy, an extremely controversial and unproven treatment. And Jenny McCarthy, who openly linked vaccines to autism in children, spread one of the worst cases of incorrect medical information. There is no medical evidence that vaccines cause autism in children.

ADD A CONCLUSION

Writing the First Draft

4.6 **Write the first draft.**

The Writer's Desk: Write the First Draft

In the previous Writer's Desk exercises, you wrote an introduction, a conclusion, and an essay plan. Now write the first draft of your essay. Also write a title for your essay.

The Writer's Room

Writing Activity 1

Choose an essay plan that you developed for Chapter 3, and write the first draft of your essay.

Writing Activity 2

Write the first draft of an essay about one of the following thesis statements.

General Topics

1. The traditional role of males in this generation has (has not) changed significantly from previous generations.
2. Movies and television shows glorify crime and criminals.
3. Lying is appropriate in certain situations.
4. I would like to improve three of my traits.

College- and Work-Related Topics

5. The following factors contribute to the academic success of college students.
6. Getting fired can be a liberating experience.
7. Learning from experience is more (less) effective than learning from books.
8. I would (would not) be a good salesperson for the following reasons.

Checklist: First Draft

When you develop the first draft, ask yourself these questions.

❑ Do I have a compelling introduction?

❑ Does my introduction lead into a clear thesis statement?

❑ Do my body paragraphs contain interesting and sufficient details?

❑ Do the body paragraphs support the idea presented in the thesis statement?

❑ Do I have an interesting title that sums up the essay topic?

❑ Does my conclusion bring my essay to a satisfactory close?

5 Revising and Editing

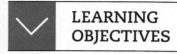

LEARNING OBJECTIVES

5.1 Follow key steps in revising and editing.

5.2 Revise for unity.

5.3 Revise for adequate support.

5.4 Revise for coherence.

5.5 Revise for style.

5.6 Edit for errors.

5.7 Write the final draft.

Revising and editing are similar to adding the finishing touches to a garden. A gardener adds new plants or transplants flowers and shrubs to enhance a garden. Similarly, a writer revises details and edits errors to improve an essay.

Key Steps in Revising and Editing

5.1 Follow key steps in revising and editing.

The revising and editing stage is the final step in the writing process. When you **revise**, you modify your writing to make it stronger and more convincing. Read your first draft critically and look for faulty logic, poor organization, and poor sentence style. Then reorganize and rewrite the draft, making any necessary changes. To **edit**, you proofread your final draft for errors in grammar, spelling, punctuation, and mechanics.

There are five key steps to follow during the revising and editing stage.

Revising and Editing

STEP 1   Revise for unity. Make sure that all parts of your work relate to the main idea.

STEP 2   **Revise for adequate support.** Determine that your details effectively support the main idea.

STEP 3   **Revise for coherence.** Verify that your ideas flow smoothly and logically.

STEP 4   **Revise for style.** Make sure that your sentences are varied and interesting.

STEP 5   **Edit for technical errors.** Proofread your work, and correct errors in grammar, spelling, mechanics, and punctuation.

Revising for Unity

5.2   Revise for unity.

All ideas in an essay clearly support the focus of the essay. If an essay lacks **unity**, then some ideas drift away from the main idea a writer has expressed in the essay. To check for unity in an essay, consider the following:

Every idea in an essay must move in the same direction just as this road goes straight ahead. There should be no forks in the road.

- Make sure that all topic sentences in the body paragraphs support the thesis statement of the essay.
- Make sure that all sentences within a body paragraph support the topic sentence of that paragraph.

ESSAY WITHOUT UNITY

The next essay plan looks at the reasons for deforestation. Topic Sentence 3 veers away from the writer's thesis or central focus (deforestation has implications for the quality of life).

Do not take a detour from your main idea.

Thesis Statement:	**Deforestation in the Amazon has tremendous implications for people's quality of life.**
Topic Sentence 1:	First, logging, mining, and agriculture displace the indigenous population in the Amazon.
Topic Sentence 2:	Also, scientists believe that deforestation in the Amazon will lead to a rapid increase in global climate change, which will affect people worldwide.
Topic Sentence 3:	Many development experts are trying to find methods to have sustainable development in the Amazon.

Practice 1

The following thesis statements have three supporting points that can be developed into body paragraphs. Circle the point that does not support the thesis statement.

1. North Americans have created a throw-away culture.

   a. First, waste from disposable containers and packaging has increased during the last one hundred years.

   b. Old appliances can be recycled.

   c. Consumers throw away about 40 percent of edible food.

2. International adoptions should be banned.

   a. Too many celebrities have adopted internationally.

   b. An internationally adopted child will often lose contact with his or her culture.

   c. By adopting from poor countries, wealthy Westerners contribute to the exploitation of mothers who cannot afford to keep their babies.

PARAGRAPH WITHOUT UNITY

Not only must your essay have unity, but each body paragraph must have unity. The details in the paragraph must support the paragraph's topic sentence. In the next paragraph, which is part of a larger work, the writer drifted away from his main idea. Some sentences do not relate to the topic sentence. If the highlighted sentences are removed, then the paragraph has unity.

> In her book *The Beauty Myth: How Images of Beauty Are Used against Women*, Naomi Wolf argues that women suffer psychologically because society indoctrinates them to value themselves based on their appearance. For example, the multibillion-dollar cosmetic and fashion industry markets its products by using very tall and thin supermodels. Most women cannot attain the physical standards of such an ideal and feel that they are failures if they cannot be thin and beautiful. Some companies depict regular and plus-sized women in their advertisements. For instance, Dove has used models of various sizes to sell some products. Even small children are affected. Many little girls idolize thin pop stars, and then become obsessed about their weight and physical appearance. Girls as young as nine years of age have been diagnosed with anorexia.

The writer detours here.

Practice 2

Paragraphs A and B contain problems with unity. In each paragraph, underline the topic sentence and cross out any sentences that do not support the controlling idea.

Paragraph A

When Gita arrived in the United States, she suffered from culture shock. On the first day of classes, Gita noticed that some American students were eating or drinking as they walked in crowded places. Such behavior would be unthinkable in India. It is considered rude to eat in front of someone and not share food. Gita also noticed that American students were on familiar terms with their college instructors. Some students even called the instructors by their first names. Indian students would never call a professor by his or her first name. I was an exchange student in Seoul, South Korea. Korean students bow to their professors and elders. I also got into the habit of bowing each time I met my professors. Gita eventually adjusted to student life in the United States and today laughingly recounts her reactions to some of the cultural differences.

Paragraph B

Academic performance weakens when students are sleep deprived. Therefore, our college should implement a few rules to help students get enough sleep. First, the college should actively promote physical exercise for students. People who exercise regularly find it easier to fall asleep and stay asleep at night. Some people don't like to exercise, and they have physical problems that prevent them from exercising. Classes could also start one hour later to give students an extra hour to sleep. Or students could have an hour free in the afternoon. Some students would take advantage of this free period to take a nap. Finally, the college could offer seminars and sleep clinics to educate students about the consequences of too little sleep. If the college implements these small changes, students' grades may improve.

Like a bridge, main ideas should have adequate support.

Revising for Adequate Support

5.3 Revise for adequate support.

A bridge is built using several well-placed beams, bars, blocks, and so on. Like a bridge, an essay requires **adequate support** to help it stand on its own. When revising an essay for adequate support, consider the following:

- Make sure that your thesis statement is broad enough to be supported by several points. You may need to revise the thesis statement to meet the length requirements of the essay.

- When you write the body paragraphs of the essay, insert specific details and try to include vivid descriptions, anecdotes, examples, facts, or quotations.

Avoid Circular Reasoning

Circular reasoning means that a paragraph restates its main point in various ways but does not provide supporting details. Like a driver aimlessly going around and around a traffic circle, the main idea never seems to progress. Avoid using circular reasoning by directing your paragraph with a clear, concise topic sentence and by supporting the topic sentence with facts, examples, statistics, or anecdotes.

Do not lead your reader in circles. Make a point and develop it.

PARAGRAPH WITH CIRCULAR REASONING

The following paragraph contains circular reasoning. The main point is repeated over and over. The writer does not provide any evidence to support the topic sentence.

> Traveling is a necessary educational tool. Students can learn a lot by visiting other countries. Many schools offer educational trips to other places for their students. Students may benefit from such cultural introductions. Clearly, traveling offers students an important educational opportunity.

This writer leads the reader in circles.

In the second version of this paragraph, the paragraph contains specific examples that help to illustrate the main point.

REVISED PARAGRAPH

> Traveling is a necessary educational tool. Students can learn a lot by visiting other places. Many schools and colleges offer educational trips. On such trips, students visit museums, art galleries, and historical sites. For example, the art department of our college sponsored a trip to Washington, D.C., and the students visited the Smithsonian. Other travel programs are work programs. Students may travel to another region or country to be involved in a community project. Students in the local high school, for instance, helped build a community center for children in a small town in Nicaragua. The students who participated in this project all said that they learned some very practical lessons, including organizational and construction skills. Clearly, traveling offers students an important educational opportunity.

Anecdotes and examples provide supporting evidence.

Practice 3

Read the following paragraphs, and write *OK* next to the ones that have adequate support. Underline the specific details in those paragraphs. Then, to the paragraphs that lack adequate support, add details such as descriptions, examples, quotations, or anecdotes. Use arrows to indicate where you should place specific details.

The next example is from an essay. In the first paragraph, the writer was repetitive and vague. After the writer added specific examples and vivid details, the paragraph was much more interesting.

Weak Support

To become a better dresser, follow the next steps. First, ask friends or family members what colors suit you. Also, don't be a slave to the latest fashion. Finally, spend money on a few good items rather than filling your closet with cheap outfits. My closet is half-full, but the clothing I have is of good quality.

Better Support with Details

To become a better dresser, follow the next steps. First, ask friends or family members what colors suit you. I love green, for instance, but when I wore an olive green shirt, a close friend said it brought out the green in my skin and made me look ill. Also, don't be a slave to the latest fashion. Although tank tops and low-rise jeans were popular for several years, I didn't have the right body type for that fashion because my belly spilled over the tops of my jeans. Instead, I wore longer shirts with fitted jeans, which highlighted my slender legs, not my muffin top. Finally, spend money on a few good items rather than filling your closet with cheap outfits. My closet is half-full, but the clothing I have is of good quality.

1. **Many cyclists are inconsiderate**. Cyclists think that they don't have to obey traffic rules and that traffic signs are just for car drivers. Also, some cyclists are pretty crazy and do dangerous things and risk their lives or the lives of others. People have ended up in the hospital after a run-in with these two-wheeled rebels. Cyclists should take safety courses before they ride on public roads.

Write OK or add details

2. **During my first job interview, I managed to overcome my fright**. I sat in a small, brightly lit room in front of four interviewers. A stern woman stared at me intently and curtly asked me why I wanted the job. Perspiration dripped into my eyes as I stammered that I had seen an advertisement. She smirked and asked me to be more specific. Feeling that I didn't have a chance anyway, I relaxed and stopped worrying about the faces gazing at me. I spoke about my first experience in a hospital, and I described the nurses who took care of me and the respectful way the orderlies treated me. I expressed my heartfelt desire to work as a patient care assistant, and I got the job.

Write OK or add details

Revising for Coherence

5.4 Revise for coherence.

Make your writing as smooth as possible by using expressions that logically guide the reader from one idea to the next. When revising an essay for **coherence**, consider the following:

- Ensure that sentences within each body paragraph flow smoothly by using transitional expressions.
- Ensure the supporting ideas of an essay are connected to each other and to the thesis statement by using paragraph links.

Transitional Expressions

Just as stepping stones can help you cross from one side of the water to the other, **transitional expressions** can help readers cross from idea to idea in an essay.

Here are some common transitional expressions.

Just as stepping stones link one shore to another, transitional expressions can link ideas in a paragraph and essay.

Function	Transitional Word or Expression		
Addition	again also besides finally first (second, third)	for one thing furthermore in addition in fact	last moreover next then
Comparison and contrast	as well equally even so however	in contrast instead likewise nevertheless	on the contrary on the other hand similarly
Concession of a point	certainly even so	indeed of course	no doubt to be sure
Effect or result	accordingly as a result consequently	hence otherwise then	therefore thus
Emphasis	above all clearly especially in fact	in particular indeed least of all most important	most of all of course particularly principally
Example	for example for instance in other words	in particular namely	specifically to illustrate
Reason or purpose	because for this purpose	for this reason the most important reason	

Space	above
	behind
	below
	beneath
	beside
	beyond
	closer in
		farther out
		inside
		near
		nearby
		on one side/the
		    other side
		on the bottom
			on the left/right
			on top
			outside
			to the north/east/
			    south/west
			under

Summary or conclusion	generally in conclusion in other words in short	on the whole therefore thus	to conclude to summarize ultimately
Time	after that at that time at the moment currently earlier eventually first (second, etc.) gradually	immediately in the beginning in the future in the past later meanwhile months after now	one day presently so far subsequently suddenly then these days

Adding Transitional Words Within a Paragraph

The next paragraph shows transitional words that link sentences within a paragraph.

Have you ever started a workout program and after a few weeks stopped doing it? There are several steps that you can take to stay motivated. **First**, try activities that you like to do. For example, if you hate exercising on machines, you could try swimming. **Next**, schedule your exercise activities in advance.

Choose a time and plan other activities around your workout times. **In addition**, participate in a variety of exercises. If you keep doing the same activity all the time, you will get bored and lose your motivation. **Finally**, promise yourself a little treat after you have completed your workout. A little self-indulgence is a good motivator, so reward yourself.

HINT: Use Transitional Expressions with Complete Sentences

When you add a transitional expression to a sentence, make sure that your sentence is complete. Your sentence must have a subject and a verb, and it must express a complete thought.

Incomplete   For example, violence on television.

Complete   For example, violence on television <u>is very graphic</u>.

Practice 4

GRAMMAR LINK
For more practice using transitions in sentences, see Chapter 21, "Sentence Combining."

Add appropriate transitional expressions to the following paragraph. Choose from the following list, and use each transitional word once. There may be more than one correct answer.

also	furthermore	in fact	for instance
first	then	for example	moreover

Counterculture is a pattern of beliefs and actions that oppose the cultural norms of a society. _____ hippies are the best-known countercultural group in the recent past, and they are known for rebelling against authority. _____ they rejected the consumer-based capitalist society of their parents in favor of communal living arrangements. _____ the hippie generation valued peace and created a massive antiwar movement. _____ there were mass protests against the Vietnam War. _____ small religious groups belong to the countercultural current. These groups live with other like-minded people and turn away from widely accepted ideas on lifestyle. _____ the Amish reject modern technology.

_____ militant groups and anarchist groups reject conventional laws. Some of these groups want to eliminate legal, political, and social institutions. There will always be countercultural movements in society.

Practice 5

The next paragraph lacks transitional expressions. Add appropriate transitional expressions wherever you think they are necessary.

The United States has witnessed profound changes in sexual attitudes and practices. In the 1920s, millions of men and women migrated from farms to cities. Living apart from their families and meeting new people in the workplace, young people enjoyed considerable sexual freedom, one reason that decade became known as the "Roaring Twenties." In the 1940s and 1950s, a researcher, Alfred Kinsey, published the first study of sexuality in the United States, which raised eyebrows everywhere because it was published during a time when Americans were uneasy talking openly about sex. Kinsey's study encouraged a new openness toward sexuality. In the late 1960s, the revolution truly came of age. Youth culture dominated public life, and expressions like "sex, drugs, and rock-and-roll" summed up a new, freer attitude toward sex.

—John J. Macionis, *Sociology*, 14th edition

Making Links in Essays

To achieve coherence in an essay, try the following methods to move from one idea to the next.

1. **Repeat words or phrases from the thesis statement in the topic sentence of each body paragraph.** In this example, *giftedness* and *ambiguity* are repeated words.

Thesis Statement	**Although many schools offer a program for** <u>**gifted**</u> **children, there continues to be** <u>**ambiguity**</u> **concerning the definition of** <u>**gifted.**</u>
Body Paragraph 1	One <u>ambiguity</u> is choosing the criteria for assessing the <u>gifted.</u>
Body Paragraph 2	Another <u>ambiguity</u> pertains to defining the fields or areas in which a person is <u>gifted.</u>

2. **Refer to the main idea in the previous paragraph, and link it to your current topic sentence.** In the topic sentence for the second body paragraph, the writer reminds the reader of the first point (*insomnia*) and then introduces the next point.

Thesis Statement	**Sleeping disorders cause severe disruption to many people's lives.**
Body Paragraph 1	<u>Insomnia</u>, a common <u>sleep disorder</u>, severely limits the <u>sufferer's quality of life.</u>
Body Paragraph 2	The <u>opposite condition of insomnia</u>, narcolepsy also causes mayhem as the sufferer struggles to stay awake.

3. Use a transitional word or phrase to lead the reader to your next idea.

Body Paragraph 3	<u>Moreover</u>, when sufferers go untreated for their sleep disorders, they pose risks to the people around them.

Revising for Style

5.5   Revise for style.

When you revise for sentence **style**, you ensure that your essay has concise and appropriate language and sentence variety. You can ask yourself the following questions.

- Have I used a variety of sentence patterns? (To practice using sentence variety, see Chapter 22.)

- Are my sentences parallel in structure? (To practice revising for parallel structure, see Chapter 25.)

- Have I used exact language? (To learn about slang, wordiness, and overused expressions, see Chapter 33.)

Cassie's Revision

In Chapter 3, you read Cassie's essay plan about finding a career path. After writing her first draft, she revised her essay. Look at her revision for unity, support, coherence, and style.

Just as paint makes a fence more attractive, revising for sentence style can make a piece of writing more appealing.

Add title

Finding the Right Career

A college degree is necessary for students to succeed in the global economy. Going to college is an expensive investment, so students wanted to make certain that their years at college will result in positive outcomes in their future goals. According to the Association of American Colleges and Universities (AACU), 85.9 percent of freshman students said that the main reason for seeking a college degree was to get a good job. **To ensure a**

Thesis statement

successful career pathway, students should discuss choices with friends and family, take advantage of career resources on their college campus, and intern or volunteer in their chosen field.

Add transition

First, college
~~College~~ students should discuss their career goals with friends and family. Parents have a vested interest in ensuring that their children make informed choices. They are in a unique position to assess their children's skills and abilities.

Add detail

In the article Parents Influence Children's Success, Nancy E. Hill, associate professor of social psychology at Duke University, states her opinion: "In order for children to reach their potential, they need their parents as informed advocates." Friends and other family members may also have usefull insights. For example, Jared is considering a career

Clarify pronoun

His friends
in business. ~~They~~ notice that he is a good leader.

Add detail

Jared's parents, who work in marketing and sales, suggested that he do some research into different types of business careers.

Furthermore, students should take advantage of career resources. Most colleges provide job counseling. And a bank of

Add transition

In addition, many
self-assessment tests. ~~Many~~ colleges have mentoring programs where parents, professors, and alumni offer advice. A student who participates in such mentoring programs may find their job

Revise for unity

search easier because of it. ~~There are many job search sites on the~~

Add detail

~~internet.~~ According to the Leeds School of Business at the University of Colorado, students who participated in the university mentoring program had a 40 percent greater chance of getting a job after graduating than those who had not.

Moreover, to find a good career match, students should ~~do~~ **participate in** • ← Find better word

internship programs or volunteer in their career field. Internships

and volunteering give students valuable information about their

career choice. By working in their preferred profession, students

learn what skills the job requires. **,and they** ~~They~~ learn about the working • ← Combine sentences

conditions. **Most importantly, by** ~~By~~ volunteering in their field, students can figure out • ← Add transition

what they like or dislike about that profession. **For instance** • ← Add detail

I volunteered in a hospital because I was considering a career in nursing.

Although hospital work can be difficult, I enjoyed working with patients.

Also, internships and volunteering can lead to networking

connections. Students may be able to use the relationships they

develop with their bosses or colleagues to help them find the

perfect entry-level job. **At my hospital job, I met a manager who promised** • ← Add detail

to give me a recommendation when I complete my nursing diploma.

Choosing a career path can be difficult. To make more

informed choices, students should involve friends and family,

assess college career resources, and volunteer or participate in an

internship. Students who follow these three practical steps will be

able to increase their employability after college. **They will also be** • ← Improve conclusion

more confident that they had made solid career choices.

HINT: Enhancing Your Essay

When you revise, look at the strength of your supporting details. Ask yourself the following questions.

- Are my supporting details interesting, and will they grab my reader's attention? Should I use more vivid vocabulary?
- Is my concluding sentence appealing? Could I end the paragraph in a more interesting way?

Editing for Errors

5.6 Edit for errors.

Before you finalize an essay, reread it to make sure that it is free of errors. Focus on the language, and look for mistakes in grammar, punctuation, mechanics, and spelling.

> **GRAMMAR LINK**
> To practice your editing skills, try the practices in Chapter 39.

The editing guide on the inside back cover of this book contains some common error codes that your instructor may use. It also provides you with a list of errors to check for when you proofread your text.

Editing Tips

The following tips will help you to proofread your work more effectively.

- Put your text aside for a day or two before you do the editing. Sometimes, when you have been working closely with a text, you might not see the errors.

- Begin your proofreading at any stage of the writing process. For example, if you are not sure of the spelling of a word while writing the first draft, either you could highlight the word to remind yourself to verify it later, or you could immediately look up the word in the dictionary.

- Use the grammar and spelling checker that comes with your word processor. However, be vigilant when accepting the suggestions. Do not always choose the first suggestion for a correction. For example, a grammar checker cannot distinguish between when to use *which* and *that*. Make sure that suggestions are valid before you accept them.

- Keep a list of your common errors in a separate grammar log. When you finish a writing assignment, consult your error list and make sure that you have not repeated any of those errors. After you have received each corrected assignment from your instructor, you can add new errors to your list.

Cassie's Edited Essay

Finding the Right Career

A college degree is necessary for students to succeed in the global economy. Going to college is an expensive investment, so students ~~wanted~~ **want** to make certain that their years at college will result in positive outcomes in their future goals. According to the Association of American Colleges and Universities (AACU), 85.9 percent of freshman students said that the main reason for seeking a college degree was to get a good job. To ensure a successful career pathway, college students should discuss career choices with friends and family, take advantage of career resources on their college campus, and intern or volunteer in their chosen field.

First, college students should discuss their career goals with friends and family. Parents have a vested interest in ensuring that their children make informed choices. They are in a unique position to assess their children's skills and abilities. In the article "Parents Influence Children's Success," Nancy E. Hill, associate professor of social psychology at Duke University, states her opinion: "In order for children to reach their potential, they need their parents as informed advocates." Friends and other family members may also have ~~usefull~~ **useful** insights. For example, Jared is considering a career in business. His friends notice that he is a good leader. Jared's parents, who work in marketing and sales, suggested that he do some research into different types of business careers.

Furthermore, students should take advantage of career resources. Most colleges provide career counseling. ~~And~~ **and** a bank of self assessment tests. In addition, many colleges have mentoring programs where parents, professors, and alumni offer advice. A student who participates in such mentoring programs may find ~~their~~ **his or her** job search easier because of it. According to the Leeds School of Business at the University of Colorado, students who participated in the university mentoring program had a 40 percent greater chance of getting a job after graduating than those who had not.

Moreover, to find a good career match, students should participate in internship programs or volunteer in their career field. Internships and volunteering give students valuable information about their career choices. By working in their preferred profession, students learn what skills the job requires, and they learn about the working conditions. Most importantly, by volunteering in their field, students can figure out what they like or dislike about that profession. For instance, I volunteered in a hospital because I was considering a career in nursing. Although hospital work can be difficult, I enjoyed working with patients. Also, internships and volunteering can lead to networking connections. Students may be able to use the relationships they develop with their bosses or colleagues to help them find the perfect entry-level job. At my hospital job, I met a manager who promised to give me a recommendation when I complete my nursing diploma.

Choosing a career path can be difficult. To make more informed choices, students should involve friends and family, assess college career resources, and volunteer or participate in an internship. Students who follow these three practical steps will be able to increase their employability after college. They will also be more confident that they ~~had~~ **have** made solid career choices.

The Writer's Desk: Revise and Edit Your Paragraph

Choose an essay that you have written for Chapter 4, or choose one that you have written for another assignment. Carefully revise and edit the essay. You can refer to the Revising and Editing checklists on the inside back cover.

Peer Feedback

After you write an essay, it is useful to get peer feedback. Ask a friend, family member, or fellow student to read your work and give you comments and suggestions on its strengths and weaknesses.

HINT: Offer Constructive Criticism

When you peer-edit someone else's writing, try to make your comments useful. Phrase your comments in a positive way. Look at the examples.

Instead of saying . . .	You could say . . .
You repeat the same words.	Maybe you could find synonyms for some words.
Your paragraphs are too short.	You could add more details here.

You can use this peer feedback form to evaluate written work.

Peer Feedback Form

Written by _____   Feedback by _____

Date: _____

1. What is the main point of the written work? _____

_____

_____

2. Which details effectively support the thesis statement? _____

_____

_____

3. What, if anything, is unclear or unnecessary? _____

_____

_____

_____

4. Give some suggestions about how the work could be improved. _____

_____

_____

_____

5. What is the most interesting feature of this written work? _____

_____

_____

_____

Writing the Final Draft

5.7   Write the final draft.

When you have finished making revisions on the first draft of your essay, write the final draft. Include all the changes that you have made during the revising and editing phases. Before you submit your final draft, proofread it one last time to make sure that you have caught any errors.

The Writer's Desk: Write Your Final Draft

You have developed, revised, and edited your essay. Now write the final draft.

HINT: Spelling, Grammar, and Vocabulary Logs

- **Keep a Spelling and Grammar Log.** You probably repeat, over and over, the same types of grammar and spelling errors. You will find it very useful to record your repeated grammar mistakes in a Spelling and Grammar Log. You can refer to your list of spelling and grammar mistakes when you revise and edit your writing.
- **Keep a Vocabulary Log.** Expanding your vocabulary will be of enormous benefit to you as a writer. In a Vocabulary Log, you can make a list of unfamiliar words and their definitions.

The Writer's Room

Writing Activity 1

Choose an essay that you have written for this course or for another course. Revise and edit that essay, and then write a final draft.

Writing Activity 2

Choose any of the following topics, or choose your own topic, and then write an essay. Remember to follow the writing process.

General Topics

1. taxing junk food
2. a problem in politics
3. curfews for teens under seventeen
4. privacy issues and social media sites

College- and Work-Related Topics

5. something you learned in college
6. adjustments new college students have to make
7. unpleasant jobs
8. mandatory second language learning

Checklist: Revising and Editing

When you revise and edit your essay, ask yourself the following questions.

- ❑ Does my essay have **unity**? Ensure that every paragraph relates to the main idea.

- ❑ Does my essay have **adequate support**? Verify that there are enough details and examples to support your main point.

- ❑ Is my essay **coherent**? Try to use transitional expressions to link ideas.

- ❑ Does my essay have good **style**? Check for varied sentence patterns and exact language.

- ❑ Does my essay have any errors? **Edit** for errors in grammar, punctuation, spelling, and mechanics.

- ❑ Is my **final draft** error-free?

Part II
Essay Patterns

What Is an Essay Pattern?

A pattern or mode is a method used to express one of the three purposes: to inform, to persuade, or to entertain. Once you know your purpose, you will be able to choose which writing pattern to use.

Patterns may overlap, and you can combine writing patterns. You may use one predominant pattern, but you can also introduce other patterns in supporting material.

CHAPTER 6   ILLUSTRATION
- Illustrate or prove a point using specific examples.

CHAPTER 7   NARRATION
- Narrate or tell a story about a sequence of events that happened.

CHAPTER 8   DESCRIPTION
- Describe using vivid details and images that appeal to the reader's senses.

CHAPTER 9   PROCESS
- Inform the reader about how to do something, how something works, or how something happens.

CHAPTER 10   DEFINITION
- Explain what a term or concept means by providing relevant examples.

CHAPTER 11   CLASSIFICATION
- Classify or sort a topic to help readers understand different qualities about that topic.

CHAPTER 12   COMPARISON AND CONTRAST
- Present information about similarities (compare) or differences (contrast).

CHAPTER 13   CAUSE AND EFFECT
- Explain why an event happened (the cause) or what the consequences of the event were (the effects).

CHAPTER 14   ARGUMENT*
- Argue or take a position on an issue and offer reasons for your position.

*Argument is included as one of the nine patterns, but it is also a purpose in writing.

6 Illustration

LEARNING OBJECTIVES

6.1 Define illustration.

6.2 Define the purpose of an illustration essay.

6.3 Explore topics for an illustration essay.

6.4 Write the thesis statement of an illustration essay.

6.5 Generate the supporting details of an illustration essay.

6.6 Develop an illustration essay plan.

6.7 Write the first draft of an illustration essay.

6.8 Revise and edit an illustration essay.

Icons show the game apps, fitness apps, shopping apps, and so on that are loaded on a smartphone. In the same way, writers have a better chance of persuading readers when they show or illustrate their ideas using examples.

Writers' Exchange

Work with a partner. You have three minutes to list as many words as you can that are examples of the following. For example, macaroni and cheese is a comfort food.

boring Facebook posts   nice compliments   comfort food

Illustration **73**

Exploring

What Is Illustration?

6.1   Define illustration.

Illustration writing includes specific examples that help readers acquire a clearer, deeper understanding of an essay's subject. You illustrate or give examples each time you explain, analyze, narrate, or express an opinion. Examples might include something that you have experienced or observed, or they may include factual information, such as a statistic.

   People use illustration every day. At home, a parent might list ways that a child's room is becoming messy. At college, classmates may share examples of how they have been given too much homework. At work, an employee could list examples of ways for the company to save money.

Practice 1: Visualizing Illustration

Brainstorm supporting ideas for the following thesis statement. List examples on the lines provided.

Thesis Statement: Many people store too much junk in their homes.

_____   _____

_____   _____

_____   _____

The Illustration Essay

6.2 **Define the purpose of an illustration essay.**

There are two effective ways to exemplify your main point and support your body paragraphs in an illustration essay.

1. Use a **series of examples**. When writing an essay about innovative commercials, you might list things that some directors do, such as using bizarre camera angles, introducing hilarious scenarios, adding amusing jingles, or creating catchy slogans.
2. Use an **extended example**, such as an anecdote or a description of an event. When writing about problems faced by first-year college students, you might tell a story about a specific student's chronic lateness.

Illustration at Work

Employment recruiter Rene Delery has written a guide to help job seekers create satisfactory résumés.

The **topic sentence** states the topic and controlling idea.

The **supporting sentences** provide details and examples.

The **concluding sentence** brings the paragraph to a close.

Most job hunters know that a résumé should be grammatically correct, with relevant and truthful details. Yet even good résumés can sink because of silly mistakes. For example, an annoying problem is the use of a tiny font. The person reading the résumé should not have to squint. The best font size is 11 or 12. Also, job seekers sometimes try to be artsy and try to stand out, but their irregular headings and inconsistent spacing can clutter up an otherwise well-done résumé. Another mistake job hunters make, hoping the employer won't notice, is to leave out dates. Doing so gives the impression that the candidate has something to hide. Finally, it's important for a résumé to look professional, yet people often neglect to use a simple and clear email address. Some silly email handles that have crossed my desk are "wakeysmile" and "razorkitty." Such addresses make the job hunter appear childish. Anyone who is looking for employment should keep these tips in mind.

A Student Essay

Read the student essay, and answer the questions that follow.

The Horrors of Black Friday Shopping

Molly Yesho

1   Growing up, I was taught that Thanksgiving is a time to spend with the family and be extra thankful for the things we have. However, as I get older, it has become clear that Thanksgiving may be a soon-forgotten holiday. The sole

Illustration **75**

reason for its near extinction is Black Friday. Every year, Black Friday shopping starts at an earlier time than the previous year. Now, most stores open on Thanksgiving night. Black Friday shopping is horrible for a lot of reasons.

2   First, the Black Friday sales are not that great. I have worked in retail for two years now, so I offer a unique perspective to the issue, including information that most people don't know. Here's a little secret: Stores have the same sales as any other time of year. If people wait until a week after Black Friday, the same products they are fighting over on Thanksgiving night will be discounted even more. Also, many consumers believe that coupons are exceptional for Thanksgiving. A coupon might advertise "30 percent off your entire purchase including sale items," and people think they are getting huge savings. However, customers rarely read the fine print. Typically, such coupons do not include "doorbusters," which are special sales. Most Black Friday deals are considered doorbusters; therefore, the coupons become invalid. So shopping on Black Friday is not a great way to save money.

3   Also, Black Friday just creates stress for people. There is a hectic environment for workers. Stores open earlier and earlier to get more customers. Employees work long shifts because it is the busiest time of the year. Cash register lines are long and stock runs out, causing anxiety for both customers and workers. I have seen many coworkers quit simply because of stress. Of course, customers play a huge role in the stressful environment. The majority of shoppers on Thanksgiving are angry, unpleasant people who act like children when they do not get their way. They cause a scene when they don't get help immediately. They throw a fit when stores run out of the item that they wanted. The built-up anger is usually taken out on the workers.

4   In fact, Black Friday shopping is extremely dangerous. The danger starts the moment the shoppers get into their cars. They drive at ridiculously high speeds to get to the store quickly. Then, at the stores, impatient customers push and shove just to get in the door before others or to get to an item first. Consumers argue with each other over an item or about who was in line first. Every year, the violent fights are broadcast on the news. A *CBS News* broadcaster stated that seven people have been killed on Black Friday, including a Walmart security worker who was trampled to death by crazy shoppers. It's sad to know that people die during a beautiful holiday period because of stressed, greedy shoppers.

5   Finally, even though Thanksgiving is a wonderful celebration, Black Friday shopping makes people ignore their families. Thanksgiving has disappeared in the media. Weeks prior to Black Friday, companies advertise the deals that they will be having, and they also produce ads saying "Merry Christmas" or "Happy Holidays." Companies don't advertise "Happy Thanksgiving" because they want people in their stores instead of staying home with their families. I cannot count the number of women who have come into my workplace on Black Friday and said, "My husband isn't very

happy that I missed dinner." Most of us workers would love to be at home, having dinner with our families. But instead, we are forced to work and to miss out on valuable time spent with relatives. The Thanksgiving holiday is no longer about giving thanks; it is about shopping.

6   America has a national holiday to give thanks for everything we have, but our celebration is cut short so people can be materialistic and buy more things that they don't need. Black Friday shopping is ridiculous because people ditch their families in order to shop, and they get hurt trying to get a deal. How many more people have to die before stores realize enough is enough and remain closed on Thanksgiving? Thanksgiving is a time to spend with family and be thankful for what we have; it isn't a time to go to the mall. Black Friday is truly the most horrible shopping day of the year.

Practice 2

1. Who is the intended audience? _____

2. Highlight the essay's thesis statement.

3. Underline the topic sentence in each body paragraph.

4. Using your own words, briefly sum up the writer's four supporting ideas.

   _____

   _____

   _____

   _____

5. The writer provides a personal anecdote at the beginning of her introduction. She also uses some anecdotes to back up some of her points. Which body paragraphs contain personal anecdotes?

   _____

6. What organizational strategy does the writer use?

   a. space order   b. time order   c. emphatic order

7. Write another example for one of the body paragraphs.

   _____

   _____

   _____

Illustration **77**

Explore Topics

6.3   Explore topics for an illustration essay.

In the Writer's Desk Warm Up, you will try an exploring strategy to generate ideas about different topics.

The Writer's Desk: Warm Up

Read the following questions, and write the first ideas that come to your mind. Think of two to three ideas for each topic.

EXAMPLE: What are some problems with online dating?

—too many choices, hard to decide

—photos are often cheesy or fake or modified

—profiles are unoriginal

1. What are some new trends or fads?

_____

_____

2. Think of some silly or unfounded fears that children have.

_____

_____

3. What are some status symbols in today's society?

_____

_____

Developing

The Thesis Statement

6.4   Write the thesis statement of an illustration essay.

The thesis statement of the illustration essay is a general statement that expresses both your topic and your controlling idea. To determine your controlling idea, think about what point you want to make. Remember to express an attitude or point of view about the topic.

     topic   controlling idea

Newlyweds often have misconceptions about married life.

     controlling idea   topic

I am unable to control **the mess in my work space.**

The Writer's Desk: Write Thesis Statements

Write a thesis statement for each of the following topics. You can look for ideas in the Warm Up on the previous page. Each thesis statement should express your topic and controlling idea.

EXAMPLE: Topic: problems with online dating

Thesis Statement: <u>Online daters make mistakes with their photos, profiles,</u>
<u>and searches.</u>

1. Topic: new trends or fads

   Thesis Statement: _____

   _____

2. Topic: children's silly or unfounded fears

   Thesis Statement: _____

   _____

3. Topic: status symbols in our society

   Thesis Statement: _____

   _____

The Supporting Ideas

6.5   Generate the supporting details of an illustration essay.

After you have developed an effective thesis statement, generate supporting ideas.

- Use prewriting strategies to generate a list of examples. Brainstorm a series of examples and extended examples that will best illustrate your main point.
- Choose the best ideas.
- Organize your ideas. Choose the best organizational method for this essay pattern.

The Writer's Desk: Generate Supporting Ideas

Choose one of your thesis statements from the previous Writer's Desk. List three or four examples that support the thesis statement.

EXAMPLE:

Thesis Statement: <u>Online daters make mistakes with their photos, profiles, and</u>

<u>searches.</u>

Illustration **79**

Supports: — use photos taken from more flattering angles

          — might alter pics using photo editing tools (e.g., Photoshop)

          — don't know what to say about themselves

          — write boring profiles

          — make quick judgments about others

Thesis Statement: _____

_____

Supports: _____

_____

_____

_____

_____

_____

The Essay Plan

6.6 Develop an illustration essay plan.

When writing an outline for an illustration essay, make sure that your examples are valid and relate to the thesis statement. Also, include details that will help clarify your supporting examples and organize your ideas in a logical order.

Thesis Statement: Online daters make mistakes with their photos, profiles, and searches.

    I.   Many daters post misleading photos.
        A. Some people use angles to look skinnier or fuller.
        B. Some people modify their appearance.
        C. People can use software like Photoshop to remove imperfections.

    II.   People don't know how to market themselves.
        A. People use ridiculous usernames.
        B. Profiles are often deceitful or vague.
        C. Everyone provides the same boring information.

    III.   People judge each other quickly based on looks.
        A. On Tinder, everyone swipes right or left without even reading the profile.
        B. Good partners get overlooked because they lack a certain trivial trait.

The First Draft

6.7 **Write the first draft of an illustration essay.**

After outlining your ideas in a plan, write the first draft using complete sentences. Also, include transitional words or expressions to help your ideas flow smoothly. Here are some transitional expressions that can help you introduce an example or show an additional example.

To introduce an example		To show an additional example	
for example	namely	also	in addition
for instance	specifically	first (second)	in another case
in other words	to illustrate	furthermore	moreover

VOCABULARY BOOST

Here are some ways to vary sentences, which will help you avoid boring readers with repeated phrases.

1. Underline the opening word of every sentence in your first draft. Check to see if some words are repeated.

2. If you notice every sentence begins the same way, try introducing the sentence with an adverb, such as *usually*, *generally*, or *luckily*, or a prepositional phrase such as *With his help* or *Under the circumstances*. In the following example, *They* is repeated too many times.

Repeated first words

People make many mistakes with their finances. They want luxuries that they cannot afford. They buy items on credit. They do not consider the high interest rates that credit card companies charge.

Variety

People make many mistakes with their finances. Desiring luxuries that they cannot afford, consumers buy items on credit. Sadly, many do not consider the high interest rates that credit card companies charge.

Illustration **81**

Revising and Editing

Revise and Edit an Illustration Essay

6.8   **Revise and edit an illustration essay.**

When you finish writing an illustration essay, review your work and revise it to make the examples as clear as possible to your readers. Make sure that the order of ideas is logical, and remove any irrelevant details. Before you work on your own essay, practice revising and editing a student essay.

A Student Essay

Read the essay, and then answer the questions that follow. As you read, correct any errors that you find and make comments in the margins.

....
Online Dating Mistakes
....

Julian Krajewski

1   Dating apps and online dating websites such as Match and Plenty of fish are extremely popular. Hundreds of millions of people across the world have tried the sites, including most of my friends. But it is hard to make a good dating profile. Online daters make mistakes with their photos, descriptions, and searches.

2   Too many online daters post misleading profile pictures. Some overweight people, frame the image a certain way to make themselves look skinnier. In real life, it would be impossible to keep up the illusion for more than a split second. My friend Sophie once went to meet her date only to discover that he weighed at least thirty pounds more than he appeared in his pictures. In other cases, people can look different in photos because they changed their haircut or got piercings. For example, on a dating site, I used a profile photo where I was clean-shaven. Later, I grew a beard. When I met a girl in a coffee shop, she grumbled that I "didn't match my picture." Also, some daters in their forties or fifties post old pictures of themselves. There is even people who Photoshop their photos to remove wrinkles or imperfections. Such strategies always backfire.

3   Second, a lot of people write silly, deceitful, or vague profiles. They don't know how to market themselves. They put crazy usernames like "Missjetset" and "MrPerfectGuy." On Tinder, some write ridiculous and pointless statements. One girl I was matched with began her description by stating that she "doesn't know how to make coffee." Also, profiles are usually too vague and boring. Almost everyone says, "I'm a positive person," and "I like music" or "I like having fun." They do not give enough details to stand out, and they

wonder why does nobody click on their profile. Also, daters will sometimes misrepresent themselves in an attempt to impress others. For example, in his profile, my friend Bashir says that he is very athletic and loves to cycle, but the truth is he rarely gets on his bike. He just wants to find a woman who is really physically fit. But some people write amazing, funny, original profiles. Those people probably find dates easily.

4   Furthermore, online daters make snap decisions based only on looks and risk missing out on good matches. On Tinder, for instance, it is tedious to read each profile. Swiping right or left, based on appearance, makes it easier to find matches quicker. People become picky and might select those with a particular hair color or body type. For instance, my cousin only wants to date muscular men, but then she complains that she's not meeting genuinely nice guys. She should stop focusing just on appearances. Good partners get overlooked because they lack a trivial trait. My friend Amanda informed me that I had matched with her friend Ashley. But after Ashley saw more photos of me, she decided that I had a "baby face" and was not interested. I will never know if Ashley is my soul mate, but her snap judgment suggests she probably isn't.

5   In conclusion, online dating has certain advantages. It's easy to meet a lot of different people. But daters should be careful with how they use dating platforms. They should post realistic photos and profiles, and they should be open minded when they search for potential partners.

Practice 3

Revising

1. Highlight the thesis statement.

2. Underline the topic sentences in paragraphs 2, 3, and 4.

3. In paragraph 3, the writer veers off course. Cross out the sentences that do not support the topic sentence.

   Explain why: _____

   _____

4. Body paragraphs 2, 3, and 4 contain what types support?

   a. an extended example   b. a series of examples

Editing

5. Paragraph 1 contains a capitalization error. Underline and correct the error.

   Correction: _____

6. Paragraph 2 contains a comma error. Underline and correct the error.

   Correction: _____

> **GRAMMAR LINK**
> See the following chapters for more information about these grammar topics:
> Capitalization, Ch. 37
> Commas, Ch. 35
> Subject–Verb
>   Agreement, Ch. 27
> Embedded
>   Questions, Ch. 22
> Adjectives and
>   Adverbs, Ch. 32

Illustration **83**

7. Paragraph 2 contains a subject–verb agreement error. Underline and correct the error.

   Correction: _____

8. Paragraph 3 contains an embedded question error. (For information about errors with embedded questions, see the Grammar Hint following this practice.) Underline and correct the error.

   Correction: _____

9. Paragraph 4 contains an error with the comparative form of adverbs. Underline and correct the error.

   Correction: _____

GRAMMAR HINT: Writing Embedded Questions

When a question is part of a larger sentence, do not use the question word order. View the next examples.

Error	I wondered how would I pay the rent.
Correction	I wondered how I would pay the rent.

The Writer's Desk: Revise and Edit Your Essay

Revise and edit the essay that you wrote for the previous Writer's Desk. You can refer to the revising and editing checklists at the end of this chapter and at the back of the book.

A Professional Essay

Al Kratina is a freelance writer and filmmaker who writes about films, music, and television. The next essay examines the way food is portrayed on television.

We're Watching What We Eat

Al Kratina

1   Television has a lot to teach us, not about actual facts, of course—learning science from *CSI* or *The Dr. Oz Show* seems about as effective as getting medical advice from a **carny**. But as a reflection of society, television can be a powerful tool, revealing our changing attitudes about gender, politics, race—and especially food. It may seem trivial, but almost every TV character

carny: a person who works for a carnival

eats or drinks on screen, even if it is just Dr. House washing down painkillers with pure vitriol. The way in which food is portrayed on television can tell us a lot about the shifting cultural attitudes.

2   The tension between healthy moderation and debauched indulgence is amplified to unhealthy extremes in contemporary television, with shows either championing near-starvation or reveling in **abject gluttony**. Some reality TV takes the former approach, molding unrealistic body types by treating hunger like a disease. With their focus on dramatic weight loss, shows like *The Biggest Loser* and *Bulging Brides* are fairly overt in their treatment of food as an almost sick, shameful necessity. Rarely does a TV character eat healthily without setting up a plot point or a punchline. In *The Big Bang Theory*, whatever nutrition the characters absorb at lunch is cancelled out by the endless pizza and Chinese takeout fueling their evening arguments over *Green Lantern* villains.

abject gluttony:
excessive eating

3   Someone basing his or her opinion of Western culture on prime-time programming might conclude that our insatiable hunger is matched only by our self-loathing. *The Simpsons* established many of its frequent fat gags in the 1990s, with Homer's severely disordered eating leading to everything from heart attacks to a spiritual journey. *Friends*, one of the biggest successes of the 1990s and early 2000s, was largely set in the fictional New York coffee house Central Perk, where characters rarely had anything more substantial than a latte in their hands. Their diet involved eating only once a year, preferably during a heartwarming Thanksgiving special, and otherwise smothering hunger pangs with a caffeine-induced ulcer.

4   Thankfully, a few shows take the opportunity to comment on our indulgence. The sitcom *Mike & Molly*, which follows an overweight couple who met in a weight-loss support group, deals with the often discriminatory and negative attitudes about obesity in North America. Although the mobster drama *The Sopranos* reveled in an endless consumption of ziti, cannoli, and capicola ham, many of the characters suffered ill effects, like capo Gigi Cestone, who died of a possibly sausage-induced heart attack. *The Sopranos* also drew a connection between food and psychology. A particularly insightful arc explored Tony's subconscious association of raw meat with violence and sexuality in one of his more traumatic therapy sessions.

5   Clearly, television can provide great insight about our eating habits. Certainly, any given block of food-related programming reveals how our eating habits are defined by often chaotic, contradictory impulses. Some shows suggest our future palates will be challenged by a variety of unique flavors, such as worm-based food in *Babylon 5* or the addictive drink made from a larval creature in *Futurama*. Those items may not be popular now, but just wait until they show up on *Diners, Drive-Ins, and Dives*.

Illustration **85**

Practice 4

1. Highlight the thesis statement.

2. Underline the topic sentences in paragraphs 2, 3, and 4.

3. In paragraphs 2, 3, and 4, what type of examples does the writer use?

   a. a series of examples   b. an extended example

4. In paragraph 2, how are *The Biggest Loser* and *The Big Bang Theory* similar and different in their portrayals of food?

   _____

   _____

   _____

5. How does the show *Mike & Molly* differ from other shows in the way in which it treats the subject of food?

   _____

   _____

   _____

6. List at least ten examples of television shows that the author uses as examples in the essay.

   _____   _____

   _____   _____

   _____   _____

   _____   _____

   _____   _____

The Writer's Room

Writing Activity 1: Topics

Write an illustration essay about one of the following topics, or choose your own topic.

General Topics

1. important historical events
2. social media friendships
3. mistakes that newlyweds make
4. great or horrible films
5. diets

College- and Work-Related Topics

6. things people should know about my college
7. examples of successful financial planning
8. qualities of an ineffective manager
9. mistakes students make
10. examples of obsolete jobs

**READING LINK
MORE ILLUSTRATION READINGS**
"Marketing New Inventions" p. 543
"Can We Talk?" p. 547

WRITING LINK
MORE ILLUSTRATION
WRITING TOPICS

Ch. 20, Writer's Room
topic 1 p. 307
Ch. 24, Writer's Room
topic 1 p. 346
Ch. 30, Writer's Room
topic 1 p. 409
Ch. 36, Writer's Room
topic 1 p. 471
Ch. 37, Writer's Room
topic 1 p. 484

Writing Activity 2: Media Writing

Write an illustration essay that focuses on the ways in which people or fictional characters help others. Provide examples showing how people extend themselves for someone else's benefit. Here are some suggestions to spark ideas:

Show: *The Doctors, The Biggest Loser, SuperNanny*

Film: *Dallas Buyers Club, 12 Years a Slave, The Book Thief*

Advertisment: The Shelter Pet Project (clips about pet adoption)

Song: "You've Got a Friend," "Help," "We are the World"

Podcast: *The Mental Illness Happy Hour*

Source: The Advertising Council
Mentalpod.com, mentalpod@gmail.com

Checklist: Illustration Essay

After you write your illustration essay, review the essay checklist at the back of the book. Also ask yourself the following questions.

❏ Does my thesis statement include a controlling idea that I can support with examples?

❏ Do I use a series of examples or an extended example in each body paragraph?

❏ Does each body paragraph support the thesis statement?

❏ Does each body paragraph focus on one idea?

❏ Do I have sufficient examples to support my thesis statement?

❏ Do I logically and smoothly connect paragraphs and supporting examples?

7   Narration

LEARNING OBJECTIVES

7.1 Define narration.

7.2 Define the purpose of a narration essay.

7.3 Explore topics for a narration essay.

7.4 Write the thesis statement of a narrative essay.

7.5 Generate the supporting ideas of a narration essay.

7.6 Develop a narration essay plan.

7.7 Write the first draft of a narration essay.

7.8 Revise and edit a narration essay.

When investigating a story, a reporter must try to find answers to the questions *who, what, when, where, why,* and *how.* You answer the same questions when you write a narrative essay.

Writers' Exchange

Try some nonstop talking. First, sit with a partner and come up with a television show or movie that you have both seen. Then, starting at the beginning, describe what happened in that episode or film. Remember that you must speak without stopping. If one of you stops talking, the other must jump in and continue describing the story.

Exploring

What Is Narration?

7.1   Define narration.

Narrating is telling a story about what happened. You generally explain events in the order in which they occurred, and you include information about when they happened and who was involved in the incidents.

People use narration in everyday situations. For instance, at home, someone might recount how a cooking accident happened. At college, students tell stories to explain absences or lateness. At work, a salesperson might narrate what happened on a business trip.

HINT: Value of Narration

Narration is useful on its own, but it also enhances other types of writing. For example, student writer Bruno Garcia had to write an argument essay about traffic laws. His essay was more compelling than it might otherwise have been because he included a story about his grandmother's eyesight and her driving accident.

Practice 1: Visualizing Narration

Brainstorm supporting ideas for the following thesis statement.

Thesis Statement: My first date with Calvin was a disaster.

_____   _____   _____

_____   _____   _____

_____

The Narration Essay

7.2   Define the purpose of a narration essay.

When you write a narrative essay, consider your point of view.

Use **first-person narration** to describe a personal experience. To show that you are directly involved in the story, use *I* (first-person singular) or *we* (first-person plural).

> When **we** landed in Boston, **I** was shocked by the white landscape.
> **I** had never seen so much snow.

Use **third-person narration** to describe what happened to somebody else. Show that you are simply an observer or storyteller by using *he*, *she*, *it* (third-person singular), or *they* (third-person plural).

> Drivers waited on the highway. **They** honked their horns and yelled in frustration. **They** did not understand what was happening.

Narration at Work

When lawyer Murray Marshall meets with clients, he records the facts and confirms those facts in writing. Here is an excerpt from one of his emails.

I will summarize the facts of your accident as you have related them to me. You stated that on March 10 at approximately 5 pm, you were driving your vehicle westbound on Main Street. The weather was sunny, and the road conditions were dry. In the 3000 block, after a dog darted in front of your vehicle, you strenuously applied your brakes, bringing your car to a sudden halt. Seconds later, the vehicle behind you made contact with the rear of your vehicle. You sustained a whiplash type injury to your neck and a sprain to your right wrist. You visited a local hospital within one hour following the accident, where you were given a brace for your neck and a compression bandage for your wrist. As a result of the pain you suffered in the days following the accident, you missed five days of work, for which you received no compensation from your employer. You have requested that our office research the likelihood of your recovering damages for your pain and suffering and loss of income, and to advise what the amount of those damages might be. If I have omitted or misunderstood any salient detail, please contact our office at your convenience.

- The **topic sentence** states the topic and controlling idea.
- The **supporting sentences** provide details and examples.
- The **concluding sentence** brings the paragraph to a close.

A Student Essay

Read the student essay and answer the questions that follow.

....

Rehabilitation

....

Jack McKelvey

1   I am the sum of all my experiences. I take away lessons from my failures and disappointments. These memories shape my view of my existence. Many individual experiences, from my first day of school to my first love, have changed me. However, one experience overshadows the rest:

prison. Although being in prison was not pleasant, the experience has made me a much better person today.

2   Before I was convicted and shipped off to jail, I was not a good person. I sold drugs, I lied, and I stole. If I thought I could get away with something, I would try. I had no respect for anyone, including myself. I harbored no ambitions or desires. I just wanted to sell drugs, spend money, and smoke pot. In April of 2003, that would all change.

3   On April 11, I was on the return leg of my usual trip to Grand Rapids for two pounds of marijuana. Flashing lights blinded me through the rearview mirror. I pulled over, and the lights followed. I had been making this trip every week or so for almost two years without incident. That day, I didn't even hide my illegal cargo. I knew the officer was going to smell the marijuana I was smoking. I knew he would find the large black trash bag on my back seat. I thought about running, but that never seems to end up well for the people who try it on television. Resigned to my fate, I enjoyed one last cigarette before I was shoved into the back of a royal blue state police cruiser.

4   "I sentence you to twenty-four to sixty months in the Michigan Department of Corrections." I had never heard a more sinister cluster of words. My stomach turned, and a single cold drop of sweat trickled from my armpit. My ears must not have been working correctly. The judge had just used the word *prison*. The worst images from prison documentaries flashed through my mind like lightning. I am five foot nothing and a buck thirty soaking wet, so how was I going to survive incarceration?

5   In prison, I had a lot of time to think. On the first day, I was expecting to see someone running with a knife sticking out of his ribs or to hear someone screaming as he was being raped. Bad things did occur but not on that first day. What did happen was nothing—just silence—and that, I believe, was even worse. Alone, I relived every mistake I had made that led to prison. As the months progressed, I thought most often of freedom and what I wanted to do the day I was released. I also thought of odd things I came to miss: adjusting the water temperature in the shower, opening a refrigerator door, and sleeping in a dark room. And I thought of how I had spent my life so far, and how little I had accomplished. I began to feel as if my life were over, and the best years of my life were sliding by. Although most inmates considered me a short timer, I felt as if my sentence was timeless eternity.

6   Two years into my incarceration, I realized that my release was on the horizon, and I became motivated to change. I began tearing through books with a vengeance. I took every college course available at the institution, and I even enrolled in a vocational skills program. I was going to have a second chance, and soon. Although I was doing all I could intellectually to

prepare myself for my release, I was most anxious to begin repairing the relationships I had labored to destroy. I often thought of what I would say to everyone I had disappointed and hurt. I soon realized that words would not prove that I had changed from the person I was before prison. I was going to have to show them, and that is exactly what I planned to do. For the first time since my early teen years, I was optimistic about my future.

7   After three years, two months, six days, eleven hours, and twenty-two minutes, I left prison. Euphoria fails to describe the feeling, and fails miserably. After readjusting to freedom, I found work at a landscaping company, one of the few places that will hire a felon with no degree, and I stayed out of trouble. Over the next year, I would spend a great deal of time with my family. I am proud to say that our relationship now is the best it has ever been. I have come to realize that life is about those we care about. Being imprisoned was what it took for me to realize what I was truly missing in life. The time we have is fleeting, even when it appears to be standing still. I don't plan to waste another second.

Practice 2

1. Highlight the thesis statement.
2. Underline the topic sentences in paragraphs 2, 5, and 6.
3. Using your own words, sum up what happened in paragraphs 3 and 4.

   Paragraph 3: _____

   _____

   Paragraph 4: _____

   _____

4. In paragraphs 3, 4, and 5, the narrative is simple: a man is arrested and jailed. Yet the power of the narrative is in the details: readers can see, hear, feel, and smell what happened. What are some of the most striking descriptions?

   Paragraph 3: _____

   _____

   Paragraph 4: _____

   _____

   Paragraph 5: _____

   _____

5. Why did Jack McKelvey write about his experience? What are some messages in this essay?

_____

_____

_____

_____

Explore Topics

7.3 **Explore topics for a narration essay.**

In the Writer's Desk Warm Up, you will try an exploring strategy to generate ideas about different topics.

The Writer's Desk: Warm Up

Read the following questions, and write the first ideas that come to your mind. Think of two to three ideas for each topic.

EXAMPLE: What are some memorable moments in your life?

__I ran away from home to meet a man I met on the Internet__.

__I came to the United States to study__.

1. What are some emotional ceremonies or celebrations that you have witnessed or been a part of?

_____

_____

_____

2. What significant experiences have changed you or taught you life lessons?

_____

_____

_____

3. What adventures have you had with a good friend? What happened?

_____

_____

_____

Developing

The Thesis Statement

7.4   Write the thesis statement of a narration essay.

When writing a narrative essay, choose a topic that you personally find very interesting, and then share it with your readers. For example, very few people may be interested if you simply list what you did during a recent vacation. However, if you write about a particularly moving experience during that vacation, you can create an entertaining narration essay.

Ensure that your narration essay expresses a main point. Your thesis statement should have a controlling idea.

        topic   controlling idea

The day I decided to get a new job, <u>my life took a dramatic turn</u>.

       controlling idea   topic

<u>Sadie's problems began</u> **as soon as she drove her new car home**.

HINT: How to Make a Point

In a narration essay, the thesis statement should make a point. To help you find the controlling idea, you can ask yourself the following questions:

- What did I learn?
- How did I change?

- How did it make me feel?
- What is important about it?

For example:

| **Topic** | <u>ran away from home</u> |
| **Possible controlling idea** | <u>learned the importance of family</u> |

                      topic   controlling idea

When I ran away from home at the age of fifteen, <u>I discovered the importance of my family</u>

Practice 3

Practice writing thesis statements. Complete the following sentences by adding a controlling idea.

1. During her wedding, my sister realized _____

_____

2. During my years with the National Guard, I learned _____

_____

3. When I graduated, I discovered _____

_____

The Writer's Desk: Write Thesis Statements

Write a thesis statement for each of the following topics. You can look for ideas in the Warm Up on page 92. Each thesis statement should mention the topic and express a controlling idea.

EXAMPLE: Topic: A memorable moment

Thesis statement: <u>I made a mistake when I ran away from home to meet my</u>

<u>boyfriend</u>.

1. Topic: An emotional ceremony

Thesis statement:_____

_____

2. Topic: A significant experience

Thesis statement: _____

_____

3. Topic: An adventure with a friend

Thesis statement: _____

_____

The Supporting Ideas

7.5   Generate the supporting ideas of a narration essay.

A narration essay should contain specific details so that the reader understands what happened. To come up with the details, ask yourself a series of questions and then answer them as you plan your essay.

- **Who** is the essay about?
- **What** happened?
- **When** did it happen?
- **Where** did it happen?
- **Why** did it happen?
- **How** did it happen?

When you recount a story to a friend, you may go back and add details, saying, "Oh, I forgot to mention something." However, when you write, you have the opportunity to clearly plan the sequence of events so that readers can easily follow the story. Organize events in chronological order (the order in which they occurred). You can also begin your essay with the outcome and then explain what happened that led to the outcome.

HINT: Narration Essay Tips

Here are some tips to remember as you develop your narration essay.

- Do not simply recount what happened. Reflect on why the event is important.
- Consider the main source of tension in your narrative. Descriptions of conflict or tension can help engage the reader.
- To make your essay more powerful, use descriptive language that appeals to the senses. For more information on using descriptive imagery, see pages 107–114 in Chapter 8.

The Writer's Desk: Develop Supporting Ideas

Choose one of your thesis statements from the previous Writer's Desk. Then generate supporting ideas. List what happened.

EXAMPLE: A memorable moment   Topic: _____

–met a man online   _____

–fell in love   _____

–decided to go to meet him   _____

–sold my things to buy a bus ticket _____

–my father came to take me back home _____

The Essay Plan

7.6   Develop a narration essay plan.

Before you write a narration essay, make a detailed essay plan. Write down main events in the order in which they occurred. To make your narration more complete, include details about each event.

Thesis Statement: I made a mistake when I ran away from home to meet my boyfriend.

    I.   Even though I met him in a virtual world, I thought our love was real.

        A. We started to correspond online.

        B. I fell in love with him.

        C. We talked all the time.

    II.   I didn't listen to my family and friends.

        A. My friends said that I was living in a fake world.

        B. I knew my parents would disapprove.

        C. I ignored everyone and took a bus to meet my boyfriend.

    III.   Very worried, my father came to bring me home.

        A. My father knocked on my hotel room door.

        B. At breakfast, my father met my boyfriend.

        C. My parents wouldn't allow me to keep in touch with my boyfriend.

        D. With no communication between us, my boyfriend and I broke up.

Concluding idea: If only I could turn back the clock, I would have done many things differently.

The Writer's Desk: Write an Essay Plan

Refer to the information you generated in previous Writer's Desks, and prepare a detailed essay plan. Include details for each supporting idea.

The First Draft

7.7   **Write the first draft of a narration essay.**

After outlining your ideas in a plan, you are ready to write the first draft. Remember to write complete sentences with some transitions to help readers understand the order in which events occur or occurred. Here are some transitions that are useful in narrative essays.

To show a sequence of events			
after that	finally	in the end	meanwhile
afterward	first	last	next
eventually	in the beginning	later	then

Enhancing Your Essay

One effective way to enhance your narration essay is to use dialogue. A **direct quotation** contains someone's exact words, and the quotation is set off with quotation marks. When you include the exact words of more than one person in a text, you must make a new paragraph each time the speaker changes.

> "Who did this?" my mom shrieked, as my brother and I stood frozen with fear.
> "Mark did it," I assured her shamelessly, as I pointed at my quivering brother.

An **indirect quotation** does not give the author's exact words, but it keeps the author's meaning. It is not set off by quotation marks.

> As Mark and I stood frozen with fear, our shrieking mother asked who had done it. I assured her shamelessly that Mark had done it, as my finger pointed at my quivering brother.

GRAMMAR HINT: Using Quotations

When you insert a direct quotation into your writing, capitalize the first word of the quotation, and put the final punctuation inside the closing quotation marks.

- Place a comma after an introductory phrase.

  Zsolt Alapi said, "Everyone was terrified."

- Place a colon after an introductory sentence.

  Zsolt Alapi described the atmosphere: "Everyone was terrified."

See Chapter 37 for more information about using quotations.

The Writer's Desk: Write the First Draft

In the previous Writer's Desk, you developed an essay plan. Carefully review your essay plan, make any necessary changes to the details or chronology, and then write the first draft of your narrative essay.

Revising and Editing

Revise and Edit a Narration Essay

7.8   Revise and edit a narration essay.

When you finish writing a narration essay, carefully review your work and revise it to make the events as clear as possible to your readers. Check that you have organized events chronologically, and remove any irrelevant details. Before you revise and edit your own essay, practice revising and editing a student essay.

A Student Essay

Read the essay, and then answer the questions that follow. As you read, correct any errors that you find, and make comments in the margins.

....
My Memorable Trip
....

by Van Nguyen

1   I became infatuated with a man I met on the Internet. When I was sixteen years old. I never dreamed that I would ever feel that way, but I became so obsessed that I made a plan to meet him. At that time, I was living in the south of Vietnam, and he was living in the north in a city I only recognized from news reports on television. I made a mistake when I ran away from home to meet my boyfriend.

2   Even though I met him in a virtual world, I thought our love was real. I used to play an online dance game called *Audition*, and we started to correspond. At that time, many people liked to play online games. And of course being young and impressionable, the outcome was inevitable: I fell in love with him. We talked online or by phone or we chatted via Yahoo messenger every day. My friends counseled me to be careful because I was living out my fantasies in a fake world full of phony people. But I was crazy about him, and I ignored their advice. I knew my parents would not allow me to date him. That was when I decided to run away to be with him.

3   One day, my parents were away from home for work and would not return until late evening. I ran to my friend's house to ask her for help to sell my things. Together, we sold my bicycle and gold ring so I can buy a bus ticket for my trip. The bus ride took two days during which I neither ate nor drank because I was feeling car sick. When I arrived at my destination, I rented a hotel room and called my best friend to tell her where I was. She was the only one who knew about my plan, and she had made me promise to phone her to tell her I was ok. What I didn't know was that at the time of my phone call, my mom was sitting beside her as she talked to me. Of course, my friend had to tell my mother the whole story.

4   Very worried, my father came to bring me home. It was 2 a.m., and someone knocked on my hotel room door. I was scared, so I opened it just a little and saw my father standing there. He had rented another room in the hotel and told me to come with him. A few hours later, my boyfriend came to the hotel to meet me. But he got a shock when he saw my father was with me. While we were eating breakfast together my father said "You do not have permission to see my daughter." After breakfast, my father bought two one-way plane tickets, and we went home. My parents wouldn't allow me to keep in touch with my boyfriend and took my phone away. To prevent

me from running away again, they dropped me off at school and picked me up every day after school. With no contact, it didn't take much time for my boyfriend and me to break up.

5   Sometimes, I think that if only I could turn back the clock, I would have done many things differently. I would have waited to be with him untill my parents had accepted him, and I would never have run away from home and worried my parents. I now live in the United States and have not returned to Vietnam since that event. My ex-boyfriend has a new girlfriend, he and I still keep in touch. I am going to Vietnam for a holiday in a couple of months, and I hope I will see him again. All though it was a sad memory, I have never forgotten the details about my adventure.

Practice 4

Revising

1. Highlight the thesis statement.

2. What type of narration is this?

  a. first person   b. third person

3. Paragraph 2 lacks unity. One sentence does not support the paragraph's topic. Strike through that sentence.

4. Paragraph 3 lacks a topic sentence. An appropriate topic sentence for paragraph 3 could be:

  a. I looked forward to meeting my boyfriend.

  b. I worried that my parents would find out where I was.

  c. To realize my dream, I made a meticulous plan.

  d. The bus ride was very uncomfortable and long.

Editing

5. A fragment is an incomplete sentence. Underline a fragment in paragraph 1.

Possible correction: When I was sixteen years old, _____

_____

6. Paragraph 3 contains a tense shift. A verb tense changes for no logical reason. Underline the sentence with the tense shift, and write a correction on the line below.

Correction: _____

7. Paragraph 4 contains a punctuation error in the quote. Circle the error, and write the correction on the line below.

Correction: _____

> **GRAMMAR LINK**
> Extra grammar help:
> Fragments, Ch. 23,
>   p. 327
> Run-Ons, Ch. 24,
>   p. 336
> Verb Consistency,
>   Ch. 29, p. 386
> Spelling and Commonly
>   Confused Words,
>   Ch. 34, p. 441
> Commas, Ch. 35,
>   p. 452

8. There are two spelling mistakes in paragraph 5. Underline the errors, and write the corrections on the lines below.

   Corrections: _____   _____

9. Paragraph 5 contains a run-on sentence. Underline the error and show three ways to correct the sentence.

   Corrections: _____

   _____

   _____

The Writer's Desk: Revise and Edit Your Essay

Revise and edit the essay that you wrote for the previous Writer's Desk. You can refer to the revising and editing checklists at the end of this chapter and at the end of this book.

VOCABULARY BOOST

Writers commonly overuse words. To make your writing more vivid and interesting, identify five common and overused verbs in your essay. Replace each verb with a more vivid and specific verb.

First draft We walked to the edge of the cliff and looked at the sea.
Revision We strolled to the edge of the cliff and gazed at the sea.

A Professional Essay

Sarah Stanfield writes and edits for publications such as *Videography Magazine* and the *New York Post*. In this essay from *Salon*, she narrates what happened while she was living in Ecuador.

....
Botched Tan
....

Sarah Stanfield

1   Baños, Ecuador, is a balmy village of waterfalls and thermal springs poised on the neck of the massive Tungurahua volcano. Normally, I would be thrilled to be there, but instead, I was half-conscious with pain. Baños was supposed to be my first stop on a trek into the Amazon rain forest. Thanks to what I would later find out were second-degree burns on my legs, it became my last stop.

2   I was living in Quito as part of my university's study abroad program, conducting anthropological fieldwork for my senior thesis. A few days before, I had accompanied my host family to its relatives' ranch just outside the city. The place had a pool, and the cloudy sky convinced me it was the perfect day to change my pale skin to brown, no sunscreen needed. Quito rises about nine thousand feet above sea level. At this elevation, the atmosphere is thinner, making skin more vulnerable to the sun's rays. I knew this, but convinced myself the clouds in the sky would temper the intensity of the sun. As my skin is fair with pink undertones, all my previous sunbathing efforts had resulted in some shade of red blooming across my skin. Self-tanners left me orange and streaky. Yet I kept striving for the miracle day when I would achieve a bronze glow. So I stretched out next to the pool with a Toni Morrison novel. Four hours later, I arose with legs the color of smoked salmon.

3   In Ecuador, almost everyone is of mixed Spanish and indigenous ancestry, with brown eyes, thick, glossy black hair, and olive skin. Like many young and naive anthropology students out in the field for the first time, I fell in love with the beauty of the people. I envied the Ecuadorans. Looks-wise, they were everything I was not. My hair was mousy brown and lank, and my skin was too **sallow**.

sallow: an unhealthy pale color

4   I was surprised when, shortly after my arrival, Diana, my fifteen-year-old host sister, complimented me on my good skin. At first, I thought she was referring to my lack of acne. But then she ran her hand through my hair, saying that I had good hair, too. She grabbed a chunk of her own hair and made a face. I figured this to be typical teen-girl self-criticism.

5   Eventually, I realized that Ecuador has plenty of image complexes. Skin-lightening cream gets top billing on pharmacy shelves, and billboards advertising everything from cigarettes to public health messages depict smiling gringos. Matinee idols are mostly white American movie stars. Of course, Ecuadorians are not alone in aspiring to gringo beauty ideals. The most notorious example is Xuxa, the Brazilian singer and actress with the second-best-selling album in the history of Brazil. Xuxa is tall and blond, yet she presides over millions of fans in a country where almost half the citizens are of mixed African, Amerindian, and European ancestry.

6   I wasn't thinking about this as I took the bus ride from Quito to Baños, though. Before the bus trip, I had spent three days unable to walk, and now dime-size blisters were sprouting up and down my legs. I was just hoping that after all of the pain I was going through, my skin would fade from pink to brown. The bus suddenly lurched forward, causing my right leg to bump the scratchy surface of the seat in front of me. One of the blisters tore open, leaking burning fluid down my leg. Its sting convinced me that this was serious. I needed medical attention.

7   In Baños, I headed straight to the medical clinic. The waiting room was packed, mostly with young, exhausted-looking women and their numerous children. Meanwhile, my blisters were growing; they were now the size of quarters. In a tiny examination room, a young woman in a nurse's uniform greeted me. Her skin was the exact shade of caramel I yearned for. She was strikingly beautiful, except for her hair color. It was the strained yellow of a botched bleach job.

8   I lifted my skirt to my thighs, displaying my blisters and explaining in Spanish what had happened. The nurse sucked in her breath and made a little clicking sound, shaking her head. "We'll need to pop the blisters and disinfect them," she said. "Then you need to go back to Quito and go to the hospital. This looks like a second-degree burn." She took out a bottle of alcohol, a needle, and some cotton balls. With that, she got to work. I whimpered, and tears brimmed up in my eyes. Over and over I felt the sting of the needle, then the feeling of fire crawling down my legs as the fluid dribbled out, then the sting of the alcohol on open wounds, which felt like a thousand needle points battering my skin.

9   The pain alone was enough for me to swear never again to go near a beach or tanning salon. But it was the comment from the nurse, as she finished her task, which made me realize the insanity of what I had done. Screwing the cap back on the bottle of alcohol, she said, "What a pity. You had such good skin."

Practice 5

1. What type of narration is this text?

   a. first person   b. third person

2. Approximately when and where do the events take place?

   _____

3. List the main events in the order in which they occur.

   _____

   _____

   _____

   _____

_____

_____

4. How does the writer's burn affect her plans in Ecuador?

_____

_____

5. The writer mentions some reasons for her decision to tan. What are her main reasons?

_____

_____

6. According to the writer, how do some people in Ecuador feel about their appearance? Provide some examples from the text.

_____

_____

_____

_____

7. Write down one example of a direct quotation from the essay. (See pages 96–97 for a definition of direct and indirect quotations.)

_____

_____

8. Write down one example of an indirect quotation.

_____

_____

9. Writers of narration essays do more than simply list a series of events. What did Stanfield learn from her experience?

_____

_____

The Writer's Room

Writing Activity 1: Topics

Choose any of the following topics, or choose your own topic, and write a narrative essay.

READING LINK
MORE NARRATION
READINGS:

"My Bully, My Best
    Friend" p. 520
"460 Days" p. 566

MORE NARRATION
WRITING ACTIVITIES:

Ch. 21, Writer's Room
    topic 1, p. 318
Ch. 27, Writer's Room
    topic 1, p. 371
Ch. 28, Writer's Room
    topic 1, p. 387

General Topics

1. a talent you have
2. a lie or a mistake
3. a good encounter with a stranger
4. a thrilling or frightening moment
5. a news event that affected you

College- and Work-Related Topics

6. a positive moment at college
7. a turning point in your life
8. an uncomfortable incident at work
9. a positive or negative job interview
10. a difficult lesson at work or school

Writing Activity 2: Media Writing

Write an essay describing what happened to a person or a main character who overcame an obstacle to be successful. Choose a person from any film, show, song, online video, or podcast. Here are some suggestions that might spark ideas:

Show: *Unbreakable Kimmy Schmidt, Marvel's Jessica Jones, Spartacus*

Film: *The Pursuit of Happyness, The Revenant, The Roosevelts*

YouTube: Fred's Channel, PewDiePie, BlueXephos

Song: Classics "I Will Survive" (Gloria Gaynor) and "We are the Champions" (Queen)

Podcast: NPR's *TED Radio Hour*, Marc Maron's *WTF*

Checklist: Narration Essay

After you write your narration essay, review the checklist at the back of the book. Also ask yourself these questions.

❑ Does my thesis statement clearly express the topic of the narration?

❑ Does my thesis statement contain a controlling idea that is meaningful and interesting?

❑ Does my essay answer most of the following questions: who, what, when, where, why, how?

❑ Do I use transitional expressions that help clarify the order of events?

❑ Do I include details to make my narration more vivid?

8 Description

Artist D. M. Phadke adds details in his work to express his aesthetic vision.
Similarly, writers use the tools of descriptive writing to create images that readers
can visualize in the mind's eye.

LEARNING OBJECTIVES

8.1 Define description.

8.2 Define the purpose of a description essay.

8.3 Explore topics for a description essay.

8.4 Write the thesis statement of a description essay.

8.5 Generate the supporting ideas of a description essay.

8.6 Develop a description essay plan.

8.7 Write the first draft of a description essay.

8.8 Revise and edit a description essay.

Writers' Exchange

Choose one of the objects from the following list. Then, brainstorm a list of descriptive words about the object. Think about the shape, texture, smell, taste, color, and so on. List the first words that come to your mind.

For example: cake   gooey, sweet, chocolate, smooth, pink icing, layered

| lizard | school bus | lake | older adult | lemon |

What Is Description?

8.1 Define description.

Description creates vivid images in the reader's mind by portraying people, places, or moments in detail. Here are some everyday situations that might call for description.

People use description every day. At home, family members might describe the style of their new apartment to a friend. At college, students could describe the results of a chemistry experiment to their classmates. At work, employees may describe a retirement party to an absent colleague.

Practice 1: Visualizing Description

Brainstorm supporting ideas for the following thesis statement. Write some descriptive words or phrases on the lines.

Thesis Statement: Historically, there have been some very unhealthy fashion trends.

corsets   tall wigs   extremely high heels

_____   _____   _____

_____   _____   _____

_____   _____   _____

Description at Work

In this observation report, an early childhood education aide expresses concern with a young boy's ability to socialize appropriately and to adapt to the classroom environment.

D.R., a three-and-half-year-old boy, struggles to use language to communicate his ideas, wishes, and needs. On the day of this observation, D.R. was well groomed and appropriately dressed for the weather; he was wearing black dress shoes, which fell off his feet several times as he was running and playing. Expressive language skills are an area of challenge for D.R., who more frequently uses gestures to communicate. He frequently pulls on his teacher's arm and points in the direction of the toy he wants. At one point, D.R. tried to join his peers who were in a playhouse. He attempted to get into the house, but other children did not make space for him. He jumped up and down and screamed, and then he started to cry. This pattern of not using words to ask for help or express what he needed was noted frequently throughout the observation.

> The **topic sentence** states the topic and controlling idea.

> The **supporting sentences** provide details and examples.

> The **concluding sentence** brings the paragraph to a close.

The Description Essay

8.2   Define the purpose of a description essay.

When you write a description essay, focus on three main points.

1. **Create a dominant impression.** The dominant impression is the overall atmosphere that you wish to convey. It can be a strong feeling, mood, or image. For example, if you are describing a casual Sunday afternoon party, you can emphasize the relaxed ambience in the room.
2. **Express your attitude toward the subject.** Do you feel positive or negative toward the subject? For instance, if you feel pleased about your last vacation, then the details of your essay might convey the good feelings you have about it. If you feel tense during a job fair, then your details might express how uncomfortable the situation makes you feel.
3. **Include concrete details.** Details will enable a reader to visualize the person, place, or situation that you are describing. You can use active verbs, adjectives, and adverbs so that the reader imagines the scene more clearly. You can also use **imagery**, which is description using the five senses. Review the following examples of imagery.

Sight   A Western Tiger Swallowtail dipped by my face. About three inches across, its lemon yellow wings were striped improbably and fluted in black. They filliped into a long forked tail with spots of red and blue.

—Sharman Apt Russell, "Beauty on the Wing"

Sound	The tree outside is full of crows and white cranes who gurgle and screech.

—Michael Ondaatje, *Running in the Family*

Smell	I think it was the smell that so intoxicated us after those dreary months of nostril-scorching heat, the smell of dust hissing at the touch of rain and then settling down, damply placid on the ground.

—Sara Suleri, *Meatless Days*

Touch	The straps from my backpack tore into my shoulder blades, and pain ran down my spine.

—Andrew Wells, "My Journey Down the Grand Canyon"

Taste	Entirely and blessedly absent are the cloying sweetness, chalky texture, and oily, gummy aftertaste that afflict many mass-manufactured ice creams.

—R.W. Apple Jr., "Making Texas Cows Proud"

A Student Essay

Read the following student essay, and answer the questions that follow.

....

Park of Personal Pleasure
....

Laura Wilson

1 Some weary individuals tune into the latest and greatest television dramas; still others befriend drugs as a means of escape. There are an extraordinary number of different ways and reasons that people want to escape from everyday life. When I want a change from my daily routine, I go to a unique place. I experience freedom, relaxation, and amusement at Maumee Bay State Park.

2 I feel liberated as I begin my adventure on a three-mile course at the pathway entrance by the "Big Hill," best known for attracting lots of eager sledders during the blustery winters of Northwest Ohio. I strap on my rollerblades and proceed on the timbered pathways of the park. The white chubby clouds dance, and the bright sunlight stings my eyes. Gliding effortlessly along the trail, I detect hints of lavender, letting me know I am in the familiar wilderness that I have come to adore. The wind caresses my hair, and I grin to myself as I reach my maximum speed. I weave from path to path, and I feel free.

3 The next leg of my expedition helps me unwind. I venture towards the "secret beach" my friends and I discovered on a previous outing. This

jewel of a beach is located along the outer part of the same rollerblade path. I change into my trusty, ever-so-comfortable Nikes and climb over the treacherous gray boulders that separate me from the beach. My first priority is to rip off my shoes, so my toes can wriggle into the warm sand. I then sit on my usual tree stump and eagerly pull out my sketchbook. I begin to draw the vast, multi-colored sky of Oregon, Ohio, as a blanket of darkness slowly covers it. Putting some finishing touches on my artwork, I ask myself, "What could be more relaxing than this moment?"

4   To complete my already perfect day, I make my way over to the park's hotel, which holds a treasure chest of amusement for me if I can gain entry. I sneak past the front desk operator, hoping she will not question which room I am staying in. Then I snake my way through the corridor to the main lobby where I hear the bings and the beeps of the arcade games from the adjacent room. The aroma of burgers—flame grilled at the hotel restaurant right around the corner—makes my mouth water.

5   Off to my left is the real reason for my break-in. I stare through enormous glass windows at the water, but I do not possess the much-**coveted** key card, so I quickly search the hallway for guests entering the pool area. Soon a couple goes through the door, and I quickly follow. As I hurry through the doors, I cannot hold in my happiness. After I am suited up to swim, I rush over to the hot tub and sink into its warm embrace. The bubbling water soothes my aching muscles.

coveted: desired

6   Prior to discovering what Maumee Bay State Park could offer me, I would always wonder, "What is there to do in this boring, suburban home town of mine?" The answer was only two miles from my house. I am overjoyed that I took the time to figure out my personal way of escaping. I feel free, relaxed, and amused when I venture into my **realm** of personal pleasure.

realm: kingdom

Practice 2

1. Highlight the thesis statement.
2. The writer recounts a story using description that appeals to the senses. Find imagery from the essay.

   a. Sight: _____

   _____

   b. Sound: _____

   _____

   c. Touch: _____

   _____

d. Smell: _____

_____

3. What dominant impression does the writer create in this essay? Underline examples in the essay to support your answer.

_____

4. The writer recounts how she sneaks into the hotel's swimming pool area. Is this ethical behavior? What is your opinion about her actions?

_____

_____

_____

Explore Topics

8.3   Explore topics for a description essay.

In the Writer's Desk Warm Up, you will try an exploring strategy to generate ideas about different topics.

The Writer's Desk: Warm Up

Read the following questions, and write the first ideas that come to your mind. Think of two or three ideas for each topic.

EXAMPLE: List some memorable events that have happened to you or someone you know.

—my trip to Costa Rica

—the time I stayed with my grandmother in Seattle

—the time a tornado tore through our town

1. Who are your best friends?

_____

_____

_____

2. What are some unattractive fashion trends?

_____

_____

_____

3. What are your unusual food preferences?

_____

_____

_____

Developing

When you write a description essay, choose a subject that lends itself to description. You should be able to describe images or objects using some of the five senses. To get in the frame of mind, try thinking about the sounds, sights, tastes, smells, and feelings you would experience in certain places, such as a busy restaurant, a hospital room, a subway car, a zoo, and so on.

The Thesis Statement

8.4   Write the thesis statement of a description essay.

In the thesis statement of a description essay, you should convey a dominant impression about the subject. The dominant impression is the overall impression or feeling that the topic inspires.

>   topic   controlling idea
> **The photograph of me as a ten-year-old** has an embarrassing story behind it.

> controlling idea   topic
> Feeling self-satisfied, **Odysseus Ramsey started his first day in public office.**

HINT: How to Create a Dominant Impression

To create a dominant impression, ask yourself how or why the topic is important.

Poor   Land developers have built homes on parkland.
              (Why should readers care about this statement?)

Better   The once pristine municipal park has been converted into
              giant estate homes that average families cannot afford.

The Writer's Desk: Thesis Statements

Write a thesis statement for each of the following topics. You can look for ideas in the Warm Up in the previous Writer's Desk. Each thesis statement should state what you are describing and contain a controlling idea.

EXAMPLE: Topic: a memorable event

Thesis Statement: <u>On that scorching day in April, I experienced the most</u>
<u>frightening moments of my life</u>.

1. Topic: a close friend

Thesis Statement: _____

_____

2. Topic: unattractive fashion trends

Thesis Statement: _____

_____

3. Topic: unusual food preferences

Thesis Statement: _____

_____

The Supporting Ideas

8.5   Generate the supporting ideas of a description essay.

After you have developed an effective thesis statement, generate supporting details.

- Use prewriting strategies such as freewriting and brainstorming to generate ideas.
- Choose the best ideas. Most description essays use imagery that describes the person or scene.
- Organize your ideas. Choose the best organizational method for this essay pattern.

Show, Don't Tell

Your audience will find it more interesting to read your written work if you show an action of a person or a quality of a place rather than just state it.

Example of Telling: Laura was angry.

Example of Showing: Laura stomped down the stairs and rushed into the kitchen. Cheeks flushed red with anger, she glared at her older brother. "Where were you? I was waiting for two hours," she hollered. Instead of waiting for his answer, she scowled at him and marched out of the kitchen, banging the door behind her.

Practice 3

Choose one of the following sentences, and write a short description that shows—not tells—the quality or action.

1. Today was a perfect day.

2. I was frightened as I entered the cave.

3. The weather did not cooperate with our plans.

Use Different Figurative Devices

When writing a description essay, you can use other figurative devices (besides **imagery**) to add vivid details to your writing.

- A **simile** is a comparison using *like* or *as*.

    My thoughts ran as fast as a cheetah.

    Let us go then you and I,
    When the evening is spread out against the sky
    Like a patient etherised upon a table
                      —from "The Love Song of J. Alfred Prufrock" by T.S. Eliot

- A **metaphor** is a comparison that does not use *like* or *as*.

    Life is sweet-and-sour soup.

    Memory is the diary we all carry about with us.
                      —by Oscar Wilde

- **Personification** is the act of attributing human qualities to an inanimate object or an animal.

    The chocolate cake winked invitingly at us.

    Love is blind.
                      —from *The Merchant of Venice* by William Shakespeare

Practice 4

Practice using figurative language. Use a simile, metaphor, or personification to describe each numbered item below. If you are comparing two things, try to use an unusual comparison.

EXAMPLE: toddler: <u>The toddler was like a monkey, climbing up and down with</u>
<u>   great agility. (simile)</u>

1. mountain: _____

_____

2. hair: _____

_____

3. ocean: _____

_____

VOCABULARY BOOST: Use Vivid Language

When you write a description essay, try to use vivid language. Use specific action verbs and adjectives to create a clear picture of what you are describing.

Use a more vivid, specific adjective. My boss was ~~angry.~~ livid

Use a more vivid, specific verb or image. The child ~~cried.~~ whimpered

Think about other words or expressions that more effectively describe these words: *laugh, talk, nice, walk.*

The Writer's Desk: List Sensory Details

Choose one of your thesis statements from the previous Writer's Desk, and make a list of sensory details. Think about images, impressions, and feelings that the topic inspires in you.

EXAMPLE: Topic: a memorable event

–scorching day   –ripped trees

–blistering sun   –smashed homes

–howling wind   –frightened people

–driving like a racecar driver

Your topic: _____

Your list of sensory details: _____

_____

_____

_____

_____

_____

_____

_____

The Essay Plan

8.6 Develop a description essay plan.

An essay plan helps you organize your thesis statement, topic sentences, and supporting details before you write a first draft. When you make an essay plan, remember to include concrete details and to organize your ideas in a logical order. If you want to emphasize some description details more than others, arrange them from least affecting to most affecting. If you want your readers to envision a space (a room, a park, and so on), arrange details using spatial order.

Thesis Statement: On that scorching day in April, I experienced the most frightening day of my life.

    I.   We were floating slowly down the river, enjoying ourselves, when we saw our parents running towards us.

        A. My parents screamed that a storm was coming.

        B. A large Force 5 tornado was tearing through the woods behind us.

        C. It tossed the trailer into the air, and the tornado ripped up the trees.

    II.   Trying to escape the clutches of the horrible storm, our parents drove like race car drivers.

        A. We drove into town.

        B. We went through a police roadblock.

        C. We drove to the garage of a friend.

    III.   We could not believe what was before our eyes.

        A. The town was gone.

        B. Houses were torn to pieces.

        C. Cars, trees, electric poles were smashed.

The Writer's Desk: Write an Essay Plan

Choose one of the ideas that you have developed in previous Writer's Desks and prepare an essay plan. Remember to use vivid details and figurative language to help create a dominant overall impression.

The First Draft

8.7   Write the first draft of a description essay.

After outlining ideas in a plan, you are ready to write the first draft. Remember to write complete sentences. Also, as you write, think about which transitions can effectively help lead your readers from one idea to the next. Description writing often uses space order. Here is a list of transitions that are useful for describing the details in space order.

To show place or position			
above	beyond	in the distance	outside
behind	closer in	nearby	over there
below	farther out	on the left/right	under
beside	in front	on top	underneath

The Writer's Desk: Write the First Draft

In the previous Writer's Desk, you developed an essay plan. Now write the first draft of your description essay. Before drafting, carefully review your essay plan and make any necessary changes.

Revising and Editing

Revise and Edit a Description Essay

8.8   Revise and edit a description essay.

When you finish writing a description essay, review your work and revise it to make the description as vivid as possible to your readers. Check that you have organized your ideas, and remove any irrelevant details. Before you work on your own essay, practice revising and editing a student essay.

GRAMMAR HINT: Using Adjectives and Adverbs

When you revise your description essay, check that you have used adjectives and adverbs correctly. For example, many people use *real* when the adjective is actually *really*.

My brother, Magnus, is ~~real~~ really tall and powerful.

See Chapter 32 for more information about adjectives and adverbs.

A Student Essay

Read the essay, and then answer the questions that follow. As you read, correct any errors that you find and make comments in the margins.

....

Tornado

....

Kelsey Spell

1   In Arkansas, April is a hot and humid month. That particular spring day, the sun was beating down hard as we searched for any shady spot we could find to keep cool. A friend suggested we go for a little dip in the river. We walked through the woods to the river and jumped in. The water on our hot skin felt cold at first, but then we became used to it. We swam, hiding from the blistering sun under shade created by the overhanging branches of the trees. But little did I know what was in store for us. On that scorching day in April, I experienced the most frightening day of my life.

2   We were floating slowly down the river, enjoying ourselves, when we saw our parents running towards us. They screamed that a storm was on the way and urged us to get out of the water. We rushed to our trailer home, put on dry clothes, and raced into vehicles to flee from the area as fast as possible. We drove in convoy: My mother and we children were in the first car, and my father was in the car behind us. By the time we were at the end of the driveway, a large Force 5 tornado was tearing through the woods behind us. We glanced back, and we saw that it was the very same woods we had just been playing in. The tornado howled as it ripped through the trees, breaking them all piece by piece within seconds. The Herculean wind tossed the trailer we had just been in into the air. It flipped upside down, spun around out of control, and slammed to the ground.

3   Trying to escape the clutches of the horrible storm, our parents drove like race car drivers. My father barely escaped the tornado because the wind grabbed the back of his car, almost tossing it into a ditch like a rag doll. As we reached the outskirts of town, two police officers were blocking off the road with their vehicles. We flew right through them. It was then that they looked up and saw what we were running from, and they too got into their cars and zipped along right behind us. We drove through town and into a garage of a friend. We scrambled out of the cars and hustled inside the house. We heard howling and crashing, and we felt the building rumbling. What had been a beautiful blue clear sky was now as black as coal. Then within five minutes it was all over.

4   We waited for the sky to clear up before we came out of the garage, and when we did, you could not believe what was before our eyes. Our town and our home were gone. The tornado had torn the houses to pieces, flipped

cars upside down, knocked over train cars, and snapped light poles in two. Uprooted trees, intertwined into one another, lay scattered on the roads. The violent storm had ripped our school building in half as if it were a piece of paper. It had tossed school buses around like children throwing toys during a temper tantrum. The town looked like the world's biggest junkyard.

5   We all survived with just scratches and bruises, and I could not be more thankful. The citizens of our town came together real quick to help the needy. Volunteers provided food, water, blankets, and clothes to those in need. Within a month, our town rose up from the ashes that awful storm had created. Although it is not the same as it once was, our town is now a place of familiarity and comfort again. It is a town filled with people who are so close that they are all like family. Our town is Marmaduke, Arkansas.

GRAMMAR LINK

Extra grammar help:
Pronouns, Ch. 31,
    p. 408
Adverbs, Ch. 32, p. 422
Spelling, Ch. 34, p. 441

Practice 5

Revising

1. Highlight the thesis statement.

2. Highlight the topic sentence of paragraphs 3 and 4.

3. Paragraph 2 lacks a topic sentence. A possible topic sentence:
   a. Our parents were frightened and yelled at us.
   b. Our primary thought was to escape the destructive force of the tornado.
   c. We children thought it was a very exciting event.
   d. The winds from the tornado ripped everything up.

4. What overall dominant impression does the writer convey in the essay? Underline examples in the essay to support your answer.

   _____

5. A simile is a comparison using *like* or *as*. Underline three examples of similes in paragraph 4.

Editing

6. Paragraph 2 has a spelling error. Underline and correct the mistake.

   Correction: _____

7. Paragraph 4 contains a pronoun shift. Underline and correct the error.

   Correction: _____

   _____

8. In paragraph 5, there are two adverb errors. Underline and correct the errors. Correction: _____

A Professional Essay

Sy Montgomery is a conservationist and award-winning writer of adult and children's books about our natural world. The next excerpt, from her book *Spell of the Tiger*, is about the tigers of the Sundarbans, a mangrove jungle on the India–Bangladesh border.

With an Open Mouth

Sy Montgomery

1   On a soft May night in West Bengal, when the sweet scent of khalsi flowers clung to the wet, warm darkness, when the moon shone round and white, and boatmen's lanterns winked at one another like fireflies up and down the river, death came with an open mouth for Malek Molla. The day's work was over. Molla and his six companions had collected five kilograms of honey from the fat combs they'd found hanging among the small, curved, downward-pointing leaves of a genwa tree. Collecting honey is one of the most dangerous jobs in Sundarbans, yet from April to June hundreds of men leave their mud and thatch houses and their rice fields and fishing nets to follow the bees into the forest.

2   In little wooden boats, they glide down the numberless channels that permeate the sodden land of Sundarbans. Barefoot, they wade through the sucking clay mud. Carefully, they step around the breathing roots of the mangroves, which spike up from the earth like bayonets. Sometimes they must pass through stands thick with hental, which is used by crocodiles to build their nests. Its stems are armored with two-inch thorns so sharp that by the time you feel one in your foot, it has already penetrated half an inch and broken off in your flesh.

3   One man always stands guard for the group because there are many dangers. Tigers hunt in these forests. Crocodiles lurk in the shallows. Vipers coil in the shade. Even the bees can kill. They are aggressive, and their sting causes muscle spasms, swelling, and fever. People who have been badly stung say that the pain can last for a year.

4   The honey itself is said to be an antidote to the bees' poison. Some who have survived attacks by bee swarms say companions saved their lives

by smearing the thin, spicy honey over the stings. Sundarbans honey is considered an elixir of sorts. Shamans say eating some each day will ensure a long life. The leaves of the khalsi, whose fragrant, white blossoms supply the pollen from which the earliest honey is made, are curative, too: A paste made from them will staunch the flow of blood.

5   The group found the first bees' nest easily, eight feet up in a genwa. One man climbed the spindly trunk. With smoke from a kerosene-soaked torch of green hental **fronds**, he drove the bees from the hive and cut loose the swollen comb with a machete. Another man below caught the comb in a ten-gallon tin that had once held mustard oil. The others waited, armed with clubs, ready in case a tiger appeared, but none did.

fronds: large leaves

6   That afternoon, they emerged from the forest safe and laden with their riches, the golden honey. In their low-bodied wooden boat, anchored in the Chamta River, beneath the palm thatch that roofed the cabin, the six tired men relaxed. Their lantern gleamed. The men talked and laughed and smoked the harsh, leaf-wrapped cigarettes called bidi. A pot of curry and India's ubiquitous dahl—lentil stew—bubbled on the boat's clay stove. One man offered a song. The notes of the Bengali melody rose and fell, full and then empty, like the tides that rise to engulf the forest every six and a half hours and then fall back, drained.

7   No one felt the boat rock. No one heard a scream. But everyone heard the splash when something very heavy hit the water beside the boat. The men pointed their flashlights into the forest, along the shore. On the far bank of the river, the light barely caught the figure of a huge, wet cat slinking into the mangroves, carrying the body of Malek Molla like a fish in its mouth. Molla had been quiet that evening; possibly, he had been asleep. The tiger may have killed him without ever waking him up. Without making a sound, without rocking the boat, a predator—possibly weighing five hundred pounds and stretching to nine feet long—had launched itself from the water, selected its victim, seized him in its jaws, and killed him instantly.

8   Molla's body was recovered the following day. The tiger had severed his spinal cord with a single bite to the back of the neck. It had eaten the soft belly first. In Sundarbans, everyone watches for the tiger. But the tiger, they say, always sees its victim first.

Practice 6

1. What is the dominant impression conveyed by the author?

_____

2. Highlight the thesis statement.

3. Why is collecting honey a dangerous occupation for the men of the Sundarbans?

_____

_____

_____

_____

4. The writer uses imagery to describe the Sundarbans. Find examples of imagery for the following senses.

Sight: _____

Smell: _____

Taste: _____

Sound: _____

Touch: _____

5. A simile is a comparison using _like_ or _as_. Underline one simile in paragraph 6 and one in paragraph 7.

6. Personification is giving human traits to nonhuman objects. Underline an example of personification in paragraph 1.

7. In the Sundarbans, what can the honey collectors do to protect themselves? You will have to infer or make a guess.

_____

_____

The Writer's Room

Writing Activity 1: Topics

Write a description essay about one of the following topics, or choose your own topic.

General Topics

1. a music concert
2. a public place that has a lot of odors
3. your dream house
4. a scene from nature
5. an exciting sports event

College- and Work-Related Topics

6. a beautiful building or area on campus
7. a frustrating day
8. an eccentric professor
9. a new person I have met
10. graduation day

READING LINK
MORE DESCRIPTION
READINGS

"Into Thin Air" p. 557
"Buried Alive" p. 561

Writing Activity 2: Media Writing

Write an essay in which you describe the setting of a past era. Using sensory details, describe the setting as you see it portrayed in a film, television show, or even an online video clip. Here are some suggestions that might spark ideas:

Show: *Mad Men, Downton Abbey, The Last Kingdom*

Film: *Lincoln, Les Misérables, Bridge of Spies*

Video: *AP Archive* (The Associated Press channel on YouTube)

Checklist: Description Essay

After you write your description essay, review the essay checklist at the back of the book. Also ask yourself these questions.

❏ Does my thesis statement clearly show what I will describe in the essay?

❏ Does my thesis statement have a controlling idea that makes a point about the topic?

❏ Does my essay have a dominant impression?

❏ Does each body paragraph contain supporting details that appeal to the reader's senses?

❏ Do I use vivid language?

9 Process

Everyone uses processes. For example, a teaching artist may need to explain to students how to shape, fire, and glaze pottery. Along similar lines, writers often need to explain to readers how to do something or how something functions.

LEARNING OBJECTIVES

9.1 Define process.

9.2 Define the purpose of a process essay.

9.3 Explore topics for a process essay.

9.4 Write the thesis statement of a process essay.

9.5 Generate the supporting ideas of a process essay.

9.6 Develop a process essay plan.

9.7 Write the first draft of a process essay.

9.8 Revise and edit a process essay.

Writers' Exchange

Choose one of the following topics, and have a group or class discussion. Describe the steps you would take to do that process.

- how to bake cookies
- how to wash a car
- how to play baseball
- how to play a card game

Exploring

What Is Process?

9.1 Define process.

A **process** is a series of steps usually done in chronological order. In process writing, you explain how to do something, how an incident took place, or how something works.

People explain processes every day. At home, parents might explain to their children how to make macaroni and cheese. At college, a professor may explain to students how they could become tutors. At work, an employer could describe to newly hired interns how to perform their daily responsibilities.

Practice 1: Visualizing Process

Brainstorm supporting ideas for the following thesis statement. Write a few words to show each step.

Thesis Statement: When you are traveling to a tropical destination, there are some important steps to follow.

 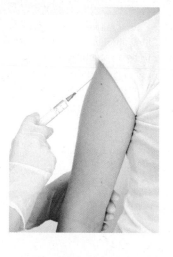 

_____   _____   _____

_____   _____   _____

_____   _____   _____

_____   _____   _____

Process at Work

Frank Morelli is a mechanic who specializes in repairing sports cars. In this pamphlet excerpt, he advises customers on how to buy a car.

Purchasing a car for the first time is both stressful and exciting. To ensure that you make the best choice, consider the following suggestions. First, identify your needs. For example, make a list of why you want a vehicle, how much you want to pay, and what color and model you want. Next, do some research. Many websites and magazines have information about the performance and reliability of different car models. For instance, the magazine *Consumer Reports* publishes reports based on laboratory tests of various vehicles. Finally, test-drive several different cars. You will know not only if the engine runs smoothly but also if you are comfortable driving the car. By following these simple steps, you will be able to make an informed decision when buying your next car.

> The **topic sentence** states the topic and controlling idea.

> The **supporting sentences** provide details and examples.

> The **concluding sentence** brings the paragraph to a close.

The Process Essay

9.2   Define the purpose of a process essay.

Before planning a process essay, you need to determine your purpose. Do you want to tell readers how to complete a process or how to understand a process?

1. **Complete a process.** This type of essay contains directions for completing a particular task. A writer might explain how to change a flat tire, how to decorate a room, or how to use a particular computer program.
2. **Understand a process.** This type of essay explains how something works or how something happens. A writer might explain how the admissions process at a college works or how food goes from the farm to the table.

A Student Essay

Read the essay and answer the questions that follow.

What's Cooking in My Kitchen?

Leander Neal

1   Every culture in the world has its own cuisine. Italy, for example, has an exciting variety of pasta dishes. My favorite food is chicken alfredo pasta. There are many different ways of making this delicious mealtime entrée. By following the next steps, you can create an amazing version of this traditional Italian dish.

2   First, you need to shop for items to make your meal. Ingredients that go into this dish include two boneless chicken breasts and a box of fettuccini noodles. You also need sauce, and it can be store-bought or homemade. I suggest you make your own sauce, as it will be tastier, and you will feel like a real chef. The sauce requires a cup and half of milk, two tablespoons of butter, two tablespoons of flour, and some salt or pepper. It also includes one-half cup of Parmesan cheese. Although it is available in cans, the best Parmesan cheese is fresh. It may be a bit expensive, but it is worth it to make the dish especially tasty. All of these items are easily available at your local grocery store.

3   Prepare the chicken. Place the chicken breasts in a large pot and cover them with water. There should be about one inch of water above the breasts. Bring the water to a boil, and then reduce the heat slightly. Cook the chicken for about twenty minutes, until it is no longer pink on the inside. Using a sharp knife, cut into the breast and check for the color. If it is white inside, it means the breast is done. Use prongs to remove the chicken from the water, and place the two pieces on a large plate or breadboard. Keep the water because you can use it to cook the pasta. Dice—or slice—the chicken into small bite-size pieces, and leave them on the side.

4   You are now ready to prepare the pasta. Make sure the pasta pot is about three-quarters full of water. You can use the water from the cooked chicken, and you can add more water if needed. Also sprinkle in a pinch of salt, and bring it back to a boil. Next, add the fettuccini noodles. Reduce the heat slightly, ensuring that the water continues to boil. Cook the noodles for about seven minutes, but refer to the instructions on the back of the pasta box to check the cooking time. Swirl a fork in the water while the pasta is cooking to make sure it breaks up and doesn't cook in large clumps. Pasta is ready when it is limp, but still slightly firm, which is called al-dente. Do not overcook it because you don't want your pasta to be soggy or gooey.

5   Finally, prepare the alfredo sauce. This is the most satisfying step because you will feel a sense of accomplishment. First, finely grate about half a cup of Parmesan cheese. You will need to use the grater that has the smallest holes. Then set the cheese on the side. (If you are pressed for time, you can always use the pre-grated store-bought variety.) Then make the roux, which consists of butter and flour. This mixture will thicken the sauce. Into a large saucepan, melt a couple of tablespoons of butter and the equivalent amount of flour. Stir it around until it starts bubbling. Turn the heat down to make sure that your roux does not stick to the pan. Then slowly pour one and a half cups of milk into the mixture and keep stirring to remove all the lumps. When it starts to thicken, add the Parmesan cheese and keep stirring. At the end, add salt and pepper to taste. The sauce is easy to make, but you have to be careful not to scorch it because if you do, it will not be pleasant to your taste buds.

6   Your dish is now ready. Add the cooked noodles and the chicken to the sauce, and then mix. Spoon the completed mixture into a beautiful serving dish. The food should smell terrific and taste delicious if you do it correctly. That is how you make one of my favorite foods. I hope you prepare this meal for your dinner tonight.

Practice 2

1. Highlight the thesis statement.
2. Underline the topic sentence in each body paragraph.
3. Add some transitional expressions to paragraph 3.
4. What type of process essay is this?
   a. complete a process   b. understand a process

Explore Topics

9.3   Explore topics for a process essay.

In the Writer's Desk Warm Up, you will try an exploring strategy to generate ideas about different topics.

The Writer's Desk: Warm Up

Read the following questions, and write the first ideas that come to your mind. Think of two or three ideas for each topic.

EXAMPLE: Imagine that you are traveling to another country. What are some steps you should take to make your vacation successful?

-get to know the language and culture

-understand the currency

-read about the geography and climate, and pack accordingly

1. How do you choose your major at college?

2. How do you prepare for a religious or cultural holiday or celebration?

3. What steps do you take to impress a date?

_____

_____

_____

Developing

When you write a process essay, choose a process that you know something about. For example, you might be able to explain how to become more environmentally conscious; however, you might not know enough to advise how to reduce nuclear waste.

The Thesis Statement

9.4   Write the thesis statement of a process essay.

In a process essay, the thesis statement states what process you will be explaining and what readers will be able to do after they have read the essay.

        topic   controlling idea

Surviving in the wilderness requires some basic knowledge.

            controlling idea   topic

Consistency, patience, and time are essential **to becoming a good parent**.

The Writer's Desk: Thesis Statements

Write a thesis statement for each of the following topics. You can look for ideas in the Warm Up in the previous Writer's Desk. Each thesis statement should state the process and contain a controlling idea.

EXAMPLE: Topic: how to prepare for a trip

Thesis Statement: <u>To have a safe and enjoyable journey, take several</u>

<u>important steps before you embark on your travels</u>.

1. Topic: how to choose a college major

Thesis Statement: _____

_____

2. Topic: how to prepare for a religious or cultural holiday or celebration

Thesis Statement: _____

_____

3. Topic: how to impress a date

Thesis Statement: _____

_____

The Supporting Ideas

9.5   Generate the supporting ideas of a process essay.

A process essay contains a series of steps. When you develop supporting ideas for a process essay, think about the main steps that are necessary to complete the process.

- Use prewriting strategies such as freewriting and brainstorming to generate ideas.
- Choose the best ideas. Clearly explain the steps of the process.
- Organize your ideas. Choose the best organizational method for this essay pattern. Process essays generally use chronological (time) order.

HINT: Give Steps, Not Examples

When you explain how to complete a process, describe each step. Do not simply list examples of the process.

Topic: How to Plan an Interesting Vacation

List of Examples	Steps in the Process
• going to a tropical island	• decide what your goal is
• riding a hot air balloon	• research possible locations
• swimming with sharks	• find out the cost
• touring an exotic city	• plan the itinerary according to a budget

The Writer's Desk: List the Main Steps

Choose one thesis statement from the previous Writer's Desk. List the main steps to complete the process.

EXAMPLE: Thesis Statement: <u>To have a safe and enjoyable journey, take several</u>

<u>important steps before you embark on your travels</u>.

Steps: <u>1.   Become familiar with the language and culture of the country.</u>

<u>2.   Educate yourself about the currency exchange rate and</u>

<u>banking system.</u>

<u>3.   Research the geography and climate of the country, and pack</u>

<u>accordingly.</u>

Thesis Statement: _____

_____

Steps: _____

_____

_____

_____

_____

_____

The Essay Plan

9.6   Develop a process essay plan.

An essay plan helps you organize your thesis statement, topic sentences, and supporting details before you write a first draft. Decide which steps and which details your reader will really need to complete the process or understand it.

Thesis Statement: To have a safe and enjoyable journey, take several important steps before you embark on your travels.

    I.   Become familiar with the language and culture of the country.
   - A. Know some key phrases.
   - B. Know the cultural norms.
   - C. Know social etiquette.

   II.   Educate yourself about the currency exchange rate and banking system.
   - A. Find out currency exchange rates.
   - B. Know the bank holidays.
   - C. Take enough funds.

  III.   Research the geography and climate of the country, and pack accordingly.
   - A. Look up the temperature during the time you are traveling.
   - B. Figure out the methods of transportation and the general geography.

The First Draft

9.7 **Write the first draft of a process essay.**

As you write your first draft, explain the process in a way that would be clear for your audience. Address the reader directly. For example, instead of writing "You should scan the newspaper for used cars," simply write "Scan the newspaper for used cars." Also, remember to use complete sentences and transitions to string together the ideas from your essay plan smoothly. Here are some time-order transitions that are useful for explaining processes.

To begin a process	To continue a process		To end a process
(at) first	after that	later	eventually
initially	afterward	meanwhile	finally
the first step	also	second	in the end
	furthermore	then	ultimately
	in addition	third	

GRAMMAR HINT: Avoid Sentence Fragments

Ensure that you do not use sentence fragments to list the steps of the process. A sentence must have a subject and a verb to express a complete idea.

> check
> Consider your airline's carry-on luggage requirements. First, the weight of your suitcase.

See Chapter 23 for more information about sentence fragments.

Revising and Editing

Revise and Edit a Process Essay

9.8 **Revise and edit a process essay.**

When you finish writing a process essay, carefully review your work and revise it to make the process as clear as possible to your readers. Check to make sure that you have organized your steps, and remove any details that are not relevant to being able to complete or understand the process. Before you revise and edit your own essay, practice revising and editing a student essay.

A Student Essay

Read the essay, and then answer the questions that follow. As you read, correct any errors that you find and make comments in the margins.

Preparations for Traveling to a Different Country

Mary Chandler Izard

1   Traveling to other countries is a wonderful learning experience. Travelers become familiar with different cultures, make friends from all over the world, have adventures, and discover new things about themselves. However, an overseas trip requires planning that goes beyond just buying a ticket and packing a suitcase. To have a safe and enjoyable journey, take several important steps before you embark on your travels.

2   First, become familiar with the language and culture of the country. If the people of the country do not speak English, then a tourist must make sure that he or she knows key phrases. To be able to communicate. Some useful phrases are the following: *How much is this*? *Do you speak English*? *Where is the bathroom*? I watch many foreign films and enjoy the translations of other languages into English. Also, the visitor must know the cultural norms of the country. For example, Americans tend to value their personal space and do not like when someone steps into it. Generally, Americans keep a couple of feet of distance when talking to someone. In other countries, however, personal space is viewed differently. For instance, Asians stand closer to one another when talking. Travelers should also know other cultural expectations. In South Asia, it is unacceptable to eat with the left hand, and in most Asian countries, it is vital that a visitor removes their shoes before entering someone's home.

3   Currency and exchange rates differ all over the world. Americans use dollars, but the British use pounds, and the French use Euros for currency. The exchange rates change daily. Since the exchange rate is so different, a tourist must be sure he or she has adequate funds while traveling. Banks charge for

cash withdrawals from ATMs (automated teller machines), especially if the visitor is using a debit card from another country. And a visitor should know the bank holidays of the destination country. In some countries, there are few ATMs, visitors may have to go into a bank to withdraw cash.

4   Research the geography and climate of the country, and pack accordingly. Tourists should be aware of the temperature of the region when they are visiting. Also, it is a good idea to know the types of public transit needed to visit different regions in the country.

5   Traveling to another country takes a lot of thought. Visitors will experience problems if they are not fully prepared. They could get lost, not have enough money, or get into a confrontation with someone from that country because of different cultural norms. So to have the best travel experiences, visitors should familiarize themselves with different aspects of the country.

Practice 3

Revising

1. Highlight the thesis statement.
2. Highlight the topic sentences of paragraphs 2 and 4.
3. In paragraph 2, cross out the sentence that does not support the topic sentence.
4. Which of the following would make an effective topic sentence for paragraph 3?
   a. It is expensive to travel to another country.
   b. Travelers should carry some cash when they travel.
   c. Educate yourself about the destination's currency exchange rate and banking system.
5. Paragraph 3 lacks transitions. Add at least three transitions to link sentences. Draw lines indicating where they should be placed.
6. Paragraph 4 lacks adequate support. Add some examples that would help flesh out the paragraph. _____

_____

_____

_____

Editing

7. Underline a sentence fragment in paragraph 2. Then correct it.

   Correction: _____

GRAMMAR LINK

Extra grammar help:

Fragments, Ch. 23,
    p. 331
Run-Ons, Ch. 24,
    p. 338
Pronouns, Ch. 31,
    p. 410

8. Underline a pronoun error in paragraph 2. Write the correction below.

Correction: _____

_____

9. Underline a run-on sentence in paragraph 3. Then correct it.

Correction: _____

_____

The Writer's Desk: Revise and Edit Your Process Essay

Revise and edit the essay that you wrote for the previous Writer's Desk. You can refer to the revising and editing checklists at the end of this chapter and at the end of the book.

VOCABULARY BOOST

Look at the first draft of your process essay. Underline the verb that you use to describe each step of the process. Then, when possible, come up with a more evocative verb. Use your thesaurus for this activity. Try not to repeat the same verb more than once.

A Professional Essay

Melinda Smith, Lawrence Robinson, and Jeanne Segal are regular contributers to *HelpGuide.org*, a website that is dedicated to writing about mental, emotional, and social health issues.

Tips for Breaking Free of Compulsive Smartphone Use

Melinda Smith, Lawrence Robinson, and Jeanne Segal

1   Online addictions can have many forms. Virtual, online friends can become more important than real-life relationships. We've all seen the couples sitting together in a coffee shop or restaurant ignoring each other and engaging with their smartphones instead. But online friends exist in a bubble, not subject to the same demands or stresses as messy real-world relationships. People also have online compulsions, such as gaming, gambling, stock trading, online shopping, or bidding on auction sites like eBay. There are also those who web surf compulsively, watching videos,

searching Google, or checking news feeds. All this compulsive use of the Internet and smartphone apps can cause you to neglect other aspects of your life, from real-world relationships to hobbies and social pursuits.

2   If you repeatedly check texts, emails, news feeds, websites, or apps, it may be time to reassess your technology use. Getting control over your smartphone use isn't a case of quitting cold turkey. Think of it more like going on a diet. Just as you still need to eat, you probably still need to use your phone for work, school, and social life. Try the following strategies to cut back to more healthy levels of smartphone usage.

3   Turn off your phone at certain times of the day and night. When you're driving, in a meeting, at the gym, having dinner, or playing with your kids, put away your phone. Also, don't bring your phone or tablet to bed. The blue light emitted by the screens can disrupt your sleep if used within two hours of bedtime. Turn devices off and leave them in another room overnight to charge.

4   Replace your smartphone use with healthier activities. If you are bored and lonely, resisting the urge to use your smartphone to play games or check social media can be very difficult. Have a plan for other ways to fill the time, such as meditating, reading a book, or chatting with friends face to face. For instance, when you spend time with other smartphone addicts, play the "phone stack" game. Ask your friends to place their smartphones face down on the table. Even as the phones buzz and beep, no one is allowed to grab his or her device. If someone can't resist checking her phone, that person has to pick up the check for everyone.

5   Remove social media apps from your phone so you can only check Facebook, Twitter and the like from your computer. What you see of others on social media is rarely an accurate reflection of their lives—people exaggerate the positive aspects of their lives, brushing over the doubts and disappointments that we all experience. Spending less time comparing yourself unfavorably to these stylized representations can help to boost your mood and sense of self-worth.

6   Remember that human beings are social creatures. Socially interacting with another person face-to-face—making eye contact, responding to body language, listening, talking—can make you feel calm, safe, and understood, and quickly put the brakes on stress. Interacting through text, email, or messaging may feel important, but it bypasses these nonverbal cues, and it can never have the same effect on your emotional well-being. Online friends can't hug you when a crisis hits, visit you when you're sick, or celebrate a happy occasion with you.

7   Ultimately, a smartphone addiction can negatively impact your health and your life. The persistent buzz, ping, or beep of your smartphone can

distract you from important tasks, slow your work, and interrupt those quiet moments that are so crucial to creativity and problem solving. Accept that by limiting your smartphone use, you're likely going to miss out on certain invitations, breaking news, or new gossip. Accepting this fact can be liberating and help break your reliance on technology.

Practice 4

1. What is the author's specific purpose? _____

   _____

2. Highlight the thesis statement. Be careful as it may not be in the first paragraph.

3. Find the topic sentence of each body paragraph and underline it.

4. In each topic sentence, the subject is implied but not stated. What is the subject? _____

5. According to the author, why should people limit their smartphone use?

   _____

   _____

   _____

   _____

6. How can smartphones affect people's sleep patterns? _____

   _____

   _____

7. Why should people engage in face-to-face interaction rather than electronic interaction? _____

   _____

   _____

8. The writer uses no transitional expressions to link the steps in the process. Add a transitional word or expression to the beginning of each body paragraph.

WRITING LINK
MORE PROCESS
WRITING TOPICS

Ch. 21, Writer's Room
   topic 2, p. 318
Ch. 25, Writer's Room
   topic 2, p. 352
Ch. 26, Writer's Room
   topic 1, p. 359
Ch. 31, Writer's Room
   topic 1, p. 422

The Writer' Room

Writing Activity 1: Topics

Write a process essay about one of the following topics, or choose your own topic.

General Topics	College- and Work-Related Topics
How to . . .	**How to . . .**

1. find a place to live
2. become a good leader
3. get a good night's sleep
4. find a roommate
5. do an activity or a hobby

6. survive a dull class
7. assemble a _____
8. become a better manager or supervisor
9. change a law
10. make a good impression at an interview

**READING LINK
MORE PROCESS
READINGS**

"The Rules of Survival"
     p. 553
"How Cults Become
     Religions" p. 576

Writing Activity 2: Media Writing

Write a process essay in which you explain how to train a dog, horse, cat, bird, or other animal. To help you plan your ideas, watch a show, movie, or online clip about training an animal. Here are some suggestions to help spark ideas:

Show: *The Dog Whisperer, Animal Planet*

Film: *The Horse Whisperer, Seabiscuit*

Online and Video: ASPCA pet training videos

Podcast: NPR's *Fresh Air* (segments from showbiz animal trainers Teresa Ann Miller and Bill Berloni)

Checklist: Process Essay

As you write your process essay, review the checklist at the back of the book. Also ask yourself these questions.

❑ Does my thesis statement make a point about the process?

❑ Do I include all of the steps in the process?

❑ Do I clearly explain each step so my reader can accomplish the process?

❑ Do I mention all of the supplies that my reader needs to complete the process?

❑ Do I use transitions to connect all of the steps in the process?

10   Definition

10.1 Define definition.

10.2 Define the purpose of a definition essay.

10.3 Explore topics for a definition essay.

10.4 Write the thesis statement of a definition essay.

10.5 Generate the supporting ideas of a definition essay.

10.6 Develop a definition essay plan.

10.7 Write the first draft of a definition essay.

10.8 Revise and edit a definition essay.

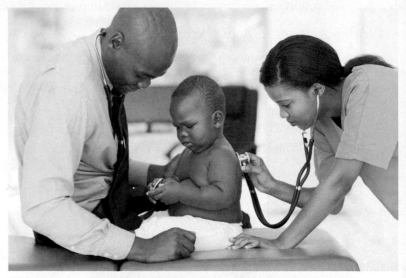

To help patients understand a diagnosis, doctors may define the illness itself or explain related medical terms. Similarly, you may write an entire essay in which you define a term.

Writers' Exchange

Brainstorm some common slang expressions. Think about words you use to express pleasure or disgust. You can also consider words describing a specific type of person. Choose one expression and define it without using a dictionary. Make your definition clear so that a nonnative speaker of English will understand the word.

Exploring

What Is Definition?

10.1 Define definition.

When you **define,** you explain the meaning of a word. Some terms have concrete meanings, and you can define them in a few words. For example, a *town* is "a small city." Other terms, such as *values*, *faith*, or *human rights*, are more abstract and require more detailed definitions. It is possible to write a paragraph, an essay, or even an entire book about such concepts.

People often try to define what they mean. For example, at home, parents might explain to their children what it means to be *reliable*. At college, a professor may ask students to define the term *poverty*. At work, a colleague could suggest that a coworker's business presentation *needs improvement*, and then explain what she means.

Practice 1: Visualizing Definition

Brainstorm supporting ideas for the following thesis statement.

Thesis Statement: An Internet addict is a person who needs to be online almost constantly.

_____   _____

_____   _____

_____   _____

_____   _____

The Definition Essay

10.2 Define the purpose of a definition essay.

When you write a definition essay, try to explain what a term means to you. For example, if someone asks you to define *overachiever*, you might give examples of overachievers and what you think those people do that goes beyond the limits. You may also explain what an overachiever is not. Also, remember the next two points.

1. **Choose a term that you know something about.** You need to understand a term to say something relevant and interesting about it.
2. **Give a clear definition.** Write a definition that your reader will easily understand, and support your definition with examples.

Definition at Work

Will Thomas is a certified home inspector. In this excerpt from a home inspection report, he defines *ice-damming*.

The **topic sentence** states the topic and controlling idea.

The **supporting sentences** provide details and examples.

The **concluding sentence** brings the paragraph to a satisfactory close.

My inspection of the attic insulation and the roof ventilation system indicate that this house may be subject to ice-damming, which can cause water to penetrate the structure. Ice-damming occurs in the winter when hot air from the heated parts of the house escapes into an insufficiently insulated and improperly ventilated attic. This hot air warms the underside of the roof, causing snow on the roof to melt. It quickly refreezes when it trickles down over a cold spot, which is typical at the edge of the roof. This ice forms a physical barrier, a dam—which holds back more meltwater, creating a pool on the roof. This growing pool of meltwater then creeps under the shingles and into the house. Ice-damming can cause serious visible damage to the interior of a house, but it can also cause hidden problems such as biological growth in finished walls and degradation of the wood frame structure of the house. It's important to know if there is ice-damming.

HINT: Consider Your Audience

Consider your audience when you write a definition essay. You may have to adjust your tone and vocabulary, depending on who will be reading the essay. For example, if you write a definition essay about cloning for your political science class, you may have to explain concepts using basic, nontechnical terms. If you write the same essay for your biology class, you may be able to use more technical terms.

A Student Essay

Read the student essay, and answer the questions that follow.

....

Have Some Manners

....

Jessica Bailey

1   The idea of good manners seems quaint, like something out of a costume drama on the BBC. In the past, the word "manners" provoked such images as a Victorian gentleman doffing his top hat to a lady wearing a bustle or placing his cape across a puddle. Surely a world that has abandoned petticoats and driving gloves in favor of jeans and cell phones has also shed manners that serve to prop up old-fashioned class hierarchies. Really good manners, however, are not empty social conventions or formalities; they are signals of mutual respect.

2   A basic lesson everyone should learn is to show respect and consideration with words. Parents and other mentors can teach that concept by example. They can insist that children say "please" and "thank you." They can remind children not to interrupt others because that implies that the other person's words are not important. They can speak to each other and to children in a calm way, without resorting to shouting or insults. A child who observes others speaking thoughtfully and choosing appropriate words will adopt the same behavior naturally. I have an acquaintance who uses swear words in every sentence. He doesn't seem to care that people might be offended by his cursing. Mutual friends wonder whether he was raised by wolves. The generous among them say that his mama should have tried to teach him manners.

3   Words are not always enough. Good manners are also shown in concrete actions. Using the correct fork or spoon is not compulsory, but eating in a pleasing way is important. At the table, one ought to eat like a civilized person to avoid disgusting other diners. Some people shove food in their mouths or talk with their mouths full, and that sickens other people at the table. Children should learn to chew slowly, with their mouth closed. Another action everyone should learn is to hold doors open for others. It takes just a second to turn and see if someone is following, so holding the door shows basic respect. Also, people should learn to cover their mouths when they cough. Furthermore, when they are using public transportation, younger people should give up their seats to their elders. When I was a child, we took the subway a lot, and my father always made us stand and let an older person take the seat.

4   The most important aspect of good manners is to have a positive and compassionate attitude. At home, children who raise an eyebrow or

roll their eyes display thoughtlessness. At school, children may ignore or isolate unpopular classmates. In classrooms, some students yawn loudly, trying to show the teacher that they are bored. A poor attitude shows a lack of manners. Parents are good role models when they extend kindness and courtesy to strangers. For example, my mother taught me to look into a server's eyes and say, "Thank you" when I received a plate of food. When we passed a homeless person on the street, she would say, "Don't look away. Look at him and smile. He deserves your respect just like everybody else does." She told us that our attitude shows.

5   Good manners reflect well not only on ourselves, but on our parents, family, and community. At the table, be poised. Remember that others are watching and also trying to enjoy their meals. At school and work, thoughtful words and actions can make coworkers or classmates get along with us. Ultimately, we should all remember the Golden Rule and treat others as we would like to be treated.

Practice 2

1. Highlight the thesis statement.
2. What point is the essay making about good manners?

   _____

3. Underline the topic sentence in paragraphs 2 to 4.
4. In your own words, list some of the specific examples that help define good manners.

   _____

   _____

   _____

   _____

   _____

   _____

Explore Topics

10.3 Explore topics for a definition essay.

In the Writer's Desk Warm Up, you will try an exploring strategy to generate ideas about different topics.

The Writer's Desk: Warm Up

Read the following questions, and write the first ideas that come to your mind. Think of two or three ideas for each topic.

EXAMPLE: What is BMX culture?

<u>—buy and alter bikes</u>

<u>—learn to do tricks</u>

<u>—share risks and get injuries</u>

<u>—strong connected community</u>

1. What is oversharing?

2. What is the American dream?

3. What is a good citizen?

VOCABULARY BOOST

Some words have neutral, positive, or negative associations. Look at each set of words and categorize each as neutral (=), positive (+), or negative (-). Do this with a partner.

1. thin, cadaverous, lean, emaciated, wiry, skinny, slender

2. home, shack, cabin, slum, stomping ground, dump, sanctuary

3. dainty, delicate, finicky, fussy, prissy, fragile, elegant, frail

4. honest, coarse, crude, open, gross, straightforward

5. brat, child, sweetheart, cutie, munchkin, delinquent, heir, mama's boy

The Thesis Statement

10.4 **Write the thesis statement of a definition essay.**

A clear thesis statement for a definition essay introduces the term and provides a definition. There are three basic ways to define a term.

Definition by Synonym

Providing a definition by synonym is useful if the original term is difficult to understand, and the synonym is a more familiar word.

> term + synonym
> A Twitter handle   is a person's username or unique identifier.

Definition by Category

When you define by category, you determine the larger group to which the term belongs. Then you determine what unique characteristics set the term apart from others in that category.

> term + category + detail
> A hot mess   is a person or thing   that is extremely unsuccessful or disordered.

Definition by Negation

When you define by negation, you explain what a term does *not* mean. You can then include a sentence explaining what it does mean.

> term + what it is not + what it is
> Obsession   is not an eccentricity;   it is a mental illness.

GRAMMAR HINT: Using Semicolons

You can join two related and complete ideas with a semicolon, as the writer has done in this example of a definition.

> Marriage is not the end of your freedom; it is the beginning of a shared journey.

See Chapter 21 for more information about using semicolons.

Making a Point

Defining a term by synonym, category, and negation is only a guideline for writing thesis statements for a definition essay. Keep in mind that your essay will be more interesting if you express your attitude or point of view in your thesis statement.

No point   Avarice means greed.
Point   Avarice, or greed, invariably leads to tragedy.

Practice 3

Write thesis statements by defining the following terms using your own words. Try to make definitions by synonym, category, and negation. Remember to indicate your controlling idea in the thesis statements.

EXAMPLE: Road rage _is not a momentary lapse of judgment; it is serious_
criminal behavior.

1. A photobomb _____

_____

2. Helicopter parents _____

_____

3. Cyberbully _____

_____

4. Crowdfunding _____

_____

5. A tweet _____

_____

HINT: Be Precise!

When you write a definition essay, it is important to use precise words to define the term. Moreover, when you define a term by category, make sure that the category for your term is correct.

    Anorexia nervosa is the <u>inability</u> to eat.
    (Anorexia nervosa is not an ability or an inability.)

    Anorexia nervosa is <u>when</u> you want to be thin.
    (*When* refers to a time, but anorexia nervosa is not a time.)

    Anorexia nervosa is <u>where</u> it is hard to eat properly.
    (*Where* refers to a place, but anorexia nervosa is not a place.)

Now look at a better definition of this illness.

    Anorexia nervosa is a tragic **eating disorder** characterized by refusing food and overexercising to achieve an extremely thin appearance.

Practice 4

Revise each sentence using precise language.

EXAMPLE: Multitasking is when you do many activities at once.

<u>Multitasking is doing many activities at once</u>.

_____

1. A spin doctor is when public opinion is influenced by manipulating information.

   _____

   _____

2. A poor loser is the inability to accept defeat graciously.

   _____

   _____

3. Unfriending is a person who removes someone from his Facebook friends list.

   _____

   _____

The Writer's Desk: Write Thesis Statements

Write a thesis statement in which you define each of the following topics. You can look for ideas in the previous Writer's Desk. Remember to make a point in your thesis statement.

EXAMPLE: Topic: BMX culture

   Thesis statement: <u>**BMX riders form a strong lifestyle community of**</u>

   <u>**risk-takers**</u>.

1. Topic: oversharing

   Thesis statement: _____

   _____

2. Topic: the American dream

   Thesis statement: _____

   _____

3. Topic: a good citizen

   Thesis statement: _____

   _____

The Supporting Ideas

10.5 Generate the supporting ideas of a definition essay.

After you have developed an effective thesis statement, generate supporting ideas. In a definition essay, you can give examples that clarify your definition. To develop supporting ideas, follow these three steps:

- Use prewriting strategies to generate ideas. Think about facts, anecdotes, and examples that will help define your term.
- Choose the best ideas. Use examples that clearly reveal the definition of the term.
- Organize your ideas. Choose the best organizational method for this essay pattern.

The Writer's Desk: Generate Supporting Ideas

Choose one of your thesis statements from the previous Writer's Desk. List three or four ideas that most effectively illustrate the definition.

EXAMPLE: Thesis Statement: <u>BMX riders form a strong lifestyle community of</u>

<u>risk-takers.</u>

Supports: <u>—can use four locations: park, street, vert, flatland</u>

     <u>—fix up bikes with better parts</u>

     <u>—help each other</u>

     <u>—learn tricks and focus on improvement</u>

Thesis Statement: _____

_____

Supports: _____

_____

_____

_____

_____

The Essay Plan

10.6 Develop a definition essay plan.

An essay plan helps you organize your thesis statement and supporting details before you write the first draft. A definition essay includes a complete definition of the term and provides adequate examples to support the central definition. When creating a definition essay plan, make sure that your examples provide varied evidence and do not just repeat the definition. Organize your ideas in a logical sequence.

Thesis Statement: BMX riders form a strong lifestyle community of risk-takers.

I.   BMX freestyle riders use four different locations.

    A. Park is a skate park.

    B. Vert is like park but with higher ramps.

    C. Flatland is a place where people climb on their bikes.

    D. Street bikers ride on stairs and railings.

II.   BMX riders are very particular about their bikes.

    A. They fix up their bikes with better parts.

    B. They add chromoly metal parts.

    C. They have sealed components.

III.   They have a strong community network.

    A. They help injured riders.

    B. They meet at jams and share information and skills.

    C. They form solid friendships.

The Writer's Desk: Write an Essay Plan

Refer to the information you generated in previous Writer's Desks and prepare a detailed essay plan.

The First Draft

10.7 Write the first draft of a definition essay.

Your essay plan is the backbone upon which you can build your first draft. As you write, remember to vary your sentence structure. Also include transitional words or expressions to help your ideas flow smoothly. Here are some transitional expressions that can help you show different levels of importance in a definition essay.

To Show the Level of Importance	
clearly	next
first	one quality . . . another quality
most important	second
most of all	undoubtedly

The Writer's Desk: Write the First Draft

Carefully review the essay plan you prepared in the previous Writer's Desk. Make any necessary changes to the definition or its supporting details, and then write your first draft.

Revise and Edit a Definition Essay

10.8 Revise and edit a definition essay.

When you finish writing a definition essay, carefully review your work and revise it to make the definition as clear as possible to your readers. You might have to adjust your definition and supporting ideas to suit their knowledge. Also keep in mind the tone of your essay. Certain words have either negative or positive connotations. Finally, check that you have organized your ideas logically and remove any irrelevant details. Before you revise and edit your own essay, practice revising and editing a student essay.

A Student Essay

Read the student essay, and then answer the questions that follow. As you read, correct any errors that you find and make comments in the margins.

BMX Culture

Kara Bruce

1   Have you seen some scruffy-looking teenagers on tiny bikes? Perhaps they are jumping down a set of stairs or spinning on one wheel. Maybe they are at a skate park racing up ramps and lifting into the air. Those riders are enjoying a sport called BMX, or bicycle motorcross. Since the 1970s, riders have altered little pedal bikes and done tricks on them. In recent years, the BMX community has grown and formed different disciplines under the title "freestyle BMX." Today, BMX is not just a sport; it is a strong lifestyle community of risk-takers.

2   BMX freestyle riders have their choice of four locations: park, vert, street, and flatland. "Park" means skate park, where there are jump boxes, flat banks, and so on. "Vert," short for vertical, is similar to park, but the ramps are higher, and it's riskier. "Street" means riding a wall, going down stairs, and riding on a ledge anywhere on public streets. "Flatland" is a perfectly flat place, like a parking lot. Flatland riders use the bike to do tricks. They turn the bike upside down or climbing over the bike while it is moving. I'm part of the BMX community, and I consider myself a street and park rider. I use the urban landscape as a playground. I love looking at a handrail, bench, or stairs in a new light.

3   BMX riders are very particular about their bikes. They may begin with an inexpensive bike but then change the parts to improve the bike's performance. Many parts have certain metals, the most commonly known

is 4130 chromoly. It is a strong and light metal, especially when compared to steel. A better type of metal helps when riders jump from high places or balance on top of rails and ledges. As you improve, you upgrade bike parts to have a lot of "sealed" components. Parts like bearings aren't left exposed to the elements, which ensures a stronger and safer bike. Bikers who are constantly doing tricks need reliable bikes. There are many types of BMX bikes depending on the chosen discipline. Flatland bikes will have very different geometry than a BMX race bike, because one is used for doing spins and tricks, while the other is mainly for stability while at high speeds.

4   BMX riders have a strong and supportive community network. For instance, the community formed Stay Strong, a charity for a professional rider who became disabled after doing a double back flip. The BMX community has supported him after medical insurance would not. Also, there are many events, called jams, where people meet and help each other. Local riders can show off their skills for prizes, teach skills to others, and make friends with other BMX enthusiasts! Once someone is part of the community, that person makes friends for life. For example, last summer, when I did a road trip to the United States, a girl from Florida let me stay at her place. She had to leave for a funeral, but she left a key for me. She trusted me. Because we share a passion for BMX.

5   BMX riders have a great community and a way of living. The sport provides physical and mental challenges; riders must be strong to overcome their fear of falling and getting hurt. Of course, there are risks, and people get injured. For instance, I've broken my collarbone, wrist, and hand. But any sport carries risks. Even inactivity is a killer! So if you want to have fun and be part of a great community, get a BMX and become a rider! The sport tests the mind as well as the body.

Practice 5

Revising

1. Highlight the thesis statement.
2. What type of definition does the thesis statement have? Circle the best answer.

   a. synonym   b. category   c. negation

3. Highlight the topic sentences in paragraphs 2, 3, and 4.
4. In paragraph 3, the writer veers off course. Cross out the sentences that do not support the topic sentence.
   Explain why: _____

   _____

5. Body paragraphs 2, 3, and 4 do not begin with transitional words and expressions. Write some possible words for each paragraph.

   Para. 2: _____   Para. 3: _____   Para. 4: _____

Editing

6. Underline and correct a verb consistency error in paragraph 2.
   Correction: _____

7. Underline and correct a run-on sentence error in paragraph 3.
   Correction: _____

8. Underline and correct two pronoun shifts in a sentence in paragraph 3.
   Correction: _____

9. Paragraph 4 contains an incomplete sentence. Identify and correct a fragment error.
   Correction: _____

> **GRAMMAR LINK**
> See the following chapters for more information about these grammar topics:
> Verbs, Ch. 29, p. 388
> Pronouns, Ch. 31, p. 410
> Run-Ons, Ch. 24, p. 338
> Fragments, Ch. 23, p. 329

The Writer's Desk: Revise and Edit Your Essay

Revise and edit the essay that you wrote for the previous Writer's Desk. You can refer to the revising and editing checklists at the end of this chapter and at the end of the book.

A Professional Essay

Tristin Hopper is an award-winning journalist. In the next essay, he discusses travellers who do volunteer work overseas.

....

Voluntourism

....

Tristin Hopper

1   "Voluntourism" is one of the world's fastest-growing travel niches. According to a 2012 report in the journal *Africa Insight*, volunteering takes up a significant share of the global youth travel industry. But all is not well with what would appear to be the **pinnacle** of altruism. In an age of mismanaged charities and shady volunteer operations, this annual tide of volunteers can harm as much as it can help.

pinnacle: highest level

2   "When I got started in 1995, the number of organizations offering international volunteer placements was so few I could count them on one hand," said Steve Rosenthal, founder of Cross-Cultural Solutions, an international volunteering nonprofit. "Now, literally every time I search on

the Internet, I'll find multiple new organizations." Much of this demand is due to a rise in the popularity of gap years. "It's become very, very, very popular for high school kids and university students to have some kind of exposure to volunteering," said Barbara Heron, a York University–based researcher on international volunteering. "And because of the proliferation, and the lack of preparation, then you start to see some more problematic things happening."

3   International volunteering used to be the exclusive domain of aid agencies such as the Peace Corps or the Rotary Club. But in the last fifteen years, an entire multi-billion-dollar industry has cropped up to meet the demand. More and more, volunteering is managed through an interlocking network of volunteer "brokers." Organizations recruit volunteers for a fee and then pay a per-head rate to entrepreneurs in developing countries who then ensure the volunteers are taken care of and paired up with a suitable volunteer stint. "The field has attracted organizations that might be more profit-driven than mission-driven, which obviously could be a problem," said Mr. Rosenthal. "And when you're dealing with children, schools, disadvantaged women, it's not an environment you want to fail in—because the consequences are real."

4   Hammer-wielding volunteers can take jobs away from local workers. Fleeting volunteer stints at orphanages can foment emotional attachment issues with children. And volunteers, especially untrained teenage volunteers, can be extraordinarily expensive to maintain. "It's not that the volunteers are demanding people, but it's more demanding to have them because you have to look after them; . . . they all get sick," said Ms. Heron. Even medical missions, if poorly organized, can undermine and bankrupt local healthcare providers.

5   Sometimes, overseas volunteer enterprises can get downright shady. In 2012, an investigation by *Al Jazeera English* in Cambodia revealed that, over a ten-year period, spiking voluntourism demand had helped to double the number of Cambodian children in orphanages, many of which operated in sub-standard conditions and with almost no supervision. At one point, reporter Juliana Ruhfus approached an orphanage director and, without once being asked for identification, convinced him to let her take four hand-picked children on a "tour" around Phnom Penh.

6   Furthermore, such orphanages can do more harm than good. A 2010 report on "AIDS orphan tourism" by the South Africa–based Human Sciences Research Council stated, "Short-term volunteer tourists are encouraged to 'make intimate connections' with previously neglected, abused, and abandoned young children. However, shortly after these 'connections' have been made, tourists leave . . . [and] many of the children they leave behind have experienced another abandonment."

7   "There are ways to do this well and there are ways to do this badly," said Karen Takacs, the executive director of Crossroads International, one of Canada's oldest international volunteer groups. Founded in the 1960s, the group's mission is to furnish carefully vetted and highly trained volunteers for foreign postings. In essence, it supplies foreign development groups with free consultants. The same goes for CUSO, a longstanding Canadian group that pairs skilled applicants—including retired judges, accountants, lawyers and other professionals—with targeted overseas postings.

8   Regardless, even a naïve, unskilled, nineteen-year-old can be harnessed for a greater good if he or she finds the right organization. Take the example of Petersfield, Jamaica, a community of 2,200 people best known as the birthplace of reggae musician Peter Tosh. Located far from the coast, the town's efforts to jumpstart a local tourism economy had repeatedly failed. That is, until they partnered with the U.S. nonprofit Amizade. They offer homestays for foreign volunteers in exchange for fees that could be distributed throughout the community. Now Petersfield has a standing corps of foreigners available to do everything from painting the local post office to running computer classes, said Eric Hartman, a voluntourism researcher.

9   In a four-year study of international volunteers, researchers found that when people decide to go abroad, the single biggest motivation was cross-cultural understanding, which was then followed by personal growth, skills development, adventure, and a chance to boost one's résumé. "Helping others," they found, was right at the bottom of the list. Their findings are certainly not an indictment of volunteering—far from it, said Heron, the study's co-chair. According to charity researcher Saundra Schimmelpfennig, if you want to volunteer, "do so with the understanding that you are the person that will benefit the most from your work."

Practice 6

1. Highlight the thesis statement of this essay.

2. What is *voluntourism*? Define the term using your own words.

_____

_____

_____

3. Why is the demand for voluntourism increasing? See paragraphs 2, 3, and 9.

_____

_____

_____

4. How does voluntourism negatively affect children in developing nations?

_____

_____

_____

_____

_____

5. List four other negative effects of voluntourism.

_____

_____

_____

6. What are ways to make voluntourism more effective?

_____

_____

_____

_____

7. After reading this essay, what advice would you give someone who wants to volunteer overseas? Think of two or three pieces of advice.

_____

_____

_____

The Writer's Room

Writing Activity 1: Topics

Write a definition essay about any of the following topics, or choose your own topic.

General Topics

1. a soul mate
2. crowdfunding
3. a culture of entitlement
4. mind games
5. an adult

College- and Work-Related Topics

6. a good team player
7. a hacktavist
8. equal opportunity
9. a start-up
10. fake news

Writing Activity 2: Media Writing

Write a definition essay in which you define or explain *common sense*. To generate some ideas, watch a show, movie, or online clip about topics that might or might not require common sense. Here are some suggestions to help spark ideas:

Show: *Dr. Phil* or *The Dr. Oz Show*

Film: *The Descendants, We Bought a Zoo, The Great Gatsby, 12 Years a Slave*

Online: *Common Sense Media* (the site's catalog includes videos about sexting, oversharing, and digital surveillance)

Podcast: *Planet Money* (e.g., episodes #466, "DIY Finance" and #283, "Why Do We Tip?")

READING LINK
MORE DEFINITION
READINGS

"Slum Tourism" by Eric Weiner p. 539
"Chance and Circumstance" by David Leonhardt p. 583

WRITING LINK
MORE DEFINITION
WRITING TOPICS

Ch. 23, Writer's Room topic 1, p. 337
Ch. 29, Writer's Room topic 2, p. 400
Ch. 33, Writer's Room topic 1 p. 442
Ch. 30, Writer's Room topic 2 p. 471

Checklist: Definition Essay

As you write your definition essay, review the checklist at the back of the book. Also ask yourself the following set of questions.

❏ Does my thesis statement contain a definition by synonym, category, or negation?

❏ Do I use concise language in my definition?

❏ Do I make a point in my thesis statement?

❏ Do all of my supporting paragraphs relate to the thesis statement?

❏ Do the body paragraphs contain enough supporting details that help define the term?

11 Classification

11.1 Define classification.

11.2 Define the purpose of a classification essay.

11.3 Explore topics for a classification essay.

11.4 Write the thesis statement for a classification essay.

11.5 Generate the supporting ideas of a classification essay.

11.6 Develop a classification essay plan.

11.7 Write the first draft of a classification essay.

11.8 Revise and edit a classification essay.

To make shopping easier for consumers, retailers organize their products according to color, size, make, model, cost, and so on. When writing a classification essay, you organize and present ideas in categories.

Writers' Exchange

Work with a partner or group. Divide the next words into three or four different categories. What are the categories? Why did you choose those categories?

art	studio	medicine
construction	stethoscope	workshop
doctor	paintbrush	hospital
hammer	welder	sculptor

What Is Classification?

11.1 Define classification.

When you classify, you divide a large group into smaller and more understandable categories. For instance, if a bookstore simply displayed books randomly on shelves, customers would have a hard time finding the books that they need. Instead, the bookstore classifies according to subject area. In classification writing, each of the categories must be part of a larger group, yet they must also be distinct. For example, you might write an essay about the most common types of hobbies and sort those into board games, sports, and crafts.

People use classification in their everyday lives. At home you sort laundry based on fabric or color before you toss it in the washer or dryer. At college, the administration classifies subjects into arts, sciences, and so on. A workplace such as an office might classify employees as managers, sales staff, support staff, and other general roles.

Practice 1: Visualizing Classification

Brainstorm supporting ideas for the following thesis statement. Divide each category into subcategories by thinking of related activities.

Thesis Statement: There are several categories of games that are good for the mind.

Board Games

Card Games

Puzzles

_____ _____ _____

_____ _____ _____

_____ _____ _____

The Classification Essay

11.2 Define the purpose of a classification essay.

To find a topic for a classification essay, think of something that you can sort or divide into different groups. Also, determine a reason for classifying the items. When you are planning your ideas for a classification essay, remember the following points.

1. **Use a common classification principle.**

   A **classification principle** is the overall method that you use to sort the subject into categories. To find the classification principle, think about one common characteristic that unites the different categories. For example, if your subject is "jobs," your classification principle might be any of the following:

   - jobs in which people work with their hands
   - dangerous jobs
   - outsourced jobs

2. **Sort the subject into distinct categories.**

   A classification essay should have two or more categories.

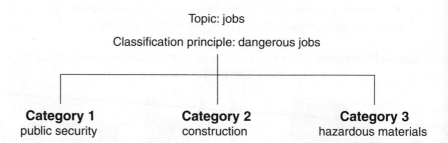

Topic: jobs

Classification principle: dangerous jobs

Category 1
public security

Category 2
construction

Category 3
hazardous materials

3. **Say something meaningful.**

   Your essay should not simply divide a topic into categories; it should say something meaningful. For instance, you can divide cars into small, medium, and large sizes. If you simply describe those categories, you will not be giving the reader any valuable information because everyone knows those three sizes exist. Instead, justify why each category is significant. For example, you can describe what a car's size tells us about the owner. Or you can categorize cars according to specific life stages (the ideal dating car, family car, and retirement car). Always consider what point you are trying to make.

   In an essay about dangerous jobs, your point could be the following: "The public should express more gratitude to those people who work in dangerous fields."

Classification at Work

Ahmad Bishr is a Web design consultant. In the next excerpt from an email to a client, he makes suggestions about classifying the content areas on a website.

> The second thing you need to do is decide how to divide your site. The opening page should contain only the most pertinent information about the cottage you are trying to rent. For instance, include the number of rooms, the location, the most spectacular traits of the cottage, and so on. Each subcategory will become a link. Because you are trying to rent your cottage, I suggest that one link contain photos of the interior, with details about each room. You will also need a link that includes a rental calendar and rates. A third section might contain information about local attractions. Remember that too many categories will confuse the viewer. You'll want a simple, uncluttered site. Keep the divisions down to four or five pages at the most. Definitely, organization is a key element in a website.

The **topic sentence** states the topic and controlling idea.

The **supporting sentences** provide details and examples.

The **concluding sentence** brings the paragraph to a close.

A Student Essay

Read the student essay and answer the questions that follow.

Discrimination in the 21st Century

Victoria Johnson

1   When the topic of discrimination is discussed, it is usually described in terms of racial, religious, or gender offenses. These types of discrimination are undeniable, but the disabled community is rarely mentioned. In 1990, Congress passed the Americans with Disabilities Act. The ADA mandated that buildings be accessible and job modifications be made to accommodate the disabled. Although this policy was a welcome beginning for people with disabilities, in practical terms, the disabled still face challenges. The disabled, specifically those in electric wheelchairs, are discriminated against in personal relationships, transportation options, and public venues.

2   Disabled people have more difficulties establishing relationships with others. I use an electric wheelchair, and a hard part of my life is not having a lot of friends. When I was little, I had friends because the other children thought it was cool to push me or to ride in my wheelchair. However, by the time I was ten, the situation had changed. As people grow up, they begin doing more and more activities; they no longer just want to go over to

someone's house to play. For people in electric wheelchairs, this is a problem. I cannot go to a friend's house unless there is a way to get inside. During my adolescence, I usually couldn't go to parties because there was no ramp. Because I was not able to take part in weekend activities like roller-skating or sports, the kids started to forget me. They saw me only at school and did not think to include me in the after-school activities. Unfortunately, people are uncomfortable around the disabled.

3   Transportation is another problem for people in electric wheelchairs because they need vans with ramps. Anyone can drive a van, but many hesitate to do so. The disabled cannot just get into any car and go to lunch. Friends need to make arrangements to take disabled people in a special van. This extra planning causes problems. Since many disabled people cannot drive and go where they want when they want, they become frustrated. In most localities, the bus system has only a few buses with wheelchair lifts, so people in wheelchairs are dependent on others to get where they want to go. The lack of independence can lead to a lack of self-esteem. People with disabilities feel they are bothering others when they ask for transportation help, and it becomes easier to stay at home.

4   People without disabilities think that things are so much better now because buildings are accessible. Of course, gaining access to buildings is important, but what happens once a disabled person is inside? Public venues often do not meet the needs of the handicapped. Whenever I go to a sports event or a concert, I have to sit near the top, and I cannot see a thing. For example, when the Clay Center in Charleston, West Virginia, was built, handicapped seating was placed in the back row instead of throughout the theater. Shopping malls are also a problem. Although the entrance is easily accessible, actual shopping is difficult. In some stores, the aisles are so narrow that the chair hits everything. Stores place too many clothes on the racks, and wheelchairs cannot get between them. The dressing rooms are also too small. The bigger department stores will have one handicapped dressing room, but usually it is filled with boxes. Grocery stores place items too high to reach. The clerks are helpful, but it is still annoying to have to ask for help.

5   For people in wheelchairs, doing activities for and by themselves is difficult. Whether the discrimination in personal relationships, transportation, and building accommodations is intentional or not, it still serves to divide people. It has been more than twenty years since the Americans with Disabilities Act was passed. The disabled should not be complacent about the steps that have been taken to improve their lives because discrimination is still a problem. Unfortunately, it may take years for the handicapped population to truly become a part of the community.

Practice 2

1. Highlight the thesis statement.

2. Highlight the topic sentence in each body paragraph. Remember that the topic sentence is not always the first sentence in the paragraph.

3. State the three categories that the writer discusses, and list some details about each category.

   a. _____

   Details: _____

   _____

   _____

   b. _____

   Details: _____

   _____

   _____

   c. _____

   Details: _____

   _____

   _____

4. Which introductory style does this essay use? Circle your answer.

   a. anecdote   c. definition

   b. historical   d. opposing position

Explore Topics

11.3   Explore topics for a classification essay.

In the Writer's Desk Warm Up, you try an exploring strategy to generate ideas about different topics.

The Writer's Desk: Warm Up

Read the following questions, and write the first ideas that come to your mind. Think of two to three ideas for each topic.

EXAMPLE: How is social media useful?

   —make friends

   —organize events

   —build workplace networking

1. What are some different dance styles?

_____

_____

_____

2. What are some different types of consumers? To get ideas, think of some people you know and the way that they shop.

_____

_____

_____

3. What are some types of heroes that people have at different times in their lives?

_____

_____

_____

Making a Classification Chart

A **classification chart** is a visual representation of a main topic and its categories. Making a classification chart can help you to identify the categories more clearly so that you will be able to write more exact thesis statements.

When you classify items, remember to find a common classification principle. For example, you can classify sports according to their benefits, their degree of difficulty, or their costs.

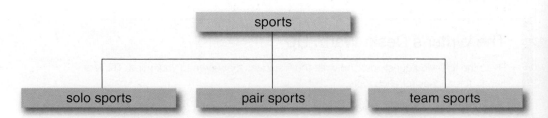

Classification Principle: psychological benefits

You can also use a pie chart to help you classify items.

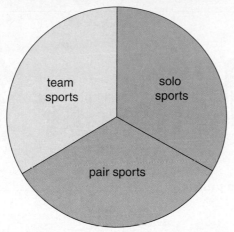

Psychological Benefits of Sports

Some students find it easier to draw or doodle pictures to help represent the categories of their classification charts. Do whatever works for you, unless your instructor asks for a specific type of chart.

HINT: Make a Point

To make interesting classification essays, try to express an attitude, opinion, or feeling about the topic. For example, in an essay about discipline, your classification principle might be types of discipline methods; however, the essay needs to inform readers of something specific about those methods. You could write about discipline methods that are most effective, least effective, ethical, unethical, violent, nonviolent, and so on.

Practice 3

In the following classification charts, a subject has been broken down into distinct categories. The items in the group should have the same classification principle. Cross out one item in each group that does not belong. Then write down the classification principle that unites the group.

EXAMPLE:

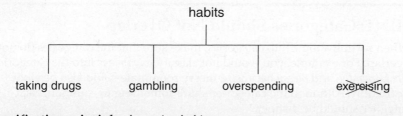

Classification principle: <u>damaging habits</u>

1.

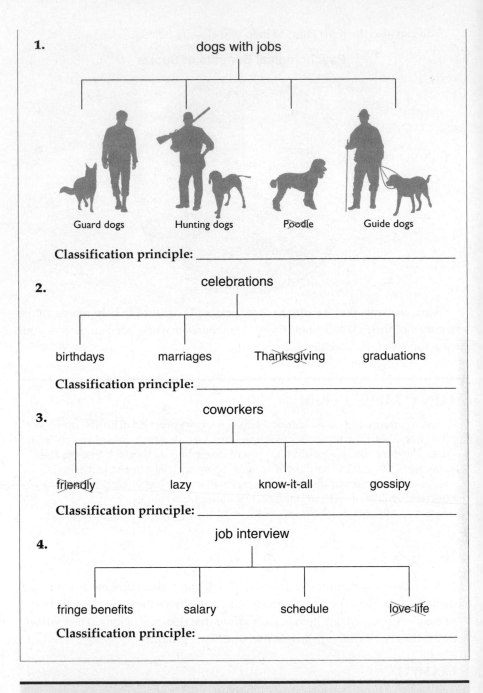

dogs with jobs

Guard dogs   Hunting dogs   Poodle   Guide dogs

Classification principle: _____

2.

celebrations

birthdays   marriages   Thanksgiving   graduations

Classification principle: _____

3.

coworkers

friendly   lazy   know-it-all   gossipy

Classification principle: _____

4.

job interview

fringe benefits   salary   schedule   love life

Classification principle: _____

HINT: Categories Should Not Overlap

When sorting a topic into categories, make sure that the categories do not overlap. For example, you would not classify *roommates* into the categories *aloof*, *friendly*, and *messy* because a messy roommate could also be aloof or friendly. Although the categories share something in common, each category should be distinct.

The Writer's Desk: Find Distinct Categories

Break down the following topics into three distinct categories. Remember to find categories that do not overlap. You can look for ideas in the Writer's Desk Warm Up on pages 165–166.

EXAMPLE:

Events organized with online tools

flash mobs | flash robs | riots

Classification principle: activities done with strangers

1.

dance styles

Classification principle: _____

2.

consumers

Classification principle: _____

3.

heroes

Classification principle: _____

The Thesis Statement

11.4 Write the thesis statement for a classification essay.

The thesis statement in a classification essay clearly indicates what you will classify. It also includes the controlling idea, which is the classification principle. You can also mention the types of categories in your thesis statement.

topic   controlling idea
Several types of coworkers can completely destroy a workplace environment.

                topic   controlling idea
Gossipy, lazy, and know-it-all coworkers can completely destroy a workplace environment.

The Writer's Desk: Write Thesis Statements

Write clear thesis statements. You can refer to your ideas in previous Writer's Desks. Remember that your thesis statement can include the different categories you will be discussing.

EXAMPLE: Topic: events organized online

Thesis statement: <u>Three types of interesting and unexpected social activities are flash mobs, flash robs, and riots.</u>

1. Topic: dance styles

   Thesis statement: _____

   _____

2. Topic: consumers

   Thesis statement: _____

   _____

3. Topic: heroes

   Thesis statement: _____

   _____

The Supporting Ideas

11.5 Generate the supporting ideas of a classification essay.

After you have developed an effective thesis statement, generate supporting ideas. In a classification essay, you can list details about each of your categories.

- Use prewriting strategies to generate examples for each category.
- Choose the best ideas.
- Organize your ideas. Choose the best organizational method for this essay pattern.

You can prepare a traditional essay plan. You can also illustrate your main and supporting ideas in a classification chart such as the one that follows.

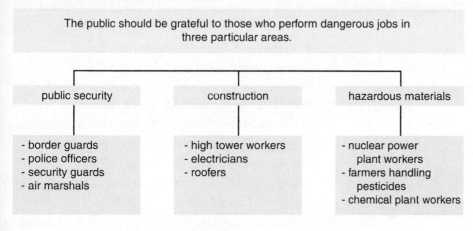

The public should be grateful to those who perform dangerous jobs in three particular areas.

public security	construction	hazardous materials

- border guards
- police officers
- security guards
- air marshals
	- high tower workers
	- electricians
	- roofers
		- nuclear power
		  plant workers
		- farmers handling
		  pesticides
		- chemical plant workers

The Writer's Desk: Develop Supporting Ideas

Choose one of the thesis statements from the previous Writer's Desk, and list supporting ideas.

Thesis statement: _____

The Essay Plan

11.6   Develop a classification essay plan.

Before you write a classification essay, make a detailed essay plan. Add supporting details for each category.

Thesis Statement: Three types of interesting and unexpected crowd activities are flash mobs, flash robs, and riots.

    I.   Flash mobs are unexpected fun activities.
        A. Someone plans a song or dance.
        B. People sign up online.
        C. They meet in public and do the activity.
        D. Members of the public are shocked but may join in.

    II.   Flash rob groups use crowds to commit theft.
        A. People connect with Facebook or Twitter.
        B. The crowd meets in a store at a particular time.
        C. The crowd members rob the store.

    III.   Riots are the most dangerous type of crowd activity.
        A. People plan to meet after a sports game or political event.
        B. Some people begin to break the law.
        C. Bystanders join in to break windows and rob stores.

The Writer's Desk: Make an Essay Plan

Refer to the information you generated in previous Writer's Desks, and prepare a detailed essay plan. Arrange the supporting details in a logical order.

The First Draft

11.7   Write the first draft of a classification essay.

After you outline your ideas in a plan, you are ready to write the first draft. Weave together the ideas you have in your essay plan. Remember to write complete sentences and to include transitional words or expressions to help your ideas flow smoothly. Here are some transitions that can help you express which category is most important and to signal movement from one category to the next.

To show importance	To show types of categories
above all	one kind . . . another kind
clearly	the first/second kind
most of all	the first/second type
particularly	the last category
the most important	

The Writer's Desk: Write the First Draft

Carefully review the classification essay plan you prepared in the previous Writer's Desk and make any necessary changes. Then, write the first draft of your classification essay.

Revising And Editing

Revise and Edit a Classification Essay

11.8   Revise and edit a classification essay.

When you finish writing a classification essay, carefully review your work and revise it to make sure that the categories do not overlap. Check that you have organized your essay logically, and remove any irrelevant details. Before reviewing your own essay, practice revising and editing a student essay.

A Student Essay

Read the essay, and then answer the questions that follow. As you read, correct any errors that you find and make comments in the margins.

....

Flash Mobs, Flash Robs, and Riots
....

Diego Pelaez

1   Facebook, Twitter, and instant messaging provide people with the information necessary to gather in public places. Most citizens use social media to meet up with family and friends. However, sometimes groups of strangers congregate using such technology, and they do harmful or illegal actions. Three types of interesting and unexpected crowd activities are flash mobs, flash robs, and riots.

2   A flash mob occurs when a group of people gather in a public place to do some type of unexpected performance. That is harmless and fun. Some credit Improv Everywhere's "Frozen Grand Central" as the clip that really ignited the flash mob revolution. Uploaded in 2008, the clip shows people who be walking around New York's Grand Central Terminal. Suddenly, about two hundred people freeze in position, looking like statues. A minute later, they walk away as if nothing has happened. The stunned expressions on the faces of onlookers helped make the video clip a Web sensation. Since then, crowds of people have gathered in public squares to have pillow fights, dance with synchronized movements, sing, and even to quack like ducks. Although such activities involve some planning, to onlookers they appear to be spontaneous acts of mass silliness.

3   A flash rob is a dangerous and illegal group activity. In 2010, American police saw the first flash robs, where large groups of people descended on stores to steal items. For instance, on July 30, 2012, a Chicago clothing store was the victim of flash robbing. About twenty people entered Mildblend Supply Company and stole high-price denim jeans. Flash robs also occur in Canada. In July 2011, a thieving mob descended on an Ottawa convenience store, showing little compassion for the local merchant. Sometimes lone thieves rob stores, and their images are captured on security cameras.

4   Riots, which are the worse group activity, include wanton destruction and violence. In the spring of 2011, disappointed Vancouver hockey fans burned cars, broke windows, and stores were robbed. That summer, England had five days of rioting. The first riot began in Tottenham, an area in North London, where a peaceful protest about a police shooting turned violent. As the riots spread, participants in different towns took advantage of the chaos to go on destructive shopping sprees. Some people lost their homes, their businesses, and even their lives. For instance, an uninsured butcher in Tottenham lost about $50,000 worth of meat and worried that this event had destroyed his life's work. Even more seriously, sixty-eight-year-old Richard Bowes was beaten to death merely because he tried to stop rioters from burning down a building, and three people were run over as they tried to defend their neighborhood.

5   Flash mobs are generally safe and fun events. Flash robs and riots, however, are much more destructive. Social media can contribute to all three types of gatherings, it can also be used to catch lawbreakers. After flash robs and riots, some outraged citizens have created "name and shame" Facebook pages, uploading cellphone images of lawbreakers and publicly humiliating them. Police forces also use the tools of social media, putting photos on Facebook and YouTube. In England, with the public's help, police identified close to two thousand looters. Perhaps the biggest wake-up call for flash robbers and rioters is to find out that social media can cut both ways.

Practice 4

Revising

1. Highlight the thesis statement and the topic sentences in the three body paragraphs.

2. The essay is organized using what type of order?

   a. time   b. space   c. emphatic

   Explain your answer: _____

   _____

3. In paragraph 3, one of the examples is not a valid support. Cross it out. Explain why it is not valid. _____

_____

4. What does the writer mean in the conclusion when he says that social media "can cut both ways." _____

_____

Editing

5. A fragment lacks a subject or a verb and is an incomplete sentence. Underline one fragment in paragraph 2. Then write the correction in the space.

Correction: _____

6. Paragraph 2 contains a verb-tense error. Underline the error, and write the correction here.

Correction: _____

7. In paragraph 4, there is an error with the superlative form of an adjective. Underline the error, and write the correction here.

Correction: _____

8. In paragraph 4, there is a parallel structure error. Underline and correct the error. (For more information about parallel structure, see the Grammar Hint below.)

_____

9. Paragraph 5 contains a run-on sentence. Underline it, and show a possible correction here.

Correction: _____

_____

> **GRAMMAR LINK**
>
> More grammar help:
> Fragments, Ch. 23
> Run-Ons, Ch. 24
> Parallel Structure, Ch. 25
> Verb Tenses, Ch. 28
> Adjectives, Ch. 32

GRAMMAR HINT: Parallel Structure

Use parallel structure when words or phrases are joined in a series. The groups of items should be balanced.

Some annoying sales methods include calling customers on the
phone, putting pop-up ads on the Internet, and ~~when they leave~~ **leaving**
text messages.

The Writer's Desk: Revise and Edit Your Essay

Revise and edit the essay that you wrote for the previous Writer's Desk. You can refer to the revising and editing checklists at the end of this chapter and at the end of the book.

Vocabulary Boost

Writers commonly overuse the same vocabulary. To make your writing more vivid and interesting, look at your first draft and underline at least ten repeated nouns and verbs. (Remember that a noun is a person, place, or thing.) Then add details or specific descriptions to five of the nouns and write more vivid verbs. Here is a brief example of how you might avoid repetition of nouns and verbs.

Dull, repetitive	Patrice likes cycling. Patrice often cycles to work at his bookstore. Often Patrice is reckless and cycles without a helmet.
Detailed, uses synonyms	**Patrice** likes **cycling** and **commutes** to work on his **bike**. Although **the 30-year-old bookstore owner** knows better, **he** often **recklessly rides** without a helmet.

A Professional Essay

Marjie T. Britz is a professor of criminal justice at Clemson University. Her research interests include street gangs, cybercrime, and organized crime. The following excerpt is from her book *Computer Forensics and Cyber Crime*.

Motivations of Terrorism

Marjie T. Britz, Ed.

1   Terrorists and terrorist groups vary widely in their longevity, methodology, sophistication, and commitment. While some groups have shown great resiliency, others have been extinguished as quickly as they were ignited. Thus, it is impossible to discuss all groups which are, have been, or will be engaging in terrorists acts. Rather, it is more appropriate to discuss the groups collectively by their motivation: individual, political-social, nationalistic, environmental, state-sponsored, and religious.

2   Individual terrorism is often overlooked in discussions of the phenomenon, as there is a collective perception that such individuals have limited impact and do not constitute a significant threat. Such individuals act independently and typically eschew group involvement. Their motivations

are as disparate as the actors themselves but are largely directed as a discontentment with society in general. Theodore "Ted" Kaczynski (aka the Unabomber) is an example of an individual terrorist.

3   Political-social terrorism is the most ambiguous because the actors are often characterized by the success of their operations. Theoretically speaking, political-social terrorism is perpetrated by groups, which are attempting to accomplish an **articulable** political agenda. Most often, such groups engage in behavior to overthrow the established order and replace it with their own. Depending upon the emergent government, groups that are successful are referred to as patriots, heroes, freedom fighters, revolutionaries, or regimes. An example of the former might include the early American colonists, while an example of the latter would include Castro's 26 of July Movement.

articulable: an idea that is able to be expressed clearly

4   Nationalist terrorism is characterized by groups that share a collective perception of oppression or persecution. Generally, the groups maintain large memberships and significant longevity due to their ability to recruit on platforms of persecution. Examples include many prominent Arab Palestinian terrorists groups like HAMAS (Islamic Resistance Movement), Hezbollah, Palestine Islamic Jihad (PIJ), and Palestine Liberation Front (PLF). Other groups are the Irish Republican Army (IRA) and the Spanish Basque separatists, Euzkadi Ta Askatasuna (ETA).

5   Commonly known as ecoterrorism, environmental terrorist groups base their ideology on the conservation of natural resources. Some groups also focus on animal rights. In the United States, the first group to engage in violent acts (i.e., arson) was *Earth First!*. However, their actions pale in comparison to later groups such as the Earth Liberation Front (ELF), which has set fire to commercial properties and private vehicles. One of the most prominent animal rights group, the Animal Liberation Front (ALF), has directed similar efforts at university research centers or industries which engage in activities which exploit or harm animals.

6   Like political terrorism, state-sponsored terrorism is defined by the established order. In today's world, it contains two broad groups of actors: (1) those governments that engage in acts of terror against their own citizens (i.e., Nazi Germany, Bosnia, etc.); (2) those governments that support or carry out terrorist acts against other governments. According to the United States, the governments of Cambodia, Rwanda, and Bosnia are currently engaging in acts of terror against their own citizens, while Cuba, Syria, and Iran continue to support international terrorist acts against other countries.

7   Perhaps the most prevalent, and certainly the most dangerous, groups of terrorists are motivated by religious ideologies. Historically, such groups have displayed the highest degree of longevity, devotion, and success. Claiming to be empowered by God and justified by scripture, they have waged war and slaughtered innocents—all in the name of religion. Their

zealotry: extremism

zealotry blinds them to human suffering, and even the most horrific acts are seen as glorious. Such ideologies are not limited to one particular faith or denomination. Although Islamic groups have garnered the most attention in the past decade, Christian and Jewish groups remain active. Some of the groups that are the most actively engaged in acts of terror include: (1) Christian: Army of God, God's Army, Nagaland Rebels, Phineas Priesthood, National Democratic Front of Bodoland; (2) Judaic: Kahane Chai, Kach, Jewish Defense League; (3) Islamic: al Qaeda, HAMAS, Jihad Rite, Turkish Hezbollah, Palestinian Islamic Jihad.

8   In conclusion, analyzing motivation is a useful tool to understanding and inhibiting terrorist organizations. In the wake of the 9/11 terror attacks, the government and the American public articulated a resolve to immediately seek out and destroy those enemies, both foreign and domestic, who sought to **rent asunder** the fabric of American society. By understanding the inspiration that encourages terrorist groups, the American government may be able to develop tools to limit them.

rent asunder: shred into bits

Practice 5

1. What is the topic of this essay? _____

2. What are the main characteristics of the following types of terrorist groups?

　a.　individual terrorism members _____

　　_____

　　_____

　b.　political-social terrorism _____

　　_____

　　_____

　c.　national terrorism _____

　　_____

　　_____

　d.　ecoterrorism members _____

　　_____

　　_____

　e.　state-sponsored terrorism _____

　　_____

　　_____

f. religious terrorism _____

_____

_____

3. What is the writer's purpose? Circle your answer.

   a. to entertain   b. to persuade   c. to inform

4. Who is the audience for this essay? _____

_____

5. Do you think that the use of terror tactics to achieve a goal is ever justified? Explain your answer.

_____

_____

_____

_____

_____

READING LINK
MORE CLASSIFICATION
READINGS

"Living Environments"
   p. 532
"How Companies
   Deceive Us" p. 524

The Writer's Room

Writing Activity 1: Topics

Choose any of the following topics, or choose your own topic, and write a classification essay. Determine your classification principle, and make sure that your categories do not overlap.

General Topics

Categories of . . .

1. computer users
2. useful websites
3. weight-loss methods
4. neighbors
5. reality shows

College- and Work-Related Topics

Categories of . . .

6. electronic modes of communication
7. help professions
8. success
9. work environments
10. customers

WRITING LINK
MORE CLASSIFICATION
WRITING TOPICS

Ch. 22, Writer's Room
   topic 1 p. 326
Ch. 26, Writer's Room
   topic 2, p. 357
Ch. 29, Writer's Room
   topic 2, p. 398
Ch. 34, Writer's Room
   topic 1, p. 451
Ch. 37, Writer's Room
   topic 2, p. 482

Writing Activity 2: Media Writing

Write an essay in which you divide crime fighters or criminals into categories. Or, you could describe different types of crimes. Use examples to support your ideas. To spark ideas, watch a show, movie, or online video or listen to a podcast.

Show: *Law & Order*, *The Jinx*, *Dexter*, *Criminal Minds*, *COPS*

Film: *The Wolf of Wall Street*, *Michael Clayton*, *The Godfather*

Video: U.S. Department of Homeland Security's public service videos

Podcast: *Serial*, *Criminal*

Checklist: Classification Essay

After you write your classification essay, review the checklist at the back of the book. Also, ask yourself these questions.

❑ Does my thesis statement explain the categories that I will discuss?

❑ Do I use a common classification principle to unite the various items?

❑ Do I offer sufficient details to explain each category?

❑ Do I arrange the categories in a logical manner?

❑ Does all of the supporting information relate to the categories that I am discussing?

❑ Do I include categories that do not overlap?

❑ Does my essay make a point and say something meaningful?

12 Comparison and Contrast

When you shop for new furnishings or home decor items, you compare the features of different items to help you make a decision. When you write a comparison and contrast essay, you examine two or more items and make conclusions about them.

Writers' Exchange

What were your goals as a child? What are your goals as an adult? Think about work, money, and family. Compare your answers with those of a partner, and discuss how childhood goals are different from adult goals.

LEARNING OBJECTIVES

12.1 Define comparison and contrast.

12.2 Define the purpose of the comparison and contrast essay.

12.3 Explore topics for a comparison and contrast essay.

12.4 Write the thesis statement of a comparison and contrast essay.

12.5 Generate the supporting ideas of a comparison and contrast essay.

12.6 Develop a comparison and contrast essay plan.

12.7 Write the first draft of a comparison and contrast essay.

12.8 Revise and edit a comparison and contrast essay.

Exploring

What Is Comparison and Contrast?

12.1 Define comparison and contrast.

When you want to decide between options, you compare and contrast. You **compare** to find similarities and **contrast** to find differences. The exercise of comparing and contrasting can help you make judgments about things. It can also help you to better understand familiar things.

People use comparison and contrast in their daily lives. For instance, at home, you might explain to a parent why Version X of a smartphone is better than Version Y. At college, students often compare two courses. In workplaces, salespeople compare their new products with competing products to highlight the differences.

Practice 1: Visualizing Comparison and Contrast

Brainstorm supporting ideas for the following thesis statement. Write some benefits of each type of sport on the lines provided.

Thesis Statement: Team sports provide different benefits than solo sports.

Team sports

Solo sports

_____

_____

_____

_____

_____

_____

The Comparison and Contrast Essay

12.2 Define the purpose of the comparison and contrast essay.

In a comparison and contrast essay, you can compare and contrast two different subjects, or you can compare and contrast different aspects of a single subject. When you write using this essay pattern, remember to think about your specific purpose.

- Your purpose could be to make judgments about two items. For example, you might compare and contrast two cars to convince your readers that one is preferable.

- Your purpose could be to describe or understand two familiar things. For example, you might compare two movies to help your readers understand their thematic similarities.

Comparison and Contrast at Work

Mr. Thomas, a supervisor, trains his employees in hospitality management. In this excerpt from his manual, he explains the difference between customer service and customer care.

The terms "customer service" and "customer care" are frequently used interchangeably, but actually mean different things. Customer service is the "minimum required" to complete a transaction and sell your product or service. It can, and should, be done politely and efficiently. Customer care, on the other hand, is the art of thinking of your customer as an individual *beyond* the immediate transaction. Consider the following scenario. A family with young children arrives at a hotel after a long day traveling. They are politely checked in and a porter helps them with their luggage, so customer service was provided. However, as they left the check-in desk, the parents were heard telling the children it was bath night. You have other guests to serve, but you quickly write a note on hotel stationary with the message "Hope this helps with bath time!" and you instruct a colleague to deliver extra-large towels and two kids' "bath bags" to the room. The bags contain tear-free shampoo, sponges, and a wind-up bath toy. The next morning, the parents tell the front desk how delighted the children were. That family will have a wonderful feeling about their stay and will be back. Good customer care will result in positive reviews, word-of-mouth recommendations, and repeat stays.

> The **topic sentence** states the topic and the controlling idea.

> The **supporting sentences** provide details and examples.

> The **concluding sentence** brings the paragraph to a close.

Comparison and Contrast Patterns

Comparison and contrast essays follow two common patterns.

Point by Point Present one point about Topic A and then present the same point about Topic B. Keep following this pattern until you have a few points for each. Go back and forth from one side to the other like tennis players hitting a ball back and forth across a net.

Topic by Topic Present all of your points about one topic, and then present all of your points about the second topic. Offer one side and then the other side, just as opposing lawyers would do in the closing arguments of a court case.

MARINA'S EXAMPLE

Marina is trying to decide whether she would prefer a part-time job in a clothing store or in a restaurant. Marina can organize her information using a topic-by-topic pattern or a point-by-point method.

Thesis Statement: The service station job is better than the restaurant job.

Point-by-Point Comparison	Topic-by-Topic Comparison
Topic sentence: Salaries	Topic sentence: Job A
Job A	♦ salary
Job B	♦ hours
Topic sentence: Working hours	♦ working environment
Job A	
Job B	Topic sentence: Job B
Topic sentence: Working environments	♦ salary
Job A	♦ hours
Job B	♦ working environment

A Student Essay

Read the student essay, and answer the questions that follow.

....

Swamps and Pesticides

....

Corey Kaminska

1   Having had many jobs in my twenty-two years, I have realized some jobs are a good experience, but many jobs turn into a horrible nightmare. I have also realized that every job has some good points. My favorite all-time job was working as a mosquito abater, and my worst was being a Crystal Hot Springs campground janitor.

2   In my best job, I worked for the Box Elder Mosquito Abatement District, and I had a very exciting routine. This may sound like an odd job, and I would not blame anyone for thinking so. I began my day by walking into the modern abatement building. I drooled over the fancy trucks and

four-wheelers that would be mine for the summer. Each morning, the abatement crew met in the conference room to discuss the day's duties. We were then set free to protect the citizens of Box Elder County.

3   Being a mosquito abater was a laid-back and pleasant job. I could work alone while enjoying the outdoors and having fun at the same time. Each day, I gathered my pesticides and supplies. I tossed the chemicals into my 2005 Chevy extended cab, and then I traveled the vast countryside for the day. Pulling my new Honda Rancher on the trailer behind, I searched for a spot where mosquito larvae might be. Then I unloaded my four-wheeler off the trailer and drove through the mucky swamp looking for the perfect spot to start treating the unpleasant larvae-infested water. When I finally found the tiny worm-like creatures swimming on top of the water, the fun began. I turned on my hopper, which spread sand-like granules into the water and killed the larvae. Bogging through the swampy water on the four-wheeler was something I would have done for fun, but now I was getting paid for it.

4   On the other hand, my job as a Crystal Springs campground janitor was horrible in almost every way. As a janitor, I would begin my day by waking up exceptionally early. Arriving at Crystal Springs, the first thing I had to do was clean out the empty pools and hot tubs. That was a nasty experience. Cleaning up human filth that lingers in the pools until evening and then sticks to the walls as the pool drains is not an appealing task. Scrubbing the walls of the pool for hours is a boring nightmare. The only thing that made it worse was the constant smell from the dairy farm directly across the street. After cleaning out the pools and refilling them with fresh water, I was required to clean out the men's and women's locker rooms. During the cleaning, I often found disgusting items. The work was boring, and the pay was horrible.

5   Although there were drastic differences between my best and my worst job, I discovered some surprising similarities. Both jobs taught me that work is work and money is money. In each job, I helped other people and made their lives just a little bit more enjoyable. I also learned that life is not always about me. Although I was not really appreciated in either job, I learned to recognize my own value. If the job had not been done, people would have suffered the consequences. They would have lived with more mosquitoes, and they would have seen the filth in the pool, hot tubs, and locker rooms.

Practice 2

1. Highlight the thesis statement.

2. Highlight the topic sentences in paragraphs 2, 3, and 4.

3. What pattern of comparison does the writer follow in the entire essay?
   a. point by point   b. topic by topic

4. In paragraphs 2, 3, and 4, what does the writer focus on?

   a. similarities   b. differences

5. List the main advantages of the mosquito abater job.

   _____

   _____

6. List reasons why the janitor job was horrible.

   _____

   _____

   _____

7. In the conclusion, the writer mentions some similarities. Use your own words to list the main similarities.

   _____

   _____

Explore Topics

12.3   **Explore topics for a comparison and contrast essay.**

In the Writer's Desk Warm Up, you will try an exploring strategy to generate ideas about different topics.

The Writer's Desk: Warm Up

Read the following questions, and write the first ideas that come to your mind. Think of two to three ideas for each topic.

EXAMPLE: What are some key differences between toys that are traditionally for girls and for boys?

girls' toys	boys' toys
–pastel colors	–noisy
–stuffed animals	–toy cars, trucks, fire engines
–dolls with clothes	–action figures

1. What were your childhood goals? What are your goals today?

childhood goals	current goals

2. What are the key features of your generation and your parents' generation?

your generation	your parents' generation

3. What are some games that you enjoy? Think about board games or online game apps. Brainstorm the key features of two different games.

Developing

The Thesis Statement

12.4   Write the thesis statement of a comparison and contrast statement.

In a comparison and contrast essay, the thesis statement indicates what you are comparing and contrasting, and it expresses a controlling idea. For example, the following thesis statement indicates that the essay will compare the myths and reality of mold to prove that it does not seriously threaten human health.

Common household mold is not as dangerous as many people believe.

Practice 3

Read each thesis statement, and then answer the questions that follow. State whether the essay would focus on similarities or differences.

1. The weather in our region is more extreme than it was in the past.

a. What is being compared? _____

b. What is the controlling idea? _____

c. What will the essay focus on? ____ similarities ____ differences

2. Commerce students and art students have some surprising traits in common.

   a. What is being compared? _____

   b. What is the controlling idea? _____

   c. What will the essay focus on? ____ similarities ____ differences

3. Before marriage, people expect to feel eternally lustful toward their "soul mate," but the reality of married life is quite different.

   a. What is being compared? _____

   b. What is the controlling idea? _____

   _____

   c. What will the essay focus on? ____ similarities ____ differences

VOCABULARY BOOST

Some prefixes mean "not" and give words opposite meanings. Examples are *il-*, *im-*, *in-*, *dis-*, *un-*, *non-*, and *ir-*. Create opposites by adding prefixes to the following words.

EXAMPLE: __un__ available

1. _____ legal		7. _____ reliable
2. _____ polite		8. _____ harmed
3. _____ toxic		9. _____ reversible
4. _____ appropriate		10. _____ necessary
5. _____ approve		11. _____ patient
6. _____ considerate		12. _____ agree

The Writer's Desk: Write Thesis Statements

For each topic, write a thesis statement that includes what you are comparing and contrasting and a controlling idea.

EXAMPLE: Topic: girls' and boys' toys

Thesis statement: <u>**Both girls' and boys' toys reinforce gender stereotypes.**</u>

1. Topic: childhood goals and current goals

   Thesis statement: _____

   _____

   _____

2. Topic: two generations

   Thesis statement: _____

   _____

   _____

3. Topic: two games

   Thesis statement: _____

   _____

   _____

The Supporting Ideas

12.5   Generate the supporting ideas of a comparison and contrast essay.

After you have developed an effective thesis statement, generate supporting ideas. In a comparison and contrast essay, think of examples that help to clarify the similarities or differences, and then incorporate some ideas in your final essay plan.

To generate supporting ideas, you might try using a Venn diagram. In this example, you can see how the writer draws two circles to compare traditional boys' and girls' toys and how some ideas fall into both categories.

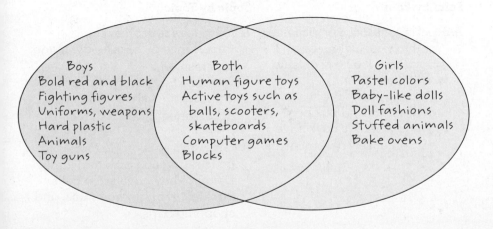

Boys
Bold red and black
Fighting figures
Uniforms, weapons
Hard plastic
Animals
Toy guns

Both
Human figure toys
Active toys such as
   balls, scooters,
   skateboards
Computer games
Blocks

Girls
Pastel colors
Baby-like dolls
Doll fashions
Stuffed animals
Bake ovens

The Writer's Desk: Develop Supporting Ideas

Choose one of your thesis statements from the previous Writer's Desk. List some similarities and differences.

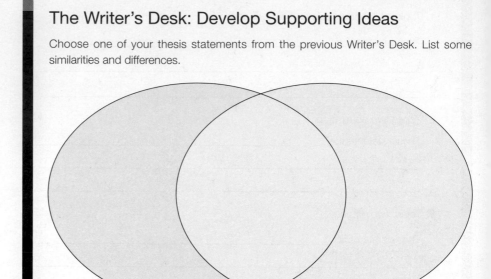

The Essay Plan

12.6   Develop a comparison and contrast essay plan.

Before you write a comparison and contrast essay, make a detailed essay plan. Decide which pattern you will follow: point by point or topic by topic. Then add supporting details. Make sure that each detail supports the thesis statement. Also think about the best way to organize your ideas.

Thesis Statement: Both girls' and boys' toys reinforce gender stereotypes.

Point by Point

A/B Girls' toys focus on activities in the home, whereas boys' toys focus on outside activities.
Details: Girls have dollhouses and baking ovens whereas boys have carpenter sets and racecars.

Topic by Topic

A Girls' toys reinforce the importance of looks, body image, and fashion.
Details: They receive fashion dolls with clothing, shoes, and other accessories.

A Girls' toys encourage nurturing by focusing on home and family.
Details: They have baby dolls, baking ovens, toy vacuums, and shopping carts.

Point by Point

A/B Girls' toys focus on physical appearance, and boys' toys focus on heroic fighters.
Details: Girls dress their Barbie dolls, and they put on child-friendly makeup. Boys have action figures such as GI Joes and superheroes.

Topic by Topic

B Boys' toys prepare them for creative careers and activities outside the home.
Details: Boys have little workshops, Lego sets, and toy cars and trucks.

B Boys' toys encourage boys to be heroes in their fantasy games.
Details: Boys receive action figures such as GI Joe, X-Men, and Superman.

The Writer's Desk: Write an Essay Plan

Refer to the information you generated in previous Writer's Desks, and prepare a detailed essay plan using a point-by-point or topic-by-topic pattern. You can use the letters A and B to indicate which side you are discussing in your plan. Include details about each supporting idea.

The First Draft

12.7   Write the first draft of a comparison and contrast essay.

After you outline your ideas in an essay plan, you are ready to write the first draft. Remember to follow the topic-by-topic or the point-by-point pattern you used in your plan. Write complete sentences and use transitions to help your ideas flow smoothly. The following transitions can be helpful for guiding readers through a comparison and contrast essay.

To show similarities		To show differences	
additionally	in addition	conversely	nevertheless
at the same time	in the same way	however	on the contrary
equally	similarly	in contrast	then again

The Writer's Desk: Write the First Draft

Write the first draft of your comparison and contrast essay. Before you write, carefully review your essay plan to see if you have enough support for your points and topics. Flesh out each body paragraph with specific details.

Revise and Edit a Comparison and Contrast Essay

12.8 Revise and edit a comparison and contrast essay.

When you finish writing a comparison and contrast essay, carefully review your work and revise it to make sure that the comparison or contrast is as clear as possible to your readers. Check that you have organized your essay logically, and remove any irrelevant details. Before you work on your own essay, practice revising and editing a student essay.

A Student Essay

Read the essay, and then answer the questions that follow. As you read, correct any errors that you find, and make comments in the margins.

Gender and Toys

Ashley Lincoln

1   As a young mother, I try to avoid gender stereotyping my children. I encourage my five-year-old daughter to play sports, and I bought my son a baby doll when he asked for one. My friends been saying they have the same concerns about gender roles. But insulating children from male or female role expectations is almost impossible. Girls' and boys' toys reinforce gender stereotypes.

2   Girls' toys reinforce the importance of looks, body image, and fashion. Parents can buy their daughters makeup sets that include child-friendly lipstick, blush, and eye shadow. Barbies and other fashion dolls fill store shelves. Hanging next to the dolls are packages with tiny clothing. Of course, none of the dolls are pudgy, pimply, large-boned, or just plain unattractive. When girls play with these toys, they are taught that beauty and the right clothes and makeup are very important.

3   If a little girl does not like fashion toys, they will surely enjoy baby dolls with their fake bottles of milk, soft little blankets, and strollers. Girls' toys encourage nurturing by focusing on the home and the family. At a very young age, girls learn to be competent mothers when they change the little diapers of their dolls. Girls can learn to cook with their Easy-Bake ovens, and they learn to shop with tiny shopping carts and cash registers. My daughter and her friends love playing "house" with one child acting as the mother.

They shop for toy groceries and feed their "babies." Girls learn about the importance of parenting quicker than boys do.

4   Boys' toys, on the other hand, emphasize jobs and activities outside the home. My son begged for, and received, a miniature workshop complete with a plastic saw, drill, screwdriver, and wrench. Lego sets prepare boys for creative occupations such as architecture and auto design. Computer and video games prepare boys for jobs in the high-tech industries. Finally, there is a lot of toy cars, trucks, and racetracks to remind boys that cars are very important to their identities.

5   Toys aimed at young males also permit boys to be the heroes in their fantasy games. In the boys' aisle of the toy store, there are rows of action figures. The GI Joes fight soldiers from other armies. Batman, Superman, and the X-Men fight fantasy villains. There is the occasional female hero, such as Rey from *Star Wars*, but most action figures depict males. Such toys encourage boys to fantasize about rescuing others and be a savior.

6   Some suggest that it is useless to fight against the male and female roles. They point out that girls in previous centuries made their own dolls out of straw and rags, and boys made weapons out of tin cans and wood. While that is true, toy stores take the stereotyping to extremes. So, how can we expand toy options for all children? Buy more gender-neutral toys such as modeling clay, painting supplies, or balls and other sporting equipment.

Practice 4

Revising

1. Highlight the thesis statement.

2. Highlight the topic sentence in each body paragraph.

3. Circle a transitional word or phrase in the topic sentence of paragraph 4. Then add transitional words or phrases to the other topic sentences.

4. What pattern does the writer use to organize this essay? Circle your response.
   a. point by point   b. topic by topic

5. The student writer uses the word "reinforce" at the end of the introduction and in the first sentence of the second paragraph. To avoid repeating the same word, what synonym could the student use?

_____

GRAMMAR LINK
More information about
grammar topics:

Subject–Verb
    Agreement, Ch. 27
Verbs, Ch. 29
Pronouns, Ch. 31
Adjectives and Adverbs,
    Ch. 32
Parallel Structure,
    Ch. 25

Editing

6. Underline the verb error in the introduction. Write the correction on the line.

Correction: _____

7. Underline and correct the pronoun–antecedent error in paragraph 3.

Correction: _____

_____

8. Underline and correct a comparative form error in paragraph 3. (For more information about comparative errors, see the Grammar Hint below.)

Correction: _____

_____

9. Underline and correct the subject–verb agreement error in paragraph 4.

Correction: _____

_____

10. Underline and correct the parallel structure error in paragraph 5.

Correction: _____

GRAMMAR HINT: Comparing Adjectives and Adverbs

When comparing or contrasting two items, ensure that you have correctly written your comparative forms. For instance, never put *more* with an adjective ending in *-er*.

Cycling to college is ~~more~~ better than taking the bus.

If you are comparing two actions, remember to use an adverb instead of an adjective.

more easily
Children learn lessons ~~easier~~ when they are treated with respect.

The Writer's Desk: Revise and Edit Your Essay

Revise and edit the essay that you wrote for the previous Writer's Desk. You can refer to the revising and editing checklists at the end of this chapter and at the end of the book.

A Professional Essay

Andrea Kuszewski is a Florida-based behavior therapist and researcher with expertise in Asperger syndrome. In the following essay, she explains the similarities and differences between sociopaths and extreme altruists.

Heroes Versus Sociopaths

Andrea Kuszewski

1   We look at heroes and do-gooders as a special sort of breed. They are people who possess extraordinary traits of altruism—selfless concern for the well-being of others—even at the expense of their own existence. On the other end, sociopaths also have an extraordinary set of traits, such as extreme selfishness, lack of impulse control, no respect for rules, and no conscience. As crazy as it sounds, there may be a closer link than most people would think between the extreme-altruistic personality and the sociopathic personality.

2   The word "altruism" conveys images of people like St. Mother Teresa or Mahatma Gandhi, passive and extremely selfless people. But extreme-altruistic people are anything but passive or meek. They are often feisty, argumentative, independent, idealistic risk takers and convention-breakers. At a first glance, one would be compelled to put the sociopath and the extreme-altruistic person on opposite ends of a personality scale. After all, the chances of a serial killer running into a burning building to save a child are pretty slim, right? And wouldn't a hero-type be one of the last people likely to break rules? Wrong!

3   Those who go out of their way to help others, even at the expense of their own welfare, are actually more likely to break rules than the average person. On 9/11, after it was apparent that the buildings were about to collapse, teams of firefighters were called back, yet they disobeyed orders and pushed on anyway, only to perish in the quest to possibly save even one more life. Those are the actions of a hero, or an extreme-altruistic personality type.

4   Extreme-altruists are compelled to do good deeds, even when doing so makes no sense and brings harm upon them. They cannot tolerate injustice and go to great lengths to help those who have been wronged, regardless of their personal relationship to them. Now, I am not speaking of the guy who helps an old lady cross the street. I am speaking of the guy who throws himself in front of a speeding bus to push the old lady out of the way, killing himself in the process. The average thoughtful person does not take those kinds of tremendous personal risks on a regular basis.

5   Both extreme-altruists and sociopaths have high impulsivity, need for novelty, and the tendency to break rules, but there is a fundamental

difference in the motivation driving their behavior. Someone who is altruistic is always looking for the way things should be in a fair and just world. They are able to empathize—feel what the other person is feeling, or imagine themselves in another's shoes. This empathy is the force that moves them to engage in heroic behaviors. They are driven by factors outside of themselves.

6   Sociopaths, on the other hand, are motivated by internal factors—selfish desires and the advancement of their own cause, rather than the causes of others or of society as a whole. They don't have the ability to empathize, so they see no logic in acting in any way other than selfishly since they cannot imagine themselves in anyone else's position. Everything they do is driven by their quest to satisfy their own needs, rather than—and often at the expense of—the needs of another person. The defining characteristic that separates the two personality types is their ability to empathize, either not at all or too much, which then drives the extreme behavior of each.

7   So while the extreme-altruistic person indeed acts for the good of other people, he or she often violates laws, breaks rules, or otherwise causes ripples in the order of society. To be a good citizen, we are expected to follow laws at all times. But we can all agree that the world needs extreme heroes; they are the ones who consistently go beyond the call of duty, even when it could mean losing their jobs, receiving hefty fines, or even serving time in jail. I want to send a message out to all of those heroic altruists out there, continually putting their butts on the line for our well-being: Thank you. The world is a better place because you dare to do good—even when it seems crazy to do so.

Practice 5

1. Highlight the thesis statement.

2. What are some traits of a sociopath?

_____

_____

3. What are some traits of the extreme-altruist?

_____

4. Underline the topic sentences in paragraphs 3 through 6.

5. What are the main similarities and differences between sociopaths and altruists? Complete the following chart.

	Sociopaths	Extreme-Altruists
Similarities	_____	_____
	_____	_____
	_____	_____
	_____	_____
Differences	_____	_____
	_____	_____
	_____	_____
	_____	_____

6. Is the average person an extreme-altruist? Explain your answer.

_____

_____

_____

7. This essay compares and contrasts two things, but it also presents an argument. What is the argument?

_____

_____

The Writer's Room

Writing Activity 1: Topics

Choose any of the following topics, or choose your own topic, and write a comparison and contrast essay.

General Topics

Compare or contrast . . .

1. two performances
2. two useful apps
3. a male and a female friend
4. two characters from film or fiction
5. two common phobias

College- and Work-Related Topics

Compare or contrast . . .

6. courage versus recklessness
7. living on campus versus living off campus
8. being self-employed versus working for others
9. online classes and traditional classes
10. expectations about a job versus the reality of the job

READING LINK
MORE COMPARISON AND CONTRAST READINGS
"The Untranslatable Word 'Macho'"
 p. 579
"The Happiness Factor"
 p. 587

Writing Activity 2: Media Writing

Write an essay in which you compare and contrast two life stages, such as childhood and adulthood or adolescence and old age. For this essay, you could compare and contrast two characters in a television soap opera or drama, a movie, or a podcast story.

Show: *House of Cards, Parenthood, Switched at Birth*

Film: *An Education, Boyhood, Inside Out*

Podcast: *Modern Love, The New Yorker Radio Hour, The Moth*

WRITING LINK
MORE COMPARISON
AND CONTRAST
WRITING TOPICS

Ch. 20, Writer's Room
   topic 2 p. 305
Ch. 23, Writer's Room
   topic 2 p. 335
Ch. 27, Writer's Room
   topic 2 p. 369
Ch. 32, Writer's Room
   topic 1 p. 431
Ch. 38, Writer's Room
   topic 2 p. 489

Checklist: Comparison and Contrast

After you write your comparison and contrast essay, review the checklist at the end of the book. Also, ask yourself the following set of questions.

❏ Does my thesis statement explain what I am comparing and contrasting?

❏ Does my thesis statement make a point about the comparison?

❏ Does my essay have a point-by-point or topic-by-topic pattern?

❏ Does my essay focus on similarities or on differences?

❏ Do all of my supporting examples clearly relate to the topics that I am comparing or contrasting?

13   Cause and Effect

Scientists explain why lightning storms occur. They also explain the effects of lightning strikes on buildings and people. Writers use the cause and effect pattern to explain the answers to these types of questions.

LEARNING OBJECTIVES

13.1   Define cause and effect.

13.2   Define the purpose of a cause and effect essay.

13.3   Explore topics for a cause and effect essay.

13.4   Write the thesis statement of a cause and effect essay.

13.5   Generate the supporting ideas of a cause and effect essay.

13.6   Develop a cause and effect essay plan.

13.7   Write the first draft of a cause and effect essay.

13.8   Revise and edit a cause and effect essay.

Writers' Exchange

Work with a group of students. Each group has two minutes to brainstorm as many reasons as possible to explain why people follow fashion fads. Then, each team will have two minutes to explain the effects of following fashion fads. The team with the most causes and effects wins.

What Is Cause and Effect?

13.1   Define cause and effect.

Cause and effect writing explains why an event happened or what the consequences of such an event were. A cause and effect essay can focus on causes, effects, or both.

People often analyze the causes or effects of something. At home, a teenager might explain to her parents why she had a car accident. At college, an administrator may be asked to give reasons for the lack of student housing on campus. At work, a boss might clarify the reasons for company downsizing to employees.

Practice 1: Visualizing Cause and Effect

Brainstorm supporting ideas for the following thesis statement. Write some details on the lines provided.

Thesis Statement: A shopping addiction has some serious effects.

_____   _____   _____

_____   _____   _____

_____   _____   _____

The Cause and Effect Essay

13.2 **Define the purpose of a cause and effect essay.**

When you write a cause and effect essay, focus on two main tasks.

1. **Indicate whether you are focusing on causes, effects, or both.** If you do decide to focus on both causes and effects, make sure that your thesis statement indicates your purpose to the reader.

2. **Make sure that your causes and effects are valid.** You should determine real causes and effects and not simply list things that happened before or after the event. Also, verify that your assumptions are logical.

Illogical	Our furnace stopped working because the weather was too cold.
	(This is illogical; cold weather cannot stop a furnace from working.)
Better	Our furnace stopped working because the filters needed replacing and the gas burners needed adjusting.

Cause and Effect at Work

In a petition to stop the expansion of an airport, Green Hills townspeople explain the effects of noise pollution on their quality of life.

> If the airport expands, increasing noise pollution would significantly alter the quality of life for our community. First, we may not be able to enjoy daily activities, such as outdoor barbecues, garden parties, or relaxing in our yards if noise increases. Next, excessive noise may affect our health. Research has shown that noise pollution can in some instances lead to hypertension, hearing loss, and sleep disruption. In addition, we may also suffer psychological effects such as stress and annoyance. Therefore, we must ensure that the expansion of the airport is stopped.

The **topic sentence** states the topic and controlling idea.

The **supporting sentences** provide details and examples.

The **concluding sentence** brings the paragraph to a close.

A Student Essay

Read the student essay, and answer the questions that follow.

College Students and the Challenge of Credit Card Debt

Katie Earnest

1   Did you know that most college students carry credit card debt? In fact, according to a Nelli Mae study, three out of four students have an outstanding balance of $2,200. My son maxed out three different credit cards by the time he was in the second semester of his junior year. He couldn't keep up with his monthly payments to the credit card companies anymore,

even though he had a part-time job on campus and a part-time job off campus. Students get into credit card debt for a variety of reasons.

2   Credit card companies have clever ways to promote their products to students. Anyone who is at least eighteen years old can get a credit card without parental consent or any source of income. According to the *Daily Emerald*, one of the many ways that major credit card companies take advantage of this situation is to offer universities generous monetary donations in exchange for the full rights to market their cards on campus. Credit card companies distribute brochures or flyers around campus and set up a booth offering free gifts to college students if they fill out a card application. Another way that credit card companies target college students is by calling them four to five times a month or continuously mailing them card applications.

3   While most college students obtain a credit card with the intention of using it only for emergencies, it doesn't always work out that way. Students start off using their credit card to buy gas, purchase a few groceries, catch a movie, or grab a late-night pizza. However, before they know it, they have reached their credit card limit. College students don't realize that fees or penalties will grow because of high interest rates. After maxing out the first credit card, many people will sign up for another credit card, still telling themselves that it will be for emergencies only. The credit card debt spirals out of control. There have been two widely reported cases of college students who took their lives because of their excessive accumulation of credit card debt. According to the *College Student Journal*, one of the students was a twenty-year-old with a debt of $10,000, and the other was a nineteen-year-old with a debt of $2,500.

4   Furthermore, students don't realize how difficult it can be to pay credit card bills. A part-time job may result in a lower than expected salary. Living expenses may be higher than expected. Thus, it is challenging for students to make their monthly payments on time. For example, my son could not keep up with his monthly payments even though he had two part-time jobs. His debt accumulated quickly.

5   In conclusion, credit cards have become a fact of life on college campuses, and they continue to be a temptation for students. College students who carry a high level of credit card debt face financial stress just as my son did. If I had known that card companies solicited students on campus, I would have educated my son about credit card usage, and I would have warned him about the challenges that he would face if he accumulated a large amount of debt.

Practice 2

1. What introductory style does the writer use?

a. general background   c. definition

b. anecdote   d. contrasting position

2. Highlight the thesis statement.

3. Does the thesis statement express causes, effects, or both?

    a. causes   b. effects   c. both

4. Highlight the topic sentences in paragraphs 2, 3, and 4.

5. Using your own words, sum up the causes for student credit card debt.

_____

_____

_____

_____

_____

6. What does the writer think she should have done to help her son?

_____

_____

Explore Topics

13.3   Explore topics for a cause and effect essay.

In the Writer's Desk Warm Up, you try an exploring strategy to generate ideas about different topics.

The Writer's Desk: Warm Up

Read the following questions, and write the first ideas that come to your mind. Think of two or three ideas for each topic.

EXAMPLE: What are some causes and effects of workplace hostility?

    –jealousy and competition _____

    –demanding bosses _____

    –employee burnout _____

1. What are some causes and effects of falling in love?

_____

_____

_____

2. What are some causes and effects of oversharing online?

_____

_____

_____

3. Why do people cheat on their spouses? What are the effects of cheating?

_____

_____

_____

Developing

The Thesis Statement

13.4 Write the thesis statement of a cause and effect essay.

When writing a thesis statement for a cause and effect essay, clearly demonstrate whether the focus is on causes, effects, or both. Also, make sure that you state a controlling idea that expresses your point of view or attitude.

controlling idea (causes)   topic

There are many valid reasons that **people declare bankruptcy**.

topic   controlling idea (effects)

A bankruptcy can have a profound effect on a person's physical and emotional health.

topic   controlling idea (causes and effects)

A bankruptcy, which could be caused by valid reasons, may have a profound effect on a person's health.

Practice 3

Look carefully at the following thesis statements. Decide if each sentence focuses on the causes, effects, or both. Look at the key words that give you the clues, and circle the best answer.

1. Poverty persists in developing countries because of lack of education, scarcity of jobs, and corruption of politicians.

   a. causes   b. effects   c. both

2. In our college, the high student dropout rate, which is triggered by the tourist industry, results in long-term problems for the community.

   a. causes   b. effects   c. both

3. A drug-pricing scandal hurt the reputation and financial success of Turing Pharmaceuticals.

a. causes   b. effects   c. both

GRAMMAR HINT: *Affect* and *Effect*

Use *affect* as a verb and *effect* as a noun. *Affect* means "to influence or change" and *effect* means "the result."

verb

How does the ban on fast food in public schools affect children's health?

noun

What effects will the ban on fast food in public schools have on children's health?

You can also use *effect* as a verb that means "to cause or to bring about a change or implement a plan."

verb

Health care professionals lobbied to effect changes in public school lunch menus.

See Chapter 34 for more information about commonly confused words.

The Writer's Desk: Write Thesis Statements

Write a thesis statement for each of the following topics. You can look for ideas in the previous Writer's Desk. Determine whether you will focus on the causes, effects, or both in your essay.

EXAMPLE: Topic: hostile work environment

Thesis Statement: <u>**A hostile workplace, which can lead to several problems, is often triggered by jealousy or an unpleasant boss.**</u>

1. Topic: falling in love

Thesis Statement: _____

_____

2. Topic: oversharing online

Thesis Statement: _____

_____

3. Topic: cheating on a spouse

Thesis Statement: _____

_____

The Supporting Ideas

13.5 Generate the supporting ideas of a cause and effect essay.

After you have developed an effective thesis statement, generate supporting ideas. In a cause and effect essay, think of examples that clearly show the causes or effects. To develop supporting ideas, follow these three steps:

- Use prewriting strategies such as freewriting and brainstorming to generate ideas.
- Choose the best ideas. Use examples that clearly reveal the causes and effects.
- Organize your ideas. Choose the best organizational method for this essay pattern.

HINT: Do Not Oversimplify

Avoid attributing a simple or general cause to a very complex issue. When you use expressions such as *it appears that* or *a possible cause is*, it shows that you are aware of the complex factors involved in the situation.

Oversimplification	Global warming is caused by cars.
Better	One possible cause of global warming is the CO_2 emissions from cars.

Identifying Causes and Effects

Imagine that you had to write a cause and effect essay on gambling. You could brainstorm and think of as many causes and effects as possible.

Causes
- need money quickly
- enticed by advertisements to buy lottery tickets
- think winning is possible
- have easy access to gambling establishments

Gambling

Effects
- bankruptcy
- problems in marriage or at work
- depression
- criminal behavior such as forging checks

The Writer's Desk: Identify Causes and Effects

Choose the topic of one of the thesis statements from the previous Writer's Desk. Then write some possible causes and effects.

EXAMPLE: Topic: <u>hostile work environment</u>

Causes	Effects
-arrogant employees	-physical problems such as insomnia
-too much work	-psychological problems such as
-jealous coworker	low self-esteem or burnout
-a very strict and demanding boss	-depression
	-diminished quality of life

Focus on: <u>causes</u>

Topic: _____

Causes	Effects

Focus on: _____

The Essay Plan

13.6   Develop a cause and effect essay plan.

In many courses, instructors ask students to write about the causes or effects of a particular subject. Take the time to plan your essay before you write your first draft. Also, think about how you would logically arrange the order of ideas. As you develop your plan, make sure that you focus on causes, effects, or both.

Thesis Statement: A hostile workplace, which can lead to several problems, is often triggered by employee jealousy or an unpleasant boss.

    I.   A hostile work environment is often caused by employee arrogance or envy.

        A. Some groups are tight-knit and don't easily accept newcomers.

      B. Some employees have high opinions of themselves.

      C. Coworkers may feel jealous of a new employee's expertise.

  II.   Another reason for a hostile workplace is a strict boss.

      A. Some employees may be frightened of a difficult boss.

      B. Some bosses may overreact if an employee makes a mistake.

      C. A strict boss generates a lot of stress for employees.

  III. People in stressful workplaces may experience physical and psychological stress.

      A. Some people may suffer from insomnia.

      B. Some employees may develop burnout or depression.

The Writer's Desk: Write an Essay Plan

Choose one of the ideas that you have developed in previous Writer's Desks, and prepare an essay plan. If you think of new details that will explain your point more effectively, include them in your plan.

The First Draft

13.7 Write the first draft of a cause and effect essay.

After you have developed and organized your ideas in your essay plan, write the first draft. Remember to write complete sentences and to use transitional words or expressions to help your ideas flow smoothly. Most writers arrange cause and effect essays using emphatic order, which means that they place examples from the most to the least important or from the least to the most important. The following transitional expressions are useful for showing causes and effects.

To show causes	To show effects
for this reason	accordingly
the first cause	as a result
the most important cause	consequently

The Writer's Desk: Write the First Draft

Carefully review and, if necessary, revise your essay plan from the previous Writer's Desk, and then write the first draft of your cause and effect essay.

VOCABULARY BOOST

Using inappropriate vocabulary in a particular context can affect the way people respond to you. For example, you would not use street language in a business meeting. Replace the following words with terms that can be used in academic or professional writing.

buddy   guy   kid   chill   stuff   crook

Revising and Editing

Revise and Edit a Cause and Effect Essay

13.8   Revise and edit a cause and effect essay.

When you finish writing a cause and effect essay, review your work and revise it to make the examples as clear as possible to your readers. Check that you have organized your ideas logically, and remove any irrelevant details. Before you work on your own essay, practice revising and editing a student essay.

A Student Essay

Read the essay, and then answer the questions that follow. As you read, correct any errors that you find, and make comments in the margins.

Workplace Hostility

Emily Dubois

1   I will always remember the very first day I started a new job. I was a little nervous, and I wondered if I would like working in a kitchen. What I dreaded the most was to meet my colleagues. Fortunately, they turned out to be very amiable. However, many people are unlucky because they have uncaring coworkers. A hostile workplace, which can lead to several problems, is often triggered by employee jealousy or an unpleasant boss.

2   First, a hostile work environment is often caused by arrogance or envy. When a person joins a working team that has been together for a long time, it is normal for that person to feel left out. Some groups are tight-knit and don't easily accept a new coworker. For example, my mother once started a new job where everyone been very close. Her coworkers never really tried to interact with her, and when they did, it was only to criticize. The situation made my mother very uncomfortable, and she quit after two months. Also,

some workers have a high opinion of themselves and want to show the new person that they deserve respect because of their superior experience. They may snub newcomers. Additionally, if the new employee has a lot of expertise, a higher salary, and better benefits, then coworkers may feel jealous. Such situations create a negative atmosphere.

3   Another reason for a hostile workplace is a very strict boss. Some employees are justifiably frightened of their superiors. Of course, employers do not tolerate major mistakes and are bothered when deadlines are not met. However, some managers overreact because their expectations are too high. For example, in the movie *The Devil Wears Prada*, Meryl Streep acts as Miranda, a terrifying boss. The movie is based on Anna Wintour, the real-life editor of *Vogue*. I have also worked under a nasty boss. At my second job, my manager was frequently in a foul mood and would scream even when I simply dropped a spoon. An angry superior generates alot of stress for the workers. Colleagues tend to snap at each other instead of collaborating, and then they start a silent competition to see who can please the boss the most. In the end, employees don't enjoy going to work.

4   A hostile workplace may cause physical and psychological problems in employees. People can experience health problems such as insomnia. A hostile workplace can also impact a worker's self-esteem and lead to burnout. When my mother had spiteful colleagues, she lost her confidence and became depressed. In today's difficult economy, people sometimes remain in unfriendly workplaces for years simply because they have no choice and cannot find another job. But such people have a diminished quality of life. However, some people in a hostile work environment benefit from doing stress-relieving activities. At my work, many of my colleagues take yoga courses.

5   In conclusion, hostile workplaces are usually caused by peer envy and nightmarish employers. The work experience become physically and emotionally draining. Every working environment should be calm and respectful. Perhaps everyone should follow the footsteps of Anne Hathaway's character in *The Devil Wears Prada*, and they should quit if a workplace is too hostile.

Practice 4

Revising

1. Does this essay focus on causes, effects, or both? _____

2. Highlight the thesis statement of the essay.

3. Underline the topic sentences in body paragraphs 2, 3, and 4.

4. What are some of the causes for workplace hostility?

_____

_____

5. What are some effects of workplace hostility?

_____

_____

6. Paragraph 4 lacks unity. Cross out any sentences that do not support the topic sentence of the paragraph.

7. What is the introductory style of this essay?

a. historical background   c. an anecdote

b. a definition   d. a contrasting position

Editing

8. Underline and correct the verb tense error in paragraph 2.

Correction: _____

9. Underline and correct a spelling error in paragraph 3.

Correction: _____

10. There is a subject–verb agreement error in paragraph 5. Underline and correct the mistake.

Correction: _____

> **GRAMMAR LINK**
> See the following chapters for more information about these grammar topics:
> Verb Tenses, Ch. 28
> Spelling, Ch. 34
> Subject–Verb Agreement, Ch. 27

The Writer's Desk: Revise and Edit Your Essay

Revise and edit the essay that you wrote for the previous Writer's Desk. You can refer to the revising and editing checklists at the end of this chapter and at the end of the book.

A Professional Essay

Diane Mapes, a contributor to *NBC News* and *Today.com*, writes about health, relationships, and lifestyle. Her essays have appeared in a variety of publications including the *Washington Post, Los Angles Times, Seattle Magazine, Southern Living,* and *CNN.com*. In the following essay, the names of certain people have been changed to protect their privacy.

Why Some People Are Accident Prone

Diane Mapes

1   Simon Redmond's catalogue of self-induced injuries reads like something out of *The Spanish Inquisition Handbook*: fractured skull, shattered fingers, broken wrists, fractured elbows, torn muscles, sulfuric acid burns, self-stabbings, multiple broken noses, and, last month, a ruptured tendon in his ankle. "I didn't trip or anything," says the forty-six-year-old attorney from Madison, Wisconsin. "I was just walking down the hall, in a hurry, and I went around the corner and it suddenly felt like somebody hit me in the ankle with a baseball bat." Hurry, worry, multitasking, and stress are the four horsemen of the accident prone.

2   Debbie Mandel, author of *Addicted to Stress*, says people who are under stress aren't living in the present—they're thinking ahead or thinking behind—and as a result, aren't paying attention to where they're going. "I have more accidents whenever I'm stressed and distracted," says Kate Rowe, a thirty-six-year-old freelance writer from Seattle. "Once, I fell into a ditch and sprained my ankle and two days later hit myself in the back with my car door and injured my shoulder blade. I've even had a bed fall on me. Maybe if I had been paying more attention, I would have seen it was teetering."

3   But Simon Redmond raises the question of whether there are other factors at play besides stress and trying to do too much. Redmond attributes his accident-prone nature to a pattern of risk-taking and attention-getting behavior that began when he was a small child. By age eleven, he had fallen out of a tree house, set himself on fire, knocked himself unconscious, and cracked his kneecap. "When I was younger, it was literally not on my radar screen to care whether I got hurt or not," he says. "If I didn't get hurt, I did something that was impressive to my friends. And if I did get hurt, I got attention from my mom. It was a win-win situation."

4   Others, such as Austin sales executive Tanya Jones, don't understand why they have accidents. Jones claims that some of her mishaps, such as getting rear-ended at a red light, have nothing to do with her behavior. Researchers at the University Medical Center Groningen in the Netherlands have found that accident-prone people actually exist. After reviewing the results of seventy-nine studies which recorded the mishaps and misfortunes of nearly 150,000 people, they determined that 1 out of every 29 people has a 50 percent or higher chance of having an accident than the rest of us. A study by the University of Delaware, which tested athletes to measure processes like spatial skills and reaction time before and after an injury, suggests that some people simply have slower reaction times and slower processing speeds.

5   Dr. Buz Swanik, associate professor of health, nutrition and exercise sciences at the University of Delaware, says that stress and anxiety slow down

a person's reaction time even further. "But the biggest issue is multitasking," says Swanick. "If you're presented with a lot of stimuli, you have to filter out what's most important to you. If you're chopping something with a knife, you have to take that seriously enough to stay focused on it. You can't let loud noises or children or anything else disturb your train of thought."

6   Traveling also seems to up your chances of an accident. Dr. Ben Koppel, a medical director of MEDEX Global Group, a Baltimore-based company that provides international travel insurance and assistance, says the most common accidents while traveling involve slips or falls. "When you travel, you have to maintain a certain degree of presence," he says. Jet lag, sleep deprivation, and inner ear issues and unfamiliarity with hotel accommodations can also contribute to accidents. "I've seen some significant burns with curling irons because of the change in voltage," Koppel says. "People rush into a hotel room and plug in a curling iron without realizing there's a current difference. At 240 volts, that first curl will snap your hair off and set it on fire."

7   Finally, a lot of accidents can also be indicative of a health issue such as a neurological disorder. "With [multiple sclerosis], the first symptom we look at is depth perception—you're walking down the street and miss the curb," says Koppel. "Parkinson's starts when you pick up your coffee and spill it all over yourself. These are significant things to tell your doctor." Claire Nimes, a forty-three-year-old mother of five, says she never thought anything about her frequent spills until she was diagnosed with MS.

8   While hidden health issues can sometimes be the culprit, most accidents are caused by those four predictable horsemen. Dr. Swanik, who studied injuries among athletes, says, "People in a hurry, trying to do things in a hurry, trying to do more than one thing at a time—that's the recipe for injuries and accidents more consistently than anything else." Planning your day so you don't end up rushing and multitasking can help. Focus on one task at a time. "It's tough," he says. "Here I am talking to you on speakerphone while I'm driving, and I'm talking about multitasking and how it causes injuries. We should have planned this phone call in the evening."

Practice 5

1. Highlight the thesis statement.

2. Which type of introduction does the writer use?
   a. historical background   b. anecdote   c. general background

3. Underline the topic sentence in body paragraphs 2–7. Be careful because the topic sentence may not be the first sentence in each paragraph.

4. In the thesis statement, the author names four causes of accident-prone behavior: hurry, worry, multitasking, and stress. But in the essay, she elaborates and includes even more causes. Describe five more causes of self-induced injuries. Mention the paragraph number of each cause.

_____

_____

_____

_____

_____

5. Mapes also provides research to support her point. Circle the names of at least four professionals or research centers.

6. In paragraph 3, Simon Redman called his attention-seeking behavior as a child "win-win." Explain what he meant.

_____

_____

7. In the conclusion, Dr. Swanik did not take his own advice. What

mistake did he make? _____

_____

READING LINK
MORE CAUSE AND
EFFECT READINGS

"The Price of Public
 Shaming in the
 Internet Age" p. 528
"Nature Returns to the
 Cities" p. 536

The Writer's Room

Writing Activity 1: Topics

Write a cause and effect essay about one of the following topics, or choose your own topic.

WRITING LINK
MORE CAUSE AND
EFFECT WRITING TOPICS

Ch. 22, Writer's Room
 topic 2 p. 326
Ch. 28, Writer's Room
 topic 2 p. 385
Ch. 33, Writer's Room
 topic 2 p. 440
Ch. 35, Writer's Room
 topic 1 p. 462

General Topics

Causes and/or effects of . . .

1. playing a sport
2. cyberbullying
3. a fear of _____
4. road rage
5. a natural phenomenon

College- and Work-Related Topics

Causes and/or effects of . . .

6. changing a career
7. becoming successful
8. raising the minimum wage
9. outsourcing jobs
10. dropping out of high school

Writing Activity 2: Media Writing

Write an essay describing the causes or effects of a physical or mental ailment, and use examples to support your point. To generate some ideas, watch a show, movie, or online clip or listen to a podcast. Here are some suggestions to help spark ideas:

Show: *House, Nip/Tuck,* or *The Big C*

Film: *Silver Linings Playbook, The King's Speech, The Elephant Man, Inside Out*

Online: "What's Disability to Me?" video series on the World Health Organization website

Podcast: The Center for Disease Control's *CDC Radio* or *Vital Signs*

Checklist: Cause and Effect Essay

As you write your cause and effect essay, review the checklist at the end of the book. Also, ask yourself the following questions.

❏ Does my thesis statement indicate clearly that my essay focuses on causes, effects, or both?

❏ Do I have adequate supporting examples of causes and/or effects?

❏ Do I make logical and valid points?

❏ Do I use the terms *effect* and/or *affect* correctly?

14 Argument

LEARNING OBJECTIVES

14.1 Define argument.

14.2 Define the purpose of an argument essay.

14.3 Explore topics for an argument essay.

14.4 Write the thesis statement of an argument essay.

14.5 Generate the supporting details of an argument essay.

14.6 Develop an argument essay plan.

14.7 Write the first draft of an argument essay.

14.8 Revise and edit an argument essay.

Medical practitioners often use argument to convince colleagues about the best treatment for a patient. In the same way, you use argument writing to convince readers to see issues from your point of view.

Writers' Exchange

For this activity, you and a partner will take turns debating an issue. To start, choose which one of you will begin speaking. The first speaker chooses one side of any issue listed below, and then argues about that issue without stopping. When your instructor makes a signal, switch speakers. The second speaker talks nonstop about the opposing view. If you run out of ideas, you can switch topics when it is your turn to speak.

Debate Topics:

The United States should build walls on its northern and southern borders.

It is better to be an only child.

Adolescence is the best time of life.

Exploring

What Is Argument?

14.1 Define argument.

When you use **argument**, you take a position on an issue, and you try to prove or defend your position. Using effective argument strategies can help you convince somebody that your point of view is a valid one.

Argument is both a writing pattern and a purpose for writing. In fact, it is one of the most common aims, or purposes, in most college- and work-related writing. For example, in Chapter 10, there is an essay called "Voluntourism," in which the writer uses definition as the predominant pattern. At the same time, the author uses argument to convince the reader that volunteer workers can have negative effects on their host country. Therefore, in most of your college- and work-related writing, your purpose is to persuade the reader that your ideas are compelling and legitimate.

People use argument in their daily lives. For instance, at home, you might argue about the distribution of housework, providing examples to support your point. At college, students argue for better equipment in the computer lab or art department. At work, salespeople make well-planned arguments to convince customers to buy a product or service.

Practice 1: Visualizing Argument

Brainstorm supporting ideas for the following thesis statement. Write some details on the lines provided.

Thesis Statement: All college students should learn a second language.

_____   _____   _____

_____   _____   _____

_____   _____   _____

The Argument Essay

14.2   **Define the purpose of an argument essay.**

When you write an argument essay, remember four key points.

1. **Consider your readers.** What do your readers already know about the topic? Will they be likely to agree or disagree with you? Do they have specific concerns? Consider what kind of evidence would be most effective with your audience.

2. **Know your purpose.** In argument writing, your main purpose is to persuade the reader to agree with you. Your specific purpose is more focused. You may want the reader to take action, to support a viewpoint, to counter somebody else's argument, or to offer a solution to a problem. Ask yourself what your specific purpose is.

3. **Take a strong position, and provide persuasive evidence.** Your thesis statement and topic sentences should clearly show your point of view. Then back up your point of view with a combination of facts, statistics, examples, and informed opinions.

4. **Show that you are trustworthy.** Respect your readers by making a serious argument. If you are condescending, or if you try to joke about the topic, your readers may be less inclined to accept your argument. You can also help readers have more respect for your ideas when you know something about the topic. For example, if you have been in the military or know people in the military, you might be able to make a very convincing argument about the lack of proper equipment for soldiers.

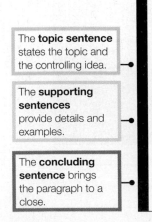

Argument at Work

The following letter was written by a social work program director assessing the needs of a mother and her children who had been the victims of family violence.

The **topic sentence** states the topic and the controlling idea.

The **supporting sentences** provide details and examples.

The **concluding sentence** brings the paragraph to a close.

   Ms. P and her children recently participated in our program. Throughout the course of her time with our program, Ms. P demonstrated herself to be a responsible, dedicated, and loving caregiver to her children. Ms. P and her children—A, S, D and Y—were referred to the agency last February. At the time of intake, they were victims of her husband's physical and verbal abuse. Mrs. P showed increased advocacy skills, both for herself and for her children, and demonstrated a commitment to raising them in a safe and healthy environment, free from exposure to violence or abuse. I strongly recommend that Ms. P receive full custody of her children.

A Student Essay

Read the student essay, and answer the questions that follow.

....

Graffiti as Art

....

Jordan Foster

1   Long ago—about 30,000 B.C.E.—people made markings on cave walls, depicting great hunts and travels. Those handprints and rough figures can still be seen today. They have withstood the test of time and give us a better idea of who our ancestors were. That ancient graffiti was the voice of early humans and their way of saying, "I exist." Today, graffiti should be accepted and celebrated.

2   First, graffiti—or street art—is a treasure trove of self-expression. There are seven billion people on this planet and counting. Cities are crowded, and a lot of people feel invisible and powerless. Graffiti is a way for some of them to proclaim, "I exist, and this is what I have to say." Some street artists feel validated when their images and words appear on public walls. Self-expression and art should belong to the world regardless of medium, not just to those who can afford $1,500 for space on a billboard. If advertisers can use the public spaces to spread their messages, then graffiti artists should be allowed to use those spaces as well.

3   Furthermore, a lot of graffiti art conveys powerful messages and makes us think. Banksy, a world-famous street artist, has risen to rock-star fame, and his politically subversive messages are in cities around the world. For instance, in England, a wall portrays a rioter throwing a bouquet of flowers. In 2005, he decorated Israel's controversial West Bank wall with images of children escaping with helium balloons and a man holding back a curtain to expose a paradise on the other side.

4   Most importantly, graffiti can also serve to decorate or beautify something ugly or plain. For sure, people's homes and places of worship and burial should remain sacred and shouldn't be touched. But a lot of graffiti is in neighborhoods and locations that nobody really cares about. Old rail cars or a train underpass might have graffiti. The explosion of colors in an otherwise drab landscape beautifies the area, especially if the artist has some talent. Many street artists are recognized for the aesthetic quality of their work. Shepard Fairey, for instance, is most famous for his stenciled blue and red image of President Obama, but his street art appears all over the country.

5   Graffiti is one of the oldest forms of self-expression. Regardless of its message, it should remain as one of the public forms of expression and art. People should have the right to convey who they are, regardless of the surface they use for their self-expression.

Practice 2

1. Highlight the thesis statement.

2. What introduction style does the writer use?
   - a. an anecdote
   - b. a definition
   - c. a contrasting position
   - d. historical background

3. Underline the topic sentences in body paragraphs 2, 3, and 4.

4. Circle the transitional expressions in the three topic sentences.

5. How does the writer organize his arguments?
   - a. time
   - b. space
   - c. emphatic

   Explain your answer?

   _____

Explore Topics

14.3   Explore topics for an argument essay.

In the Writer's Desk Warm Up, you will try an exploring strategy to generate ideas about different topics.

The Writer's Desk: Warm Up

Read the following questions, and write the first ideas that come to your mind. Think of two or three ideas for each topic.

EXAMPLE: Does age matter in a relationship?

   I don't know. Love is love, but there could be problems.

   What if the older person doesn't want children?

1. What should children learn about cell phone, email, and online etiquette?

   _____

   _____

   _____

2. Should college students be permitted to carry concealed weapons on campus? Why or why not?

_____

_____

_____

3. What are some of the major controversial issues in your neighborhood, workplace, college, state, or country? List some issues.

_____

_____

_____

Developing

The Thesis Statement

14.4   Write the thesis statement of an argument essay.

In the thesis statement of an argument essay, state your position on the issue.

       topic   controlling idea (the writer's position)

Many corporate executives are overpaid for very substandard work.

A thesis statement should be debatable; it should not simply be a fact or a statement of opinion.

Fact   In American restaurants, people generally tip for service.

          (This is a fact. It cannot be debated.)

Opinion   I think that tipping for service should be abolished in U.S. restaurants.

          (This is a statement of opinion. Nobody can deny that you feel this way. Therefore, do not use phrases such as _In my opinion, I think,_ or _I believe_ in your thesis statement.)

Argument Tipping for service should be abolished in U.S. restaurants.

          (This is a debatable statement.)

HINT: Be Direct

Many students feel reluctant to take a stand on an issue. They may feel that it is too personal or impolite to do so. However, in academic writing, it is perfectly acceptable, and even desirable, to state an argument in a direct manner and then support it.

Practice 3

Evaluate the following statements. Write *F* for a fact, *O* for an opinion, or *A* for an argument.

1. In our state, many youths drop out of school. _____

2. I think that our town needs more police officers. _____

3. There are three effective strategies to reduce the high school dropout rate. _____

4. Oil companies should not be permitted to drill in deep oceans. _____

5. I don't think it is safe to drill in deep ocean waters. _____

6. Many Internet sites have pop-up advertising. _____

7. In my opinion, country music is predictable and repetitive. _____

8. Our mayor should resign for three reasons. _____

HINT: Making a Guided Thesis Statement

Your instructor may want you to guide the reader through your main points. To do this, mention your main and supporting ideas in your thesis statement. In other words, your thesis statement provides a map for the readers to follow.

High school students should receive art education because it promotes their creativity, enhances their cultural knowledge, and develops their analytical skills.

The Writer's Desk: Write Thesis Statements

Write a thesis statement for the next topics. You can look for ideas in the Warm Up on pages 216–217. Make sure that each thesis statement clearly expresses your position on the issue.

Example: Topic: age in relationships

Thesis statement: <u>Age matters in relationships</u>.

1. Topic: etiquette in our technological age

Thesis statement: _____

_____

2. Topic: concealed weapons on campus

Thesis statement: _____

_____

3. Topic: a controversial issue

Thesis statement: _____

_____

The Supporting Ideas

14.5 Generate the supporting details of an argument essay.

To make a logical and reasoned argument, support your main point with facts, examples, and statistics. (For details about adding facts, examples, and statistics, see page 45 in Chapter 4.)

You can also include the following types of support.

- **Quote informed sources.** Sometimes experts in a field express an informed opinion about an issue. An expert's thoughts and ideas can add weight to your argument. If you want to argue that people are becoming complacent about sexually transmitted infections, you might quote an article published by a respected national health organization.

- **Consider logical consequences.** When you plan an argument, think about long-term consequences of a proposed solution to a problem. Maybe you oppose a decision to drill for oil off the coast of California. A long-term consequence could be an environmental disaster if there is an earthquake near the rig.

- **Acknowledge opposing viewpoints.** Anticipating and responding to opposing views can strengthen your position. If you argue that school uniforms should be mandatory, you might address those who feel that students need freedom to express themselves. Try to refute some of the strongest arguments of the opposition.

Making an Emotional Appeal

Generally, an effective argument appeals to the reader's reason, but it can also appeal to his or her emotion. For example, you could use certain words or descriptions to encourage a reader's sense of justice, humanity, or pride. However, use emotional appeals sparingly. If you use **emotionally charged words** such as *wimp* or *thug*, or if you appeal to base instincts such as fear or prejudice, then you may seriously undermine your argument. Review the next example of an emotional appeal.

Overemotional	Our democracy is under threat! Dangerous demagogues are calling news organizations, such as CNN, "fake news" simply because those outlets report embarrassing or inconvenient truths. Real fake news is created by despicable online publications. Fools post wild accusations against people they perceive to be enemies, or they write propaganda. To survive, we must support reputable media outlets and denounce horrible fake news.
Reasonable and more neutral	A healthy democracy needs a free, independent press that can hold people in positions of power accountable. Most mainstream media outlets, such as CNN, present well-researched, carefully articulated information. Fake news outlets, on the other hand, cynically invent information and present it to the public as factual. Critical readers should question whether news is fact or fiction.

HINT: Avoid Common Errors

When you write your argument essay, avoid the following pitfalls.

Do not make generalizations. If you begin a statement with *Everyone knows* or *It is common knowledge*, then the reader may mistrust what you say. You cannot possibly know what everyone else knows or does not know. It is better to refer to specific sources.

Generalization	American children are spoiled brats.
Better	Parents should not overindulge their children for several reasons.

Do not make exaggerated claims. Make sure that your arguments are plausible.

Exaggerated	If marijuana is legalized, drug use will soar in schools across the nation.
Better	If marijuana is legalized, drug use may increase in schools across the nation.

Practice 4

You have learned about different methods to support a topic. Read each of the following thesis statements, and think of a supporting idea for each item. Use the type of support suggested in parentheses.

1. Junk food should be banned from college campuses.

(Logical consequence) _____

_____

2. Online dating is a great way to meet a potential mate.

(Acknowledge an opposing view) _____

_____

3. Children should not be spanked.

(Emotional appeal) _____

_____

4. The college dropout rate is too high in our state.

(Logical consequence) _____

_____

VOCABULARY BOOST

Some words can influence readers because they have positive or negative connotations, which are implied or associated meanings. The meaning often carries a cultural value judgment with it. For example, *macho* may have negative connotations in one country and positive connotations in another country. For the word *thin*, synonyms like *skinny* or *skeletal* have negative connotations, while *slender* and *svelte* have positive ones.

Using a thesaurus, try to come up with related terms or descriptions that have either positive or negative connotations for the words in bold.

Gloria is **large**. _____

Calvin is **not assertive**. _____

Mr. Wayne **expresses his opinion**. _____

Franklin is a **liberal**. _____

Identify terms you chose that might be too emotionally loaded for an argument essay.

Consider Both Sides of the Issue

Once you have decided what issue you want to write about, try to think about both sides of the issue. Then you can predict arguments that your opponents might make, and you can plan your answer to the opposition. Here are examples.

Topic: Age matters in relationships

For	Against
♦ People have different levels of maturity.	♦ Love is love, and age doesn't matter.
♦ The desire to have children is strong at certain ages.	♦ People can adapt to each other.
♦ Such relationships will probably not last when one person gets ill.	♦ Other factors (finances, culture) may be more important than age.
♦ Society condemns couples with large age differences.	♦ People must be free to choose their own partners.

The Writer's Desk: Consider Both Sides of the Issue

Choose one of the topics from the previous Writer's Desk, and write arguments showing both sides of the issue.

Topic: _____

For	Against
_____	_____
_____	_____
_____	_____
_____	_____
_____	_____

HINT: Strengthening an Essay with Research

In some courses, your instructors may ask you to include supporting ideas from informed sources to strengthen your essays. You can find information in a variety of resources, including textbooks, journals, newspapers, magazines, or the Internet. When researching, make sure that your sources are from legitimate organizations. For example, for information about the spread of AIDS, you might find statistics on the World Health Organization website. You would not go to someone's personal rant or conspiracy theory site.

For more information about evaluating and documenting sources, refer to Chapter 17, The Research Essay.

The Essay Plan

14.6   Develop an argument essay plan.

Before you write your argument essay, outline your ideas in a plan. Include details that can help illustrate each argument. Make sure that every example is valid and relates to the thesis statement. Also think about your organization. Many argument essays use emphatic order and list ideas from the least to the most important.

Thesis Statement: Age matters in a relationship.

I.   Two people with a large age difference may have conflicting values and cultural experiences.
  A. Music, movies, politics, etc. change over time.
  B. People raised in different generations may see gender roles differently.
  C. Such differences can lead to breakups (Rick and Barbara example).

II.   People's goals change as they age.
  A. One person may want to retire when the other doesn't.
  B. The younger partner may want children, but the older partner already has kids.
  C. The younger partner might still want to party when the older partner is more career oriented.

III.   Other people judge such couples.
  A. Young wives are called "trophy wives" and "gold diggers."
  B. Older men are called "sugar daddies."
  C. Older women are called "cougars."
  D. Actress Demi Moore was judged harshly when she married a younger man.

IV.   Couples break up when the older one starts getting frail.
  A. People get more fragile and unhealthy as they age.
  B. The younger partner may not want to become a nursemaid.
  C. Barbara and Rick broke up after Rick had a stroke.

Concluding idea: People should look for age-appropriate partners.

The Writer's Desk: Write an Essay Plan

Choose one of the ideas that you have developed in the previous Writer's Desk, and write a detailed essay plan.

The First Draft

14.7 Write the first draft of an argument essay.

Now that you have a refined thesis statement, solid supporting details, and a roadmap of your arguments and the order in which you will present them, you are ready to write the first draft. Remember to write complete sentences and to include transitional words or expressions to lead readers from one idea to the next. Here are some transitions that introduce an answer to the opposition or the supporting ideas for an argument.

To answer the opposition		To support your argument	
admittedly	of course	certainly	in fact
however	on one hand/other hand	consequently	obviously
nevertheless	undoubtedly	furthermore	of course

The Writer's Desk: Write the First Draft

Write the first draft of your argument essay. Include an interesting introduction. Also, add specific details to flesh out each body paragraph.

Revising and Editing

Revise and Edit an Argument Essay

14.8 Revise and edit an argument essay.

When you finish writing an argument essay, carefully review your work and revise it to make the supporting examples as clear as possible to your readers. Check that the order of ideas is logical, and remove any irrelevant details. Before you revise and edit your own essay, practice revising and editing a student essay.

A Student Essay

Read the essay, and then answer the questions that follow. As you read, correct any errors that you find and make comments in the margins.

Age Matters

Chloe Vallieres

1   In 2003, the American Association of Retired Persons (AARP) published a study revealing that 34 percent of women over forty were dating younger men. Having a younger spouse is becoming more and more popular. However, statistics also demonstrate that couples separate more

often when the age gap between the two lovers exceeds ten years. Important age gaps in relationships can lead to considerable conflicts; therefore, age matters in a relationship.

2   Two people with a large age difference may have conflicting values and cultural experiences. Your views about religion and gender roles may differ. Also, politics, music, and movies change with time, so it may be hard to find topics to talk about if partners grew up in different eras. They might not have none of the same tastes. Imagine that a forty-year-old woman is dating a sixty-year-old man. The woman loves hip hop. She was raised to believe that her job is as important as her spouse's job and that childrearing should be shared. Her older partner might hate her musical tastes, and he could assume that his wife should be the primary caretaker of their children. Our family friends Rick and Barbara had this experience. Barbara, who is much younger than Rick, often complained about Rick's chauvinism. He hated her clothing styles and music. Their fifteen-year relationship ended last year.

3   Partners with an age gap are likely to have different goals. When Rick turned sixty-two, he retired, but Barbara still had professional ambitions. He wanted to travel every winter, she hoped to build her career. Damon and Sherrie, another May–December couple, disagree about having children. Damon, who is in his fifties, already has three adult children, but Sherrie, who is just thirty-five, wants to have a baby. Even younger couples can have problems. A twenty-five-year-old woman who has finished university might want to settle down and focus on her career, but her younger partner might still want to party.

4   Couples with age differences have to face other people's bad opinions. "Cougar" and "dirty old man" are common negative terms. There are other unflattering stereotypes: The girl dates the older man (her "sugar daddy") to get her hands on his money, and the mature man marries his young girlfriend (his "trophy wife") to have sexual favors and to appear virile. For example, Demi Moore. The actress was judged harshly when she married Ashton Kutcher, who was fifteen years her junior. Then she was humiliated when he cheated on her with younger women. People pitied her, and some bloggers said that it was "inevitable" that Kutcher would find a more age-appropriate partner.

5   Finally, some couples break up when the older partner develops health problems. Bone injuries or a weak heart. For example, Rick has high blood pressure and, three years ago, he suffered a minor stroke. Barbara recently left the marriage, confiding to my mother that she did not want to spend the next years being a nursemaid for an old man.

6   Those who proclaim that love can overcome everything are naïve bozos. Age matters, and people should look for age-appropriate partners. When spouses have huge age differences, the relationship is doomed. Dave, a popular blogger on the Intro2u Web site, writes, "It's elements like maturity and life experience, which tend to correlate with age, that can make or break a relationship's long-term potential."

Practice 5

Revising

1. Highlight the thesis statement.

2. Highlight the topic sentences in paragraphs 2, 3, 4, and 5.

3. In the margins next to the essay, add transitional words or expressions to each topic sentence in paragraphs 2 to 4.

4. In the concluding paragraph, the writer uses emotionally charged words and exaggerates. Give examples of these two problems.

   Emotionally charged language: _____

   Exaggeration: _____

   _____

Editing

GRAMMAR LINK

More grammar help:
Fragments, Ch. 23
Run-Ons, Ch. 24
Double Negatives,
  Ch. 29
Pronouns, Ch. 31

5. Paragraph 2 contains a pronoun shift error. (See the explanation in the Grammar Hint below.) Circle the incorrect pronoun, and write your correction here.

   _____

6. Paragraph 2 contains a double negative. Underline it and correct it here.

   _____

7. Paragraph 3 contains a run-on sentence. Two complete ideas are incorrectly joined. Underline the run-on sentence, and correct it on the lines provided.

   _____

   _____

8. Underline fragments in paragraphs 4 and 5 and correct them here.

   Paragraph 4: _____

   Paragraph 5: _____

GRAMMAR HINT: Keeping Pronouns Consistent

In argument writing, make sure that your pronouns do not switch between *they*, *we*, and *you*. If you are writing about specific groups of people, use *they* to refer to those people. Change pronouns only when the switch is logical.

Many hunters argue that they need large collections and varieties of guns.
                    they
Yet why would ~~you~~ need a semi-automatic to go hunting?

See Chapter 31 for more information about pronoun usage.

The Writer's Desk: Revise and Edit Your Essay

Revise and edit the essay that you wrote for the previous Writer's Desk. You can refer to the revising and editing checklists at the end of this chapter and at the back of the book.

A Professional Essay

In this essay, journalist Audra Williams argues that cheerleaders should be compensated fairly. Read the essay and answer the questions that follow.

....

Why Cheerleaders Should be Paid
....

1   Football players and football cheerleaders have a lot in common. Both groups are made up of incredible athletes who perform astonishing acts of strength and mastery to adoring fans. Both groups say they have dreamt of doing this work as long as they can remember and have been going to early morning and after-school rehearsals since they were kids. Both groups have been engrossed in gruelling team practices leading up to the start of football season. But only the players are paid for their time. Cheerleaders, despite the hundreds of hours they spend working to bring value to the team and the brand, are still largely volunteers. There is no reason for this, of course, other than this is how it has always been. But that does not mean it should stay that way. Cheerleading is a highly skilled, dangerous activity, and the women who do this work should be well paid to do it.

2   The wage discrepancy in the United States would be comical if it were not so horrifying. The average NFL player has an annual salary of $2 million, while many cheerleaders are paid less than $1000 a year. A long-simmering issue, this disparity has received attention over the past month as cheerleaders' legal battles have grown in number and success. California just passed a minimum wage requirement for cheerleaders that will come into effect on January 1, and New York State is considering similar legislation. Even with such advances, NFL cheerleaders will still earn nowhere near a living wage. After winning a wage-theft lawsuit, for example, the Oakland Raiderettes have seen their wages increase from $125 a game to $9 an hour; this brings each of their salaries up to $3,250 a year. Mascots, by the way, earn up to $65,000 per season, and concession workers are paid between $12 and $18 an hour.

3   It's hard not to wonder how much this pay gulf has to do with the gender divide between players and cheerleaders. The players demonstrate agility and endurance through excruciatingly masculine tasks like running,

crashing into each other, and throwing a ball. Cheerleaders, on the other hand, show those same skills through the typically feminine art form of dance and gymnastics, all while giving one hundred megawatt smiles. Beauty and enthusiasm are expected of women in the public eye, while being simultaneously used as evidence of their lack of **gravitas** and worth.

gravitas:
seriousness

4   Many people feel that cheerleader work is unskilled, just smiling and jumping around and shaking pom poms. I invite anyone who feels that way to look up some routines online, and see how much luck they have mastering them. Alongside complex choreography and gymnastics, many teams also have routines that involve physically rigorous and potentially dangerous activities such as lifting, tossing, and (arguably most important) catching each other. A study out of the University of Montreal earlier this summer suggests that hospital-treated injury rates for cheerleaders in Canada has tripled in the last twenty years. While that research focused on university and high school teams, it is reflective of the increasing dangers of the sport overall. As a matter of fact, a cheerleading injury likely means unpaid time away from a cheerleader's day job. You know, the one that she needs to make a living.

5   The pop culture portrayal of the cheerleader is at best eye-candy and, at worst, airhead. In reality, they are incredibly talented and driven athletes. A quick glance through the cheerleader bios on the teams' websites will introduce you to women who are studying to be lawyers, social workers, behavioral therapists, and dance teachers. They love their moms, they love their kids, and they seem to love animals universally. They want to make the fans happy and be part of a team.

6   Cheerleaders pay out of pocket to do work that strengthens the NFL brand, which benefits players and team owners alike. Cheerleaders take classes in gymnastics, dance, and aerobics. They also spend money on tights and shoes. Then there are the costs of gym memberships, haircuts, makeup, and tanning, which are required. Maintaining specific beauty standards is the norm. Weigh-ins are routine, as are hair and makeup checks.

7   Why does anyone become a cheerleader, then? The reasons are largely the same as with any sport. Cheerleaders, like football players, are good at what they do and enjoy doing it in front of a stadium of cheering fans. They like being part of a team. They enjoy traveling around the country. They like the social status of being part of a nationally recognized franchise. Those things are profitable for players, but not for cheerleaders.

8   There is no reason being part of that team shouldn't come with a living wage, other than someone at some point just decided not to bother paying them. Cheerleaders are not part of some **hardscrabble** community theatre troupe or members of a fledgling dance company hoping to one day get funding. They are part of the brand, and their work is making money for everyone from team owners to sportscasters. It is only fair that they start to see some of that profit.

hardscrabble:
struggling

Practice 6

1. Highlight the thesis statement.
2. What introductory style does the writer use to introduce the topic?
   a. general background information   b. anecdote   c. definition
3. What financial sacrifices do cheerleaders make?

   _____

   _____

4. How are cheerleaders and professional football players similar, according to the writer?

   _____

   _____

5. What is the difference in pay between cheerleaders and NFL players?

   _____

   _____

6. What reasons does the author offer to explain the wage gap between cheerleaders and football players? Give two reasons.

   _____

   _____

   _____

7. Underline two sentences that present negative opinions of cheerleaders.
8. Who is the audience for this essay?

   _____

> **READING LINK
> ARGUMENT**
>
> "The Paradox of New
>   Technologies"
>   p. 550
> "Nudge" p. 572

The Writer's Room

Writing Activity 1: Topics

Choose any of the following topics, or choose your own topic, and write an argument essay. Remember to narrow your topic and to follow the writing process.

General Topics

1. Should online gambling be banned?
2. Should children be spanked?
3. Should voting be compulsory?
4. Should tipping for service be abolished?
5. What is the biggest problem in your town or city?

College- and Work-Related Topics

6. Should students work while going to college?
7. Should all college disciplines include apprenticeship or intern programs?
8. Should service workers create unions?
9. Should some college courses be removed from the curriculum?
10. What is the most underappreciated profession?

WRITING LINK
See the next grammar sections for more argument writing topics.

Ch. 24, Writer's Room topic 2, p. 344
Ch. 30, Writer's Room topic 2, p. 407
Ch. 31, Writer's Room topic 2, p. 420
Ch. 32, Writer's Room topic 2, p. 431
Ch. 34, Writer's Room topic 2, p. 451
Ch. 35, Writer's Room topic 2, p. 462

Writing Activity 2: Media Writing

Write an argument essay discussing a controversial issue, perhaps one that revolves around war or sociopolitical conflict. Look online, watch some programs or movies, or listen to podcasts to help spark ideas. Here are some suggestions:

Show: *Homeland, Narcos*

Film: *Zero Dark Thirty, Schindler's List, The Last Days in Vietnam, The Imitation Game*

Online: The United Nations site (e.g., UN WebTV videos and interactive maps)

Podcast: *Stuff You Missed in History Class*, the BBC's *World War One* and *History Extra*

Checklist: Argument Essay

After you write your argument essay, review the checklist at the end of the book. Also, ask yourself the following set of questions.

❏ Does my thesis statement clearly state my position on the issue?

❏ Do I make strong supporting arguments?

❏ Do I include facts, examples, statistics, and logical consequences?

❏ Do my supporting arguments provide evidence that directly supports the thesis statement?

❏ Do I acknowledge and counter opposing arguments?

❏ Do I use valid arguments? (Do I avoid making broad generalizations? Do I restrain any emotional appeals?)

❏ Do I use a courteous tone?

Part III
More College and Workplace Writing

In the next chapters, you learn about college and workplace writing. Chapter 15 provides valuable information about writing essay exams. Chapters 16 and 17 guide you through the process of synthesizing material and writing a research essay. Chapter 18 focuses on the response essay, and Chapter 19 gives you some important workplace writing strategies.

CHAPTER 15
The Essay Exam
- Prepare for essay exams.

CHAPTER 16
Summarizing
- Practice summary-writing strategies.

CHAPTER 17
The Research Essay
- Plan a research essay and avoid plagiarism.

CHAPTER 18
The Response Essay
- Develop responses to literature and film.

CHAPTER 19
The Résumé and Letter of Application
- Learn to write résumés and letters.

15   The Essay Exam

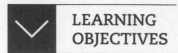
15.1 Prepare for exams.

15.2 Write essay exams.

Just as athletes rigorously train to win an important race, successful students follow specific strategies to ace exams.

Writers' Exchange

Tell a partner about your study habits. Discuss the following questions.

1. When you are given an assignment, how do you react? Do you procrastinate or start working right away?

2. When you are told about a test, what do you do? Do you panic? Do you plan study times? Do you give yourself enough time to study?

3. How do you balance your college, home, and work lives? Do you put too much emphasis on your social life? Do you spend too much time at a part-time job?

After you discuss the questions, brainstorm a list of steps students can take to become successful at college.

Preparing for Exams

15.1   Prepare for exams.

In many of your college courses, you will be asked to write essay exams. You will be expected to show what you know in an organized and logical manner. To be better prepared for such exams, try the following strategies.

Take Meaningful Notes

In class, listen carefully and take notes about key points. Your instructor might signal important ideas with phrases such as "and most importantly." Also, remember to date your notes. You will want a record of when you wrote them during the semester. The dates might help you to know what to focus on while you are studying.

Choose a note-taking method that works best for you. Possible methods are handwriting on paper, typing on a laptop, writing with a stylus on a tablet, or recording thoughts on an audio device. If you are visual, you might even draw images along with your notes, which could help you "see" concepts and remember them more easily. Place your notes in a consistent location so you can easily find and review them.

HINT: Using Abbreviations

Many abbreviations we use in English derive from Latin terms. Here are some abbreviations to help you take notes more efficiently.

Abbreviation	English	Latin
e.g.	for example	exempli gratia
etc.	and so on	et cetera
i.e.	that is	id est
N.B.	important	nota bene
vs., v.	against	versus

Keep in mind that these abbreviations are useful for note taking. When you write an essay, use the complete English words, not the abbreviations.

Review Course Material

Cramming is an ineffective, short-term strategy for college success. Instead, reviewing your course material *regularly*, perhaps every second day or each week, will ensure that you know your subjects well.

- **Study with a classmate or friend.** Set a particular time each week, which will motivate you to study during times when you want to do something else. Ask each other questions on key concepts, or proofread each other's written work.

- **Ask questions.** When you don't understand something in class, speak up. Chances are great that others in the class also have problems understanding the material. Also consider speaking with your instructors during their office hours. Prepare questions about concepts that you do not understand. Waiting until the day before the exam will be too late.

- **Predict exam questions.** Look for important themes in your course outline. Also review your notes and identify what information is of particular importance. Look over previous exams and answer those questions. Finally, predict what types of questions will be on the exam. Write down possible questions, and practice answering them.

Practice 1

Imagine that your English instructor will give you an exam next week. The exam will cover material from the past three weeks. What types of questions might your instructor ask? Brainstorm some ideas here.

_____

_____

_____

_____

_____

Writing Essay Exams

15.2 Write essay exams.

In many of your courses, you will have to answer exam questions with a paragraph or essay to reveal how well you understand information. Although taking any exam can be stressful, you can reduce exam anxiety and increase your chances of doing well by following some of the preparation and exam-writing strategies outlined in this chapter.

Schedule Your Time

Before you write the exam, find out exactly how much time you have, and then plan how much time you will need to answer the questions. For example, if you have a one-hour exam, and you have three questions worth the same value, try to spend no more than twenty minutes on each question.

Determine Point Values

As soon as you get an exam, scan the questions and determine which questions have a larger value. For example, you might respond to the questions with the largest point value first, or you might begin with those that you understand well. Then go to the more difficult questions. If you are stuck on a certain answer, skip to another question, and then go back to that question later.

Carefully Read the Exam Questions

In an exam question, every word counts. Here are two ways you can read actively.

1. **Identify key words and phrases.** When you read an exam question, underline or circle key words and phrases to understand exactly what you are supposed to do. In the next example of an essay question, the underlined words highlight two different tasks.

        Discuss cost-plus pricing, and analyze its importance to a company.

1. Define the term.

2. Explain why it is important.

2. **Pay attention to common question words.** Directions for exam questions often use specific verbs (action words). The following chart gives you several common words that you will find in essay-style questions.

Verb	Meaning
describe discuss review	Examine a subject as thoroughly as possible. Focus on the main points.
narrate trace	Describe the development or progress of something using time order.
evaluate explain your point of view interpret justify take a stand	State your opinion and give reasons to support your opinion. In other words, write an argument essay.
analyze criticize classify	Explain something carefully by breaking it down into smaller parts.
enumerate list outline	Go through important facts one by one.
compare contrast distinguish	Discuss important similarities and/or differences.
define explain what is meant by	Give a complete, accurate definition that demonstrates the meaning of or your understanding of the concept.
explain causes	Analyze the reasons for an event.
explain effects	Analyze the consequences or results of an event.
explain a process	Present all of the steps needed to do a task.
illustrate	Demonstrate your understanding by giving examples.
summarize	Write down the main points from a larger piece of work.

Practice 2

What tasks are students expected to do in each essay exam? Choose the best key words.

Topic

Key Word

1. Explain how a country calculates its gross domestic product (GDP). _____
2. Discuss the repercussions of social media bullying on high school students. _____
3. Provide examples of alternative energy sources. _____
4. Distinguish between universal health care and privatized medicine. _____
5. Discuss whether capital punishment should be abolished. _____
6. Explain what crowdfunding is. _____

a. compare and contrast

b. define

c. explain a process

d. argue

e. explain causes or effects

f. give examples

Practice 3

The following is an exam from a sociology course. Read the instructions, and then answer the questions that follow the sample.

Answer both parts A and B. You will have two hours to complete the evaluation.

Part A   Define two of the following terms. (5 points each)

1. democracy
2. theocracy

3. fascism
4. communism

Part B   Write a 300-word essay about one of the following topics. (40 points)

1. How will economic development in low-income countries improve if women are given a higher social status? Explain your answer.
2. How does poverty in developing nations compare with poverty in the United States?
3. Some consider the United States a "middle-class society." Explain how true you believe this claim to be.
4. Explain the causes of homelessness in this nation.

1. What is the total point value of the exam? _____
2. How many definitions should you write? _____
3. How many essays should you write? _____

4. Which part of the exam would you do first? Explain why.

_____

_____

5. How much time would you spend on Part A and Part B? Explain why.

_____

_____

Follow the Writing Process

Treat an essay exam as you would any other writing assignment by following the three main steps of the writing process.

Explore   Jot down any ideas that you think can help you answer the question. Try the prewriting activities suggested in Chapter 1 of this book, such as brainstorming or clustering. Prewriting will help you generate some ideas for your essay.

Develop   Use the exam question to guide your thesis statement and topic sentences. List supporting ideas, organize your ideas using an essay plan or outline, and then write an essay. Remember to include an introduction with a clear thesis statement and to use transitions such as _first_, _moreover_, or _in addition_ to link your ideas.

Revise and Edit   Read over your essay to verify that all ideas support the thesis statement and to ensure that you have adequate details to support your topic sentences. Also check spelling, punctuation, and mechanics.

HINT: Writing a Thesis Statement

In an essay exam, your thesis statement should be very clear. A good strategy is to write a guided thesis statement that includes the main ideas or concepts that you will cover in the essay. Review the essay topic and sample thesis statement.

Essay topic   Explain the key pricing strategies that companies use.

Thesis statement   The most common pricing strategies are **cost-plus pricing, target pricing,** and **yield-management pricing.**

Practice 4

Write thesis statements for the following exam questions. Remember that your thesis must have a controlling idea.

EXAMPLE: Discuss the dangers of armed militias in our nation.

Thesis statement: <u>Armed militias can destroy lives, break social order, and lead</u>
<u>to chaos.</u>

1. Compare viral marketing with traditional print marketing. Point out the advantages and disadvantages of each type.

_____

_____

_____

2. Explain the steps needed to reduce texting while driving casualties.

_____

_____

_____

3. Are social media addictions a growing problem? Defend your viewpoint.

_____

_____

_____

Practice 5

College student John Marshall wrote the following essay for a business course. Read the essay and answer the questions that follow.

The Value of Corporate Social Responsibility

1.   Business corporations exert an immense influence on society. Companies such as Facebook or Google influence social trends, public opinion, the government, and the economy. Given their influence, what responsibilities do corporations have to society? Traditionally, the standard objective of a corporation has been to make as much profit as possible. Higher profits facilitate growth, attract investors, and appease shareholders. While corporations still strive to make profits, *how* they do it has changed. Corporate social responsibility (CSR) has become an important marketing technique that leads to greater customer loyalty, better employee morale, and higher profits.

2.   First, corporations that do good deeds positively influence the consumer's perception of the corporation, which leads to more customer loyalty. For example, in the United States, Toms Shoes donates one pair of shoes to someone in need for every pair that a customer buys. Consumers respond positively to the company's initiative. In Canada, Mountain Equipment Coop donates tents to families who have lost their homes following a natural disaster. Customers have the sense that they are personally contributing aid to the disadvantaged. Such donation initiatives help consumers feel more generous and compassionate. As a consequence, they are more likely to trust corporations that are involved in socially responsible activities. For the corporation, this trust results in increased brand loyalty.

3.   But corporate responsibility doesn't end with consumers. It also helps to increase employee morale and create a more loyal workforce. For example, when a coffee shop buys fair trade coffee, socially-conscious employees enjoy knowing that their livelihoods are not damaging those of coffee growers or harming the environment. Another example is Google, which has several responsibility initiatives. The company donates money as well as computers and other technology. In "Corporate Philanthropy," Adam Weinger says that in 2015, "Google employees volunteered nearly 80,000 hours of service. In total, Google has matched $21 million in employee donations." Employees feel better about the work they do when they know they are also contributing to a better world. For the corporation, better morale translates into higher worker productivity.

4.   Finally, when corporations show that they are socially responsible, they gain financially. Many modern corporations advertise their philanthropic efforts, energy efficiency, and/or care for social well-being as much as they do their products or services. A recent study conducted at the University of South Florida reported that 80 percent of respondents believed firms should engage in pro-social behaviors, and 52 percent of respondents would boycott a firm that they perceived as socially irresponsible. Companies benefit when they have a more altruistic image. For example, a café can sell a greater quantity of coffee because it is advertised as fair trade. Toms Shoes generated positive news coverage for its shoe donation program, and customers flocked to the stores. Thus, when customers feel more loyal and employees have higher morale, companies reap financial rewards for being perceived as socially responsible.

5.   CSR campaigns have become a leading marketing strategy in North America because the perception of corporate social responsibly

is beneficial for the firm and the consumer. When consumers buy from corporations that they perceive as socially responsible, they receive psychological benefits in the forms of greater self-esteem and self-actualization. Employees also feel better about their work. Therefore, corporations receive indirect benefits; they have a better reputation. But they also receive direct financial benefits.

Comprehension

1. This student essay is in response to which test question? Choose the best answer.
   a. Distinguish between companies with good and bad social reputations.
   b. Trace the development, over time, of corporate social responsibility.
   c. Explain possible benefits of corporate social responsibility.
   d. Define the term "corporate social responsibility."

2. Highlight the thesis statement in the introduction. Also highlight the topic sentences in body paragraphs 2–5.

3. On a separate sheet of paper or on the computer, create a plan for this essay. For the details, just use words or phrases.

The Writer's Room

1. Predict at least three essay exam questions for one of your courses. Then develop an informal essay plan for one of the questions.

2. Look at an exam that you completed previously. Write a paragraph explaining what you could have done to receive a higher mark.

Checklist: An Essay Exam

As you prepare for your essay exam, ask yourself the following questions.

❏ Have I taken clear notes during lectures?

❏ Have I reviewed my notes on a regular basis?

❏ Have I organized study time?

❏ Have I asked my instructor questions when I didn't understand a concept?

❏ Have I asked my instructor what material the exam will cover?

16 Summarizing

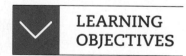
A stylist trims away excess hair to reveal a client's new style. In the same way, when you summarize, you keep the key points and discard unnecessary details.

Writers' Exchange

Work with a partner. In a couple of minutes, describe the contents of an article or essay that you have read for this course. What were the key points?

What Is a Summary?

16.1 Define summary.

A summary is a logical shortened form of a longer reading. It provides a clear and precise snapshot of an author's ideas and arguments. Writing a summary is not as simple as it seems. First, there is a discovery phase: You must thoroughly understand what an author wishes to convey. Then, after you have a clear understanding of the key points, you must express the author's ideas in a fair and unbiased way. It is essential to put aside your own reactions and opinions.

A summary is a snapshot of a more complete work.

Summaries matter: They demonstrate to instructors that you can convey another person's ideas accurately and fairly—without plagiarizing or copying that person's exact words. In college courses, you often write summaries. An instructor may ask you to sum up the main ideas of an article or book. In response and analysis reports, a summary can provide background information before you make your own arguments. And in research essays, brief synopses of other people's ideas can add weight to your arguments.

Additionally, people in many professions are asked to write summaries. For instance, companies hire people to read articles and compress detailed information into basic components. These summaries help work teams identify the issues quickly and decide which actions to take. Science labs summarize important findings. Even the minutes of a meeting are essentially summaries of the key ideas that were discussed. Thus, the ability to summarize properly is useful in many contexts.

How to Write a Summary

16.2 Write a summary.

Here are ways to summarize an original text to its basic elements:

1. **Read the original text carefully** because you will need a complete picture before you write.
2. **Underline or highlight key ideas** to help you visualize the main ideas.
3. **Make an outline of the original piece**. Ask yourself *who, what, when, where, why,* and *how* questions to help you identify the central ideas.
4. **Write a first draft** from memory and with the help of your notes.
5. **Mention the author and title of the original source** early in your summary.
6. **Use your own words to restate the main ideas**. Keep specialized words, common words, and the names of people or places. For all other words, find synonyms in a dictionary or a thesaurus.
7. **Maintain the original author's meaning and intent**. Remind readers that you are summarizing by using phrases such as *The writer explains* or *The author suggests*. Do not add your own opinions unless your instructor asks you to do so.

8. **Respect the length requirements**. Summaries are generally about one-quarter the length of the original piece, but requirements may vary. For instance, to summarize an article, you could write a paragraph. To summarize an entire book, you might need a page or two. Ask your instructor for details about length.

9. **Write your final draft.** Ensure that you have explained the critical ideas and used your own words.

In written summaries, readers should be able to understand the essential message. The complete document would contain more details and examples, but readers would not require the original to make sense of the central ideas.

Citing the Source in a Summary

In a summary, you can cite the source in the opening sentence. Mention the author and title of the work. If you are summarizing from a print source, then you can include the page number in the first sentence, or you can place the page number, in parentheses, at the end of the summary. If you are summarizing a large work such as a novel, or if the source is Web based, generally no page numbers are necessary. For more detailed information about citing sources, see Chapter 17, "The Research Essay."

HINT: Avoid Direct Quotations

A summary should not include any phrases or sentences from the original piece. The point is to condense the original item using your own words as much as possible. If you feel that you must use some of the writer's words, put quotation marks around them. Otherwise, you could be accused of plagiarism. (For more information about plagiarism, see page 267 in Chapter 17.)

> Additionally, according to Williams, cheerleaders are not **"eye candy"** and **"air heads."** They are often smart students in difficult programs such as law.

SAMPLE SUMMARY

Review this summary of an essay that appears in Chapter 14 on page 231.

In "Why Cheerleaders Should Be Paid" (231), Audra Williams says that cheerleaders do highly skilled jobs and deserve better treatment by the football industry. Williams compares the salaries of NFL players and cheerleaders

> In your topic sentence, mention the source. Include the page number, when available.

Use your own words to explain the main ideas.

Remind readers that it is a summary by frequently referring to the writer.

Use transitional expressions.

and points out that cheerleaders do not earn a living wage. Even mascots and concession workers earn more than the athletic women who entertain spectators. A possible reason for the low salaries could be gender inequality. Williams makes the point that a female's ability to dance and do gymnastics is not as valued as a male's capacity to slam into another man. The writer explains that cheerleading requires complex and hazardous movements. In fact, many cheerleaders are hospitalized for injuries such as a fall. Additionally, according to Williams, cheerleaders are not dumb. They are often smart students in difficult programs such as law. Moreover, each cheerleader has to spend money on the profession. Gym memberships and hair and wardrobe requirements can be expensive. They have to be beautiful and extremely fit to maintain their position on the squad. The writer concludes with a call to action, arguing that cheerleaders are a vital part of a team's image, so the athletic women should also benefit from the profitable football industry.

Conclude your summary.

Practice 1

Summarize the next selections. Your summary should be much shorter than the original selection. Remember to cite the source and to use your own words.

1. Developing a friendship with a co-worker who has a work ethic and who can "keep it zipped" is a must-have. No matter how great your significant other, friends, and neighbors are at solving problems or listening to your work concerns, they are not your best option. Why? Because they don't work where you do. Only a co-worker can completely understand the personalities and culture of your workplace.

—Goddard, Stephanie. "Top Ten Ways to Beat Stress at Work." *Work-Stress-Solutions*, 14 May 2010, www.work-stress-solutions.com/stress-management-tips.html.

Summary

_____

_____

_____

_____

_____

2.   And credit-card companies have changed their lending policies in ways that make credit more accessible—but also more complicated. . . . Instead of charging everyone the same, companies adjust the interest rates according to customers' credit scores. They also charge special fees for late payments, purchases that exceed a credit limit, foreign-currency transactions, phone payments, and so forth. This structure makes it profitable to extend credit to high-risk borrowers, including those with low incomes.

—Postrel, Virginia. "The Case for Debt." *Atlantic*, Nov. 2008, pp. 44–47.

Summary

_____

_____

_____

_____

3.   The progression of skateboarding went from a cult-like activity with rebellious undertones to a mainstream hobby. The originators of skateboarding in 1970s Southern California, who were portrayed in the popular documentary *Dogtown and Z-Boys*, wouldn't recognize the sport today. At that time, boarders were outlaws; as one of the main characters in the film says, "We get the beat-down from all over. Everywhere we go, man, people hate us." Nowadays, skateboarding is about as countercultural as *The Simpsons*. More kids ride skateboards than play basketball, and many of them snap up pricey T-shirts, skate shoes, helmets, and other accessories. In fact, boarders spend almost six times as much on "soft goods," such as T-shirts, shorts, and sunglasses (about $4.4 billion in a year), than on hard-core equipment, including the boards themselves.

—Solomon, Michael R. *Consumer Behavior.* 10th ed., Pearson, 2013, p. 557.

Summary

_____

_____

_____

_____

_____

Practice 2

The following adapted essay appeared on page 534 of *Sociology* by John J. Macionis. Read the essay and then write a one-paragraph summary. Remember to follow the summary-writing guidelines in this chapter.

The Twenty-First-Century Campus: Where Are the Men?

1.   A century ago, the campuses of colleges and universities across the United States might as well have hung out a sign that read "Men Only." Almost all of the students and faculty were male. There were a small number of women's colleges, but many more schools—including some of the best known U.S. universities such as Yale, Harvard, and Princeton—barred women outright. Since then, women have won greater social equality. By 1980, the number of women enrolled at U.S. colleges finally matched the number of men.

2.   In a surprising trend, however, the share of women on campus has continued to increase. As a result, in 2011, men accounted for only 43 percent of all U.S. undergraduates. The gender gap is evident in all racial and ethnic categories and at all class levels. Among African Americans on campus, only 37 percent are men. The lower the income level, the greater the gender gap in college attendance.

3.   Meg DeLong noticed the gender imbalance right away when she moved into her dorm at the University of Georgia at Athens; she soon learned that just 39 percent of her first-year classmates were men. In some classes, there were few men, and women usually dominated discussions. Out of class, DeLong and many other women soon complained that having so few men on campus hurt their social life. Not surprisingly, most of the men felt otherwise.

4.   What accounts for the shifting gender balance on U.S. campuses? One theory is that many young men are drawn away from college by the lure of jobs, especially in high technology. This pattern is sometimes termed the "Bill Gates syndrome," after the man who dropped out of college and soon became the world's richest person by helping to found Microsoft. Thus, many boys have unrealistic expectations about their earning power if they don't have an education.

5.   In addition, analysts point to an anti-intellectual male culture. More young women are drawn to learning and seek to do well in school, whereas some young men attach less importance to studying. According to Judith Kleinfeld, in the journal *Gender Issues*, stereotyping is also holding boys back. Because girls generally have more developed social

skills and are better behaved than boys, they perform better in school, which then prepares them for college. Boys, on the other hand, are often labeled as less cooperative and more likely to act out in classrooms, which can affect their grades. Rightly or wrongly, more men seem to think they can get a good job without investing years of their lives and a considerable amount of money in getting a college degree.

6.   Many college officials are concerned about the lack of men on campus. In an effort to attract more balanced enrollments, some colleges are adopting what amounts to affirmative action programs for males. But courts in several states have already ruled such policies illegal. Many colleges, therefore, are turning to more active recruitment; admissions officers are paying special attention to male applicants and stressing a college's strength in mathematics and science—areas traditionally popular with men. In the same way that colleges across the country are striving to increase their share of minority students, the hope is that they can also succeed in attracting a larger share of men.

The Writer's Room

Writing Activity

Choose one of the following activities:

1. Summarize a paragraph from a newspaper or magazine article.
2. Summarize the essay "Discrimination in the 21st Century" from Chapter 11 (page 163).
3. Summarize Chapter 15, "The Essay Exam."
4. Summarize the plot of a television program, online series, or movie.
5. Summarize a text that you have read for another course.
6. Choose an essay from Chapter 41 of this book, and summarize it.

Checklist: Summarizing

When you paraphrase or summarize, ask yourself these questions.

❑ Have I kept the original intent of the author?
❑ Have I kept only the key ideas?
❑ Have I used my own words when summarizing?
❑ Have I mentioned the source when summarizing?

17   The Research Essay

When preparing a new meal, you may follow the recipe of an experienced chef and add your own touches. In the same way, when you write a research essay, you cite other people's ideas and combine them with your own to make a more convincing paper.

Writers' Exchange

Work with a partner. Match the word in Column A with a word that has a similar purpose or meaning in Column B. Then discuss the differences between the two words in each pair.

A	B
MLA	Footnote
Works Cited	Plagiarism
Copying	Indirect quotation
Parenthetical documentation	APA
Paraphrase	Bibliography

Planning a Research Essay

17.1 Plan a research essay.

Conducting **research** means looking for information that will help you better understand a subject. Knowing how to locate, evaluate, and use information from other sources is valuable in your work and day-to-day activities. It is also crucial in college writing because, in many of your assignments, you are expected to include information from outside sources. In this chapter, you learn some strategies for writing a research paper.

Determining Your Topic

In some courses, your instructor will ask you to write a research paper about a specific topic. However, if you are not assigned one, you will need to think about issues related to your field of study or to your personal interests.

The scope of your topic should match the size of the assignment. Longer essays may have a broader topic, but a short research essay (of three or four pages) must have a rather narrow focus. If you have a very specific focus, you will be able to delve more thoroughly into the topic. To help find and develop a topic, try exploring strategies such as freewriting, questioning, or brainstorming. (See Chapter 1 for more information about prewriting strategies.)

Finding a Guiding Research Question

The point of a research essay is not simply to collect information and summarize it; the idea is to gather information that relates directly to your guiding research question. To help you determine your central question, brainstorm a list of questions that you would like your research to answer.

For example, John Cary Nuez wants to write about the military, so he could ask himself some questions to narrow his topic.

What are the major dangers for U.S. soldiers?

Are women effective in combat mission roles?

What types of people make the best soldiers?

Nuez's next step is to find a guiding research question that can become the focus of his essay.

Should women have combat roles in war zones?

Gathering Information

17.2 Gather information.

Once you know what information you seek, you can begin gathering ideas, facts, quotations, anecdotes, and examples about the research topic you have chosen. Before you begin to gather information, consider how to find it and how to sort the valid information from the questionable information.

The Writer's Desk: Find a Research Topic

Choose a general topic that you might like to write about.

Topic: _____

Now ask five or six questions to help you narrow the topic.

_____

_____

_____

_____

_____

_____

Decide which question will become your guiding research question, and write it here.

_____

_____

_____

Consulting Library-Based Sources

Today's technological advances in both print and electronic publishing make it easier than ever to access information. For sources, you can consult encyclopedias, online catalogs in libraries, periodicals, and the Internet. Here are some tips for finding information about your topic through library resources.

- **Ask a reference librarian** to help you locate information using various research tools, such as online catalogs, CD-ROMs, and microfiches. Before meeting with the librarian, write down some questions that you would like the answers to. Possible questions might be *Can I access the library's online databases from my home computer?* and *Can you recommend a particular online database?*

- **Search the library's online holdings.** You can search by keyword, author, title, or subject. Using an online catalog, a student typed in the key words *addiction* and *biology* and found the following book.

Author	Goldstein, Avram
Title	Addiction: from biology to drug policy
Imprint	New York: Oxford University Press, 2001
Call Number	RC564.G66 2001
Location	NRG – Book Shelves
Status	Available
Description	353 p.; 24 cm.
ISBN	0195146638

Notice that the listing gives the call number, which helps you locate the book on the library shelves. If the catalog is part of a library network, the online listing explains which library to visit. Because books are organized by topic, chances are good that you will find other relevant books near the one you have chosen.

- **Use online periodicals in libraries.** Your library may have access to EBSCOhost® or INFOtrac. By typing keywords into EBSCO, you can search through national or international newspapers, magazines, or reference books. When you find an article that you need, print it or cut and paste it into a word processing file, and then email the document to yourself. Remember to print or copy the publication data because you will need that information when you cite your source.

Searching the Internet

Search engines such as Google and Yahoo! can rapidly retrieve thousands of documents from the Internet. However, most people do not need as many documents as those engines can generate. Here are some tips to help make your Internet searches focused and efficient.

- **Choose your keywords with care.** Imagine you want information about new fuel sources for automobiles. If you type the words *alternative energy* in Google's keyword search space, you will come up with ten million entries (also known as "hits"). Think about more precise terms that could help you limit your search. For instance, if you are really interested in fuel sources for automobiles, you might change your search request to *alternative car fuel*. If you do not find information on your topic, think about synonyms or alternative ways to describe it.

- **Use quotation marks to limit the search.** Remember that you are driving the search, and you can control how many hits you get. By putting quotation marks around your search query, you limit the number of sites to those that contain all of the words that you requested. For example, when you input the words *alternative car fuel* into Google, you will have more than three million hits. When the same words are enclosed within quotation marks, the number of hits is reduced significantly.

- **Use bookmarks.** When you find information that might be useful, create a folder where you can store the information in a "bookmark" or "favorites" list. Then you can easily find it later. (The bookmark icon appears on the toolbar of your search engine.)
- **Use academic search engines.** Sites such as *Google Scholar* or *Virtual Learning Resources Center* help you look through academic publications such as theses, peer-reviewed papers, books, and articles. To find more academic sites, simply do a search for "academic search engines."

Conducting Interviews or Surveys

You can support your research essay with information from an interview. Speak to an expert in the field or someone who is directly affected by an issue. If you record the interview, ensure that your subject gives you permission to do so. Remember to plan the interview before you meet the person and list key questions that you would like answered. Include the person's complete name and qualifications in your research notes.

Another source of information can be a **survey**, which is an assessment of the views of many people. For example, if you are writing about a tuition fee increase, you can survey students to gather their opinions. When you plan your survey, follow some basic guidelines:

- **Determine your goal.** What do you want to discover?
- **Determine the age, gender, and status of the respondents** (people you will survey). For example, you might decide to survey equal-sized groups of males and females or those over and under twenty-five years of age.
- **Decide how many people you will survey.** Survey at least ten people (or a number determined by your instructor).
- **Determine the type of survey you will do.** Will you survey people using the phone, email, or written forms? Keep in mind that people are more likely to obscure the truth when asked questions directly, especially if the questions are embarrassing or very personal. For example, if you ask someone whether he agrees or disagrees with legalized abortion, he might present a viewpoint that he thinks you or nearby listeners will accept. The same person might be more honest in an anonymous written survey.
- **Plan your survey questions.** If gender, age, marital status, or job status are important, place questions about those items at the beginning of your survey. When you form your questions, do not ask open-ended, essay-type questions

because it will be difficult to compile the results. Instead, ask yes/no questions or provide a choice of answers. Sample questions:

What is your gender?   male _____ female _____

How often do you use the public transit system (the bus, subway, or train)?

_____ weekdays   _____ about once a week

_____ rarely or never   _____ about once a month

If you want to determine your respondents' knowledge about a topic, include an "I don't know" response. Otherwise, people will make selections that could skew your survey results.

Has Jackson Monroe done a good job as student union leader?

_____ yes   _____ no   _____ I don't know

TECH LINK
There are many online survey tools that help you draft questions easily and distribute surveys electronically. Two examples are Google Forms and SurveyMonkey.

Evaluating Sources

17.3   Evaluate sources.

When you see sources published in print or online, especially when they are attention-grabbing with color or graphics, you may forget to question whether those sources are reliable. For instance, a company's website advertising an alternative cancer therapy might be less reliable than an article in a scientific journal by a team of oncologists (doctors who treat cancer).

HINT: Questions for Evaluating a Source

Each time you find a source, ask yourself the following questions:

- Will the information support the point that I want to make?
- Is the information current? When was the site last updated? Ask yourself if the date is appropriate for your topic.
- Is the site reliable and highly regarded? For instance, is it from a well-respected newspaper, magazine, or journal? Is the English grammatically correct?
- Is the author an expert on the subject? (Many sites provide biographical information about the author.)
- Does the writer present a balanced view, or does he or she clearly favor one viewpoint over another? Ask yourself if the writer has a political or financial interest in the issue.
- Is there advertising on the site? Consider how advertising might influence the site's content.
- Do different writers supply the same information on various sites? Information is more likely to be reliable if multiple sources cite the same facts.

Practice 1

Imagine that you are conducting research about the safety of bottled water. Answer the questions by referring to the list of Web entries that follows the questions.

1. Write the letters of three Web hits that are **not** useful for your essay. For each one you choose, explain why.

   _____

   _____

   _____

   _____

2. Write the letters of the three Web hits that you should investigate further. Briefly explain how each one could be useful.

   _____

   _____

   _____

   _____

A. **Should I stop drinking bottled water? | Life and style | The ...**
   www.theguardian.com › Lifestyle › Health & wellbeing
   Jun 1, 2015 - There is no evidence bottled water is better for you and, indeed, it may be less safe than tap water.

B. **There Can Be Dangers Of Drinking Bottled Water | Water Purifiers**
   http://www.home-water-distiller.com/waterpurifiers/drinkingwater/
   there-can-be-dangers...62/
   22 Aug 2008 . . . Water is an excellent way to keep your mind sharp and your body in excellent shape as most everyone in the world already knows.

C. **Healthy Diet Info Zone: BOTTLED WATER - DANGER!!!**
   http://health-diet-info.blogspot.com/2008/05...html
   BOTTLED WATER - DANGER!!! Posted by Martin | 6:55 AM.
   Healthy Drinks · 0 comments. Bottled water in your car . . .
   very dangerous, woman! . . .

D. **Bottled vs. Tap**
   http://pediatrics.about.com...a/080702_ask_3.htm
   Is the extra cost of bottled water vs. tap water worth it? . . . "consumers should feel confident of the safety of their water," says Stew Thornley, a water quality health educator with the Minnesota Department of Health. . . .

E. City still in shock over water danger
http://www.chinadaily.com.cn/china/2009-02/23...htm
City still in shock over water danger. By Qian Yanfeng (China Daily)
"... but I'm still drinking bottled water and only use tap water for
washing," he said. ...

F. ABC News: Study: Bottled Water No Safer Than Tap Water
http://abcnews.go.com...id=87558&page=
Bottled water users were twice as likely as others to cite health for
their choice of beverage, the study found. Fifty-six percent of
bottled water users ...

HINT: Do Not Pay for Online Articles

Ignore websites that offer to sell articles or essays. There are many free online
journals, magazines, and newspapers that contain articles suitable for a
research project. Also find out if your college has access to extensive online
databases such as EBSCO.

The Writer's Desk: Research Your Topic

Using the guiding research question that you developed in the previous Writer's Desk,
list some keywords that you can use to research your topic.

_____

_____

_____

_____

Using the library and the Internet, find some sources that you can use for your research
essay. You might also conduct interviews or prepare a survey. Print out relevant online
sources, and keep track of your source information.

Taking Notes

17.4 Take notes.

As you research your topic, keep careful notes on paper, on note cards, or in
computer files. Do not rely on your memory! You would not want to spend
several weeks researching, only to accidentally plagiarize because you had not
adequately acknowledged some sources.

Look for sources that support your thesis statement. Each time you find a source that seems relevant, keep a detailed record of its publication information so that you can easily cite the source when you begin to write your research essay. You will find important information about preparing in-text citations and a Works Cited (MLA) list later in this chapter.

For example, a student created the following note card after finding source material in the library.

Author: Morris, Charles G. and Albert A. Maisto

Title: *Understanding Psychology*, 11th ed.

Publisher: Pearson

Date: 2016

Page 406: Wartime experiences often cause soldiers intense and disabling combat stress that persists long after they have left the battlefield.

Finding Complete Source Information

Source information is easy to find in most print publications. It is usually on the copyright page, which is often the second or third page of the book, magazine, or newspaper. On many Internet sites, however, finding the same information can take more investigative work. When you research on the Internet, look for the home page to find the site's title, publication date, and so on. Record as much information from the site as possible.

Book, Magazine, Newspaper	Website
Author's full name	Author's full name
Title of article or chapter	Title of article
Title of book, magazine, or newspaper	Title of site
Publishing information (name of publisher and date of publication)	Publisher of site Date of publication or update date that you accessed the site
Volume and number of a series, and page numbers used	Complete website address

HARPER'S

HARPER'S MAGAZINE/JANUARY 2014

YOU RANG?
Mastering the Art of Serving the Rich
By John P. Davidson

THE PIOUS SPY
A Taliban Intelligence Chief's Death and Resurrection
By Mujib Mashal

SUBJECT TO SEARCH
A story by Lorrie Moore

Also: Lydia Davis, Lauren Groff, Gordon Lish

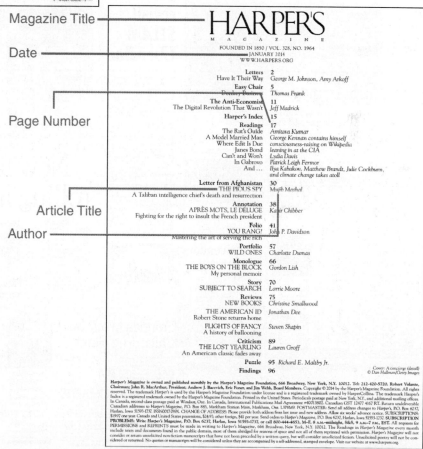

Magazine Title ——

HARPER'S
M A G A Z I N E

FOUNDED IN 1850 / VOL. 328, NO. 1964

Date ——— JANUARY 2014
WWW.HARPERS.ORG

Page Number ——

Article Title ——

Author ———

Cover: A concierge (detail)
© Dan Hallman/Getty Images

Harper's Magazine is owned and published monthly by the Harper's Magazine Foundation, 666 Broadway, New York, N.Y. 10012. Tel: 212-420-5720. Robert Volante, Chairman; John R. MacArthur, President; Andrew J. Bacevich, Eric Foner, and Jim Webb, Board Members. Copyright © 2014 by the Harper's Magazine Foundation. All rights reserved. The trademark Harper's is used by the Harper's Magazine Foundation under license and is a registered trademark owned by HarperCollins. The trademark Harper's Index is a registered trademark owned by the Harper's Magazine Foundation. Printed in the United States. Periodicals postage paid at New York, N.Y., and additional mailing offices. In Canada, second-class postage paid at Windsor, Ont. In Canada, International Publications Mail Agreement #40013802. Canadian GST 12477 4167 RT. Return undeliverable Canadian addresses to Harper's Magazine, P.O. Box 885, Markham Station Main, Markham, Ont. L3P8M9 POSTMASTER: Send all address changes to Harper's, P.O. Box 6237, Harlan, Iowa 51593-1737. ISSN0017-789X. CHANGE OF ADDRESS: Please provide both address from last issue and new address. Allow six weeks' advance notice. SUBSCRIPTIONS: $19.97 one year Canada and United States possessions, $24.97; other foreign, $41 per year. Send orders to Harper's Magazine, P.O. Box 6237, Harlan, Iowa 51593-1737. SUBSCRIPTION PROBLEMS: Write Harper's Magazine, P.O. Box 6237, Harlan, Iowa 51593-1737, or call 800-444-4653. M-F, 8 A.M.–midnight, S&S, 9 A.M.–7 P.M., EST. All requests for PERMISSIONS and REPRINTS must be made in writing to Harper's Magazine, 666 Broadway, New York, N.Y. 10012. The Readings in Harper's Magazine every month include texts and documents found in the public domain, most of them abridged for reasons of space and not all of them reprinted with permission. Harper's Magazine will not consider or return unsolicited non-fiction manuscripts that have not been preceded by a written query, but will consider unsolicited fiction. Unsolicited poetry will not be considered or returned. No queries or manuscripts will be considered unless they are accompanied by a self-addressed, stamped envelope. Visit our website at www.harpers.org

Date

Newspaper Title

Page Number

Article Title

Author

Title of Site

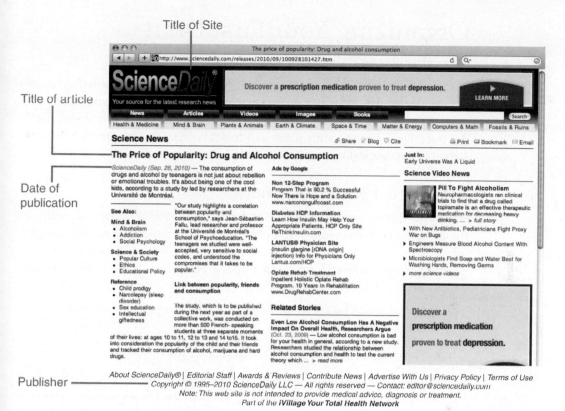

Title of article

Date of publication

Publisher

HINT: Avoid Plagiarism

Do not plagiarize. Plagiarism is using someone else's work without giving that person credit—even if you did it unintentionally. Such an act is considered stealing and is a very serious offense. Always make sure that your notes contain detailed and clear source information. Then, when you later quote, paraphrase, or summarize another's work, you can cite the source. For more information about summarizing, see Chapter 16.

The Writer's Desk: Take Notes

Use your topic from the previous Writer's Desk. Take notes from the sources that you have found. In your notes, include direct quotations, paraphrases, and summaries. Organize your sources, and keep a record of them. For more information about quoting, paraphrasing, and summarizing, see pages 263–265 in this chapter. Also see Chapter 16: Summarizing.

Organizing Your First Draft

17.5 Organize your first draft.

For research essays, as for any other type of essay, planning is essential. After you have evaluated the material that you have gathered, decide how you will organize your material. Group your notes under the main points that you would like to develop. Then arrange your ideas in a logical order. You might choose to use spatial, chronological, or emphatic order.

Writing a Thesis Statement

After taking notes, plan your thesis statement. Your thesis statement expresses the main focus of your essay. You can convert your guiding research question into a thesis statement. For instance, John Cary Nuez wrote the guiding research question: Should women have combat roles in war zones? After researching and gathering material, he reworked his question to create a thesis statement.

> Women should be retained only for combat support roles and not for direct combat engagements.

Creating an Outline

An **outline** or **plan** will help you organize your ideas. Write your main points, and list supporting details and examples. You can mention the sources you intend to use to support specific points. After looking at your preliminary outline, check if there are any holes in your research. If necessary, do more research to fill in those holes before writing your first draft. (For more samples of essay plans and for reminders about the writing process, see Chapters 1–5.)

JOHN'S PRELIMINARY OUTLINE

Thesis: Women should be retained only for combat support roles and not for direct combat engagements.

1. Women acquire combat training–related injuries more than men.

    —Women have a greater risk of injury than men. (UK Ministry of Defense)

    —Injured female combatants may cause problems for entire unit.

2. Women cannot meet the same physical training standards as required by men.

    —Very few women qualified for the first phase of courses (Kamarck).

    —Female marines cannot equal men in training performance (Leiby).

3. Women are essential to combat missions in their combat support roles.

    —They are exposed to similar danger and stress as men (Morris).

    —They participate in meaningful actions.

    —They have special and useful skills (Mulrine).

Incorporating Visuals

17.6 Incorporate visuals.

Visuals—such as charts, maps, graphs, photos, or diagrams—can help to clarify, summarize, emphasize, or illustrate certain concepts in research essays. For example, a graph showing the falling crime rate can be an effective way to support an argument that policing methods have become increasingly successful. Remember to use visuals sparingly and to cite them properly.

Most word processing programs offer templates for many visuals. For example, the toolbar in MS Word allows you to select *Chart* under *Insert* to create line, bar, pie, and other types of charts. Simply input your own data, and the program will create the chart for you. The following charts are standard templates from MS Word.

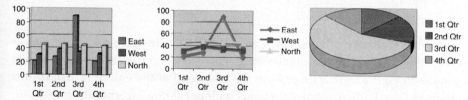

Other visuals can be useful for illustrating concepts. Often, readers prefer seeing an object or idea in context rather than trying to understand it in writing. Basic diagrams, like the one shown here, can be especially useful for scientific and technical writing.

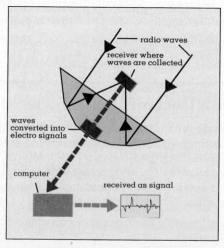

HINT: Using Visuals

Here are some recommendations for using visuals in an academic research essay:

- Ask your instructor whether you are permitted to use visuals in your essay and, if so, where you need to insert them (in the body of your essay or in an appendix).

- Include a label above each visual to clearly identify it. For example, you can number figures and tables sequentially: *Figure 1, Figure 2*, or *Table 1, Table 2*, and so on.

- Place a caption alongside or under the visual to help the reader understand it.

- Acknowledge the source of any visual that you borrow.

- Explain in the text how the visual supports a specific point. For example, in the body of your paper, you might write *Figure 2 illustrates how the crime rate has fallen steadily since the 1990s.*

Citing Sources

17.7 Cite sources.

Each time you borrow someone's words, ideas, or images, you must **cite** or credit the source to avoid plagiarizing. There are two places you need to cite sources in your research essays—in the essay and at the end of it. Use **in-text citations** (also known as **parenthetical citations**) as you incorporate quotations, paraphrases, or summaries. Then, cite the sources in an alphabetized list at the end of your essay. The title of this source list depends on the documentation style you choose. For example, the Modern Language Association (MLA) refers to the list as Works Cited and the American Psychological Association (APA) refers to it as References. This chapter presents MLA guidelines. For information about APA guidelines, see Appendix 2 (pages 609–614). You can also check each organization's website.

HINT: Choose a Documentation Style

A **documentation style** is a method of presenting the material that you have researched. Three common sources for documenting style are the Modern Language Association (MLA), the American Psychological Association (APA), and the *Chicago Manual of Style* (CMS). Before writing a research essay, check with your instructor about which documentation style you should use and where you can find more information about it.

Avoid Plagiarism

17.8   Avoid plagiarism.

Plagiarism is the act of using someone else's **words** or **ideas** without giving that person credit. Plagiarism is a very serious offense and can result in expulsion from a course or termination from work. Always acknowledge the source when you borrow material.

The following actions are examples of plagiarism.

- copying and pasting text from an Internet source without using quotation marks to properly set off the author's words

- using ideas from another source without citing that source

- making slight modifications to an author's sentences but presenting the work as your own

- buying another work and presenting it as your own

- using another student's work and presenting it as your own

HINT: Be Careful

The Internet has made it easier to plagiarize, but it is also easier for instructors to catch cheaters. To avoid plagiarism, always cite the source when you borrow words or ideas.

Integrating Paraphrases, Summaries, and Quotations

17.9   Integrate paraphrases, summaries, and quotations.

In a research essay, you can support your main points with paraphrases, summaries, and integrated quotations. They strengthen your research paper and make it more forceful and convincing.

- A **paraphrase** is an indirect quotation. It is roughly the same length as the author's original words. When you paraphrase, restate someone's ideas using your own words.

- A **summary** is another type of indirect quotation. It is shorter than a paraphrase and includes only the main ideas of the original work.

- A **direct quotation** contains the exact words of the speaker or writer, and it is set off with quotation marks.

All of these strategies are valid ways to incorporate research into your writing, as long as you give credit to the author or speaker. Review examples of a paraphrase, summary, and quotation.

Original Selection

Identity marketing is a promotional strategy whereby consumers alter some aspects of themselves to advertise for a branded product. A British marketing firm paid five people to legally change their names for one year to "Turok," the hero of a video game series about a time-traveling Native American who slays bionically enhanced dinosaurs. In another case, the Internet Underground Music Archive (IUMA) paid Kansas parents $5,000 to name their baby boy Iuma. Body art is the most common form of identity advertising. Air New Zealand created "cranial billboards" in exchange for a round-trip ticket to New Zealand; thirty Los Angeles participants shaved their heads and walked around with an ad for the airline on their skulls. Some companies pay people to display more permanent body art. The Casa Sanchez restaurant in San Francisco gives free lunches for life to anyone who gets its logo tattooed on his or her body. The Daytona Cubs baseball team awards free season tickets for life to anyone who will tattoo the Cubs logo on his or her body.

—Solomon, Michael R. *Consumer Behavior*. 12th ed., Pearson, 2016, p. 557.

Paraphrase

In his book *Consumer Behavior*, Michael R. Solomon discusses a marketing trend called identity marketing. Citizens receive a financial incentive to promote a company in some way. For example, an advertising company paid people to briefly rename themselves after a popular game's lead character. An online music archive offered cash to parents who would name their baby after the company. The most widespread form of identity marketing occurs when people agree to have their head shaved or their body tattooed in exchange for some reward, such as a free flight, a lifetime supply of baseball tickets, or unlimited free lunches (557).

Summary

Mention source

Michael R. Solomon, in his book *Consumer Behavior*, discusses a marketing trend called identity marketing. Examples include some firms who pay people to adopt the company's name and companies who give rewards such as free lunches or sports tickets to those who agree to be tattooed with the business's name (557).

Quotation

In his book *Consumer Behavior*, Michael R. Solomon discusses identity marketing, which is "a promotional strategy whereby consumers alter some aspects of themselves to advertise for a branded product" (557).

GRAMMAR LINK
To find out more about using quotations, see Chapter 37.

How to Summarize and Paraphrase

When you paraphrase or summarize, you restate someone's ideas using your own words. The main difference between a paraphrase and a summary is the length. A paraphrase can be close to the same length as the original selection, but a summary is much shorter.

To paraphrase or summarize, do the following:

- Paraphrase if your audience needs detailed information about the subject.
- Summarize if the audience needs to know only general information.
- A summary is generally a maximum of 30 percent of the length of the original selection.
- Restate the main ideas using your own words. You can keep specialized words, common words, and names of people or places. However, find synonyms for other words, and use your own sentence structure.
- Maintain the original author's ideas and intent.
- Acknowledge the source. Mention the author or title of the work. When available, also include the page number.
- Proofread your writing to ensure that you have expressed the message in your own words.

Note: Chapter 16 contains more information about summary writing.

HINT: Should I Paraphrase, Summarize, or Quote?

In a research essay, include some quotations, but do not overwhelm your reader with other people's direct speech. Instead, sprinkle in very short paraphrases, summaries, and quotations, when needed, to back up your arguments.

MLA Style: In-Text Citations

17.10 Use MLA style.

When you paraphrase, summarize, or quote, you must cite the source in the body of the essay. You must also cite the source in a Works Cited page at the end of your essay. See the Hint box on page 274 to view the Works Cited page for the following quotations.

You can do in-text citations in two different ways. Note that these methods must be used with paraphrases, summaries, and quotations.

1. Cite the source in the sentence.

Mention the author's name in the sentence. If you are using a print source, then put the page number in parentheses at the end of the sentence.

Author's name   page number in parentheses
Virginia Postrel mentions that the crisis became a national obsession **(44)**.

For online sources, mention the author's name. No page number is necessary.

> **Michelle Singletary** mentions the misconception: "If you have a federal student loan, it can't be discharged in bankruptcy."

If an online source does not provide an author's name, mention the article's title or the website title in the sentence.

> According to **"Student Debt Assistance,"** too many students have extremely high credit card balances.

2. **Cite the source in parentheses following the sentence.**
   In parentheses after the selection, put the author's last name and the page number, with no punctuation in between.

> The crisis was on everyone's mind: "On the subject of credit, bad news
>   Name and page number
> sells" **(Postrel 44)**.

For online sources, put the author's last name in parentheses. For e-books, include the chapter number if possible.

> Students cannot simply refuse to pay a student loan from the federal government **(Singletary)**.

If the online source does not provide an author's name, write a short form of the title in parentheses.

> The student debt load is worrisome: "Today, the average time it takes to retire undergraduate loans is 19.7 years" **("Student")**.

GRAMMAR LINK
To find out more about writing titles, see page 480 in Chapter 37.

HINT: Quoting from a Secondary Source

Some works include quotations from other people. If an author is quoted in a secondary source, then put the abbreviation qtd. in, meaning "quoted in," in parentheses.

> Hillel Black describes a "consumer credit explosion that makes the population explosion seem small" (qtd. in Postrel 45).

See Chapter 37 for more information about using quotations.

Practice 2

Read the next selection and then write a paraphrase, a summary, and a direct quotation. Remember to acknowledge the source. If you are unsure about how to punctuate a quotation, refer to pages 470–471 in Chapter 37.

Original Selection

Although fewer Americans are smoking (down to about 25 percent from over 40 percent in the sixties), women and teenagers are actually smoking more than before. This is alarming news when one considers the toxic nature of nicotine: In the 1920s and 1930s, it was used as an insecticide and is considered to be highly toxic and fast acting. Although the amount of nicotine in a cigarette is low, first-time smokers often experience nausea as a result of the toxic effects after just a few puffs.

—Ciccarelli, Saundra K. *Psychology*. Pearson, 2009, pp. 148–149.

1. Write a paraphrase.

_____

_____

_____

_____

_____

_____

2. Write a summary.

_____

_____

_____

_____

3. Write a direct quotation.

_____

_____

_____

Practice 3

Practice identifying plagiarism. Read the following selection, and then determine if the paraphrase and summaries contain plagiarized information. Check for copied words or phrases, and also determine if the source is properly mentioned.

Original Selection

Having children can affect marital satisfaction. Studies show that parents report lower levels of satisfaction compared to nonparents. Mothers of infants, however, show the greatest difference in marital contentment when compared to women with no children at all. In general, the data show that satisfaction for both men and women decreases after the birth of the first child. Researchers suggest that this is, in large part, due to conflicts that come about from parenting and decreased levels of personal freedom. Children demand attention and force a shift in roles from husband/wife to father/mother. Regardless of the form of the study, parents exhibit lower levels of a sense of well-being while expressing more frequent negative emotions than do peers who are without children.

—Carl, John D. *Think: Social Problems*. 2nd ed., Pearson, 2013, p. 219.

1. **Paraphrase**

   In *Think: Social Problems*, John D. Carl writes that parents have a lower rate of marital happiness than couples without children. Mothers of infants show the greatest difference in marital happiness, perhaps because there are many conflicts that are caused by the presence of children. For instance, children demand attention and couples experience a shift in roles from spouses to parents. Also, parents have decreased levels of personal freedom. They express more frequent negative emotions than nonparents (219).

   Is this an example of plagiarism? yes _____ no _____

   Why? _____

2. **Summary**

   In *Think: Social Problems*, John D. Carl writes that childless couples are actually more satisfied than those with children. The decline in happiness may partially be due to the stresses involved in parenting. Mothers and fathers see their liberty eroded as they expend a lot of time and energy taking care of their offspring (219).

   Is this an example of plagiarism? yes _____ no _____

   Why? _____

   _____

3. **Summary**

   Studies show that parents do not feel as content as nonparents, mainly because there are many stresses involved in raising children. Mothers and fathers have a lot of restrictions on their personal time, and their role as spouse is taken over by the role of caretaker. Thus, they have a more pessimistic outlook than child-free couples.

   Is this an example of plagiarism? yes _____ no _____

   Why? _____

MLA: Preparing a Works Cited List

An MLA-style Works Cited list appears at the end of a research essay. It gives readers details about each source from which you have borrowed material to write your essay. Works Cited is not the same as a running bibliography, which lists all of the sources you consulted while you were researching your essay topic. In a Works Cited list, include only works that you have quoted, paraphrased, or summarized.

To prepare a Works Cited list, follow these basic guidelines.

1. A Works Cited list always starts on a new page. Put your name and page number in the upper right-hand corner, as you do on all other pages of the essay.
2. Write "Works Cited" at the top of the page and center it. Do not italicize it, underline it, or put quotation marks around it.
3. List each source alphabetically, using the author's last name.
4. Indent the second line and all subsequent lines of each entry five spaces.
5. Double-space all lines.

Parts of a Works Cited Reference

A work cited reference has the following parts.

1. Author	Complete last name, first name
2. Title of Source:	
Title of short work	"Article" or "Short Story"
Title of long work	*Book* or *Magazine* or *Website Name*
3. Container (information to identify the location of the source)	
–Title of container where the source can be found	Title of *Book, Series, Journal,* or *Website*
–Other contributors	Edited by, Translated by, Illustrated by, Adapted by, Directed by, and Narrated by
–Version	2nd ed., 3rd ed., or Updated ed.
–Volume and issue numbers	Vol. 8, no. 4
–Publisher	Complete Name of Company or Organization (unless the website name is essentially the same as the publisher's name)
–Date of publication	2016
–Time of publication for a Webpage	12:34 a.m.
–Page number(s) in print sources	p. 21 or pp. 419–422
–Website URL (omit the http://) or digital object identifier (DOI)	

EXAMPLE

> Miller, Barbara. *Cultural Anthropology in a Globalizing World.*
> 4th ed., Pearson, 2017, pp. 205–243.

Sample MLA-Style Works Cited Entries

The following are a few sample entries for various publications. The *MLA Handbook for Writers of Research Papers* has a complete list of sample entries. As you look at the samples, notice how they are punctuated.

Model Entries

BOOKS

> comma   period   period   comma   comma   period
> Last name, First name. *Title of Book.* edition, Publisher, Year.

One author

> Carl, John D. *Think: Social Problems.* 2nd ed., Pearson, 2013.

Two authors

After the first author's last and first name, write the first and last name of the second author. Write *and* before the second author name.

> Wade, Carole, and Carol Tavris. *Psychology.* 12th ed., Pearson, 2016.

Three or more authors

Put the first author's name followed by *et al.*, which means "and others."

> Manza, Jeff, et al. *The Sociology Project 2.0.* Pearson, 2016.

Editor instead of an author

Write the editor's name followed by *editor*.

> Gansworth, Eric, editor. *Sovereign Bones: New Native American Writing.*
> Nation, 2007.

Two or more books by the same author

Write the author's name in the first entry only. In subsequent entries, type three hyphens followed by a period. Then add the title.

> Angelou, Maya. *I Know Why the Caged Bird Sings.* Random House, 1969.
> ---. *Mother: A Cradle to Hold Me.* Random House, 2006.

A work in an anthology

For articles or essays taken from an anthology or edited collection, mention the author and title of the article first. Then write the anthology's title followed by *edited by* and the name of the editor. End with the publisher, year, and page numbers of the piece you are citing.

> Weaskus, Jeanette. "A Ghost Dance for Words." *Sovereign Bones: New Native American Writing*, edited by Eric Gansworth, Nation, 2007, pp. 129–134.

A previously published article in a collection

Some collections give information about a previously published article on the page where the article appears. After the title of the work, include the date of the original publication. Then include the title of the collection.

> Buchenwald, Art. "The Hydrogen Bomb Lobby." 1981. *Controversy: Issues for Reading and Writing*, edited by Judith J. Pula, et al., 3rd ed., Pearson, 2005, pp. 178–180.

A book in a series

If the book is part of a series, then end your citation with the series name (but do not italicize it or set it off in any way).

> Fiorina, Morris P., et al., editors. *Culture War?* 3rd ed., Pearson, 2011. Great Questions in Politics.

Encyclopedia and dictionary

When encyclopedias and dictionaries list items alphabetically, you can omit volume and page numbers. It is sufficient to list the edition and year of publication.

> "Democracy." *New Oxford American Dictionary*. 3rd ed., 2016.

PERIODICALS

> Last name, First name. "Title of Article." *Title of Magazine, Newspaper, or Journal*, volume, number, date, pages.

Note: If the pages are not consecutive, put the first page number and a plus sign (81+).

Newspaper article

> Gillis, Justin. "In Zika Epidemic, a Warning on Climate Change." *The New York Times*, 21 Feb. 2016, pp. 6–7.

Magazine article

> Goodell, Jeff. "The Rise of Intelligent Machines." *Rolling Stone*, 10 Mar. 2016, pp. 44–51.

Editorial

Put the editor's name first. If the editorial is unsigned, begin with the title. Put "Editorial" after the title.

> "Gun Ownership Does Not Make Women Safer." Editorial, *Boston Globe*, 10 Feb. 2016, p. A19.

Journal article

> Seligman, Martin. "The American Way of Blame." *APA Monitor*, vol. 29, no. 7, 1998, p. 97.

ELECTRONIC (INTERNET) SOURCES

When using a source published on the Internet, include as much of the following information as you can find. Keep in mind that some sites do not contain complete information. Put a comma after the publisher or sponsor. **Include the complete URL address** or DOI (digital object identifier) of scholarly articles. Leave out "http://" from the URL address and end the citation with a period.

> Last name, First name. "Title of Article." *Title of Site* or *Online Publication*, Publisher or Sponsor (if available), Date, URL or DOI.

Personal website article

> Winterson, Jeannette. "Gnomon." *Jeannette Winterson*, 31 Jul. 2015, jeanettewinterson.com/category/stories/.

E-Book

Format the e-book reference like you would if it were a print version, but add the URL.

> Heywood, Ian, et al. *An Introduction to Geographical Information Systems*. 4th ed., Pearson, 2011, *Amazon Digital Services*, www.amazon.ca/Introduction-Geographical-Information-Systems-4th/dp/027372259X.

Online newspaper article

> Macdonald, Nancy. "Canada's Prisons are the 'New Residential Schools.'" *Maclean's*, Rogers Digital Media, 18 Feb. 2016, www.macleans.ca/news/canada/canadas-prisons-are-the-new-residential-schools/.

> Sisson, Paul. "Flue Caseload Spikes in San Diego County." *San Diego Union-Tribune*, 17 Feb. 2016, 5:50 p.m., www.sandiegouniontribune.com/news/2016/feb/17/flu-week6-spike/.

Online magazine article

> Alos-Ferrer, C., et al. "Inertia and Decision Making." *Frontiers in Psychology*, vol. 7, no. 169, 16 Feb. 2016, PMC, doi: 10.3389/fpsyg.2016.00169.

Online dictionary

"Prescient." *Dictionary.com*, 26 Apr. 2016, www.dictionary.com/browse/
    prescient.

Web-only article

Leonard, Andrew. "America Favors the Rich." *Salon*, 28 Aug. 2012, www
    .salon.com/2012/08/28/the_class_warfare_trap/.

No listed author

If the site does not list an author's name, begin with the title of the article.

"Mass Layoff Summary." *Bureau of Labor Statistics*, 13 May 2013, www
    .bls.gov/news.release/mslo.nr0.htm.

OTHER TYPES OF SOURCES
Film or online video

For a film, include the names of the most relevant contributors to the project. For
instance, you could include the name of the the director and/or main performers.
Also mention the studio and the year of release. For an online video, include the
website link.

Note: If the video is long, include the exact time of the video that you are
referencing in your in-text citation.

Batman v Superman: Dawn of Justice. Directed by Zack Snyder,
    performance by Ben Affleck, Warner Bros. Pictures, 2016.

"A New Direction on Drugs." *60 Minutes.* Interview by Scott Pelley,
    CBSnews, 13 Dec. 2015, www.cbsnews.com/news/60-minutes-a-new-
    direction-on-drugs-2/.

Radio or television program

Include the segment title, title of the series, creator, season, episode, and date.

"The Real Killer." *The Catch*, created by Jennifer Schuur and Helen
    Gregory, performance by Mireille Enos, season 1, episode 2,
    Shondaland ABC Studios, 2016.

Sound recording

Include the name of the performer or band, the title of the song, the title of the
CD, the name of the recording company, and the year of release. If it is a digital
source, include the URL.

Beyoncé. "Daddy Lessons." *Lemonade*, Beyoncé Knowles, 2016, iTunes.
    apple.com/us/album/lemonade/id1107429221.

Social Media

For a tweet, copy the full text and place in quotation marks. For a Facebook post, just use the first line of the post as your title. Include the time of the posting as well as the date.

> Last name, First name (or in a Tweet, the user name). "Entire tweet or first few words of Facebook update." *Twitter* or *Facebook*, Date posted, Time viewed, URL.

@StLouisBlues. "Thanks to all our fans for making 2015–16 another incredible season." *Twitter*, 27 May 2016, 10:00 a.m., twitter.com/hashtag/WeAllBleedBlue?src=hash&lang=en.

@dottynixon. "For my next writing project, finally got around to reading the Canadian Constitution. Funny what work you put off." *Twitter*, 15 Oct. 2017, 10:15 a.m., twitter.com/dottynixon.

Paranjape, Meghana. "Monkeying around in the forest . . . ." *Facebook*, 30 Mar. 2015, 2:18 p.m., www.facebook.com/meghana.paranjape?fref=ts.

HINT: Placement and Order of Works Cited

The Works Cited list should be at the end of the research paper. List sources in alphabetical order of the authors' last names. If there is no author, put the title in the alphabetized list. The example is a Works Cited page for the quotations listed on pages 265–266.

Works Cited

Postrel, Virginia. "The Case for Debt." *The Atlantic,* Nov. 2008, pp. 44–47.

Singletary, Michelle. "The Color of Money." *The Washington Post,* 28 Apr. 2016, www.washingtonpost.com/people/michelle-singletary.

"3 Unexpected Stats Proving College Loans Confound Both Students and Administrators." *American Student Assistance,* 26 Apr. 2016, www.asa.org/for-partners/schools/content-pages/3-unexpected-stats-proving-college-loans-confound-both-students-and-administrators/.

Practice 4

Imagine that you are using the following sources in a research paper. Arrange the sources for a Works Cited list using MLA style. Remember to place the items in alphabetical order.

- You use a definition of "stress" from the online dictionary Dictionary.com. The year of publication is 2016. You accessed the site today.

- You quote from the 12th edition of the textbook *Society: The Basics* by John J. Macionis. The book was published by Pearson in 2017.

- You use statistics from the article "Sleeping Disorder Statistics." It is on the website *Statistic Brain Research Institute*. The data on the website is from April 12, 2015. There is no author. The URL is www.statisticbrain.com/sleeping-disorder-statistics/.

- You quote from the article "Is Stress Contagious?" by Beth Levine from the magazine *O, The Oprah Magazine*. The article is on page 81 in the June 2014 issue.

- You quote from the article "How Stress Harms the Heart" by Alexandra Sifferlin. It appeared in *Time*. It was published on March 24, 2016. The URL is time.com/4270655/how-stress-harms-the-heart/.

Works Cited

_____

_____

_____

_____

_____

_____

_____

_____

The Writer's Desk: Write a Research Essay

Write your research essay. After you write your first draft, revise and edit it. Remember to double-space your essay and include a Works Cited page.

Sample Research Essay

17.11 Review a sample research essay.

Title Pages and Outlines

Although MLA does not insist on an outline for a research essay, your instructor may request one.

Outline

Thesis: For the Armed Forces to be battle ready and effective, women should be retained only for combat support roles and not for direct combat engagements.

I.   Women acquire combat training related injuries more than men.
   A. Women have a greater risk of MSK injury than men.
   B. Such injuries can cause a loss in duty time.
   C. High level of injury of female combatants may cause problems for entire unit.
II. Women cannot meet the same physical training standards as required by men.
   A. Congress is reviewing standards to establish gender-neutral tests.
   B. Very few women qualified for the first phase of the course at Army Ranger School.
   C. Female marines cannot equal men in training performance.
III. Women are essential to combat missions in their combat support roles.
   A. They are exposed to similar danger and stress as men.
   B. Women participate in meaningful actions.
   C. Women have special and useful skills.

The Research Essay

Write your last name and page number in the top right corner of each page.

Double-space your identification information.

Center the title without underlining, italics, quotation marks, or boldface type.

Nuez 1

John Cary Nuez

Professor Travis Lockwood

English 102

May 26, 2017

Women in Combat

For over six decades, women have been joining the U.S.
military. In 2013, the Department of Defense rescinded the rule

Nuez 2

that prohibited women from serving in the combat divisions, thus exposing more and more women to direct combat environments. The U.S. Department of Defense reported that over 14,000 assignments in ground combat units were opened to women in 2015 (Roulo). In his report, David Burrelli provides a definition of ground combat: "Direct ground combat is engaging an enemy on the ground with individual or crew served weapons while being exposed to hostile fire and to probability of physical contact with hostile force's personnel" (4). Despite the fact that there are more positions for women on the frontline, critics have expressed concerns about female participation in direct combat. Indeed, for the Armed Forces to be battle ready and effective, women should be retained only for combat support roles and not for direct combat engagements.

First, women acquire combat training–related injuries more than men. It is true that some women are very strong and fit, and combat training may prepare such women to face a high level of physical demands. However, women face a greater risk of being injured than men. A study by the United Kingdom's Ministry of Defence on Musculoskeletal injury (MSK) shows that "women with the same aerobic fitness and strength as men are still likely to have a greater risk of MSK injury due to the inherent differences in their physiology and anatomy" (*Women* B1). Such injuries can cause a loss in duty time, thereby affecting training. Additionally, if many female combatants suffer from training injuries, then this could cause problems for the entire unit. For instance, the unit may not be able to deploy if several members are injured.

Furthermore, some studies show that women cannot meet the same physical training standards as required by men.

Annotations (right margin):

- Double-space your essay.
- Cite the source of a paraphrase.
- You can introduce a quotation with a complete sentence.
- End your introduction with your thesis statement.
- You can acknowledge opposing viewpoints and then refute them.
- You can integrate a quotation into a sentence.
- If the author is not known, put the first word of the title in parentheses.

Cite the source
of summarized
information.

You can identify the
source in the phrase
introducing the
quotation.

It is not necessary
to document your
common knowledge.

Include the page
number of a print
source.

The military has been encouraging women to participate in training courses required for direct combat duty. Only twenty-nine women took part in the Infantry Officer Course but none graduated, and as of May 2015, of the over one hundred women who participated in the elite Army Ranger School Course, only twenty qualified for the initial part of the course (Kamarck 18). In addition, reporter Richard Leiby in *The Seattle Times* writes, "It's official. Men rule at pullups. Most female Marines can't even do three lousy pullups!" The physical difference between men and women could potentially affect the output required of military personnel in combat engagements. In 2016, the U.S. military includes women in all units, and the U.S. Congress is reviewing how to establish standards for physical testing that are gender neutral. Despite the military's efforts to adjust the physical standards for women, the result of failed training completion is an indication that women are not be able to perform at the same level as men in physical endurance.

Women are essential to the combat mission with their role in combat support. Even though women serve in the support capacity, they are still exposed to as much danger as men, such as vulnerability to live fire or explosives. And like their male counterparts, women soldiers may also feel the long-term effects of combat missions, such as posttraumatic stress disorder (PTSD). Morris and Maisto state, "Wartime experiences often cause soldiers intense and disabling combat stress that persists long after they have left the battlefield" (406). In their supporting role, women would participate in meaningful action and do essential service to aid those on the front line. Women should not feel as if they are being sheltered because they would be subject to equal risk as male soldiers. Instead, women should

Nuez 4

be proud of their contributions in combat support. Referring to women's capabilities, Col. David Fivecoat, commander of the Airborne and Ranger Training Brigade, says, "You may not be able to hump the extra weight because you're a small person, but if you can do a great job planning, or going to get the water, or if you're seen as value-added—that's how you do well . . . " (qtd. in Mulrine). Most men in the military acknowledge that women are a valuable asset when it comes to winning a war.

Taking into consideration women's potential for injuries and their lower level of performance and training outcomes, they do not seem suited for direct combat roles. Women have been instrumental in the effectiveness of the military for a long time, and their participation continues to be essential in times of war. Women have demonstrated their excellence and their unique skills, and there is nothing more for them to prove. Women should be proud of their work in the military.

> Three spaced periods indicate that part of the quotation has been deleted.

> Use "qtd. in" to show that the quotation appeared in a secondary source.

> End with a quotation, prediction, or suggestion.

Nuez 5

Works Cited

Burrelli, David F. *Women in Combat: Issues for Congress.* Congressional Research Service, 9 May 2013, *Library of Congress,* www.dtic.mil/cgi-bin/GetTRDoc?AD=ADA590333.

Kamarck, Kirsty N. *Women in Combat: Issues for Congress.* Congressional Research Service, 3 Dec. 2015, *Library of Congress,* fas.org/sgp/crs/natsec/R42075.pdf.

Leiby, Richard. "Why Most Female Marines Struggle to Pass Pullup Test." *The Seattle Times,* 12 Jan. 2014, www.seattletimes.com/life/wellness/why-most-female-marines-struggle-to-pass-pullup-test/.

Morris, Charles G. and Albert A. Maisto. *Understanding Psychology.* 11th ed., Pearson, 2016.

> Put the Works Cited list on a separate page.

> Center the Works Cited heading.

> List sources in alphabetical order.

> Double-space throughout, and indent the second line of each source.

Nuez 6

Mulrine, Anna. "Breaking Military's Ultimate Glass Ceiling?: Women Start Ranger Training." *The Christian Science Monitor*, 30 Apr. 2015, www.csmonitor.com/USA/ Military/2015/0430/Breaking-military-s-ultimate-glass- ceiling-Women-start-Ranger-training.

Roulo, Claudette. "Defense Department Expands Women's Combat Role." *DoD News*, U.S. Department of Defense, 24 Jan. 2013, archive.defense.gov/news/newsarticle .aspx?id=119098.

Women in Ground Close Combat (GCC) Review Paper. United Kingdom Ministry of Defence, 1 Dec. 2014, www.gov.uk/ government/uploads/system/uploads/attachment_data/ file/389575/20141218_WGCC_Findings_Paper_Final.pdf.

Practice 5

Answer the following questions by referring to the research essay.

1. How many magazines or books were used as sources? _____

2. How many Internet articles were used as sources? _____

3. When the student used a quotation that appeared as a quotation in another source, how did he show that fact? (See the fourth paragraph.)

_____

4. In the Works Cited page, how many sources do not mention an author? _____

5. On the Works Cited page, are the sources listed in alphabetical order? yes _____ no _____

Indicate if the following sentences are true (T) or false (F). Look at the Works Cited page to answer each question. If the sentence is false, write a true statement under it.

6. The second row of each citation should be indented. T F

_____

7. The title of articles should be set off with italics.   T   F

_____

8. Place periods after the author's first name and the title of the work.   T   F

_____

9. For Internet sources, no dates are necessary.   T   F

_____

10. For Internet sources, include the URL.   T   F

_____

HINT: APA Website

To get some general information about some basic style questions, you can view the APA's website. Use the menu on the left side of the page to direct you to specific style questions and answers.

On the same website, there is a link to information about online or "electronic" sources. Because the information about online sources is continually being updated, the site has comprehensive information about the latest citation methods.

The Writer's Room

Writing Activity 1

Write a research paper about one of the following topics. Ask your instructor what reference style you should use. Put a Works Cited page at the end of your assignment.

1. Write about a contemporary issue that is in the news.
2. Write about any issue in your career choice or field of study.

Writing Activity 2

Write a research paper about one of the following topics. First, brainstorm questions about your topic and find a guiding research question. Then follow the process of writing a research essay.

Affirmative action	Health-care reform
Animal testing	Holistic healing
Assisted suicide	Home schooling
Attention-deficit disorder	Immigration
Body image	Legitimate vs. fake news
Censorship of the Internet	Mandatory drug testing
Childhood obesity	News media and bias
Consequences of war	Prison reform
Date rape	Privacy and the Internet
Executive salaries	Technology and pollution (e-waste)
Fertility treatments or planned parenthood	Teen pregnancy
Foreign adoptions	Tobacco industry
Gambling	Violence in the media
Genetically modified food	Volunteer work
Government-sponsored gambling	Youth gangs

Checklist: Research Essay

When you plan a research essay, ask yourself these questions.

❑ Have I narrowed my topic?

❑ Have I created a guiding research question?

❑ Are my sources reliable?

❑ Have I organized my notes?

❑ Have I integrated source information using quotations, paraphrases, and summaries?

❑ Have I correctly documented my in-text or parenthetical citations?

❑ Have I correctly prepared and punctuated my Works Cited page?

18 The Response Essay

18.1 Respond to film
and literature.

Music critics respond to the skill of the performer and the quality of the acoustics.
They also notice the concert venue and the costumes. You take similar elements
into consideration when you interpret works of film and literature.

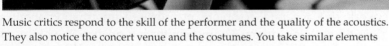

Writers' Exchange

Work with a partner. Discuss films or stories that you love. Make a "top-five" list.

Writing a Response Essay

18.1 Respond to film and literature.

As a college student, you are often asked to state your opinion, to interpret issues,
and to support your ideas. In some of your courses, your instructor may ask you to
respond to another work with a **response essay**, which can also be called a **report**.

Parts of a Response Essay

When writing such an essay, include a brief summary of the original work,
showing that you have a clear understanding of it. Then explain your reactions
to the work. Review the four parts of a response essay: Introduction, Summary,
Responses, and Conclusion.

INTRODUCTION

In the introductory paragraph, identify the source of the work you are analyzing. For instance, if you are writing about a print piece, such as a book or an e-magazine, identify the author, title, and publication date. If you are responding to a film, identify the title, director, and date of release. You can complete the introduction with general background information about the work. End the introduction with your thesis, which includes the topic and your controlling idea.

SUMMARY

Write a **brief synopsis** of the work. Include the main points, and do not go into great detail. Summarize the work so that readers can clearly understand the main storyline. At this point, do not make any personal value judgments. Simply state what happened. (To learn more about summary writing, see Chapter 16, "Summarizing".)

REACTIONS

After the summary, include several reaction paragraphs. Remember that each body paragraph should develop one main point. (Review the model response essays on the next pages and notice that each body paragraph has a single focus.) To find ideas for your reaction paragraphs, you can ask yourself the following questions.

- Is the subject relevant to any of my academic studies? Does it relate to topics we have discussed in this class or in another course?

- Does the work give accurate, complete, or unbiased information about a subject? Does the author or filmmaker present the information in a balanced way? Or is the point of view somewhat slanted?

- Can I relate to the characters? What do they tell me about human nature?

- Does the work have technical merits? Does the author have a vivid writing style? Does the film have beautiful camera work or impressive special effects?

- What is the work's message? Has it changed my understanding about an issue? Is it related to a real-world problem?

- Would I recommend the work to other people? If so, why?

   Note: Always support your reactions with specific examples.

CONCLUSION

Sum up your main points. End with a recommendation or a final thought.

Follow the Writing Process

When preparing your response essay, remember to follow the writing process.

- Use exploring strategies to generate ideas.

- Organize your ideas in distinct paragraphs that each have a central focus. Ensure that each body paragraph has unity, adequate support, and coherence.

- Back up your reactions with specific details from the work. Avoid vague statements such as *I like the movie* or *The book is interesting*. Instead, explain why you like the work or find it interesting, and support your point with details and examples.

- Edit your work, and correct any errors.

Include Quotations

You may decide to include direct quotations in your summary and your reaction paragraphs. Ensure that any quotations include a page reference, if available. Also ensure that you punctuate quotations correctly. (For more information about using quotations, see pages 470–473 in Chapter 37.)

HINT: Citing the Work

Your instructor might ask you to cite the work at the end of your response essay. For instance, the two response essays in this chapter would have the following MLA "Works Cited" information.

Works Cited

Star Wars: Episode VII - The Force Awakens. Directed by J. J. Abrams, performance by Harrison Ford, Mark Hamill, and Carrie Fisher, Lucasfilm, 2015.

Hemingway, Ernest. *For Whom the Bell Tolls*. Scribner, 1995.

For more information about MLA guidelines, see Chapter 17. For information about APA Guidelines, see Appendix 2 on pages 609–613.

A SAMPLE RESPONSE TO A FILM

College student Yarrum Seib wrote the following response to one of his favorite films. Notice how he structured his response.

Star Wars VII: The Force Awakens

1. In 2015, a popular sci-fi series returned with *Star Wars: Episode VII - The Force Awakens*. I was never a huge *Star Wars* fan, but I lined up on a drizzly night to see the latest installment of the franchise. It was so difficult to get tickets that I had to go to the midnight screening. Luckily, I had no problems staying awake. Directed by J. J. Abrams, who had also directed *Lost*, a popular TV series, *The Force Awakens* easily kept my attention. The entertaining film contains

Introduction
- Begins with general background information about the film
- Identifies the film's title, release date, and director.

Thesis statement
- Expresses the main focus of the essay

Summary
- Briefly describes the film's main events
- Uses the present tense to summarize the story

Reaction
- Responds to the film's characters

- Supports the topic sentence with specific examples

Reaction
- Responds to the film's visual effects

familiar *Star Wars* characters, stunning visual effects, and a reminder that good will prevail over evil.

2.   The movie opens thirty years after the death of the wicked Emperor. An evil leader is still intent on destroying the New Republic (formerly the Alliance). The mysterious and frightening Supreme Leader Snoke leads the First Order and has absolute command over his troops. "There's been an awakening. Have you felt it?" Snoke asks his second in command, setting the stage for the Order's evil plans. Their weapon of mass destruction is Star Killer Base. The Resistance is a group of soldiers and pilots who try to stop the First Order. Both the Order and the Resistance are desperate to find Luke Skywalker, so much of *Star Wars VII* revolves around the search for him.

3.   The movie has colorful characters from previous episodes and some great new heroes. Carrie Fisher returns as General (formerly Princess) Leia Organa. Feisty and determined, she leads the Resistance in its attempt to defend the New Republic. "Chewie, we're home!" exclaims the heroic pilot Han Solo as he and his long-suffering sidekick co-pilot Chewbacca thrill audiences with their first on-screen appearance since *Return of the Jedi* in 1983. Leia and Han have some of the most moving scenes as they affectionately tease each other. Also reprising their roles are the lovable robotic duo C3PO and R2D2. Of course, Luke Skywalker returns as an older bearded recluse. New heroes are Rey, a strong female character who is a talented but tormented scavenger, and Finn, a conflicted ex-soldier. Although Finn was raised to be an aggressive stormtrooper for the First Order, he flees after witnessing the brutality of his peers. Viewers also meet Poe, the best pilot in the Resistance—after Han Solo, of course. Poe's adorable robot sidekick BB8 also plays an important role.

4.   Amazing sets and special effects contribute to the believability of *The Force Awakens*. The filmmakers built massive sets and detailed models. Han Solo's space craft, the Millennium Falcon, may be creaking with age, but it can still out-maneuver the Order's new and improved TIE fighters. There is no shortage of CGI fireworks, especially during the battle scenes. For example, the final light saber duel, with flares of red and blue light, is riveting.

5.   The movie continues the tradition of pitting good against evil; however, it throws in a surprise twist. The good characters—particularly Han, Leia, and Rey—are honest, have pure motivations, and remember to use the higher power of the "force." Snoke, General Hux, and Kylo Ren are ugly representations of evil. Snoke is a skeletal monster. Hux is a Hitler-type dictator who screams and spits at his

troops. And Ren, a depressed warrior in an iron mask, flies into violent rages. But for the first time in *Star Wars'* history, a faceless stormtrooper has a human face. Finn, feeling morally conflicted, refuses an order to kill defenseless villagers. When he joins the Resistance, he becomes one of the good guys. Perhaps Finn's rejection of evil will spark a wider rebellion of stormtroopers in later sequels.

Reaction
- Reflects on the film's depiction of good and evil

6.   *The Force Awakens* is a worthy addition to the *Star Wars* legacy. The entertaining film combines a strong storyline, a colorful array of old and new characters, and dazzling effects. It also breaks new ground by showing the compassionate side of a stormtrooper, allowing viewers to reflect on the moral conflicts that soldiers face. This is a great movie even for those who are not science fiction fans.

Conclusion
- Sums up the film's strongest points and makes a recommendation

A SAMPLE RESPONSE TO A NOVEL

College student Diego Pelaez responded to the novel *For Whom the Bell Tolls*. Review how he structured his response.

Lessons from *For Whom the Bell Tolls*

1.   Robert Jordan says to himself, "You have only one thing to do, and you must do it" (45). He plans the strategic destruction of a bridge in Ernest Hemingway's novel *For Whom the Bell Tolls*. The story, published in 1940, contains a relevant message. The novel follows Robert Jordan, an American university teacher and weapons expert, as he fights with Spanish republican forces against the fascist army led by Francisco Franco. *For Whom the Bell Tolls* asks difficult, relevant questions about the necessity of war, and it graphically depicts the consequences.

Introduction
- Begins with general background information about the novel.
- Identifies the title and date of publication.

Thesis statement
- Expresses the main focus of the essay.

2.   The novel opens with Jordan planning a strategic demolition of a bridge. The rest of the novel explains the preparations required for the risky operation. Jordan is a cold military strategist. He falls in love with Maria, a beautiful young woman. She had been brutalized by fascist forces and was then rescued and nurtured back to health by the guerrilla band. Pablo, the previous leader of the band, makes it clear that he wants nothing to do with the blowing up of the bridge, and his refusal is considered a sign of cowardice. In the meantime, Jordan's love for Maria and his growing loyalty to the guerrillas make his mission more difficult. Knowing that the enemy forces are too numerous, Jordan's attack on the bridge becomes more and more doomed as the story progresses.

Summary
- Briefly describes the book's main events.
- Uses the present tense to narrate actions that happen within the story.

Reaction
- Responds to the book's depiction of war.
- Indicates in parentheses the page of each direct quotation.

3. The honest depictions of war in the novel are greatly moving and at times horrifying. For example, there is a description of an earlier attack by Pablo's band. Pablo orders all the fascists to be brutally whipped, and members of his band make fun of their fascist captives. "Should we send to the house for thy spectacles?" (115) the crowd asks Don Guillermo, one of the fascist sympathizers. Then they attack him with flails (instruments used for cutting down grain), and they throw him over a cliff. The scene shows the excessive brutality involved in war, even wars that can be justified.

Reaction
- Responds to the characters.

4. A particularly sympathetic character in this novel is Robert Jordan. At first, Jordan views the guerrilla band at his disposal as means to an end. His priority is the mission more than the well-being of the guerrillas. However, as the story progresses, Jordan becomes conflicted. His love for Maria grows, and he realizes that he has something to live for. While lying beside Maria, "he held her, feeling she was all of life there was" (253).

5. The other characters are also diverse and fascinating. Pablo's wife, Pilar, is a voice of conscience, and she strongly condemns the treatment Don Guillermo receives. She says, "Nobody can tell me that such things as the killing of Don Guillermo in that fashion will not bring bad luck" (117). Also, the guerrilla band is a very likeable group, with a wise-cracking gypsy and the honorable old Anselmo, among others. Pledging allegiance to the cause, Anselmo says, "I am an old man who will live until I die" (19). Despite Jordan's growing affection for the group, he keeps planning the dangerous mission knowing that a lot of his new friends could die while carrying it out.

Support
- Provides specific examples to show that the characters are varied and interesting.

6. *For Whom the Bell Tolls* shows the horrors of war. The desire to drive the fascists out is seen as a worthy goal, even if there will be many deaths. However, the futility of war is also shown. Robert Jordan's single-minded determination becomes eroded by his newfound love and desire for life. As his death approaches, Jordan thinks, "The world is a fine place and worth fighting for, and I hate very much to leave it" (440).

Reaction
- Responds to one of the book's messages.

7. In the end, war is presented as neither good nor bad, but rather as a simple fact of life. In the final scene of the novel, after the attack on the bridge, Jordan falls and critically injures himself. He tells the rest of the group to move on. Jordan waits for the fascists to come up the path and tries to remain conscious long enough to go out in a blaze of glory. Jordan can "feel his heart beating against the pine needle floor of the forest" (444). Ultimately, this excitement is as much a reason for war as any ideals.

Conclusion
- Ends with a final insight about the book.

The Writer's Room

Write a response essay (or "report") about one of the following topics. Remember to include an introduction, a summary, and several paragraphs explaining your reaction to the work.

1. In an essay, respond to "The Veldt" on page 590.

2. Write about a short story, novel, or film of your choice.

Checklist: Response to a Literary Work or a Film

After you write your response, review the checklist at the end of the book. Also, ask yourself these questions:

❏ Have I considered my audience and purpose?

❏ In the introduction, have I identified the title, author, and date?

❏ Have I given a short summary of the work?

❏ Have I described my reactions to the work?

❏ Have I integrated specific quotations and examples?

❏ Have I summed up my main arguments in the conclusion?

Chapter 19 The Résumé and Letter of Application

LEARNING OBJECTIVES

19.1 Prepare a résumé.

19.2 Write a letter of application.

A menu can help you decide whether to try a new restaurant. In the same way, a well-written résumé and application letter can help an employer determine whether you are a good candidate for a job.

Writers' Exchange

Work with a partner and discuss your past work experience. Write down your job titles. Then brainstorm the duties you performed, skills you developed, or accomplishments you achieved. You can use the list of action verbs to get ideas.

EXAMPLE: Waiter—handled cash, interacted with customers, developed autonomy

Some action verbs

advertised	collaborated	facilitated	inspected	overhauled
assembled	compiled	forecasted	interacted	oversaw
assisted	coordinated	handled	managed	resolved
budgeted	evaluated	implemented	negotiated	served

Preparing a Résumé

19.1   Prepare a résumé.

The word *résumé* comes from a French word meaning "to summarize." Essentially, a résumé is a short summary of your work-related experience. Your résumé should be customized for each employer. Review the following example of a skills-focused résumé.

A Sample Résumé

TEANA BUTLER
9001 Naples Drive
Jacksonville, Florida 32211
Telephone: (904) 555-4567
E-mail: teana27@gmail.com

OBJECTIVE
Position as a respiratory therapist in a long-term care facility

QUALIFICATIONS SUMMARY
Experience with senior citizens
Knowledge of hospitality management
Strong teamwork and leadership skills
Computer skills (Word and Excel)

EDUCATION
Respiratory Therapy Diploma   **June 2017**
Concorde Career Institute, Jacksonville, Florida
Relevant courses: Ventilator and Airway Management / Home Respiratory Care

EXPERIENCE
Sunrise Care Facility, Jacksonville, FL   **2017 to present**
Cafeteria Manager

- Handle cash and calculate end-of-day sales
- Work well under high pressure
- Negotiate patiently with elderly residents
- Manage a team of three coworkers

Gray's Children's Camp, Orlando, FL   **Summer 2016**
Activities Coordinator

- Organized a variety of summer sports activities for ten-year-olds
- Settled disagreements and led children with gentle authority
- Provided one-on-one help to a child with special needs

Meals on Wheels, Jacksonville, FL   **April–June 2015**
Volunteer

- Helped prepare and deliver meals to seniors

*Include contact information but **not** your birthplace, birth date, nationality, or a personal photo.*

Summarize your most pertinent qualifications and skills.

Put the most recent schooling first. If you have more than a high school education, it is not necessary to list your high school.

Outline your most recent job experience. If you have not had any paying jobs, you could mention any volunteer work that you have done. For each job that you list, mention the tasks that you completed and the aptitudes you developed.

Ideally, your résumé should be only one page long. If you have extra space, you can end with Awards, Volunteer Work, or Activities.

It is not necessary to list references. Most employers ask for references at the interview stage.

HINT: Use Parallel Structure

When you describe your work experience, begin with parallel action verbs.

Not parallel	Parallel verbs
-greet customers	**-greeted** customers
-I took inventory	**-took** inventory
-handling cash	**-handled** cash

Practice 1

Refer to the sample résumé to answer the questions.

1. Should you write *Résumé* at the top of your résumé?

yes _____ no _____

2. In the résumé, where should you mention your strongest skills?

_____

_____

3. In what order should you list your work experience?
   a. from past to present
   b. from present to past

4. In the Experience section, should you use the word *I*?

yes _____ no _____

5. What information should you include in the Experience section? Choose the best answers.

   a. job title   d. salary
   b. boss's phone number   e. skills and accomplishments
   c. job dates (when you worked)   f. all of the above

Writing a Letter of Application

19.2   Write a letter of application.

Sometimes called a cover letter, a letter of application accompanies a résumé. It explains how you learned about the position and why you are a good candidate for the job. It complements your résumé and doesn't repeat it. In your letter, include specific examples to demonstrate why you are right for the job. Maintain a direct, confident tone. Remember that the letter provides a chance to demonstrate your communication skills.

Sample Letter of Application

Review the parts of the next letter.

Teana Butler
9001 Naples Drive
Jacksonville, FL 32211
(904) 555-4567
teana27@gmail.com

July 5, 2017

Alexia Anders
Cedars Long-Term Care Facility
225 Meadowland Boulevard
Jacksonville, FL 32101

Subject: Position as a respiratory therapist

Dear Ms. Anders:

I am applying for the position of respiratory therapist that was posted in the *Florida Times-Union*. I am completing my diploma in Respiratory Therapy and am very enthusiastic about a career in this field.

I have heard about your facility's strong reputation in elder care, and I believe that I could be a valuable asset to your team. In my recently completed courses at the Concorde Career Institute, I learned about ECGs, arterial blood gas analysis, pulmonary function testing, and NICU monitoring. In addition, my experience at a nursing home has taught me to show patience and empathy when communicating with elderly patients. Furthermore, I have strong teamwork skills. For example, in a protracted dispute over shifts, I was able to negotiate an agreement between my colleagues and defuse an unhappy workplace atmosphere. Within months of being hired, I was rewarded with the manager's position.

I would appreciate the opportunity to speak with you in detail about my qualifications. I am available for an interview at your convenience and could start work immediately. Thank you for your consideration.

Sincerely yours,

Teana Butler

Teana Butler

Sender's address
Capitalize street names. Put a comma between the city and state or country. Do not put a comma before the zip code.

Date
Put a comma between the full date and the year.

Recipient's address
Capitalize each word in a company name.

Subject line (optional)
Briefly state your reason for writing.

Salutation
Find the name of the recruiter or write the following:
• Dear Sir or Madam:
• Attention: Human Resources Manager

Introductory paragraph
Explain the position you are applying for. Also mention where you heard about the job.

Body
Sell yourself! Do not just repeat what is in your résumé. Explain how you meet or exceed the job's requirements, and highlight your strongest skills.

Conclusion
Mention the interview and end with polite thanks.

Closings
Some possible closings are *Yours truly* or *Respectfully yours*.

Letter Basics

When you write a letter of application, remember the following points:

- Be brief! Employers may receive large numbers of applications. Your letter should be no longer than four short paragraphs.

- Follow the standard business letter format. Most businesses use full block style, in which all elements of the letter are aligned with the left margin. Do not indent any paragraphs. Instead, leave an extra space between paragraphs.

- To make a favorable impression, ensure that your letter is free of grammar, spelling, or punctuation errors. Proofread your letter very carefully before you send it. If possible, ask someone else to look it over for you, too.

- Follow the prospective employer's directions for how to send your résumé and application letter (in person, by mail, by email, or through the company's online career portal).

HINT: Job Portals

Often, companies have an online career portal. Candidates log in and build résumés by filling in several fields. Even if you use the "résumé builder," most systems will still prompt you to upload a file with a proper résumé and application letter. Moreover, employers expect candidates to bring a printed copy of the résumé to an interview. So, despite automated digital résumé builders, it is still very important to know how to craft these documents.

Stick to basic typefaces and use minimal formatting. Design flourishes can make files large and difficult to transmit. Also, systems and software differ, so a document can end up looking different on the employer's screen than it does on yours.

Practice 2

Answer the following questions. Refer to the sample letter of application on page 294.

1. The date should be _____ the recipient's address.
   a. above   b. below

2. If you do not know the name of the person in human resources, how should you address your letter of application?

   _____

3. Should you place a comma at the end of each line in the recipient's address?

   yes _____ no _____

4. In a letter of application, why are the next closings inappropriate?

   a. Bye for now.   _____

   b. Please accept my most gracious sentiments.   _____

5. In the sample application letter, why would Teana avoid mentioning her job at the children's camp?

   _____

   _____

Practice 3

The next letter contains twelve errors. Correct six capitalization and six punctuation errors.

Joel Mazzotti
44 Kemp Hills Drive
Bear Creek TX 78744
Email: jmazz@gmail.com

May 14 2017

Scoles and Klein Law firm
10 Congress avenue
Austin, TX, 78701

Subject, Volunteer Position

Dear mr. Klein

I would like to volunteer in your legal office. I hope to become a lawyer one day, and I would like to be exposed to the environment in a legal firm. I am willing to answer phones or do any types of errands.

I am a first-year student at Austin Community College at 1212 Rio Grande street. I will be available weekday afternoons starting in june. You can contact me at (512) 555-4567.

Respectfully Yours

Joel Mazzotti

Joel Mazzotti

The Writer's Room

Résumé and Letter

Find a job listing in the newspaper, at an employment center, through an app, or on the Internet. Write a résumé and a letter of application.

Checklist: The Résumé and the Letter of Application

When you write a résumé or letter of application, ask yourself these questions:

❏ Have I used correct spelling and punctuation?

❏ In my résumé, have I included my work experience and my education beginning with the most recent?

❏ In my letter of application, have I indicated the position for which I am applying and where or how I heard about the job?

❏ Is my letter concise? Have I used standard English?

Part IV
Editing Handbook

When you speak, you have tools such as tone of voice and body language to help you express ideas. When you write, however, you have only words and punctuation to get your message across. If your writing includes errors in style, grammar, and punctuation, you may distract readers from the message, and they may focus on your inability to communicate clearly. Increase your chances of succeeding in your academic and professional life by writing in clear, standard English.

The chapters in this Editing Handbook can help you understand important grammar concepts and ensure that your writing is grammatically correct.

SECTION 1 Effective Sentences
THEME: Conflict

 CHAPTER 20 Subjects and Verbs in Simple Sentences

 CHAPTER 21 Sentence Combining

CHAPTER 22 Sentence Variety

SECTION 2 Common Sentence Errors
THEME: Urban Development

 CHAPTER 23 Fragments

 CHAPTER 24 Run-Ons

 CHAPTER 25 Faulty Parallel Structure

20 Subjects and Verbs in Simple Sentences

SECTION THEME: Conflict

Is violence learned or genetic? In this chapter, you learn about the sources of aggressive behavior.

LEARNING OBJECTIVES

20.1 Identify subjects.

20.2 Identify verbs.

Identifying Subjects

20.1 Identify subjects.

A **sentence** contains one or more subjects and verbs, and it expresses a complete thought. The **subject** tells you who or what the sentence is about.

- Subjects may be **singular** or **plural**. A subject can also be a **pronoun**.

  Detective Marcos will interview the suspects.
  Many **factors** cause people to break laws.
  It is an important case.

- A **compound subject** contains two or more subjects joined by *and*, *or*, or *nor*.

  Reporters and **photographers** were outside the prison gates.

- Sometimes a **gerund** (*-ing* form of the verb) is the subject of a sentence.

  Listening is an important skill.

299

HINT: *Here* and *There*

Here and *There* are not subjects. In sentences that begin with *Here* or *There*, the subject follows the verb.

There are several **ways** to find a criminal.

Here is an interesting **brochure** about the police academy.

How to Find the Subject

To find the subject, ask yourself *who* or *what* the sentence is about. The subject is the noun or pronoun or the complete name of a person or organization.

The **Federal Bureau of Investigation** is a large organization. **It** has branches in every state.

When identifying the subject, you can ignore words that describe the noun.

> adjectives   subject
> The pompous and rude **sergeant** left the room.

Practice 1

Circle the subject in each sentence. Be careful because sometimes there is more than one subject.

EXAMPLE: A behavioral (study) examines genetics and behavior.

1. Political scientist Rose McDermott co-authored a study on the "warrior gene" at Brown University.

2. She found that individuals with this gene were more likely to display aggressive or violent behavior.

3. More than seventy volunteers participated in the study.

4. People with the warrior gene and those without the gene were separated into two groups.

5. A vocabulary test and money were given to students.

6. Punishing other participants with hot sauce was encouraged.

Prepositional Phrases

A **preposition** is a word that links nouns, pronouns, and phrases to other words in a sentence. It expresses a relationship based on movement or position. A **prepositional phrase** is made up of a preposition and its object (a noun or a pronoun).

Because the object of a preposition is a noun, it may look like a subject. **However, the object in a prepositional phrase is never the subject of the sentence**.

prepositional phrase   subject
With the parents' approval, the **experiment** began.

Common Prepositions							
about	among	beside	during	into	onto	toward
above	around	between	except	like	out	under
across	at	beyond	for	near	outside	until
after	before	by	from	of	over	up
against	behind	despite	in	off	through	with
along	below	down	inside	on	to	within

If you have trouble identifying the subject in a sentence, put parentheses around prepositional phrases, as shown below. Notice that a sentence can contain more than one prepositional phrase.

(Without considering the consequences), **Adam** punched another man.

The **courthouse**, (an imposing building), was in the city center.

(In 2013), (after several months of waiting), **he** appeared before a judge.

HINT: Using *of the*

In most expressions containing *of the*, the subject appears before *of the*.

subject
Each (of the parents) has agreed to participate.

One (of the fathers) was uncomfortable with the process.

Practice 2

Circle the subject in each sentence. Also add parentheses around any prepositional phrases that are near the subject.

EXAMPLE: (For many years,) ⟨Rose McDermott⟩ studied the warrior gene.

1.   In McDermott's study, half of the test subjects had the MAOA gene, also known as the "warrior gene." The others in the group did not possess this gene. During the study, the unsuspecting subjects

completed a vocabulary quiz for a cash prize. The psychologists performing the study really wanted to provoke the subjects and study their response. For example, after the quiz, the researchers lied to each participant that someone else had "stolen" some of their winnings.

2.   One of the main differences between the two groups was their response to this provocation. Each of the participants had the option to punish the other subjects who "stole" part of their reward. The punishment for the "thieves" was forced ingestion of hot sauce. The response of the group with the warrior gene was generally much more aggressive.

Identifying Verbs

20.2 Identify verbs.

Every sentence must contain a verb. The **verb** expresses what the subject does, or it links the subject to other descriptive words.

- An **action verb** describes an action that a subject performs.

  Detective Rowland <u>attended</u> a seminar. He <u>spoke</u> to some officials.

- A **linking verb** connects a subject with words that describe it, and it does not show an action. The most common linking verb is *be*, but other common linking verbs are *appear*, *become*, *look*, and *seem*.

  Kim Rossmo <u>is</u> a former detective. His methods <u>seem</u> reliable.

- When a subject performs more than one action, the sentence has a **compound verb**.

  In 2003, Rossmo <u>wrote</u> and <u>spoke</u> about his methods.

Helping Verbs

The **helping verb** combines with the main verb to indicate tense, negative structure, or question structure. The most common helping verbs are forms of *be*, *have*, and *do*. **Modal auxiliaries** are another type of helping verb, and they indicate ability (*can*), obligation (*must*), and so on. For example, here are different forms of the verb *ask*, and the helping verbs are underlined.

<u>is</u> asking	<u>had</u> asked	<u>will</u> ask	<u>should</u> have asked
<u>was</u> asked	<u>had</u> been asking	<u>can</u> ask	<u>might</u> be asked
<u>has</u> been asking	<u>would</u> ask	<u>could</u> be asking	<u>could</u> have been asked

The **complete verb** is the helping verb and the main verb. In the following examples, the main verb is double underlined. In **question forms**, the first helping verb usually appears before the subject.

Criminal profiling techniques <u>have been <u>spreading</u></u> across the continent. <u>Should</u> the detective <u>have <u>studied</u></u> the files? <u>Do</u> you <u>agree</u>?

Interrupting words such as *often*, *always*, *ever*, and *actually* are not part of the verb.

Rossmo <u>has</u> often <u>returned</u> to Vancouver.

HINT: Infinitives Are Not the Main Verb

Infinitives are verbs preceded by *to*, such as *to fly*, *to speak*, and *to go*. An infinitive is never the main verb in a sentence.

verb   infinitive

The network <u>wanted</u> **to produce** a show about geographic profiling.

Practice 3

In each sentence, circle the subject and underline the complete verb. Hint: You can cross out prepositional phrases that are near the subject.

EXAMPLE: (According to Professor Saundra K. Ciccarelli,) many (factors) <u>contribute</u> to aggressive behavior.

1.   Should teen offenders be treated like adults? Why are some teenagers aggressive? Experts in cognitive development have discovered interesting facts about the adolescent brain. First, changes in hormone levels can have profound effects on a teen's behavior. Testosterone is linked with aggressiveness. According to *Scientific American* magazine, an injection of testosterone motivated study participants to want to dominate others.

2.   Furthermore, experts in brain development have discovered new information about the frontal lobe. That part of the brain is crucial in

decision making and impulse control. In teenagers, the frontal lobe is not fully connected to the rest of the brain. Thus, teens are more likely to act without consideration of consequences. In a *CBS News* article, Temple University professor Laurence Steinberg compares the teen brain to "a car with a good accelerator but a weak brake." Thus, treating a juvenile in the same way as an adult offender is unfair and unjust.

Final Review

Circle the subjects and underline the complete verbs in the following sentences.

EXAMPLE: The study (about role models) is fascinating.

1. There are many ways to modify a person's behavior. Young children can be influenced by aggressive characters on television. Young adults may be pressured or manipulated by peers. One of the most interesting influences on behavior is social roles.

2. In the autumn of 1971, psychologist Philip Zimbardo conducted an experiment at Stanford University. Seventy healthy middle-class students were recruited. Each of the young men was given the role of a prison guard or a prisoner. Volunteers with the role of prisoner were kept in cells. The student guards wore uniforms and carried batons.

3. Very quickly, students in both roles modified their behavior. The prisoners became meek and resentful. There were also noticeable differences in the guards' attitudes. On the second day, the prisoners revolted. The guards aggressively crushed the rebellion. Then, with increasing intensity, the guards humiliated and physically restrained the prisoners. The behavior of the young men had changed.

4. Zimbardo was forced to end the experiment early. Why did the guards act so cruelly? According to psychologists, a uniform and a specific social role can have powerful influences on people's behavior.

The Writer's Room

Topics for Writing

Write about one of the following topics. When you finish writing, identify your subjects and verbs.

1. List various ways in which social roles influence people's behavior. Support your points with specific examples.

2. Some experts suggest that personality traits are partly inherited. Are your character traits similar to a family member's traits? Compare and contrast yourself with someone else in your family.

21   Sentence Combining

SECTION THEME: Conflict

LEARNING OBJECTIVES

21.1 Identify parts of a sentence and sentence types.

21.2 Make compound sentences.

21.3 Make complex sentences.

In this chapter, you read about eyewitness testimony, profiling techniques, and wrongful convictions.

The Parts of a Sentence and Sentence Types

21.1 Identify parts of a sentence and sentence types.

When sentences vary in length and type, writing flows more smoothly and appears more interesting. You can vary sentences and create relationships between ideas by combining sentences. Before you learn about the types of sentences, it is important to understand some key terms.

A **phrase** is a group of words that is missing a subject, a verb, or both, and is not a complete sentence.

in the morning   acting on her own   the excited witness

A **clause** is a group of words that contains a subject and a verb. There are two types of clauses.

- An **independent clause** is also called a simple sentence. It stands alone and expresses one complete idea.

  The victims asked for compensation.

- A **dependent clause** has a subject and a verb, but it cannot stand alone. It "depends" on another clause to be complete. A dependent clause usually begins with a subordinator such as *after*, *although*, *because*, *unless*, and *when*.

  . . . because they had lost a lot of money.

Practice 1

Write *S* next to each complete sentence. If the group of words is not a complete sentence—perhaps it is a phrase or a dependent clause—then write *X* in the blank.

EXAMPLE: Eyewitness testimony is often very powerful as evidence. __S__
           Although it can be unreliable. __X__

1. Eyewitness testimony often contributes to wrongful convictions. _____

2. Because this testimony is often unreliable or misleading. _____

3. Officers unconsciously influence witnesses to pick certain suspects. _____

4. Witnesses may also feel pressure to point out a perpetrator. _____

5. When they are not confident in their choice. _____

6. Unless reforms are enacted. _____

7. Eyewitness testimony has too much influence in criminal convictions. _____

8. Although sometimes this evidence still may be useful. _____

Types of Sentences

As you learned in Chapter 20, a **simple sentence** contains one independent clause that expresses a complete idea.

      independent clause
The trial lasted for three months.

In this chapter, you learn about compound and complex sentences as well. A **compound sentence** contains two or more independent clauses.

> independent clause   independent clause
> [The trial was long], and [the jurors became bored.]

A **complex sentence** contains at least one dependent clause joined with one independent clause.

>   dependent clause   independent clause
> After the crime occurred, [reporters visited the town.]

Compound Sentences

21.2 Make compound sentences.

Use a Coordinating Conjunction

There are several ways to create compound sentences. One method is to use a **coordinating conjunction**, which joins two complete ideas and indicates the connection between them. The most common coordinating conjunctions are *for, and, nor, but, or, yet,* and *so.*

> Complete idea   **, coordinating conjunction**   complete idea.

The detective collected the evidence, **and** the lab analyzed it.

Review the following chart showing coordinating conjunctions and their functions.

Conjunction	Function	Example
and	to join two ideas	Anna went to school, **and** she became a forensics expert.
but	to contrast two ideas	The courses were difficult, **but** she passed them all.
for	to indicate a reason	She worked very hard, **for** she was extremely motivated.
nor	to indicate a negative idea	The work was not easy, **nor** was it pleasant.
or	to offer an alternative	She will work for a police department, **or** she will work for a private lab.
so	to indicate a cause and effect relationship	She has recently graduated, **so** she is looking for work now.
yet	to introduce a surprising choice	She wants to stay in her town, **yet** the best jobs are in a nearby city.

HINT: Recognizing Compound Sentences

To be sure that a sentence is compound, place your finger over the coordinator, and then ask yourself if the two clauses are complete sentences. In compound sentences, always place a comma before the coordinator.

Simple   The witness was nervous **but** very convincing.

Compound   The witness was nervous, **but** she was very convincing.

Practice 2

Insert coordinating conjunctions in the blanks. Choose from the following list, and try to use a variety of coordinators. (Some sentences may have more than one answer.)

but   or   yet   so   for   and   nor

EXAMPLE: In 1969, the FBI introduced criminal profiling as an investigative strategy, _____*and*_____ it has been quite successful.

1.   Kim Rossmo is a renowned geographic profiler, _____ he is also an excellent detective. Rossmo examines the movements of criminals, _____ he searches for specific patterns. According to Rossmo, criminals attack in places they know, _____ they generally don't work in their own neighborhoods. Most people don't want to travel long distances for their jobs, _____ they are lazy. Criminals work the same way, _____ they stay relatively close to home.

2.   Rossmo developed a fascinating mathematical formula, _____ many police departments were skeptical about his ideas. Basically, he inputs the addresses of suspects into a computer, _____ he also inputs details about the crime scenes. His program looks for a "hot" area. Suspects may live directly in the center of the hot area, _____ they may live within a few blocks. For example, in the late 1990s, there were several sexual assaults in a town in Ontario, Canada, _____ Rossmo and his associates created a profile map. One particular suspect's home was compared with the location of the crime scenes, _____ it was placed in Rossmo's

computer program. Originally, the main offender's name was low on a list of 316 suspects, _____ it rose to number 6 on the list after the profiling. The suspect was eventually tried and convicted for the crimes, _____ he went to prison.

GRAMMAR LINK
For more practice using semicolons, see Chapter 24, "Run-Ons."

Use a Semicolon (;)

Another way to form a compound sentence is to join two complete ideas with a semicolon. The semicolon replaces a coordinating conjunction.

Complete idea	;	complete idea.

The eyewitness was certain; she pointed at the suspect.

HINT: Use a Semicolon to Join Related Ideas

Use a semicolon to link two sentences when the ideas are equally important and closely related. Do not use a semicolon to join two unrelated sentences.

Incorrect   Some eyewitnesses make mistakes; I like to watch criminal trials.
(The second idea has no clear relationship with the first idea.)

Correct   One eyewitness misidentified a suspect; the witness was not wearing contact lenses that day.
(The second idea gives further information about the first idea.)

Practice 3

Make compound sentences by adding a semicolon and another complete sentence to each simple sentence. Remember that the two sentences must have related ideas.

EXAMPLE: Last year, Eric joined a gang ____ *; he regretted his decision.*

1. Eric rebelled against his parents _____

_____

2. At age fifteen, he acted like other teens _____

_____

3. His friends tried to influence him _____

_____

4. Some people don't have supportive families _____

_____

Use a Semicolon and a Transitional Expression

You can also create compound sentences by joining two complete ideas with a semicolon and a transitional expression. A **transitional expression** links the two ideas and shows how they are related. Most transitional expressions are **conjunctive adverbs** such as *however* or *furthermore*.

Some Transitional Expressions

Addition	Alternative	Compare or Contrast	Time	Example or Emphasis	Result or Consequence
additionally	in fact	equally	eventually	for example	consequently
also	instead	however	finally	for instance	hence
besides	on the contrary	nevertheless	frequently	namely	therefore
furthermore	on the other hand	nonetheless	later	of course	thus
in addition	otherwise	similarly	meanwhile	undoubtedly	
moreover		still	subsequently		

If the second clause begins with a transitional expression, put a semicolon before it and a comma after it.

> Complete idea   **; transitional expression,**   complete idea

Stephen Truscott was not guilty; **nevertheless,** he was convicted.

Practice 4

Combine sentences using the following transitional expressions. Choose an expression from the list, and try to use a different expression in each sentence.

in fact	~~frequently~~	however	thus
therefore	moreover	nevertheless	eventually

EXAMPLE: DNA evidence is useful. It has helped clear innocent people.
(above "useful. It" is handwritten: ; frequently, it)

1. In the early 1990s, a comparison of hair samples could deliver a conviction. Scientists developed more sophisticated techniques.

2. Dr. Edward Blake is a leading authority on DNA evidence. He often testifies at trials.

3. According to Dr. Blake, microscopic hair analysis is not precise. It has secured convictions in many cases.

4. Billy Gregory's hair matched a hair found at a crime scene. Both strands of hair appeared identical.

5. The strands of hair had exactly the same color and width. They were genetically different.

6. Today, conventional hair comparison evidence is no longer allowed in most courtrooms. It may become an obsolete science.

Complex Sentences

21.3 Make complex sentences.

When you combine a dependent and an independent clause, you create a **complex sentence**. An effective way to create complex sentences is to join clauses with a **subordinating conjunction**. "Subordinate" means secondary, so subordinating conjunctions—or subordinators—are words that introduce secondary ideas.

If you use a subordinator at the beginning of a sentence, put a comma after the dependent clause. Generally, if you use a subordinator in the middle of the sentence, you do not need to use a comma.

Main idea	subordinating conjunction	secondary idea
The police arrived	**because**	the alarm was ringing.

Subordinating conjunction	secondary idea,	main idea
Because	the alarm was ringing,	the police arrived.

MEANINGS OF SUBORDINATING CONJUNCTIONS
Subordinating conjunctions create a relationship between the clauses in a sentence.

Subordinating Conjunction	Indicates	Example
as, because, so that, since	a reason, cause, or effect	He paid a lot **because** he wanted a reliable virus scanner.
after, before, since, until, when, whenever, while	a time	**After** he bought it, he installed it.
as long as, even if, if, provided that, so that, unless	a condition	The scanner won't work **unless** he activates it.
although, even though, though	a contrast	**Although** the scanner works well, new viruses can evade it.
where, wherever	a location	**Wherever** there are computers, there are cyber criminals.

HINT: More About Complex Sentences

Complex sentences can have more than two clauses.

<u>Although males commit most violent crimes</u>, <u>more and more females</u>
1   2

<u>engage in violent acts</u> <u>after they have joined gangs</u>.
3

You can also combine compound and complex sentences. The next example is a **compound-complex sentence**.

complex

<u>Although Alicia is tiny</u>, <u>she is strong</u>, and <u>she is a dedicated police officer</u>.

compound

Practice 5

Add a missing subordinating conjunction to each sentence. Use each subordinating conjunction only once. The first one is done for you.

| although | when | because | since |
| even though | if | after | ~~whenever~~ |

1. _____Whenever_____ DNA evidence does not match a suspect's DNA, that person is usually released from custody. However, some people can have more than one type of DNA in their bodies. Chimeras are people with two types of DNA. _____ chimeras are rare, they do exist.

2. Lydia Fairchild separated from her partner _____ they fought too much. To receive financial help from the government, Fairchild had to prove that she was the biological mother of her children. _____ she had given birth to her two children, her DNA showed no link to them. Eventually, scientists discovered matching DNA _____ they tested her internal organs.

3.   Chimerism occurs _____ two separate

eggs fuse during the first few days of pregnancy. The judge in the

Fairchild case expressed concern _____ he often

denies paternity rights to fathers based on DNA evidence. Also,

_____ a criminal is a chimera, his or her DNA will

not necessarily match the evidence in a crime scene.

Practice 6

Combine the sentences by adding a subordinating conjunction. Use a different subordinating conjunction in each sentence. Properly punctuate your sentences.

EXAMPLE: He entered the courthouse. Photographers snapped photos.
       As he entered the courthouse, photographers snapped photos.
       Or **The photographers snapped photos as he entered the courthouse.**

1. Stephen was fourteen years old. He was arrested.

_____

_____

2. He proclaimed his innocence. The police refused to believe him.

_____

_____

3. He was extremely nervous. He appeared to be guilty.

_____

_____

4. He was in jail. He finished high school.

_____

_____

5. New evidence surfaced. He was released.

_____

_____

Final Review

The following paragraphs contain only simple sentences. When sentences are not varied, the essay is boring to read. To give the paragraphs more sentence variety, combine at least ten sentences. You will have to add some words and delete others.

EXAMPLE: ~~Everyone~~ Although everyone accused of a crime in America gets a lawyer. Some lawyers are not as effective as others.

1.   On a Saturday night, Kalief Broder was walking home from a party. Police arrested him and charged him with robbery. The police found no evidence. Browder said he was innocent. He was never convicted of a crime. His case never even officially made it to trial. Yet Browder spent three years in prison. He was finally freed in 2013. Prosecutors lost contact with the witnesses against him and dropped the case. Browder had dozens of court appearances in front of nine different judges. A judge finally released him.

2.   Many people in Browder's position are counseled to accept plea deals even when they are innocent. Overworked public defenders have very little time to review each case or speak to their clients. As a result, a staggering 95 percent of criminal cases are resolved through plea bargaining. Browder was offered several plea bargains to be able to leave prison. He declined every time. He was innocent. He refused to admit any guilt. Other inmates heard of Browder's decision to reject a plea deal. They thought he was crazy.

3.   Public defenders have a lot of clients. They often spend as little as one hour on each case. Almost three-quarters of public defenders handle more than the maximum suggested number of cases per year. Many municipalities do not allow public defenders to reduce their workloads due to budget cuts. Former Attorney General Eric Holder addressed the crisis. Both federal and state governments have been slow to respond. The issue is critical for people of limited incomes. They cannot afford high-paid attorneys or exorbitant bail costs. Hopefully, a solution will be found.

The Writer's Room

Write about one of the following topics. Include some compound and some complex sentences.

1. Do you watch crime shows or read about crime? Narrate what happened in your favorite crime show, movie, or book.
2. What can people do to reduce the risk of being robbed? List several steps that people can take.

22 Sentence Variety

SECTION THEME: Conflict

In this chapter, you read about revolutionaries and rule breakers.

What Is Sentence Variety?

22.1 Vary your sentences.

In Chapter 21, you learned to write different types of sentences. In this chapter, you learn to vary your sentences by consciously considering the length of sentences, by altering the opening words, and by joining sentences using different methods.

Consider the following example. The first passage sounds choppy because the sentences are short and uniform in length. When the passage is rewritten with sentence variety, it flows more smoothly.

317

No Sentence Variety

It was 1789. France was in crisis. Grain prices rose. Bread became more expensive. Many French citizens were hungry. They began to complain publicly. They were frustrated. They protested in the streets.

Sentence Variety

In 1789, France was in crisis. As grain prices rose, bread became more expensive. Feeling hungry, many French citizens began to complain publicly. Frustrated, they protested in the streets.

HINT: Be Careful with Long Sentences

If your sentence is too long, it may be difficult for the reader to understand. Also, you may accidentally write run-on sentences. If you have any doubts, break up a longer sentence into shorter ones.

Long and complicated	In France, at the time of the 1789 revolution, Marie Antoinette was the queen, and she lived a life of wealth and consumption and had very little contact with ordinary people and did not know or care about the poor, so when a journalist complained about her, everyone believed the journalist.
Better	In France, at the time of the 1789 revolution, Marie Antoinette was the queen. Living a life of wealth and consumption, she had very little contact with ordinary people. Additionally, she did not know or care about the poor. Thus, when a journalist complained about her, everyone believed the journalist.

Practice 1

Combine the following sentences to provide sentence variety. Create some short and some long sentences.

Marie Antoinette was twelve years old. Her family made a decision. The girl would marry her second cousin. His name was Louis Auguste. He was fourteen years old. He would be king of France. Marie Antoinette moved from Austria to France. She had to adapt to a new culture. She lived in a palace. Excessive luxury was evident. She became one of the most famous queens in history. It was not for a good reason. She was quoted as saying, "Let them eat cake." Some historians don't believe that she said it. The phrase appeared in a book eight years before her birth. She could not have said the phrase first.

Varying the Opening Words

22.2 Vary your opening words.

An effective way to make your sentences more vivid is to vary the opening words. Instead of beginning each sentence with the subject, you could try the following strategies.

Begin with an Adverb (-*ly* Word)

An **adverb** is a word that modifies a verb, and it often (but not always) ends in -*ly*. *Quickly* and *frequently* are adverbs. Non -*ly* adverbs include words such as *sometimes* and *often*.

> <u>Quickly</u>, the crowd grew.

Begin with a Prepositional Phrase

A **prepositional phrase** is a group of words made up of a preposition and its object. *In the morning* and *at dawn* are prepositional phrases.

> <u>On state television</u>, the president addressed the nation.

Begin with a Present Participle (-*ing* Verb)

You can begin your sentence with a **present participle**, or -*ing* word. Combine sentences using an -*ing* modifier only when the two actions happen at the same time.

> <u>Posting</u> information on Facebook, the group organized a protest.

> **GRAMMAR LINK**
> For a list of irregular past participles, see Appendix 1.

Begin with a Past Participle (-*ed* Verb)

You can begin your sentence with a **past participle**, which is a verb that has an -*ed* ending. There are also many irregular past participles such as *gone, seen*, and *known*.

> <u>Raised</u> in luxury, the king did not understand the people's complaints.

Practice 2

Combine the sets of sentences. Begin your new sentence using the type of word indicated in parentheses.

EXAMPLE: (-*ly* word) The protesters gathered in Ukraine. They were anxious.

Anxiously, the protesters gathered in Ukraine.

1. (-*ing* verb) Protestors opposed new constitutional amendments. Protesters gathered in Kiev in November 2014.

   _____

   _____

2. (prepositional phrase) They demanded the resignation of Ukrainian President Yanukovich. They did so without violence.

   _____

   _____

3. (-*ed* verb) Protestors were tired of the corruption and poor economy. They wanted changes.

   _____

4. (-*ly* word) The police acted quickly. Police attacked protestors with live ammunition.

   _____

   _____

5. (prepositional phrase) A civil war developed between pro-Russian and pro–European Union factions. It was to everyone's dismay.

   _____

   _____

Combining Sentences with an Appositive

22.3 Combine sentences with an appositive.

An **appositive** is a word or phrase that gives further information about a noun or pronoun. It often describes or renames a noun. You can combine two sentences by using an appositive. In the example, the italicized phrase could become an appositive because it describes the noun *Wael Ghonim*.

> **Two sentences** Nadia Tolokonnikova protested at the 2014 Sochi Olympics. She is a musician.

You can place the appositive directly before the word that it refers to or directly after that word. Notice that the appositives are set off with commas.

appositive

Combined   A musician, **Nadia Tolokonnikova** protested at the 2014 Sochi Olympics.

appositive

Nadia Tolokonnikova, a musician, protested at the 2014 Sochi Olympics.

Practice 3

Combine the following pairs of sentences. In each pair, make one of the sentences an appositive. Try to vary the position of the appositive.

EXAMPLE: The woman ~~was a Russian citizen. She~~ co-founded a
, a Russian citizen,
revolutionary music group.

1. Pussy Riot is a performance art group. The group formed in 2011.

2. The band, was a collective of activists. It was upset with Putin's government.

3. The members perform in colorful dresses and ski masks. The members are young beautiful women.

4. In February 2012, Pussy Riot sang a protest song in a Moscow cathedral. The song was called "Chase Putin Away."

5. Vladimir Putin reacted strongly to the group's criticism. He is a controversial leader.

6. The judge sentenced the women to two years in jail. He was a stern man.

Combining Sentences with Relative Clauses

22.4 Combine sentences with relative clauses.

A **relative pronoun** describes a noun or pronoun. You can form complex sentences by using relative pronouns to introduce dependent clauses. Review the most common relative pronouns.

    that   which   who   whom   whomever   whose

Which

Use *which* to add nonessential information about a thing. Generally use commas to set off clauses that begin with *which*.

    The crime rate, **which** peaked in the 1980s, has fallen in recent years.

> **GRAMMAR LINK**
> For more information about punctuating relative clauses, refer to Chapter 35.

That

Use *that* to add information about a thing. Do not use commas to set off clauses that begin with *that*.

The car **that was stolen** belonged to a police officer.

Who

Use *who* (*whom, whomever, whose*) to add information about a person. When a clause begins with *who*, you may or may not need a comma. Put commas around the clause if it adds nonessential information. If the clause is essential to the meaning of the sentence, do not add commas. To decide if a clause is essential or not, ask yourself if the sentence still makes sense without the *who* clause. If it does, the clause is not essential.

Many of the youths **who protested in the streets** were arrested.
(The clause is essential. The sentence needs the "who" clause to make sense.)

Dr. Hassein, **who was a kind man**, saved the wounded child.
(The clause is not essential.)

HINT: Using *That* or *Which*

Both *which* and *that* refer to things, but *which* refers to nonessential ideas. Also, *which* can imply that you are referring to the entire subject and not just a part of it. Compare the next two sentences.

Explosives that are not legal were sold to violent protesters.
(The sentence suggests that some might be legal.)

Explosives, which are not legal, were sold to violent protesters.
(The sentence suggests that all are not legal.)

Practice 4

Using a relative pronoun, combine each pair of sentences. Read both sentences before you combine them. Having the full context will help you figure out which relative pronoun to use.

EXAMPLE: Crime , which varies from culture to culture. ~~It~~ can force societies to change.

1. Sociologist Emile Durkheim was from France. He believed that deviant behavior can sometimes help societies.

2. Definitions of criminal behavior are agreed on by citizens. The definitions can change over time.

3. In many countries, people express their opinions about the government. These people are breaking the law.

4. Last year, some citizens in Iran criticized government policies. They were imprisoned.

5. In the 1960s, Americans who broke Jim Crow laws. They were arrested.

6. Sometimes activists are treated as criminals. They actually help change society.

Practice 5

Add dependent clauses to each sentence. Begin each clause with a relative pronoun (*who*, *which*, or *that*). Add any necessary commas.

EXAMPLE: The story __that was about the American revolution__ was made into a documentary.

1. The boy _____ wanted to join the soldiers and fight in the American Revolutionary War.

2. The gun _____ was on his front porch.

3. The boy did something _____

4. The neighbors _____ heard a loud bang.

5. The large crabapple tree _____ was hit by the shotgun blast.

Writing Embedded Questions

22.5 Write embedded questions.

It is possible to combine a question with a statement or to combine two questions. An **embedded question** is a question that is set within a larger sentence.

Question	Embedded question
How old were the victims?	Onlookers wondered <u>how old the victims were</u>.

In questions, there is generally a helping verb before the subject. However, when a question is embedded in a larger sentence, remove the helping verb or place it after the subject. As you read the following examples, pay attention to the word order in the embedded questions.

1. **Combine two questions**.

   Separate   Why **do** people take risks? Do you know?
   (In both questions, the helping verb is *do*.)

   Combined   Do you know why people take risks?
   (The helping verb *do* is removed from the embedded question.)

2. **Combine a question and a statement**.

   Separate   How **should** society treat violent extremists? I wonder about it.
   (In the question, the helping verb *should* appears before the subject.)

   Combined   I wonder how society should treat violent extremists.
   (In the embedded question, *should* is placed after the subject.)

HINT: Use the Correct Word Order

When you edit your writing, ensure that you have formed your embedded questions properly.

Dr. Alvarez wonders why ~~do~~ people commit crimes. I asked her what
she thought
~~did she think~~ about the issue.

Practice 6

Correct six errors involving embedded questions.

EXAMPLE: The writer explains how ~~can~~ people _{can} hold on to power for
so long.

1.   Around the world, citizens wonder why are so many nations run

by dictators and authoritarian regimes. They also question how were

certain leaders able to accumulate their wealth. For example, people

want to know how did former Egyptian president Hosni Mubarak

become so wealthy.

2.   To understand the former Egyptian president's wealth, people should consider why was Mubarak admired and supported by the international political community during his reign. Around the world, democratic Western nations tend to support undemocratic regimes when it is good for international business. For example, if someone wonders how could Mubarak remain in power for eighteen years, he or she should evaluate the situation. About 4 percent of the world's oil supply must pass by boat through the Suez Canal in Egypt. Perhaps that explains why did Mubarak make sure business went smoothly for the companies and nations that needed to use the canal.

Final Review

The next essay lacks sentence variety. Use the strategies that you have learned in this chapter, and create at least ten varied sentences.

            Having
EXAMPLE: ~~People have~~ a lot of Facebook friends. ~~It~~ is not a sign of
            popularity.

READING LINK
The following essays contain more information about law, order, and conflict.

"Rehabilitation"
   p. 89
"Discrimination in the
   21st Century"
   p. 159
"Motivations of
   Terrorism" p. 172
"How Companies
   Deceive Us" p. 524
"The Price of Public
   Shaming in the
   Internet Age" p. 528
"My Bully, My Best
   Friend" p. 520

1.   I sometimes wonder. How do revolutions begin? Malcolm Gladwell is a respected author. He wrote an article called "Small Change" for the *New Yorker*. According to Gladwell, Facebook and Twitter are important. They do not have a significant impact on revolutions. He believes the following idea. Social media sites were given too much credit for uprisings in Egypt, Libya, and other nations.

2.   Gladwell gives examples. Something happened on February 1, 1960. Four black college students sat at a counter in a North Carolina Woolworth's. They ordered coffee. They were not served because of their skin color. They were determined. They sat at the counter all day.

A crowd gathered eventually. Thirty-one protestors sat in the coffee shop the next day. Then the protest grew. It was to everyone's surprise. Soon neighboring cities had sit-ins. About seventy thousand students were protesting at the end of the month. People organized without Facebook or Twitter.

3.   Gladwell has a theory. Revolutions require sacrifice and strong ties. People form "weak ties" with social media. Most Twitter and Facebook users don't know their online friends. Such websites make communication easier. The sites don't create social change.

The Writer's Room

Write about one of the following topics. Use a variety of sentence lengths.

1. What are some categories of criminals? Classify criminals into different types.

2. Why does criminal life seem exciting to some people? What factors contribute to make crime appealing?

23 Fragments

SECTION THEME: Urban Development

In this chapter, you read about the development of suburbs and cities.

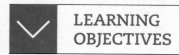

LEARNING OBJECTIVES

23.1 Define fragments.

23.2 Identify phrase fragments.

23.3 Correct fragments with *-ing* and *to*.

23.4 Identify explanatory fragments.

23.5 Identify dependent-clause fragments.

What Are Fragments?

23.1 Define fragments.

A **fragment** is an incomplete sentence. It lacks either a subject or a verb, or it fails to express a complete thought. You may see fragments in newspaper headlines and advertisements (e.g., "Overnight Weight Loss"). You may also use fragments to save space when writing a text message. However, in formal writing, it is unacceptable to write fragments.

Sentence	More and more people are moving to urban centers.
Fragment	In developing countries.

Phrase Fragments

23.2 Identify phrase fragments.

Phrase fragments are missing a subject or a verb. In each example, the fragment is underlined.

No verb	<u>The history of cities</u>. It is quite interesting.
No subject	Ancient civilizations usually had one major city. <u>Specialized in trades.</u>

How to Correct Phrase Fragments

To correct phrase fragments, add the missing subject or verb, or join the fragment to another sentence. The following examples show how to correct the previous phrase fragments.

Join sentences	The history of cities is quite interesting.
Add words	Ancient civilizations usually had one major city. **The citizens in that city** specialized in trades.

HINT: Incomplete Verbs

The following example is a phrase fragment because it is missing a helping verb. To make this sentence complete, you must add the helping verb.

Fragment	Modern cities growing rapidly.
Sentence	Modern cities <u>are</u> growing rapidly.

Practice 1

Underline and correct eight phrase fragments.

EXAMPLE: King Abdullah City. ~~It~~ is an entirely planned city that will open in 2035.

1. Most large cities grow organically over time. New York City, Beijing, and Mexico City. They grew over a period of hundreds, or even thousands, of years. However, recently some countries have tried to build cities entirely from scratch. King Abdullah City in Saudi Arabia is one such city. Gujarat Financial Tech City in India. It is another. King Abdullah City is being built in the desert, and it will be roughly the

size of Washington, D.C. When it is completed. Saudi Arabia hopes the new city will attract tourism and business investment to a previously desolate part of the country.

2.　　However, it is still unclear if these planned cities will be beneficial. For individual nations. Many previous grandiose plans for planned cities have failed. For example, Dubai Waterfront, a planned city in the United Arab Emirates, imploded after the global financial crisis. In the early twenty-first century. A lack of demand for the properties being built in the city led to the collapse of the project. Nano City, a planned mega-city in India, also ran into problems during the planning stage. The planned city proved to be much more costly than originally anticipated, and the firm that started the project failed to submit detailed plans. In a timely manner. The Indian government cancelled the project in 2010.

3.　　During the last century. People have migrated in increasing numbers to big cities. However, it is unclear if governments are able to create cities. Out of thin air. Perhaps the culture and history that are such an important part of the appeal of big cities must develop naturally.

Fragments with -*ing* and *To*

23.3 Correct fragments with -*ing* and *to*.

A fragment may begin with a **present participle**, which is the form of the verb that ends in -*ing* (*running, talking*). It may also begin with an **infinitive**, which is *to* plus the base form of the verb (*to run, to talk*). These fragments generally appear next to another sentence that contains the subject. In the examples, the fragments are underlined.

-*ing* **fragment**	Reacting to urban sprawl. City planners started a new movement in the 1980s and 1990s.
to **fragment**	Urban designers believe in the new urbanism. To help people live better lives.

How to Correct *-ing* and *To* Fragments

To correct an *-ing* or *to* fragment, add the missing words or join the fragment to another sentence. The following examples show how to correct the two previous fragments.

Join sentences Reacting to urban sprawl, city planners started a new movement in the 1980s and 1990s.

Add words Urban designers believe in the new urbanism. **They want** to help people live better lives.

HINT: When the *-ing* Word Is the Subject

Sometimes a gerund (*-ing* form of the verb) is the subject of a sentence. In the example, *cycling* is the subject of the sentence.

Correct sentence <u>Cycling</u> is a great form of exercise in urban areas.

A sentence fragment occurs when the *-ing* word is part of an incomplete verb string or when you mention the subject in a previous sentence. In the example, the fragment is underlined.

Fragment Many city dwellers get exercise. <u>Cycling on bike paths</u>.

Practice 2

Underline and correct eight *-ing* and *to* fragments.

EXAMPLE: The new urbanism movement has many principles. ~~Designing~~ **One principle is designing**
<u>walkways in neighborhoods.</u>

1. New urbanism is a suburban planning movement. To create people-friendly neighborhoods. Urban planners design self-contained neighborhoods. To limit the use of cars. Believing in the need to curtail urban sprawl. Architects plan areas where people can walk to work.

2. The new urbanism movement is a reaction against older suburban areas. After World War II, architects designed suburbs that relied heavily on cars. Living in traditional suburbs. Most people must drive to the city centers to go to work. The commute causes traffic congestion

and air pollution. Suburban dwellers waste a lot of time. Traveling in their cars. Urban sprawl also creates problems for people who do not drive. Limiting their daily activities. Nondrivers must find other means of transport. To do errands downtown or at the mall.

3.   Since 1990, the new urbanism movement has become very popular. City planners design beautiful and functional areas. To improve the quality of suburban life.

Explanatory Fragments

23.4 Identify explanatory fragments.

An **explanatory fragment** provides an explanation about a previous sentence and is missing a subject, a complete verb, or both. These types of fragments begin with one of the following words.

also	especially	for example	including	particularly
as well as	except	for instance	like	such as

In the examples, the explanatory fragment is underlined.

Fragment	Planners in the 1960s influenced the new urbanism movement. For example, Jane Jacobs.
Fragment	New urbanism planners take into consideration many factors. Especially reducing the use of the automobile.

How to Correct Explanatory Fragments

To correct explanatory fragments, add the missing words, or join the explanation or example to another sentence. The following examples show how to correct the previous explanatory fragments.

Join sentences	New urbanism planners take into consideration many factors, especially reducing the use of the automobile.
Add words	Planners in the 1960s influenced the new urbanism movement. For example, Jane Jacobs **was an important authority on urban planning**.

Practice 3

Underline and correct eight explanatory fragments. You may need to add or remove words.

EXAMPLE: Some new urbanism towns are famous: Such as Celebration.

1. Seaside, Florida, became the first community built using new urbanism principles. The town started in 1981 and became very famous. For example, *The Atlantic Monthly*. It featured Seaside on its cover. Developer Robert Davis hired experts in new urban planning. Such as architects and designers.

2. Seaside was easy to build because the area did not have traditional rules for developing land. For instance, no zoning regulations. The buildings in the town have uniform designs. Particularly the houses. They all have certain features. Porches, for example, must be sixteen feet from the sidewalk. Also, the streets. They must be made of bricks so cars cannot speed. Other towns are based on the same principles. Especially Celebration, Florida.

3. Many people criticize such communities. Particularly the conformity of design. On the other hand, some people hope to live in an ideal locale. For instance, no crime. However, critics point out that all communities have some social problems. In fact, in 2010, Celebration had its first murder.

Dependent-Clause Fragments

23.5 Identify dependent-clause fragments.

A **dependent clause** has a subject and a verb, but it cannot stand alone. It relies on another clause to be a complete sentence. Dependent clauses may begin with subordinating conjunctions or relative pronouns. The following list contains some of the most common words that begin dependent clauses.

Common Subordinating Conjunctions				Relative Pronouns
after	before	though	whenever	that
although	even though	unless	where	which
as	if	until	whereas	who(m)
because	since	what	whether	whose

In each example, the fragment is underlined.

Fragment	<u>Before William Levitt built Levittown.</u> Many people lived in congested neighborhoods.
Fragment	In the city, houses are close together. <u>Whereas in the suburbs, houses have large yards.</u>

How to Correct Dependent-Clause Fragments

To correct dependent-clause fragments, join the fragment to a complete sentence, or add the necessary words to make it a complete idea. You could also delete the subordinating conjunction. Here are two ways to correct the dependent-clause fragments in the previous examples.

Join sentences	Before William Levitt built Levittown, many people lived in congested neighborhoods.
Delete subordinating conjunction	In the city, houses are close together. In the suburbs, houses have large yards.

Practice 4

Underline and correct eight dependent-clause fragments.

EXAMPLE: William Levitt and his brother built Levittown<u>. ᵇ~~B~~ecause of a shortage of affordable housing.</u>

1.   In 1948, developer William Levitt built a community on Long

Island. That has been designated the first traditional suburb. Levitt

wanted to give returning soldiers the opportunity to participate in

the American dream. He called his community Levittown. The town

consisted of similarly built single-family homes. That attracted young

families. People wanted to escape the crowds of big cities like New

York and Philadelphia. The community grew to approximately 17,000

houses. Which led to the beginning of urban sprawl. Eventually, the

Levitts built three more Levittowns.

2.   Some people criticized Levittown. They felt it was badly designed. Because all of the houses looked similar. There were only four different house styles. Critics also complained about inequality. Although Levittown promised affordable housing for everyone. Levittown initially did not permit nonwhites to buy houses in the community. Eventually, Levittown abandoned its "whites-only" policy. In 1957, the first African Americans to buy a house in Levittown, Pennsylvania, were Bill and Daisy Myers. Who had rocks thrown at them by the other residents.

3.   Because Levittown is getting older. It has become a more attractive suburb. Many homeowners have remodeled their homes, and the saplings have grown into mature trees. Although many other suburbs have developed. Levittown remains a model of traditional suburban living.

Final Review

The following text contains the four types of fragments: phrase, *-ing* and *to*, explanatory, and dependent clause. Correct twelve fragment errors. You may need to add or delete words to make the sentences logical.

EXAMPLE: Slums lack basic services. ,s Such as electricity, sewage systems, or numbered houses.

1.   During the nineteenth and twentieth centuries. Great numbers of people moved from rural regions to urban areas. To look for work. Governments failed to provide affordable housing. For the migrants. Although they moved to the cities to improve their lives. People were forced to live in slums. Therefore, shantytowns grew at an alarming rate. Today, over one billion people live. In slums.

2.   Dharavi. It is located in Mumbai. It was originally an island. In the nineteenth century, the water around the island was filled in. Causing the area to become a part of Mumbai. Presently, around one million residents live in the Dharavi slum. People come to the shantytown. Because they can find cheap housing. Dharavi also has thousands of small businesses. Such as pottery shops and leather goods stores. Dharavi is really a city within a city.

3.   Politicians want to transform Mumbai into a modern city. Like Shanghai or Hong Kong. Thus, the government intends to convert the slum into a modern subdivision. For instance, business complexes, high rises, shopping malls, schools, and parks. Wanting to remain in their homes. Dharavi residents are fighting government plans to relocate them.

The Writer's Room

Topics for Writing

Write about one of the following topics. Check that there are no sentence fragments.

1. Describe your ideal town. What characteristics would it have?
2. What are some similarities and differences between living in a city and living in a suburb?

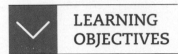

LEARNING OBJECTIVES

24.1 Identify run-ons.

24.2 Correct run-ons.

In this chapter, you read about architects and architecture.

What Are Run-Ons?

24.1 Identify run-ons.

A **run-on sentence** occurs when two or more complete sentences are incorrectly joined. In other words, the sentence runs on without stopping.

There are two types of run-on sentences.

1. A **fused sentence** has no punctuation to mark the break between ideas.

   Incorrect Skyscrapers are also called "supertall" buildings the Taipei 101 tower is among the tallest.

   Correct Skyscrapers are also called "supertall" buildings. The Taipei 101 tower is among the tallest.

2. A **comma splice** uses a comma incorrectly to connect two complete ideas.

   Incorrect The Burj Khalifa stands at 2,717 feet, it is located in Dubai, U.A.E.

   Correct The Burj Khalifa stands at 2,717 feet. It is located in Dubai, U.A.E.

Practice 1

Write *C* beside correct sentences, *FS* beside fused sentences, and *CS* beside comma splices.

Example: The White House contains 132 rooms and 35 bathrooms, it also has a tennis court and a jogging track. _____CS_____

1. The White House is the official residence of the American president, the first president, George Washington, never lived in it. _____

2. In 1790, George Washington moved the capital from New York to the District of Columbia he chose Pierre L'Enfant to plan the city. _____

3. Washington and L'Enfant chose a site for the presidential residence, they held a competition for the best design. _____

4. A young architect, James Hoban, won the competition he was inspired by a villa in Dublin, Ireland. _____

5. The corner stone was laid in 1792, and many people came to watch the construction. _____

6. John Adams was the first president to live in the house he and his wife took up residence in 1800. _____

7. During the War of 1812, the British set fire to the house, it was painted white to hide the damage. _____

8. Originally, the residence was called the President's Palace, but Theodore Roosevelt called it the White House in 1901. _____

Correcting Run-Ons

24.2 Correct run-ons.

You can correct both fused sentences and comma splices in a variety of ways. Read the following run-on sentence, and then review the four ways to correct it.

Run-on   Antoni Gaudí began his career as a secular architect he eventually became very religious.

1. Make two separate sentences by adding end punctuation, such as a period.

   Antoni Gaudí began his career as a secular architect. **He** eventually became very religious.

2. Add a semicolon (;).

   Antoni Gaudí began his career as a secular architect**;** he eventually became very religious.

3. Add a coordinating conjunction (*for, and, nor, but, or, yet, or so*).

   Antoni Gaudí began his career as a secular architect**,** **but** he eventually became very religious.

4. Add a subordinating conjunction such as *although, because, when, before, while, since,* or *after*.

   Although Antoni Gaudí began his career as a secular architect, he eventually became very religious.

Practice 2

Correct the run-ons by making two complete sentences.

EXAMPLE: Antoni Gaudí designed very interesting works, ̶h̶e̶ is .H
                considered to be a genius.

1. Antoni Gaudí was born in 1852 in Tarragona, Spain he is Catalonia's greatest architect.

2. Gaudí designed the Sagrada Familia he wanted to express his Catholic faith in his work.

3. Nature fascinated Gaudí, he incorporated nature's images into his creations.

4. Classical design used geometric shapes Gaudí's designs mimicked shapes from nature.

5. Gaudí's style evolved from Gothic influences, he created intricate, flowing, asymmetrical shapes.

6. Businessmen in Barcelona commissioned Gaudí to design a modern neighborhood, he constructed many buildings such as the Casa Milà.

7. Gaudí employed the *trencadis* style this style involves the use of broken tiles to decorate surfaces.

8. Many people initially laughed at Gaudí's vision, seven of his creations are now recognized as World Heritage Sites.

HINT: Semicolons and Transitional Expressions

Another way to correct run-ons is to connect sentences with a transitional expression. Place a semicolon before the expression and a comma after it.

EXAMPLE: The construction costs were too high; **therefore,** the town abandoned plans to build city hall.

The design was beautiful; **nevertheless,** it was rejected.

Some common transitional expressions are the following:

additionally	meanwhile	of course
furthermore	moreover	therefore
however	nevertheless	thus

To practice combining sentences with transitional expressions, see Chapter 21.

Practice 3

Correct the run-ons by joining two sentences with a semicolon.

EXAMPLE: The Palm Islands were finished in 2006 ; the islands are completely man-made.

1. The Palm Islands are an artificial group of islands off the coast of Dubai currently, only one of the two planned islands has been completed.

2. Dubai is a small city with only thirty-five miles of coastline the islands were designed as a way to maximize beachfront territory.

3. The Palm islands were also intended to house luxury hotels and villas for millionaires however, the islands may be slowly eroding.

4. According to the construction company lawyer, Richard Wilmot, the islands might be slowly sinking into the sea nonetheless, over seventy percent of the available villas on the islands have already been sold.

5. A few prominent celebrities have purchased luxury homes on the islands for example, British soccer star David Beckham was one of the first to purchase a villa on Palm Jumeirah Island in 2007.

6. Palm Jumeirah Island looks like a crown surrounded by an eleven-kilometer crescent the island was built between 2001 and 2006.

7. A personal island can cost anywhere from seven to thirty-five million dollars unfortunately, this cost is obviously out of the reach of average citizens.

8. There is some concern that developments like the Palm Islands may be causing serious damage to the surrounding ecosystem in Dubai the World Wildlife Fund claims that the U.A.E is by far the most unsustainable country on Earth.

Practice 4

Correct the run-ons by joining the two sentences with a comma and a coordinator (*for*, *and*, *nor*, *but*, *or*, *yet*, *so*).

EXAMPLE: Maya Lin's most famous design is the Vietnam Veterans
Memorial Wall‸ she has also created many other projects.
, but

1. American soldiers fought courageously in the Vietnam War the war was controversial.

2. A Vietnam War veteran, Jan Scruggs, pressured Congress to build a memorial he wanted to recognize the valor of American soldiers.

3. A competition for the best design was held in 1980 more than 2,500 people submitted ideas for the memorial.

4. The competitors could not be under eighteen could they be foreign citizens.

5. Maya Lin was only an undergraduate architect student she won the competition.

6. Lin's parents came from China she was born in Ohio.

7. Her design was a wall made of polished black granite the names of soldiers who lost their lives are etched on the wall.

8. The wall, which juts out of the earth, is an unconventional memorial it initially caused controversy.

Practice 5

Correct the run-ons by joining the two sentences with a subordinating conjunction. Use one of the following subordinators: *because, before, although, when, even though,* and *after*. If the dependent clause comes at the beginning of the sentence, remember to add a comma after it.

EXAMPLE: Millions of people have visited Rockefeller Center ^because^ it is one of the most famous landmarks in New York City.

1. Many people from China have the means to travel to famous landmarks around the world some Chinese construction firms have built replicas of those landmarks in China.

2. A copy of Manhattan was built near Beijing it was intended to be a new financial capital for the country.

3. However, the planned city ran into serious problems the financial collapse of 2008 seriously limited the original vision for the city.

4. The city is impressively built, very few of the available buildings are actually inhabited.

5. A replica of Paris in China is known as a "ghost town" very few people live in the city.

6. Many such projects are not economically profitable the replica of Florence in Tianjin has had some success attracting luxury brand stores.

7. Most of these projects failed one would think that Chinese developers would no longer have an interest in copying famous European and American cities.

8. Chinese companies should think about whether anyone wants or needs those properties they continue to build those planned cities.

Practice 6

Use a variety of methods to correct eight run-on errors. Add commas when necessary.

EXAMPLE: Many new buildings are being erected all over China,^and^ modern building designs are very popular.

1. The Chinese Revolution dominated politics, China's government developed policies to minimize class differences. As a result, new buildings were designed for utility with no regard for beauty.

2. Now, China is industrializing at a great rate businesses are asking architects to design practical but beautiful buildings. The National Theatre building, for example, is controversial, it is also intriguing. It was designed by French architect Paul Andreu, many people have criticized its design. It is shaped like an egg. It has three halls and a lake, it has a bridge. Another highly discussed building in Beijing is the CCTV tower. It looks like the letter Z, many Chinese think it is an eyesore.

3. The Beijing skyline has changed, not everybody has liked the changes. In China, some people complain about the ugly architecture, others believe the new buildings are beautiful. Average citizens are eager for Beijing to join the ranks of the most beautiful cities in the world.

The CCTV tower in Beijing

Final Review

Correct ten run-on errors.

EXAMPLE: The construction industry is the largest in the world, ^{and} public and private buildings consume a lot of energy.

1.   When most people envision cities, they think about houses, roads, and skyscrapers built above ground they do not think about subterranean cities. However, many people use underground public and private buildings every day. In North America, there are at least five hundred public and private underground buildings for example, the Engineering Library at the University of Berkeley and the Vietnam Veterans Memorial Education Center are only two such subterranean structures. More are being built every day.

Entrance to tunnels in Cappadocia

2.   Some of the oldest subsurface cities are located in Cappadocia, Turkey the first underground city in that area was constructed around 2000 b.c.e. Archaeologists believe that at one time, up to twenty thousand people lived in those Turkish cities the early Christians used them as a means to escape persecution.

3.   Montreal, Canada, contains an extremely large subterranean network. It was designed by I. M. Pei in the 1960s other architects have contributed to its expansion. It is located downtown and has around 26 miles of tunnels with about 120 exterior access points. More than 500,000 people use it each day they want to avoid Montreal's very cold temperatures in the winter.

4.   There are many reasons to build underground. First, subterranean buildings benefit from better climate control architects say that such

structures can be heated and cooled more efficiently than aboveground buildings. Also, building below the earth reduces the impact on the environment, forests and fields do not have to be cleared. Moreover, the wind, snow, and rain do not erode the walls, well-constructed underground buildings are resistant to fire and earthquakes.

5.   Perhaps in the future, there will be more underground public and private buildings, they are more environmentally friendly and more energy efficient. Certainly it is time to rethink how urban planners design cities.

The Writer's Room

Write about one of the following topics. Edit your writing, and ensure that there are no run-ons.

1. Give examples of any buildings or areas in your neighborhood, town, or country that you find attractive or unattractive. Describe these buildings, and explain why you believe they are beautiful or unsightly.

2. Are there any changes or additions that you would make to the town or city where you live, such as adding a new park or a museum? What suggestions would you make to city planners?

25 Faulty Parallel Structure

SECTION THEME: Urban Development

In this chapter, you read about landscapes and gardens.

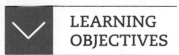

LEARNING OBJECTIVES

25.1 Define parallel structure.

25.2 Correct faulty parallel structure.

What Is Parallel Structure?

25.1 Define parallel structure.

Parallel structure occurs when pairs or groups of items in a sentence are balanced. Notice how the following sentences repeat grammatical structures but not ideas.

Parallel Nouns	<u>Books</u>, <u>stores</u>, and <u>catalogs</u> give gardeners information.
Parallel Tenses	Gardeners <u>dig</u> and <u>plant</u> in the soil.
Parallel Adjectives	Kew Garden is <u>large</u>, <u>colorful</u>, and <u>breathtaking</u>.
Parallel Phrases	You will find the public garden <u>down the road</u>, <u>over the bridge</u>, and <u>through the field</u>.
Parallel Clauses	There are some gardens <u>that have just trees</u>, and some <u>that have only flowers and plants</u>.

345

Correcting Faulty Parallel Structure

25.2 Correct faulty parallel structure.

Use parallel structure for a series of words or phrases, for paired clauses, for comparisons, and for two-part constructions. If you see "//" or "faulty parallelism" written in one of your marked essays, try the following tips for correcting those errors.

Series of Words or Phrases

Use parallel structure when words or phrases are joined in a series.

Not Parallel	The English, the Chinese, and people from Japan create luxurious gardens.
Parallel Nouns	<u>The English</u>, <u>the Chinese</u>, and <u>the Japanese</u> create luxurious gardens.
Not Parallel	I like to read books about gardens, to attend lectures about gardening, and buying plants for my garden.
Parallel Verbs	I like <u>to read</u> books about gardens, <u>to attend</u> lectures about gardening, and <u>to buy</u> plants for my garden.

Series of Clauses

Use parallel structure with a series of dependent clauses.

Not Parallel	He designed a garden that was beautiful, that was well planned, and was unique.
Parallel *That* Clause	He designed a garden <u>that was beautiful</u>, <u>that was well planned</u>, and <u>that was unique</u>.
Not Parallel	We met a designer who was friendly, who had a lot of experience, and was available.
Parallel *Who* Clause	We met a designer <u>who was friendly</u>, <u>who had a lot of experience</u>, and <u>who was available</u>.

HINT: Use Consistent Voice

When joining two independent clauses with a coordinating conjunction, use a consistent voice. For example, if the first part of the sentence uses the active voice, the other part should also use the active voice.

Not parallel	The bees <u>flew</u> [active] to the flowers, and then the nectar <u>was tasted</u> [passive] by them.
Parallel active voice	The bees <u>flew</u> [active] to the flowers, and then they <u>tasted</u> [active] the nectar.

Practice 1

Underline and correct the faulty parallel structure in each sentence.

EXAMPLE: City officials want to design gardens, to plant trees, and
~~should be~~ developing green spaces.
       to develop

1. Planting gardens on urban rooftops can help to insulate homes, to provide a habitat for local wildlife, and prevent rain runoff.

2. Rooftop gardens have been designed and built by many cultures, including Japanese, Americans, and people from Canada.

3. These gardens can be useful for people in big cities who like to plant flowers, who enjoy a brief respite from the concrete urban landscape, and like to grow their own fruits or vegetables.

4. Rooftop gardens are found on apartment buildings, schools, and places where people shop.

5. One farm in Brooklyn covers over 2.5 acres on two rooftops, yields nearly half-a-million pounds of produce, and jobs are provided for local farmers.

6. This farm produces plants that are practical, that are organic, and can be grown on previously unused spaces.

7. Rooftop farms can also prevent problems associated with excessive rainfall that will cause damage to homes, that will flood sewage systems, and can overflow onto city streets.

8. These spaces are also a venue for recreation, a place to entertain guests, and they are an additional outdoor living space for city dwellers.

9. Some people in the city can walk out the door, up the stairs, and go onto the roof to relax in their own private garden.

Comparisons

Use parallel structure in comparisons containing *than* or *as*.

| **Not Parallel** | Designing an interesting garden is easier than to take care of it. |
| **Parallel -*ing* Forms** | Designing an interesting garden is easier than taking care of it. |

| **Not Parallel** | The rock garden looks as colorful as planting roses. |
| **Parallel Noun Phrases** | The rock garden looks as colorful as the rose garden. |

Two-Part Constructions

Use parallel structure for the following paired items.

| either . . . or | not . . . but | both . . . and |
| neither . . . nor | not only . . . but also | rather . . . than |

| **Not Parallel** | The lecture on landscaping was both enlightening and of use. |
| **Parallel Adjectives** | The lecture on landscaping was both enlightening and useful. |

| **Not Parallel** | My choice was either seeing the bonsai exhibit or to go to a film. |
| **Parallel Verbs** | My choice was either seeing a bonsai exhibit or going to a film. |

HINT: Keep Lists Parallel

After a colon, ensure that your lists of words and phrases are parallel.

We completed the following assignment: learn about a plant species, take
~~taking~~ photographs of the plant, and create a poster.

Practice 2

Underline and correct ten errors in parallel construction.

EXAMPLE: City planners build parks to create green areas, to prevent
overcrowding, and ~~people can use them for recreation.~~ to develop recreational facilities

1.   During the Industrial Revolution, urban life changed rapidly and

was drastic. City planners realized that more people were moving to the cities. Planners, politicians, and people who immigrated saw city life transforming. Urban designers wanted to create green space rather than filling cities with concrete buildings.

2. One of the most important advocates of city beautification was Frederick Law Olmsted. He was born in 1822, in Hartford, Connecticut. He not only promoted urban planning, but he also was designing beautiful city gardens. He and his collaborator Calvert Vaux designed New York's Central Park. Olmsted wanted the park to have the following elements: open spaces, beautiful views, and paths that are winding.

3. Olmsted and Vaux designed many other projects. An important design was the Niagara Falls project. At that time, the falls were not completely visible to tourists. Olmsted wanted to create a harmonious landscape, to allow greater tourist accessibility, and conservation of the area was important to him. Such a park required a great deal of planning. Goat Island separates Canada from the United States. Either the landscapers could buy the island, or it was continuing to be an eyesore. Olmsted and Vaux bought the island and restored it.

4. For Olmsted, contributing to the community was more important than to have fame. He wanted not only the rich but also people who were poor to enjoy the tranquility of nature. He was known as much for his sense of beauty as respecting the environment. Olmsted died in 1903, but thousands of people continue to enjoy his legacy.

Final Review

Underline and correct ten errors in parallel construction.

EXAMPLE: Walking through a garden is more fun than ~~to read~~ a book.
_{reading}

1. Urban ecosystems refer to how cities affect their surrounding environment and vice versa. Urban planners, engineers, and people

in politics have incorporated the idea of the urban ecosystem. Many big cities require a great deal of farmland and fresh water to support them. These cities are often wasteful, inefficient, and are filled with pollution. Viewing a city as part of a larger ecosystem is a better way to plan urban areas for these reasons: it is more efficient, it integrates environmental issues into urban planning, and factors in the socioeconomic environment.

2.   Bill Moyers is a journalist, a television personality, and he comments on politics. He wrote an article detailing urban ecosystems and the problems they face. "Urban forests" are the trees that grow on hills, beside residential properties, and are found in parks. These trees are affected by salt, concrete, and substances that are toxic found in cities. Agricultural scientists, climatologists, and people who study biology have studied the effects of the air pollution and ground pollution caused by cities. These lessons have not only guided scientific experts but these experts were also alarmed.

3.   Several ways to improve urban ecosystems have been proposed. For example, academics and people who study economics have found that planting more trees in cities can greatly reduce air-conditioning costs. According to Moyers, the rapid growth of urban populations will be the biggest challenge to these ecosystems. People want their cities to be safe, environmentally diverse, and they also want cleanliness. By better integrating cities with the surrounding environment, urban planners and all citizens can achieve these goals.

The Writer's Room

Choose one of the following topics, and write a paragraph. Make sure your nouns, verbs, and sentence structures are parallel.

1. If you could be anywhere right now, where would you be? Describe that place. Include details that appeal to the senses.
2. What do you do to relax? List some steps.

26 Mistakes with Modifiers

SECTION THEME: Urban Development

In this chapter, you read about pollution and other urban issues.

LEARNING OBJECTIVES

26.1 Avoid misplaced modifiers.

26.2 Avoid dangling modifiers.

Misplaced Modifiers

26.1 Avoid misplaced modifiers.

A **modifier** is a word, a phrase, or a clause that describes or modifies nouns or verbs in a sentence. To use a modifier correctly, place it next to the word(s) that you want to modify.

>   modifier   words that are modified
> <u>Trying to combat pollution</u>, **city planners** have launched an anti-littering campaign.

A **misplaced modifier** is a word, a phrase, or a clause that is not placed next to the word that it modifies. When a modifier is too far from the word that it is describing, the meaning of the sentence can become confusing or unintentionally funny.

> I saw a pamphlet about littering waiting in the mayor's office.
> (How could a pamphlet wait in the mayor's office?)

351

Commonly Misplaced Modifiers

As you read the sample sentences for each type of modifier, notice how the meaning of the sentence changes depending on where the modifier is placed.

PREPOSITIONAL PHRASE MODIFIERS

A prepositional phrase is made of a preposition and its object.

Confusing	Helen read an article about electric cars <u>in a cafe</u>.
	(Who was in the cafe: Helen or the cars?)
Clear	<u>In a cafe</u>, Helen read an article about electric cars.

PARTICIPLE MODIFIERS

A participle modifier is a phrase that contains an *-ing* verb or an *-ed* verb.

Confusing	Jamal Reed learned about anti-littering laws <u>touring Singapore</u>.
	(Can laws tour Singapore?)
Clear	While <u>touring Singapore</u>, Jamal Reed learned about anti-littering laws.

RELATIVE CLAUSE MODIFIERS

A modifier can be a relative clause or phrase beginning with *who, whose, which,* or *that.*

Confusing	The company received a fine for the contaminated water <u>that was $100,000</u>.
	(What was $100,000, the water or the fine?)
Clear	The company received a fine <u>that was $100,000</u> for the contaminated water.

LIMITING MODIFIERS

Limiting modifiers are words such as *almost, nearly, only, merely, just,* and *even.* In the examples, notice how the placement of *almost* changes the meaning of each sentence.

Almost all of the citizens took the steps that solved the littering problem.
(Some of the citizens did not take the steps, but most did.)

All of the citizens **almost** took the steps that solved the littering problem.
(The citizens did not take the steps.)

All of the citizens took the steps that **almost** solved the littering problem.
(The steps did not solve the littering problem.)

HINT: Correcting Misplaced Modifiers

To correct misplaced modifiers, follow these steps:

1. First, identify the modifier.

   Armando saw the oil slick **standing on the pier**.

2. Then, identify the word or words being modified.

   Armando

3. Finally, move the modifier next to the word(s) being modified.

   Standing on the pier, Armando saw the oil slick.

Practice 1

Underline and correct the misplaced modifier in each sentence.

                              who forgot to flush the public toilet
EXAMPLE: The man paid the $500 fine to the health officer <u>who forgot to
flush the ^public toilet</u>.

1. Experts recognize Singapore as the cleanest city in the world from the
   United Nations.

2. Singaporean police officers will immediately arrest litterbugs who
   patrol city streets.

3. After littering, officers give a $1,000 fine to polluters.

4. For a second littering offense, a polluter must clean a public area such
   as a park or school yard wearing a bright yellow vest.

5. In 1992, Singapore politicians debated a new law that prohibited the
   importation, selling, or chewing of gum in Parliament.

6. Because gum was stuck on them, passengers could not close the doors
   to the subway trains.

7. In 2004, the law was revised to allow gum into the country that has
   medicinal purposes.

8. Singaporeans with no litter are proud of their city.

Dangling Modifiers

26.2 Avoid dangling modifiers.

A **dangling modifier** opens a sentence but does not modify any words in the sentence. It "dangles" or hangs loosely because it is not connected to any other part of the sentence. To avoid having a dangling modifier, make sure that the modifier and the first noun that follows it have a logical connection.

Confusing	While eating a candy bar, the wrapper fell on the ground. (Can a wrapper eat a candy bar?)
Clear	While eating a candy bar, **Zena dropped** the wrapper on the ground.
Confusing	To attend the conference, a background in environmental work is necessary. (Can a background attend a conference?)
Clear	To attend the conference, **participants need** a background in environmental work.

HINT: Correcting Dangling Modifiers

To correct dangling modifiers, follow these steps:

1. First, identify the modifier.

When traveling, public transportation should be used.

2. Then, decide who or what the writer aims to modify.

Who is traveling? **People**

3. Finally, add the missing subject (and in some cases, also add or remove words) so that the sentence makes sense.

When traveling, people should use public transportation.

Practice 2

Underline the dangling modifier in each sentence. Then, rewrite the sentence keeping the meaning of the modifier. You may have to add or remove words to make the sentence logical.

EXAMPLE: Breathing polluted air, concerns about health develop.

 Breathing polluted air, citizens develop concerns about their health.

1. Hoping to improve air quality, many strategies are being discussed in China.

_____

2. Without realizing their impact, photos showing Beijing's poor air quality circulated online in 2015.

_____

_____

3. While examining the photos, November had only four days of clean air.

_____

_____

4. To provide advance warning, all public buildings closed when the air quality Red Alert was issued.

_____

_____

5. Profiting from the situation, many products such as air purifiers, masks, and oxygen tanks have been sold.

_____

_____

6. Seeing increasing public pressure, alternative forms of energy are being explored.

_____

_____

7. Breathing in polluted air, many respiratory diseases have developed in China.

_____

_____

8. By paying more attention to air pollution, the nation's air quality will improve in the coming years.

_____

_____

Practice 3

Correct the dangling or misplaced modifiers. If the sentence is correct, write C next to it.

EXAMPLE:
              Keisha saw that
Walking by the sea, plastic bags were caught in the rocks.
                        ^

1. Using plastic bags, a lot of pollution is created.

2. Blown by the wind, sidewalks are frequently littered with plastic bags.

3. Clogging drains, plastic bags often cause sewage to overflow.

4. Choking on plastic, harm is caused to birds.

5. DeShawn Bertrand teaches the public about composting garbage with enthusiasm.

6. Taking public transportation, gas costs and parking fees are saved.

7. Environmental activists lobby oil industry managers who promote the green movement.

8. Following a few rules, communities can reduce pollution.

Final Review

Identify fifteen dangling or misplaced modifier errors in this selection. Then correct each error. You may need to add or remove words to ensure that the sentence makes sense.

EXAMPLE:
                                      we encountered different issues
While studying new fuel sources, ~~different issues came up~~.

1.   We discovered that there is a huge controversy about the development of natural shale gas in ecology class. People are searching for solutions who worry about the country's reliance on foreign energy sources. Many states have huge shale gas fields, so companies are exploiting those fields that want to make a profit.

2. Called fracking, oil and gas companies use a method to pump liquid into holes in shale rock to obtain natural gas. Companies have kept knowledge about shale gas extraction hidden from the public wanting to make huge profits. Containing hazardous chemicals, people's health can be affected by fracking liquids that leak into drinking wells. Also, fracking fluid can lubricate underground fault lines.

3. After enduring drilling for several years, many problems have been experienced by citizens. Showing concern, a connection between fracking and earth tremors has been confirmed by scientists. For example, near Youngstown, Ohio, fracking methods have been linked to over one hundred earthquakes. Drilling has also caused problems near Dimock, Pennsylvania. Floating upside down, fishers saw many fish. Polluted, the townspeople could not use the water. Then in 2009, a water well caused damage to a resident's property exploding suddenly. All of the homeowners almost became upset because property values have fallen.

4. Since 2011, facing hostility from citizens, access to information about fracking has been mandated. Shale gas production continues in many states by fracking. Clearly, the government needs to commission more studies on how fracking affects the environment.

> **READING LINK**
> More readings about urban issues.
> "Graffiti as Art" p. 215
> "Living Environments" p. 532
> "Nature Returns to the Cities" p. 536
> "Slum Tourism" p. 539

The Writer's Room

Write about one of the following topics. Proofread your text to ensure that there are no modifier errors.

1. What are some steps that your neighborhood or town could take to combat a littering or pollution problem?

2. What are some types of polluters? Write about three categories of polluters.

27 Subject–Verb Agreement

SECTION THEME: Travel and Survival

LEARNING OBJECTIVES

27.1 Practice basic subject–verb agreement rules.

27.2 Maintain subject–verb agreement with more than one subject.

27.3 Review special subject forms.

27.4 Maintain subject–verb agreement when the verb comes before the subject.

27.5 Maintain subject–verb agreement when there are interrupting words and phrases.

In this chapter, you read about cultural differences, travel etiquette, and safety tips.

Basic Subject–Verb Agreement Rules

27.1 Practice basic subject–verb agreement rules.

Subject–verb agreement simply means that a subject and verb agree in number. A singular subject needs a singular verb, and a plural subject needs a plural verb.

Simple Present Tense Agreement

Writers use **simple present tense** to indicate that an action is habitual or factual. Review the following rules for simple present tense agreement.

Third-person singular form: When the subject is *he, she, it,* or the equivalent (*Mark, Carol, Miami*), add an *-s* or *-es* ending to the verb.

> **Maria Orlon** <u>works</u> as a marketing researcher.

Base form: When the subject is *I, you, we, they,* or the equivalent (*women, the Rocky Mountains*), do not add an ending to the verb.

> Many **businesses** <u>rely</u> on marketing research.

HINT: Gerunds Are Singular Subjects

Sometimes a gerund (*-ing* form of the verb) is the singular subject of a sentence.

> **Fishing** <u>is</u> a popular activity.

Agreement in Other Tenses

In the past tense, almost all verbs have one past form. The only past tense verb requiring subject–verb agreement is the verb *be*, which has two past forms: *was* and *were*.

> **I** <u>was</u> tired. **Edward** <u>was</u> also tired. That day, **we** <u>were</u> very lazy.

In the present perfect tense, which is formed with *have* or *has* and the past participle, use *has* when the subject is third-person singular and *have* for all other forms.

> The **travel service** <u>has raised</u> its booking fees. Other **agencies** <u>have not raised</u> their fees.

> **GRAMMAR LINK**
> For more information about using the present perfect tense, see Chapter 28.

Note: In the future tense and with modal forms (*can, could, would, may, might, must,* and *should*), use the base form of the verb with every subject.

> **I** <u>will work</u>. **She** <u>should work</u> with me. **We** <u>can work</u> together.

HINT: Use Standard English

In casual conversations and in movies, you may hear people misuse the verbs *be, have,* and *do*. In professional and academic situations, use the standard forms of these verbs.

>   is   has   doesn't
> Karim ~~be~~ busy. He ~~have~~ a large family. He ~~don't~~ have free time.

Practice 1

Underline the correct form of the verbs in parentheses.

EXAMPLE: Travelers (<u>need</u> / needs) to learn about cultural differences.

1.   Although several countries (share / shares) the English language, some linguistic details (be / is / are) different. For example, Americans and Canadians (put / puts) gas in their cars, whereas British citizens (use / uses) petrol. In England, you (do / does) not phone people, you ring them. Australians also (use / uses) interesting expressions. A *chalkie* (is / are) a teacher, and a *mozzie* (is / are) a mosquito. Using proper terms (is / are) important.

2.   Spelling also (differ / differs) among English-speaking nations. The word *flavor* (have / has) an *our* ending in Canada and Great Britain. Also, the word *theater* (become / becomes) *theatre* in England and Australia.

3.   Business travelers should (learn / learns) about such differences. For example, Jeremiah Brown (do / does) the marketing for an American company. He (have / has) been with the company for two years. Last year, he visited London, England. One day, he (was / were) with a client. They (was / were) unable to agree on a price. When the client said, "That is too much dosh," Jeremiah (was / were) confused. Then he learned that *dosh* (is / are) a British slang word for money.

More Than One Subject

27.2 Maintain subject–verb agreement with more than one subject.

Special agreement rules apply when there is more than one subject.

And

When two or more subjects are joined by *and*, use the plural form of the verb.
    <u>Colleges</u> and <u>universities</u> **prepare** students for the job market.

Or / Nor

When two subjects are joined by *or* or *nor*, the verb agrees with the subject that is the closest to it.
                        singular
    The owner or the <u>manager</u> **decides** how the rooms will look.

                                        plural
    Neither the decorator nor her <u>assistants</u> **make** changes to the design.

HINT: *As Well As* and *Along With*

The phrases *as well as* and *along with* are not the same as *and*. They do not form a compound subject. The real subject is before the interrupting expression.

<u>Japan</u>, <u>China</u>, and <u>South Korea</u> **develop** high-tech computer products.

<u>Japan</u>, as well as China and South Korea, **develops** high-tech computer products.

Practice 2

Underline the correct verb in each sentence. Make sure the verb agrees with the subject.

Example: Ramon and Alicia (<u>take</u> / takes) many risks.

1. Ramon and Alicia Cruz (go / goes) to interesting places.
2. Right now, Ramon, along with his wife, (is / are) in a Turkish tea shop.
3. Generally, the owner or her son (greet / greets) the customers.
4. Neither Ramon nor Alicia (drink / drinks) coffee.
5. Strong black tea or herbal mountain tea (come / comes) on a special tray.
6. Sometimes, guitarists or singers (entertain / entertains) the customers.
7. The guests, along with the host, (sing / sings) Turkish songs.
8. Turkey, as well as Iran and Iraq, (have / has) a lot of tea shops.

Special Subject Forms

27.3 Review special subject forms.

Some subjects are not easy to identify as singular or plural. Two common types are indefinite pronouns and collective nouns.

Indefinite Pronouns

Indefinite pronouns refer to a general person, place, or thing. Carefully review the following list of indefinite pronouns.

Indefinite Pronouns				
Singular	another	each	no one	other
	anybody	everybody	nobody	somebody
	anyone	everyone	nothing	someone
	anything	everything	one	something
Plural	all, both, few, many, others, several, some			

SINGULAR INDEFINITE PRONOUNS

In the following sentences, the verbs require the third-person singular form because the subjects are singular.

> Almost <u>everyone</u> **knows** about tsunamis.

You can put one or more singular nouns (joined by *and*) after *each* and *every*. The verb is still singular.

> <u>Every</u> passenger **likes** the new rule. <u>Each</u> man and woman **knows** about it.

PLURAL INDEFINITE PRONOUNS

Both, few, many, others, and *several* are all plural subjects. The verb is always plural.

> A representative from the United States and another from Mexico are sitting at a table. <u>Both</u> **want** to compromise.

Collective Nouns

Collective nouns refer to groups of people or things. Review the following list of common collective nouns.

Common Collective Nouns				
army	class	crowd	group	population
association	club	family	jury	public
audience	committee	gang	mob	society
band	company	government	organization	team

Generally, each group acts as a unit, so you must use the singular form of the verb.

> The <u>team</u> **is** ready to travel to London.

HINT: *Police* Is Plural

Treat the word *police* as a plural noun because the word "officers" is implied but not stated.

> The police **have** a protester in custody.

Practice 3

Underline the correct verb in each sentence.

Example: Every society (honor / <u>honors</u>) the dead.

1.   Each nation (have / has) cultural traditions to honor the dead. In most western countries, the family (have / has) a funeral and (pay / pays) final respects to the deceased. Occasionally, the public (is / are) allowed to attend the funeral. During an open-casket ceremony, everyone (view / views) the deceased for one last time.

2.   Different societies (mourn / mourns) their dead in very interesting ways. For example, the Mexican population (celebrate / celebrates) the Day of the Dead every November. Each family (build / builds) an altar and (place / places) salt, spices, and their loved one's favorite alcoholic drinks at the foot of the altar. Nobody (forget / forgets) to buy skull-shaped candies. Others (visit / visits) the graves of their relatives to leave gifts, such as flowers or candies. A similar tradition occurs in Taiwan. Taiwanese citizens (honor / honors) their dead by cleaning the graves on Tomb-Sweeping Day. Almost everyone (offer / offers) food, tea, and wine to the family ancestors. Other individuals (fly / flies) kites shaped like animals or (pray / prays) for their loved ones.

3.   In Japan, people (travel / travels) to visit relatives during the *Obon* festival in July. At the festival, a band (play / plays) music. Everyone (dance / dances) and (welcome / welcomes) the spirits of the dead. If somebody (want / wants) to learn all the different songs and dances associated with the festival, he or she (need / needs) to visit every region of Japan. Each area (have / has) a different dance or style of music.

4.   Every cultural group (feel / feels) the need to commemorate the deceased in some way. Obviously, nobody (like / likes) to dwell on death. However, celebrating the lives of loved ones (is / are) essential for people in all societies.

Verb Before the Subject

27.4 Maintain subject–verb agreement when the verb comes before the subject.

Usually the verb comes after the subject, but in some sentences, the verb is before the subject. In such cases, you must still ensure that the subject and verb agree.

There or *Here*

When a sentence begins with *there* or *here*, the subject always follows the verb. *There* and *here* are not subjects.

V   S   V   S

Here **is** the <u>menu</u>. There **are** many different <u>sandwiches</u>.

Questions

In questions, word order is usually reversed, and the main or helping verb is placed before the subject. In the following example, the main verb is *be*.

V   S   V   S

Where **is** the nearest <u>restaurant</u>? **Is** the <u>food</u> good?

In questions in which the main verb is not *be*, the subject agrees with the helping verb.

HV   S   V   HV   S   V

When **does** the <u>café</u> **close**? **Do** <u>students</u> **work** there?

Practice 4

Correct any subject–verb agreement errors. If there are no errors, write *C* for "correct" in the space.

           Have
EXAMPLE: ~~Has~~ you ever tried backpacking?   _____

1. Is there different ways to travel inexpensively?   _____

2. Do each nation require a visa?   _____

3. There be specific ways to save money while traveling.   _____

4. In America, couch surfing are popular among student travellers.   _____

5. There is affordable home-sharing services like Airbnb.   _____

6. In Europe, there is a strong tradition of "backpacking."   _____

7. Why do that tourist have so much luggage?   _____

8. Many airlines has been raising their luggage fees lately.   _____

Interrupting Words and Phrases

27.5 Maintain subject–verb agreement when there are interrupting words and phrases.

Words that come between the subject and the verb can cause confusion. In such cases, look for the subject and then make sure that the verb agrees with it.

> S   interrupting phrase   V
>
> Some travel <u>companies</u> that advertise online **are** very reliable.

Be particularly careful with interrupting phrases that contain *of the*. In the next examples, the subject appears before *of the*.

> <u>One</u> of the most common travel-related ailments **is** dysentery.

> <u>Each</u> of the travelers **has** a backpack.

Exception: Expressions of Quantity

Expressions of quantity don't follow the preceding *of the* rule. When the subject is an expression of quantity—*the majority of, one-third of, a part of, 10 percent of, the rest of*—the verb agrees with the noun that follows *of the*.

> The majority of the <u>audience</u> **likes** the dance show.

> About 70 percent of <u>tourists</u> **buy** flight tickets online.

HINT: Identify Interrupting Phrases

When you revise your writing, place words that separate the subject and the verb in parentheses. Then you can check to see if your subjects and verbs agree.

> S   interrupting phrase   V
>
> An <u>employee</u> (in my brother's company) **annoys** his coworkers.

Practice 5

Circle the subject and place any words that come between each subject and verb in parentheses. Then underline the correct form of the verb. (Two possible verb choices are in bold.)

EXAMPLE: Most (people) (in my class) <u>like</u> / **likes** to visit other places.

1.   Almost everybody in the world **want** / **wants** to experience an airline flight. Being above the clouds **is** / **are** exciting. But one of a traveler's biggest fears **is** / **are** a plane crash. In fact, there **is** / **are** many incorrect beliefs about air travel. According to George Bibel's book *Beyond the Black Box*, the odds of being in a crash **is** / **are** extremely low.

2.   A graph about air travel statistics **appear** / **appears** in Bibel's book. The majority of crashes **happen** / **happens** during takeoff or landing. For example, about 45 percent of accidents **occur** / **occurs** on landing, but only 2 percent of passengers **die** / **dies** during such events. The worst catastrophes in aviation **occur** / **occurs** when the plane is climbing or cruising. Each of Bibel's examples **is** / **are** interesting. Apparently, an aisle seat **is** / **are** not safer than any other seat in the event of a plane crash. However, according to *Popular Mechanics* editors, the back of an airplane **is** / **are** the safest place to sit. Passengers in the rear of the plane **have** / **has** a 40 percent better chance of surviving.

3.   One of the biggest myths about plane crashes **is** / **are** that they are usually deadly. In fact, plane crashes **have** / **has** very high survival rates. For example, between 1983 and 2000, 53,000 people **was** / **were** in plane accidents, and 51,000 survived. The majority of the population **don't** / **doesn't** know that fact.

Interrupting Words—*Who, Which, That*

If a sentence contains a clause beginning with *who, which,* or *that,* then the verb agrees with the subject preceding *who, which,* or *that.*

A <u>woman</u> who **lives** in my neighborhood loves BMX cycling.

Sometimes a complete dependent clause appears between the subject and the verb.

interrupting clause

The <u>problem</u>, which we discussed, **needs** to be solved.

Practice 6

Underline and correct ten subject–verb agreement errors.

appears

EXAMPLE: Some travel information that <u>appear</u> online is not useful.

1.   A website that I frequently visit provide a lot of travel information. TripAdvisor, which have millions of viewers, has been online since 2000. It provides reviews of hotels, B&Bs, restaurants, and airlines. TripAdvisor notifies any establishment that receive a negative review. Average people who live in different parts of the world also shares ideas in travel forums.

2.   One of TripAdvisor's most popular and controversial features are the ratings. Critics argue that a minority of hotels pays tourists to provide positive reviews. For example, a hotel that is in Cornwall, England, could bribes guests to write positive comments online, according to the British site *The Mirror.* Also, many businesses that work in hospitality complains about biased and unedited reviews. Any person who is having a bad day have the opportunity to ruin a hotel's reputation.

3.   TripAdvisor, which is in many countries, have changed its slogan on the United Kingdom site. This change occurred because of complaints to the Advertising Standards Authority. The slogan, which used to be "Reviews you can trust," is now "Reviews from our community."

Final Review

Underline and correct twenty errors in subject–verb agreement.

includes
EXAMPLE: Traveling <u>include</u> certain dangers.

1.   Different countries have specific driving rules. For instance, in fifty-five countries, everyone drive on the left side of the road instead of the right! Some of the nations is England, Kenya, Japan, Thailand, Australia, Guyana, and Jamaica. In those nations, steering wheels is on the right side of cars. Also, those countries have many "roundabouts." In North America, the majority of the population don't know how to use a traffic circle, which have special rules. For instance, when a driver enters a roundabout, everyone in the outside lane have the right of way.

2.   Certainly, knowing a country's driving rules are important. Otherwise, accidents can occur. In fact, last summer, during a trip to Australia, Arizona resident Kate Willis absentmindedly drove on the wrong side of the road, swerved to miss a car, and drove off a bridge. Kate, along with her two passengers, were scared because the car started to sink into deep water. Annually, there is over ten thousand car-immersion accidents. To survive such an accident, drivers should do the following steps.

3.   First, if a car lands in water, the occupants should stay calm and exit the car quickly. There is many people who reach for their cell phone first, but every second counts. Andy Zhang, a safety expert, says, "Don't waste precious time calling 911." Some passengers, while the car is sinking, forgets to remove their seatbelts. They open the window and panics because they are strapped in. Also, either the

driver or an adult passenger have to free the children from their seat restraints. Kate, along with her two passengers, still have nightmares about being underwater inside a car.

4.   According to various websites, someone in a submerged car should wait until the car hits the bottom before he or she try to leave the car. However, neither Andy Zhang nor his colleagues agrees. Zhang says, "What if someone don't know the depth of the water? Also, the electric motors that operates the windows can stop working." Once the lower part of the door is under water, it can be almost impossible to open. In such cases, Zhang suggests that passengers use their feet to push the window out. One of his best ideas are to keep a small tool in the glove compartment and use it to break the window.

5.   Car submersion accidents occur for many reasons. Floods and driver inattention are two causes. Anyone who learn to drive should know how to escape from a submerged car.

The Writer's Room

Write about one of the following topics. Proofread your text to ensure that your subjects and verbs agree.

1. Describe a visit that you made to a culturally different restaurant. What happened? Use language that appeals to the senses.

2. Compare two cities that you have visited. How are they similar or different?

28　Verb Tenses

SECTION THEME: Travel and Survival

In this chapter, you learn about survival facts and stories.

What Is Verb Tense?

28.1 Define verb tense.

Verb tense indicates when an action occurred. Review the various tenses of the verb *work*. (Progressive, or *-ing*, forms of these verbs appear at the end of this chapter.)

Simple Forms

Present　　　　I <u>work</u> in a large company. My sister <u>works</u> with me.

Past　　　　　We <u>worked</u> in Cancun last summer.

Future　　　　My sister <u>will work</u> in the Middle East next year.

Present perfect　We <u>have worked</u> together since 2001.

Past perfect　　When Maria lost her job, she <u>had worked</u> there for six years.

Future perfect　By 2020, I <u>will have worked</u> here for twenty years.

HINT: Use Standard Verb Forms

Nonstandard English is used in everyday conversation and may differ according to the region in which you live. **Standard English** is the common language generally used and expected in schools, businesses, and government institutions in North America. In college, you should write using standard English.

| **Nonstandard** | He don't have no money. | She be real tired. |
| **Standard** | He <u>does not have any</u> money. | She <u>is really</u> tired. |

Present and Past Tenses

28.2 Define present and past tenses.

Present Tense Verbs

The simple present tense indicates that an action is a general fact or habitual activity. Remember to add *-s* or *-es* to verbs that follow third-person singular forms.

| **Fact** | Our fee **includes** transportation and hotel costs. |
| **Habitual Activity** | Carmen Cruz **teaches** Spanish every Saturday. |

PAST   Saturday   Saturday   Saturday   Saturday   FUTURE

She **teaches.** She **teaches.** She **teaches.** She **teaches.**

Past Tense Verbs

The past tense indicates that an action occurred at a specific past time. Regular past tense verbs have a standard *-d* or *-ed* ending. Use the same form for both singular and plural past tense verbs.

Yesterday morning, we **discussed** the cruise.

Yesterday morning   Today

We **discussed** the cruise.

> **GRAMMAR LINK**
> For more information about subject–verb agreement, see Chapter 27.

Practice 1

Write the present or past form of each verb in parentheses.

EXAMPLE: The tornado (occur) <u>occurred</u> at 4 P.M.

1.   Most people (have) _____ very little knowledge about certain storms. When a tornado (hit) _____ the ground, it makes a continuous rumble that doesn't fade after a few seconds, like thunder. In tornado zones, people (need) _____ to have a plan. They should have a predetermined place to hide, such as a basement. Also, they should avoid windows. Flying debris (be) _____ the most common cause of death during tornados.

2.   In December 2015, a tornado (land) _____ in the Dallas area. At first, people (notice) _____ flashes of light near the ground as power lines (snap) _____ in the fierce winds. There was a low rumble. Josh White (move) _____ his family away from the windows. They (use) _____ a mattress to protect themselves from flying objects. Luckily, White and his family (survive) _____. Tragically, the tornado (cause) _____ the deaths of eleven people. It also (damage) _____ many buildings. Afterward, in an interview with *CNN*, White (express) _____ his sadness. He (realize) _____ how fragile life is.

Irregular Past Tense Verbs

Irregular verbs change internally. Because their spellings change from the present to the past tense, these verbs can be challenging to remember. For example, the irregular verb *go* becomes *went* when you convert it to the past tense.

GRAMMAR LINK
See Appendix 1 for a list of common irregular verbs.

> The hotel **sold** its furniture. (*sold* = past tense of *sell*)
> Consumers **bought** travel insurance. (*bought* = past tense of *buy*)

BE (WAS OR WERE)
Most past tense verbs have one form that you can use with all subjects. However, the verb *be* has two past forms: *was* and *were*. Use *was* with *I*, *he*, *she*, and *it*. Use *were* with *you*, *we*, and *they*.

> The packing box **was** not sturdy enough. The plates **were** fragile.

Practice 2

Write the correct past form of each verb in parentheses. Some verbs are regular, and some are irregular.

EXAMPLE: In 2004, Tilly Smith (know) _____ *knew* _____ about tsunamis.

1.   On December 26, 2004, a catastrophic tsunami affected Thailand. In

Phuket, ten-year-old Tilly Smith (be) _____ the only

person at her hotel to recognize the warning signs of a tsunami. In a

panic, she (tell) _____ her parents that a giant wave

was approaching. They (think) _____ that their

daughter was exaggerating, and they (be, not) _____

worried. Tilly's mother (choose) _____ to ignore

her daughter, and she continued to walk along the beach. Mr. Smith,

however, (make) _____ the decision to bring his

daughter back to the hotel.

2.   At the steps to the hotel, Tilly and her father (meet) _____

a security guard. Tilly (mention) _____ the word

"tsunami." A Japanese guest nearby (hear) _____

the conversation and then (say) _____ that a

large earthquake had just occurred in the ocean. Tilly, who (feel)

_____ certain a giant wave would come, convinced

the guard. Several guards then evacuated the beach. In Thailand,

roughly 230,000 people (die) _____ during the

tsunami. But at Mai Khao Beach on Phuket, everyone (survive)

_____ because of a ten-year-old schoolgirl. There (be,

not) _____ one casualty!

HINT: Use the Base Form After *Did* and *To*

Remember to use the base form:
- of verbs that follow *did* in question and negative forms.
- of verbs that follow the word *to* (infinitive form).

                            have   survive

The guests wanted to **had** a nice vacation. Did everyone **survived**?

Practice 3

Underline and correct nine verb tense and spelling errors.

                                          capsize

EXAMPLE: The strong winds managed to <u>capsized</u> the boat.

1.   An incredible canine survival story occurred near Queensland, Australia. In 2009, Jan Griffith decided to took a boat ride with her dog Sophie. The weather turned stormy. Far from the shore, in choppy seas, the dog slipped and falled overboard. Jan didn't knew if the dog was dead or alive. She searched for her dog unsuccessfully.

2.   Sophie, however, be a good swimmer. The dog swum five nautical miles, through shark-infested water, to St. Bees Island. Sophie then managed to survived for several months by eating baby goats.

3.   Four months later, a ranger on St. Bees Island seen the dog. At first, the ranger thought that Sophie was wild. Then he noticed that the dog obeyed commands and was tame. A week after that, Sophie meeted her master again. According to Jan Griffith, the dog quickly readjusted to a life of ease.

Past Participles

28.3 Identify past participles.

A **past participle** is a verb form, not a verb tense. The past tense and the past participle of regular verbs are the same. The past tense and the past participle of irregular verbs may be different.

	Base Form	**Past Tense**	**Past Participle**
Regular verb	talk	talked	talked
Irregular verb	begin	began	begun

HINT: Using Past Participles

You cannot use a past participle as the only verb in a sentence. You must use it with a helping verb such as *have*, *has*, *had*, *is*, *was*, or *were*.

	helping verb	past participle	
TripAdvisor	**was**	<u>**founded**</u>	in 2000.
Tourists	**have**	<u>**rated**</u>	thousands of hotels.

> **GRAMMAR LINK**
> For a list of irregular past participles, see Appendix 1.

Practice 4

In the next selection, the past participles are underlined. Correct ten past participle errors, and write *C* above four correct past participles.

EXAMPLE: Top athletes have often <u>try</u> to break speed records.
tried

1. The human body is capable of much more than we have previously <u>thinked</u>. Over the years, athletes have <u>broke</u> many world records. For instance, in 1954, Sir Roger Bannister ran a mile in just under four minutes, a feat that doctors had <u>proclaimed</u> was impossible. By 1999, Moroccan runner Hicham El Guerrouj had <u>did</u> it in 3 minutes and 43 seconds. Since then, athletes have <u>beaten</u> the record over and over. In life and death situations, survivors have also <u>teached</u> experts about the body's limits.

2. Some survival specialists have <u>quote</u> the rule of three—the principle that a person can survive about three minutes without air, three days without water, and three weeks without food. However, over the years, many true-life cases have <u>demonstrate</u> that human bodies can surpass expectations. For instance, in 2009, after Haiti's earthquake, Evans Monsigrace was <u>trapped</u> under a market for twenty-seven days with

nothing but some fruit to sustain him. When he was <u>remove</u> from the rubble, he was <u>dehydrated</u> but alive.

3. Dr. John Leach has <u>being</u> in charge of survival research for the Norwegian military for many years. He has <u>finded</u> that the brain has a major role in survival. If people cannot adapt to their new environment during a disaster, the brain may start shutting the body down. Psychological trauma is <u>consider</u> the biggest problem for disaster victims.

Present Perfect Tense

(*Have* or *Has* + Past Participle)

28.4 Define present perfect tense.

A past participle combines with *have* or *has* to form the **present perfect tense**.

> Kate **has been** a tourist guide for six years.
> Since 2001, adventure tourism **has been** popular.

You can use this tense in two different circumstances.

1. Use the present perfect to show that an action began in the past and continues to the present time. You will often use *since* and *for* with this tense.

PAST
(The website
began in 2000.)
NOW

TripAdvisor **has been** popular since 2000.

2. Use the present perfect to show that one or more completed actions occurred at unspecified past times.

PAST
? ? ? ?
NOW

Anton **has visited** Cambodia four times.
(The time of the four visits is not specified.)

HINT: Use Time Markers

When you try to identify which tense to use, look for time markers. **Time markers** are words such as *since*, *for*, or *ago* that indicate when an action occurred.

Simple past	Three weeks **ago**, Parker launched her new adventure magazine.
Present perfect	**Since then**, her adventure magazine has been selling very well.

Choosing the Simple Past or the Present Perfect

Look at the difference between the past and the present perfect tenses.

Simple past   In 2002, Kumar Jain **went** to Shanghai.
(This event occurred at a known past time.)

Present perfect   Since 2002, Jain **has owned** a factory in China.
(The action began in the past and continues to the present.)

He **has made** many business contacts.
(Making business contacts occurred at unknown past times.)

HINT: Simple Past or Present Perfect?

Use the past tense when referring to someone who is no longer living or to something that no longer exists. Only use the present perfect tense when the action has a relationship to someone or something that still exists.

                        wrote
Jules Verne ~~has written~~ many adventure novels.

Practice 5

Write the simple past or present perfect form of the verb in parentheses.

EXAMPLE: For the past few years, I (be) _____ have been _____ very careful at the beach.

1.   Rip currents are narrow channels of fast-moving water. Over the years,

rip currents (occur) _____ in large bodies of water.

Since 2000, lifeguards (rescue) _____ thousands

of swimmers from rip tides. In previous centuries, most people (know, not) _____ what to do when a current pulled them out to sea. But for the last fifty years, safety experts (teach) _____ people about water safety. Even so, since 2000, rip currents (cause) _____ over one thousand fatalities in American coastal communities.

2.   If you are caught in a rip current, remain calm and do not try to swim directly to shore. According to the National Ocean Service, a rip tide can move faster than an Olympic swimmer. In 2013, Melanie Hayes was swimming with her sons when a rip current (pull) _____ them out to sea. Luckily, they (know) _____ what do to. They (remain) _____ calm as the current pulled them away from the beach, and then they (swim) _____ parallel to the shore. After a short distance, the current (lose) _____ strength, so they could return to the beach. Since the incident, Hayes (speak) _____ to others about rip current safety.

Past Perfect Tense
(*Had* + Past Participle)

28.5 Define past perfect tense.

The **past perfect tense** indicates that one or more past actions happened before another past action. It is formed with *had* and the past participle.

PAST PERFECT		PAST	NOW
▼		▼	▼

A thief **had snatched** my purse, so I bought a new one.

Notice the differences between the simple past, the present perfect, and the past perfect tenses.

Simple past In 2007, Taiwan **introduced** a high-speed rail service. (The action occurred at a known past time.)

Present perfect Taiwan **has had** high-speed trains since 2007. (The action began in the past and continues to the present.)

Past perfect The train **had left** the station by the time we arrived. (The action happened in the past, but the train left before we arrived.)

Practice 6

Underline the correct verb form in each sentence. You may choose the simple past tense or the past perfect tense.

EXAMPLE: The 2004 bus accident (<u>occurred</u> / had occurred) several years ago.

1. In 2004, bus driver Edward Jones had to drive a group of students to George Washington's house, a trip he (made / had made) many times.

2. On the route, there (was / had been) a bridge on Alexandria Avenue that (survive / had survived) since the early 1930s.

3. Jones (drove / had driven) right past the large yellow warning sign that he (saw / had seen) on several previous occasions.

4. In the right lane, the arched bridge was only 10 feet high, but it (was / had been) 13 feet high in the center lane.

5. Another bus in front of Jones (already moved / had already moved) to the middle lane when Jones (arrived / had arrived) at the bridge.

6. Jones's bus (smashed / had smashed) forcefully into the bridge, and the collision (destroyed / had destroyed) the roof of the bus.

7. Glass and metal (rained / had rained) down on students, but luckily nobody was killed.

8. Later, investigators determined that Jones (tried / had tried) to multitask by driving and speaking on a cell phone at the same time.

Passive Voice

(*be* + past participle)

28.6 Define passive voice.

In sentences with the **passive voice**, the subject receives the action and does not perform the action. To form the passive voice, use the appropriate tense of the verb *be* plus the past participle. Look carefully at the following two sentences.

Active The passenger **gave** her documents to the customs officer.
(This is active because the subject, *passenger*, performed the action.)

Passive Several documents **were given** to the customs officer.
(This is passive because the subject, *documents*, was affected by the action and did not perform the action.)

HINT: Avoid Overusing the Passive Voice

Generally, try to use the active voice instead of the passive voice. The active voice is more direct and friendly than the passive voice. For example, read two versions of the same message.

Passive voice No more than two pills per day should be ingested. This medication should be taken with meals. It should not be continued if headaches or nausea are experienced.

Active voice Do not ingest more than two pills per day. Take this medication with meals. Do not continue taking it if you experience headache or nausea.

Practice 7

Complete the following sentences by changing the passive verb to the active form. Do not alter the verb tense. Sometimes you must determine who or what is doing the action.

EXAMPLE: The vaccine is given by a nurse.
            A nurse gives the vaccine.

1. The trip was planned by us three months ago.

   _____

2. Free food is not provided by the airline on the flight.

   _____

3. Complaints about the service are often ignored by airline companies.

_____

4. Our hotel reservation was made in January.

_____

5. The hotel has been renovated several times by skilled workers.

_____

HINT: When *Be* Is Suggested, Not Written

In the passive voice, sometimes the verb *be* is suggested but not written. The following sentence contains the passive voice.

A book **written** in 2006 describes the adventure.
    ↑
(that was)

Practice 8

Underline and correct ten errors with past participles.

                  found
EXAMPLE: The snake was <u>find</u> under a rock.

1.   Last summer, Maya was invite on a camping trip to the Arizona desert. The eighteen-year-old city girl, force to sleep in a tent, was not happy. Then, on her second day, her ankle was bit by a rattlesnake. What should people do if they are attack by a poisonous snake?

2.   Many people are teached that venom should be suck out, but that is not a good strategy. First, if there is an open wound in the rescuer's mouth, the venom can enter the bloodstream. Also, a human mouth is fill with germs that can infect the wound. Luckily, Maya's friend Alex knew what do to. First, the limb was immobilize. A small piece of wood was tie to Maya's lower leg, but not too tightly. Then Alex told Maya to keep the area of the snakebite lower than her heart. When they arrived at the hospital thirty minutes later, Maya was quickly saw by a doctor.

Progressive Forms

(-*ing* verbs)

28.7 Identify progressive forms.

Most verbs have progressive tenses. The **progressive tense**, formed with *be* and the *-ing* form of the verb, indicates that an action is, was, or will be in progress. For example, the present progressive indicates that an action is happening right now or for a temporary period of time. The following time line illustrates both the simple and progressive tenses.

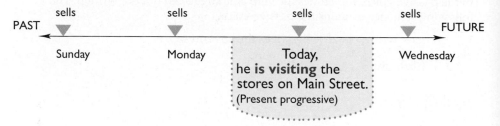

Every day, he **sells** leather wallets. (Simple present)

PAST	sells	sells	sells	sells	FUTURE
	Sunday	Monday	Today, he **is visiting** the stores on Main Street. (Present progressive)	Wednesday	

To form the progressive, use the appropriate tense of the verb *be* with the *-ing* verb.

Present progressive	Right now, I **am** <u>**working**</u>.
Past progressive	We **were** <u>**sleeping**</u> when you phoned us.
Future progressive	Tomorrow, at noon, I **will be** <u>**driving**</u>.
Present perfect progressive	The flight attendant **has been** <u>**flying**</u> since 8:00 A.M.
Past perfect progressive	The British tourist **had been** <u>**driving**</u> on the wrong side of the road when the officer stopped her.
Future perfect progressive	Next year, when Enrique retires, he **will have been** <u>**working**</u> for thirty years.

Common Errors in the Progressive Form

- Do not use the progressive form when an action happens regularly.

  Every day he ~~is complaining~~ complains about the weather.

- In the progressive form, use the correct form of the verb *be*.

  Right now, Ron ~~be~~ is visiting the pyramids.

- In the progressive form, always include the complete helping verb.

            is   have

  Right now, the tourist discussing the problem. They been talking for hours.

- Only use the past progressive tense when an action was ongoing at a specific past time or was interrupted.

                  agreed

  Yesterday, I ~~was agreeing~~ to ride a camel.

HINT: Nonprogressive Verbs

Some verbs do not take the progressive form because they indicate an ongoing state or a perception rather than a temporary action.

Examples of Nonprogressive Verbs

Perception Verbs	Preference Verbs	State Verbs	Possession
admire	desire	believe	have*
care	doubt	know	own
hear	feel	mean	possess
see	hate	realize	
seem	like	recognize	
smell*	look	suppose	
taste*	love	think*	
	prefer	understand	

*Some verbs have more than one meaning and can be used in the progressive tense. Compare the following pairs of sentences.

Nonprogressive	Progressive
He **has** an expired passport. (expresses ownership)	He **is having** a new photo taken.
He **think** it is a nice photo. (expresses an opinion)	He **is thinking** about posting it on Instagram.

Practice 9

Underline and correct one verb error in each sentence.

           had

EXAMPLE: Elisa <u>been</u> preparing for weeks for the zombie run.

1. For many years, people been sharing zombie stories.

2. The television series *The Walking Dead* been playing to huge audiences since 2010.

3. Presently, the Zombie Research Society is having over 300,000 members.

4. The society's website is describing the organization as "dedicated to the historic, cultural, and scientific study of the living dead."

5. These days, many people preparing for the so-called "zombie apocalypse."

6. Some zombie preparation websites are humorous, such as the ones I been reading lately.

7. For people who be planning for the zombie apocalypse, access to clean drinking water and easy-to-use weapons are important.

8. Right now, my friends and I are assemble a zombie survival kit.

9. Ha! At this moment, my friend pretending to be a zombie!

Final Review

Underline and correct fifteen errors in verb form or tense.

trampled

EXAMPLE: Many people were <u>trample</u> that night.

1.   Since the early 1900s, nightclubs been popular. Nightclubs pose fire safety problems because people are pack together in dark rooms. Additionally, some countries have poor safety rules. For example, on January 27, 2013, a terrible fire was occurring at Kiss nightclub in Santa Maria, Brazil. The fire was one of the worst nightclub fires in modern history. Municipalities should strictly enforce fire safety regulations in nightclubs.

2.   At 2:30 A.M. in Santa Maria, a local band be preparing to play its

sixth song. Before the song, their crew been setting up sparklers as part

of the act. The sparklers accidentally ignited the foam insulation in the

club's ceiling. At first, nobody knowed that the situation was serious.

Some people seen the flickering flames, but they didn't reacted. They

thought everything was under control. Moments later, while the room

was fill with smoke, everyone panicked and rushed toward the club's

only exit. Then someone fell in the hallway and blocked the exit.

Unfortunately, the legal limit of one thousand people had been ignore

by the club owners. In fact, nearly double that number were attempt to

flee while the fire was burning. Over two hundred people losed their

lives in the blaze.

3.   Fire safety should be teached to everyone. For instance, people

should look for alternate exits or windows instead of running toward

the main exit. Unfortunately, nightclub fires are happening every few

years, and safety regulations are often overlooked.

The Writer's Room

Write about one of the following topics. Proofread your writing, and ensure
that your verbs are formed correctly.

1. Describe a moment when you thought you were in danger. What
   happened? Use imagery that appeals to the senses.
2. What are the reasons that people travel? How does a trip outside the
   country affect people? Describe the causes and effects of traveling.

29 Problems with Verbs

SECTION THEME: Travel and Survival

LEARNING OBJECTIVES

29.1 Maintain verb consistency.

29.2 Avoid double negatives.

29.3 Avoid nonstandard verb forms *gonna*, *gotta*, *wanna*, and *ain't*.

29.4 Recognize problems in conditional forms.

29.5 Avoid nonstandard verb forms *would of*, *could of*, and *should of*.

29.6 Recognize gerunds and infinitives.

In this chapter, you read about travel destinations and tourism controversies.

Verb Consistency

29.1 Maintain verb consistency.

A verb tense gives your readers an idea about the time that an event occurred. A **faulty tense shift** occurs when you shift from one tense to another for no logical reason. When you write essays, ensure that your tenses are consistent.

Faulty tense shift	Jean Roberts traveled to Santiago, Chile, where she interviews a salon owner.
Correct	Jean Roberts traveled to Santiago, Chile, where she **interviewed** a salon owner.

HINT: *Would* and *Could*

When you tell a story about a past event, use *would* instead of *will* and *could* instead of *can*.

couldn't

Last summer, Jill wanted to travel. She ~~can't~~ afford to fly anywhere.

would

She knew that it ~~will~~ be too expensive.

Practice 1

Underline and correct ten faulty tense shifts in the next paragraphs.

rode

EXAMPLE: He climbed onto his bike and <u>rides</u> down the hill.

1.   In 1995, Rob Penn started a three-year bicycle odyssey throughout

Europe and Asia. At that time, he decided that he will ride a bike

because he can't afford a car, and he didn't want to take public transit.

For three years, Penn traveled to thirty-one different countries. Quickly,

Penn realized that others trusted him because he is on a bicycle.

2.   One day, while Penn was riding through rural Kyrgyzstan, he

falls off his bicycle while going down a steep hill. Limping badly, Penn

decided that he will go to the nearest farm for help. At first, the farmer

pointed to his gun and speaks in a menacing manner. But when the

farmer noticed the bicycle, Penn can see the difference in the old man's

attitude. The farmer put away his gun, invited Penn indoors, and offers

him food.

3.   During his travels, Penn noticed that people will treat him

differently as soon as they saw his bicycle. Perhaps others recognized

that he had to work hard to get from one place to another, and they can

appreciate his effort.

Avoiding Double Negatives

29.2 Avoid double negatives.

A double negative occurs when a negative word such as *no* (*nothing, nobody, nowhere*) is combined with a negative adverb (*not, never, rarely, seldom,* and so on). The result is a sentence that has a double negative. Such sentences can be confusing because the negative words cancel each other.

Double negative	Mr. Lee <u>doesn't</u> want <u>no</u> problems.
	(According to this sentence, Mr. Lee wants problems.)
	He <u>didn't</u> know <u>nothing</u> about it.
	(According to this sentence, he knew something about it.)

How to Correct Double Negatives

There are two ways to correct double negatives.

1. Completely remove *one* of the negative forms. Remember that you may need to adjust the verb to make it agree with the subject.

   Mr. Lee **doesn't** want ~~no~~ problems.

   Mr. Lee ~~doesn't~~ wants **no** problems.

2. Change *no* to *any* (*anybody, anything, anywhere*). Also change *never* to *ever*.

   Mr. Lee doesn't want ~~no~~ (*any*) problems. He doesn't ~~never~~ (*ever*) complain.

HINT: Words with Negative Meanings

Remember that words such as *barely, scarcely,* and *hardly* function as negative words, so don't use "not" with them.

   I ~~didn't~~ (*hardly spoke*) ~~hardly speak~~ during the tour.

Practice 2

Underline and correct eight errors with double negatives. There are two ways
to correct most of the errors.

have no or don't have any

EXAMPLE: Some tourists <u>don't have no</u> respect for the places they visit.

1.   Ko Phangan is one of Thailand's small and beautiful islands.

Forty years ago, tourists didn't have no idea that the island existed.

There weren't no hotels or hostels. One day in 1978, a young American

backpacker made his way to the island and spent a month living on

Haad Rin beach. He knew that there wouldn't be no electricity, but he

didn't care. He loved the silence and the starry nights. When he left the

island, he decided that he wouldn't tell nobody about his adventure.

But in a small restaurant in Bangkok, he became friends with a

young German couple. He decided to tell them about the little spot of

paradise that he had visited. He warned, "Don't tell nobody else!" Of

course, they spread the word.

2.   Today, thousands of young backpackers visit Ko Phangan. They

come to "Full Moon Parties," and leave behind bottles and garbage.

Previous island politicians didn't have no development plan, so the

sewage facilities can't handle the large crowds. Haad Rin beach is lined

with hotels. Often, there isn't nowhere to stay during the most popular

season. Some local residents resent the massive increase in tourism and

the rise in beachfront and water pollution, but there isn't no way to

turn back the clock.

Nonstandard Forms—*Gonna, Gotta, Wanna, Ain't*

29.3 Avoid nonstandard verb forms *gonna, gotta, wanna,* and *ain't*.

Some people commonly say *I'm gonna, I gotta, I wanna,* or *I ain't*. These are
nonstandard forms, so avoid using them in written communication.

- Write *going to* instead of *gonna*.

  My friend is ~~gonna~~ visit Montana.
  <small>going to</small>

- Write *have to* instead of *gotta* or *got to*.

  We ~~gotta~~ bring our tents.
  <small>have to</small>

- Write *want to* instead of *wanna*.

  We ~~wanna~~ camp.
  <small>want to</small>

- Write the correct form of *be* or *have* instead of *ain't*.

  Kendra ~~ain't~~ traveled. She ~~ain't~~ going to take a vacation this year.
  <small>hasn't</small> <small>isn't</small>

Practice 3

Underline and correct nine nonstandard verbs.

EXAMPLE: I <u>gotta</u> work, so I can't travel.
<small>have to</small>

1.   What can you do if you wanna travel, but you don't have a lot of money? First, you gotta plan where you'll stay. Hotels ain't cheap. But there is a new alternative: Airbnb. Ordinary people rent out rooms in their homes for very affordable rates. Hotel operators ain't too pleased with the spread of Airbnb. They say such "illegal hotels" aren't regulated. But it appears that sites like Airbnb are here to stay.

2.   If you decide to rent a room or part of your home on Airbnb, you gotta keep the place very clean. You definitely don't wanna have a bad reputation! If someone gives your place a poor rating, it could be difficult to get future renters. However, homeowners can also rate the renters, so everyone needs to behave well. Such alternative hotels are gonna continue to grow in popularity because they offer a great service.

3.   If you wanna travel on a budget, it's important to evaluate all of your options. You don't gotta spend a fortune to have a good time.

Problems in Conditional Forms

29.4 Recognize problems in conditional forms.

In **conditional sentences**, there is a condition and a result. There are three types of conditional sentences, and each type has two parts, or clauses. The main clause depends on the condition set in the *if* clause.

First Form: Possible Present or Future

The condition is true or very possible. Use the present tense in the *if* clause and the present or future tense in the result clause.

    condition (*if* clause)   result

    If you **ask** her, she **will travel** with you.

Second Form: Unlikely Present

The condition is not likely, and probably will not happen. Use the past tense in the *if* clause and use *would* or *could* in the result clause. In formal writing, when the condition contains the verb *be*, always use "were" in the *if* clause.

    condition (*if* clause)   result

    If I **had** more money, I **would** (or **could**) **visit** New Zealand.

Third Form: Impossible Past

The condition cannot happen because the event is over. Use the past perfect tense in the *if* clause, and use the past form of *would* (*would have* + past participle) in the result clause.

    condition (*if* clause)   result

    If Samson **had taken** that flight, he **would have been** in the plane crash.

    If I **were** younger, I **would cycle** across the country.

HINT: Be Careful with the Past Conditional

In "impossible past" sentences, the writer expresses regret about a past event or expresses the wish that a past event had worked out differently. In the "if" part of the sentence, remember to use the past perfect tense.

    if + past perfect tense   ,   would have (past participle)
          had
    If the driver ~~would have~~ panicked, the accident would have been worse.

Practice 4

Write the correct conditional forms of the verbs in parentheses.

EXAMPLE: If he (make) _____had made_____ a travel blog, others would have enjoyed it.

1.   Some people try risky travel adventures because they want to break a world record. For instance, in 2010, sixteen-year-old Abby Sunderland wanted to be the youngest person to sail around the world unaccompanied. Her parents permitted her to try the adventure. If they (know) _____ about the outcome, perhaps they (reconsider) _____ their decision.

2.   On February 6, 2010, the young sailor set out from Marina Del Rey, California. At that time, if anyone (ask) _____ to accompany her, she would have said "no." To break the record, she had to sail alone. For three months, she passed through rough waves and strong storms. Then when she was about 3,000 miles from Australia, gale-force winds knocked down her mast. If the boat (capsize) _____, she (be) _____ in extreme danger. Luckily, it didn't capsize. A beacon was set off, and the Australian government sent out search planes. A French fishing vessel rescued the girl. Even though she didn't break the record, she was satisfied. Of course, if she (break) _____ the record, she (be) _____ happier.

3. If people get into trouble while doing an adventure sport, should they pay for their own rescue? Sunderland's rescue was estimated to cost about $300,000. Perhaps if her family had had the money, they (pay) _____ for it, but they didn't. Instead, French and Australian taxpayers picked up the tab.

4. If you (have) _____ a sailboat, would you sail

around the world? Even if someone (pay) _____ me,

I wouldn't do it.

Nonstandard Forms—*Would of, Could of, Should of*

29.5 Avoid nonstandard verb forms *would of, could of,* and *should of.*

Some people commonly say *would of, could of,* or *should of.* They may also say *woulda, coulda,* or *shoulda.* These are nonstandard forms, and you should avoid using them in written communication. When you use the past forms of *should, would,* and *could,* always include *have* with the past participle.

                                        should have

Dominique Brown is a nurse, but she really loves real estate. She ~~should of~~

                    would have

become a real-estate agent. She ~~woulda~~ been very successful.

Practice 5

Underline and correct nine errors in conditional forms or in the past forms of *could* and *should.*

                       have
EXAMPLE: Calvin should <u>of</u> stayed home.

1.   If you search the Internet, you would find information about

"orphan tourism." In 2008, Calvin Rice went to Siem Reap, Cambodia.

He saw an organized group of orphans begging in a tourist area. He

coulda just visited the temples, but instead, he chose to work in that

orphanage. If he woulda known about the problems related to orphan

tourism, perhaps he would of done something else.

2.   First, he noticed that many visitors just came to look at the orphans, so it sometimes felt like a zoo. The orphanage even permitted a man to take out an orphan for a day, with no supervision, so anything coulda happened to the child. Rice also learned that many of the taxi drivers, tour operators, and orphanage directors make a lot of money from orphan tourism. In 2012, UNICEF said that of the nearly 12,000 children living in Cambodian orphanages, 72 percent have at least one living parent.

3.   In the past, some desperate parents coulda sold their children to an orphanage. If Rice would of known about the greed and corruption in the orphanage industry, he woulda done another type of volunteer work. He says that he should of learned about orphan tourism before he took that volunteer job. These days, issues related to orphan tourism are being debated openly.

Recognizing Gerunds and Infinitives

29.6 Recognize gerunds and infinitives.

Sometimes a main verb is followed by another verb. The second verb can be a gerund or an infinitive. A **gerund** is a verb with an *-ing* ending. An **infinitive** consists of *to* and the base form of the verb.

> verb + gerund
> Edward <u>finished</u> **repairing** his bicycle.

> verb + infinitive
> He <u>wants</u> **to take** weekends off.

Some verbs in English are always followed by a gerund. Do not confuse gerunds with progressive verb forms.

Progressive verb	Julie is working now.
	(Julie is in the process of doing something.)
Gerund	Julie finished **working**.
	(*Working* is a gerund that follows *finish*.)

Some Common Verbs Followed by Gerunds or Infinitives

Some Common Verbs Followed by Gerunds			
acknowledge	deny	keep	recall
admit	detest	loathe	recollect
adore	discuss	mention	recommend
appreciate	dislike	mind	regret
avoid	enjoy	miss	resent
can't help	finish	postpone	resist
consider	involve	practice	risk
delay	justify	quit	suggest

Some Common Verbs Followed by Infinitives			
afford	decide	manage	refuse
agree	demand	mean	seem
appear	deserve	need	swear
arrange	expect	offer	threaten
ask	fail	plan	volunteer
claim	hesitate	prepare	want
compete	hope	pretend	wish
consent	learn	promise	would like

Some common verbs can be followed by gerunds or infinitives. Both forms have the same meaning.

> begin   continue   like   love   start

> Elaine <u>likes</u> **to read**. Elaine <u>likes</u> **reading**.

> (Both sentences have the same meaning.)

Stop, Remember, and *Used to*

Some verbs can be followed by either a gerund or an infinitive, but there is a difference in meaning depending on the form you use.

Term	Form	Example	Meaning
Stop	+ infinitive	He often stops <u>to buy</u> gas every Sunday.	To stop an activity (driving) to do something else.
	+ gerund	I stopped <u>smoking</u> five years ago.	To permanently stop doing something.
Remember	+ infinitive	Please remember <u>to lock</u> the door.	To remember to perform a task.
	+ gerund	I remember <u>meeting</u> him in 2004.	To have a memory about a past event.
Used to	+ infinitive	Jane used <u>to smoke</u>.	To express a past habit.
	+ gerund	Jane is used to <u>living</u> alone.	To be accustomed to something.

Prepositions Plus Gerunds

Many sentences have the structure *verb + preposition + object*. A gerund can be the object of a preposition.

> verb + preposition + gerund
> I dream **about** <u>traveling</u> to Greece.

Some Common Words Followed by Prepositions plus Gerunds			
accuse of	(be) excited about	(be) good at	prohibit from
apologize for	feel like	insist on	succeed in
discourage <u>him</u> from*	fond of	(be) interested in	think about
dream of	forbid <u>him</u> from*	look forward to	(be) tired of
(be) enthusiastic about	forgive <u>me</u> for*	prevent <u>him</u> from*	warn <u>him</u> about*

*Certain verbs can have a noun or pronoun before the preposition.

Practice 6

Complete the sentence with the appropriate verb. Underline either the gerund or the infinitive form.

1.   Some travelers can't afford (to stay / staying) in hotels. Today, they have many other options. For instance, they can consider (to couch surf / couch surfing), which means "to sleep on someone's couch or in a spare bedroom." There are many "free hospitality" websites, including *Couchsurfing* and *BeWelcome*. Couch surfing has become a relatively safe and inexpensive way to travel.

2.   If you decide (to try / trying) couch surfing, there are a few things you should do. First, read profiles carefully, as couch-surfing hosts are rated by users. Also, remember (to give / giving) back in some way. For instance, I recommend (to cook / cooking) and (to clean / cleaning) up after meals. Also, be prepared (to contribute / contributing) to the host's food bill. Don't expect to receive free meals.

3.   Finally, if you like the couch-surfing experience, you may become a couch-surfing host. Last summer, Mila Gomeshi was excited (to go / going / about going) to Dallas, Texas. She looked

forward (to stay / staying / to staying) in someone's apartment.
Jennifer, a translator, hosts guests in her home because she enjoys
(to meet / meeting) new people from different places and cultures. At
first, Mila was nervous, but soon she stopped (to worry / worrying /
to worrying) about staying with a stranger. Today, Mila remembers
(to be / being) surprised by Jennifer's hospitality. She is interested (to
become / becoming / in becoming) a couch-surfing host one day.

Final Review

Underline and correct fifteen errors with verbs and with double negatives.

EXAMPLE: The tourists should not <u>of</u> painted so quickly.
                                         have

1.   Many people enjoy to travel and wanna do volunteer work overseas.
They look online for an organization, but often they don't know nothing
about the issues involved in the "voluntourism" industry. If youths
really hope to help others, they gotta do some research first.

2.   Some tour operators make money from travel volunteers. They
charge their idealistic workers a fee for housing, and then the money
ain't distributed to those in need. For instance, Natalia Morova worked
in Ghana for an organization that helped AIDS orphans. She didn't
know that the money was only gonna help the organization's founder.
She met children who didn't receive nothing from the charity, yet their
names were on the charity's list.

3.   In another case, Daniela Papi was an eager volunteer who looked
forward to help others. In Thailand, she paid for a bike tour that was
done with an aid organization. The young bikers painted a school

in a rural area. Papi believed that her team will make a difference.
According to Papi, everyone was tired after a long day of riding, so a
lot of the paint ends up on the floor. After they left, someone finished
to paint the walls properly because the volunteers had done such
shoddy work. In retrospect, Papi says that they should of given the
money to the school. The school needed teachers and supplies, not
paint. The school coulda hired another teacher with the money that the
cyclists contributed.

4.   According to Papi, people shouldn't stop to believe in the value of
volunteer work. However, they should be realistic and see volunteer
work as a learning opportunity. Also, there are good organizations, but
people should learn choosing wisely.

The Writer's Room

Write about one of the following topics. Ensure that your verbs are correctly
formed.

1. If you had lived one hundred years ago, what job would you have
   done? Describe the job using details that appeal to the senses.
2. Describe the different types of thrill seekers. You might begin by
   defining the term and then dividing it into categories. To get ideas, see
   the following photos.

30 Nouns, Determiners, and Prepositions

SECTION THEME: Inventions and Discoveries

In this chapter, you read about some of the inventions in the first decade of the new century.

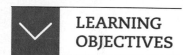

LEARNING OBJECTIVES

30.1 Distinguish count and noncount nouns.

30.2 Use determiners correctly.

30.3 Use prepositions correctly.

Count and Noncount Nouns

30.1 Distinguish count and noncount nouns.

In English, nouns are grouped into two types: count nouns and noncount nouns.

Count nouns refer to people or things that you can count such as *tree, house,* or *dog*. Count nouns have both a singular and plural form.

> She wrote <u>three</u> **articles** about famous inventors.

Noncount nouns refer to people or things that you cannot count because you cannot divide them, such as *sugar* and *imagination*. Noncount nouns have only the singular form.

> **Oil** has become a very expensive commodity.

Here are some examples of common noncount nouns.

Common Noncount Nouns					
Categories of Objects		**Food**	**Nature**	**Substances**	
clothing	machinery	bread	air	chalk	paint
equipment	mail	fish	electricity	charcoal	paper
furniture	money	honey	energy	coal	
homework	music	meat	environment	fur	
jewelry	postage	milk	heat	hair	
luggage	software	rice	ice	ink	
			radiation		
			weather		
Abstract Nouns					
advice	education	health	knowledge	proof	
attention	effort	help	logic	research	
behavior	evidence	history	peace	speculation	
creativity	extinction	information	progress	violence	

HINT: Latin Nouns

Some nouns that are borrowed from Latin or Greek keep the plural form of the original language.

Singular	**Plural**	**Singular**	**Plural**
millennium	millennia	paparazzo	paparazzi
datum	data	phenomenon	phenomena

Determiners

30.2 Use determiners correctly.

Determiners are words that will help you determine or figure out whether a noun is specific or general. Examples of determiners are articles (*a*), demonstratives (*this*), indefinite pronouns (*many*), numbers (*three*), possessive nouns (*Maria's*), and possessive adjectives (*my*).

The **students** are working on four new robotics **projects**.

Commonly Confused Determiners

Some determiners can be confusing because you can use them only in specific circumstances. Review the following commonly confused determiners.

A, AN, THE

A and *an* are general determiners and *the* is a specific determiner. **Use *a* and *an*** before singular count nouns but not before plural or noncount nouns. Use *a* before nouns that begin with a consonant (*a storm*), and use *an* before nouns that begin with a vowel (*an institute*).

Use *the* before nouns that refer to a specific person, place, or thing. Do not use *the* before languages (*He speaks Italian*), sports (*They watch tennis*), or most city and country names (*Two of the coldest capital cities in the world are Ottawa and Moscow*). Two examples of exceptions are *the United States* and *the Netherlands*.

> A **friend** bought a new hybrid **car**. The **car** can run for 60 miles on a **tank** of gas.

MANY, FEW, MUCH, LITTLE

Use *many* and *few* with count nouns.

> Many **people** invent products, but few **inventions** are really successful.

Use *much* and *little* with noncount nouns.

> Scientists are spending too much **time** on the project. They are making little **progress**.

THIS, THAT, THESE, THOSE

This and *these* refer to things that are physically close to the speaker or at the present time. Use *this* before singular nouns and *these* before plural nouns. *That* and *those* refer to things that are physically distant from the speaker or in the past time. Use *that* before singular nouns and *those* before plural nouns.

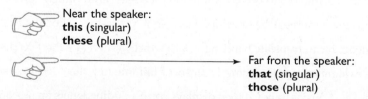

Near the speaker:
this (singular)
these (plural)

Far from the speaker:
that (singular)
those (plural)

> This **report** on my desk is about new satellite technology. The year 1957 was an important time. In that **year**, the Russians launched the first artificial satellite into space. In those **days**, Americans worried that the Russians were winning the space race. These **days**, the United States is making fantastic advances in satellite technology.

Practice 1

Underline the correct noun or determiner in parentheses. If the noun does not require a determiner, underline X.

EXAMPLE: The twenty-first century may be referred to as (<u>the</u> / a / X) Age of Communication.

1. Although (this / that) century is still young, (many / much) interesting (invention / inventions) are changing how we communicate. (These / Those) days, (few / little) people in (a / the / X) United States have never used (a / an / X) smartphone or tablet. There has been (many / much) progress in other methods of mass communication. For example, in 2005, online video sharing was rare, but (this / that) year, three friends from (a / the / X) California created YouTube. (This / That / These) days, over one hundred million YouTube videos are watched daily. In fact, some people believe that there is too (much / many) (information / informations) on that site.

2. Some other inventions are less well known. Ryan Patterson is interested in electronics. In 2001, when he was seventeen years old, he had (a / an / the) idea. While eating at (a / an / X) restaurant, Ryan saw (a / the / X) group of people who were hearing impaired. They communicated in sign language with their translator, who then repeated their order to their server. Ryan started to think of ways to help people with hearing loss to become more independent. With (little / few) (money / monies), he developed (a / an / X) product called the Braille Glove. It can translate hand signs into words. When (a / the / X) person uses sign language, electronic sensors built into (a / the / X) glove signal (a / an / X) computer. It then displays corresponding letters on (a / an / X) small screen. People who have (a / the / X) problems communicating may find Ryan's glove very convenient. Ryan received the top prize for (a / an / X) invention from Intel's 2002 Science Talent Search contest.

Prepositions

30.3 Use prepositions correctly.

Prepositions are words that show concepts such as time, place, direction, and manner. They show connections or relationships between ideas.

> In 2014, Fred bought an electric car.
> In March, his sister borrowed it for a few days.

Prepositions of Time and Place

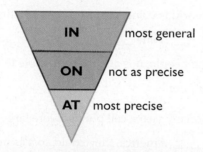

	Prepositions of Time	Prepositions of Place
in	in a year, month, or century (in February)	in a city, country, or continent (in Phoenix)
on	on a day of the week (on Monday) on a specific date (on June 16) on a specific holiday (on Memorial Day)	on a specific street (on Lacombe Ave.) on technological devices (on TV, on the radio, on the phone, on the cell phone, on the computer)
at	at a specific time of day (at 9:15) at night at breakfast, lunch, dinner	at a specific address (at 18 Oriole Crescent) at a specific building (at the hospital, at home)
from . . . to	from one time to another (from 10 AM to 1 PM)	from one place to another (from Fort Lauderdale to Orlando)
for	for a period of time (for five hours)	for a distance (for two miles)

Commonly Confused Prepositions

TO VERSUS *AT*

Use *to* after verbs that indicate movement from one place to another. Use *at* after verbs that indicate being or remaining in one place (and not moving from one place to another). Exception: Do not put *to* directly before *home*.

> Every day, the inventor **drives** to his office and **sits** at his desk.

DURING, FOR, SINCE

Use *during* to explain when something happens, *for* to explain how long it takes to happen, and *since* to indicate the start of an activity.

> During **the semester,** students study robotics for **five weeks.**

> Since **2012,** we have been doing surveys during **the fall semester.**

Practice 2

Write the correct preposition in the blanks.

EXAMPLE: I have access to 5G _____on_____ my new smartphone.

1.   _____ a presentation for Apple _____ a Tuesday
     _____ early 2007, the late Steve Jobs called the new iPhone
     a "revolutionary and magical product." Nowadays, it seems
     everyone in the world is using a smartphone, whether they are
     travelling_____ home _____ work or going out with
     friends. For young people, it is almost impossible to remember a world
     without the smartphone.

2.   _____ many years, cell phones were large and bulky. During
     the 1980s _____ America, they could cost as much as $4,000.
     The first cell phone with limited Internet access and features of the
     modern smartphone was called the Simon Personal Communicator.
     _____ 1992, _____ November 23, _____ exactly
     9 A.M., a representative of the COMDEX computer industry trade show
     unveiled its smart phone. People could check their email _____
     this device, which also had applications for a calendar and a calculator.
     _____ that time, the device was known as a personal digital
     assistant (PDA). The term "smartphone" would not be coined
     _____ several years.

3.   _____ 2007, Google launched the Android operating system
     to compete with Apple's iPhone technology. _____ then, Apple's
     iOS and Google's Android have been the two most popular operating
     systems for smartphones. People _____ nearly every country use
     smartphones all the time. People play games, surf the Internet, check
     Facebook, or use hundreds of other applications _____ their
     phones.

Common Prepositional Expressions

Many common expressions contain prepositions. These types of expressions usually express a particular meaning. The meaning of a verb will change if it is used with a specific preposition. Examine the difference in meaning of the following expressions.

to turn on—to start a machine or switch on the lights
to turn off—to stop a machine or switch off the lights
to turn down—to decline something
to turn over—to rotate
to turn up—to arrive

Some Common Prepositional Expressions

accuse (somebody) of	depend on	insulted by	responsible for
acquainted with	dream of / about	interested in	satisfied with
afraid of	escape from	long for	scared of
agree with	excited about	look forward to	search for
apologize for	familiar with	participate in	similar to
apply for	fond of	patient with	specialize in
approve of	forget about	pay attention to	stop (something) from
associate with	forgive (someone) for	pay for	succeed in
aware of	friendly with	prevent (someone) from	take advantage of
believe in	grateful for	protect (someone) from	take care of
capable of	happy about	proud of	thank (someone) for
comply with	hear about	provide (someone) with	think about / of
confronted with	hope for	qualify for	tired of
consist of	hopeful about	realistic about	willing to
count on	innocent of	rely on	wish for
deal with	insist on	rescue from	worry about

Practice 3

Write the correct prepositions in the next paragraphs. Use the preceding list of prepositional expressions to help you.

EXAMPLE: Many people are afraid _____of_____ spiders.

1. Spider web material is stronger and more flexible than steel. Until recently, textile makers could only dream _____ making cloth from spider webs. But not too long ago, two British experts succeeded _____ creating an eleven-foot-long cloth made from spider threads.

2.   The two designers specialize _____ developing different types of textiles. The designers became interested _____ making spider silk cloth after they heard that priests in Madagascar had made such a cloth in the 1800s. It took the British designers about four years and seventy thousand helpers to make the spider silk. Every day, they searched _____ golden orb spiders and harvested the silk. About fourteen thousand spiders make one ounce of silk, and the textile cloth weighs about two and a half pounds. So the textile experts had to be realistic _____ the time and effort required to make the silk.

3.   Manufacturers became excited _____ this project because they want to produce material that is as tough and pliable as spider silk. But they will have to forget _____ such a scheme because it is not cost effective. Scientists have not been able to duplicate spider silk in laboratories.

FINAL REVIEW

Correct fifteen errors in nouns, determiners, and prepositions.

                       Many   with
EXAMPLE: ~~Much~~ science fiction fans are acquainted ~~in~~ artificial intelligence.

1.   In a film *Star Wars: The Force Awakens*, robots exhibit human characteristics. BB-8, R2-D2, and C-3PO travel from one planet in another and give their owners useful advices. As technology progresses, the fantastic innovations in the world of science fiction may soon become reality.

2.   People have been fascinated with androids since a long time. Scientists are making much advances in the field of artificial intelligence (AI). Currently, researchers are searching with ways to build machines that have human intellectual abilities such as logics. On February 2011, a robot named Watson appeared at television. This day was unforgettable for fans of *Jeopardy!* because Watson defeated his two opponents, the quiz show's champions. The audience was astonished that the robot had so many knowledge.

3.   In fact, artificial intelligence has been advancing at a rapid rate. Chatterbots are robots that communicate with humans. And, at 2014, a hitchbot successfully hitchhiked across Canada. Moreover, the military is experimenting with killer robots that can perform much difficult tasks.

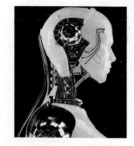

4.   As technology advances, however, society will be confronted about ethical issues. If robots can develop intelligence, will they also develop feelings? Will society grant intelligent robots legal rights? Or will robots become human slaves? Right now, there is very few information about these topics.

The Writer's Room

Write about one of the following topics. Proofread your text to ensure that there are no errors in singular or plural forms, determiners, and prepositions.

1. Have you ever bought any useless gadgets? Give some examples.
2. Is there a gadget or invention you could not live without? Explain your reasons, or describe how the object affects your life.

31 Pronouns

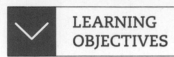

LEARNING OBJECTIVES

31.1 Practice pronoun–antecedent agreement.

31.2 Use indefinite pronouns correctly.

31.3 Avoid using vague pronouns.

31.4 Avoid unnecessary pronoun shifts.

31.5 Use the three main pronoun cases correctly.

31.6 Use relative pronouns correctly.

In this chapter, you will read about profitable inventions.

Pronoun–Antecedent Agreement

31.1 Practice pronoun–antecedent agreement.

Pronouns are words that replace nouns (people, places, or things) and phrases. Use pronouns to avoid repeating nouns.

He
Gary Dahl is an inventor. ~~Gary Dahl~~ invented the Pet Rock.

A pronoun must agree with its **antecedent**, which is the word to which the pronoun refers. Antecedents are words that the pronouns have replaced, and they always come before the pronoun. Pronouns must agree in person and number with their antecedents.

Sarah played games on **her** computer when **she** was young.

Compound Antecedents

Compound antecedents consist of two or more nouns joined by *and* or *or*. When nouns are joined by *and*, use a plural pronoun to refer to them.

James and Reid use **their** satellite phones regularly.

When singular nouns are joined by *or*, use a singular pronoun. When plural nouns are joined by *or*, use a plural pronoun.

Does the radio station or the TV station have **its** own program on new inventions?

Do environmentalists or activists update **their** websites?

Collective Nouns

GRAMMAR LINK
For a list of common collective nouns, see page 368 in Chapter 27.

Collective nouns refer to a group of people or things. The group usually acts as a unit; therefore, most of the time, the collective noun is singular.

The company was fined for copyright infringement. **It** had to pay a large sum of money.

Practice 1

Circle each pronoun and underline its antecedent.

EXAMPLE: Although many inventions are useless, (they) are popular.

1. In 1975, Gary Dahl's friends complained about their German Shepherd.

2. Ursula and Mickey Thibo did not want to take care of their dog.

3. So Dahl invented the Pet Rock, and his invention became very popular.

4. The Pet Rock was a great pet because it did not have to be fed or walked.

5. Dahl established a company, and it made a huge profit from the Pet Rock.

6. Does eBay or ThinkGeek sell the Pet Rock on its website?

Indefinite Pronouns

31.2 Use indefinite pronouns correctly.

Use **indefinite pronouns** when you refer to people or things whose identities are not known or are unimportant. This chart shows some common singular and plural indefinite pronouns.

Indefinite Pronouns				
Singular	another	each	no one	other
	anybody	everybody	nobody	somebody
	anyone	everyone	nothing	someone
	anything	everything	one	something
Plural	both, few, many, others, several			
Either singular or plural	all, any, half (and other fractions), none, more, most, some			

Singular

When you use a singular indefinite antecedent, use a singular pronoun to refer to it.

<u>Nobody</u> remembered to bring **his** or **her** laptop.

Plural

When you use a plural indefinite antecedent, use a plural pronoun to refer to it.

The two men rushed into the street, and <u>both</u> carried **their** own smartphones.

Either Singular or Plural

Some indefinite pronouns can be either singular or plural depending on the noun to which they refer.

Many scientists spoke at the conference. <u>All</u> gave important information about **their** research.
(*All* refers to scientists; therefore, the pronoun is plural.)

I read <u>all</u> of the newspaper and could not find **its** business section.
(*All* refers to the newspaper; therefore, the pronoun is singular.)

HINT: Avoid Sexist Language

Terms like *anybody*, *somebody*, *nobody*, and *each* are singular antecedents, so the pronouns that follow must be singular. At one time, it was acceptable to use *he* as a general term meaning "all people." However, today it is more acceptable to use *he or she*.

Sexist	<u>Everyone</u> should bring **his** laptop to the meeting.
Solution	<u>Everyone</u> should bring **his** or **her** laptop to the meeting.
Better Solution	<u>People</u> should bring **their** laptops to the meeting.
Exception	In the men's prison, <u>everyone</u> has **his** own cell.
	(If you know for certain that the subject is male or female, then use only *he* or only *she*.)

Practice 2

Correct eight errors in pronoun–antecedent agreement by changing either the antecedent or the pronoun. If you change any antecedents, make sure that your subjects and verbs agree.

EXAMPLE: Some customers buy ~~his~~ ^{their} Chia Pets online.

1.   Everyone feels embarrassed when they buy a useless product. One huge fad was the Chia Pet. Chia Pets are animal-shaped terracotta pots that sprout tiny plants. The plants look like the animal's fur. In 1982, many people bought Chia Pets. Some especially loved his first Chia Pet. Anybody who forgets to water their Chia gets a surprise: The Chia's "fur" dies.

2.   Since the 1980s, some people have become enthusiastic Chia collectors, and he can buy and sell the pets on the Internet. Anyone can add to their collection. Some Chias are cartoon characters such as Bugs Bunny. Others take its image from popular culture. For example, there are Chia Presidents, Chia Statues of Liberty, and so on.

3.   Someone gave me two Chia Pets as a present. Both are on my desk, and its "fur" is green and growing. The Chias are unique, and nobody else I know has one of their own.

Vague Pronouns

31.3 Avoid using vague pronouns.

Avoid using pronouns that could refer to more than one antecedent.

Vague   My father asked my brother where <u>his</u> instruction manual was.
(Whose instruction manual? My father's or my brother's?)

Clearer   My father asked my brother where **my brother's** instruction manual was.

Avoid using confusing pronouns such as *it* and *they* that have no clear antecedent.

Vague   <u>They</u> say that millions of people have bought the new iPad.
(Who are *they*?)

Clearer   **Reporters** say that millions of people have bought the new iPad.

Vague	<u>It</u> stated in the newspaper that robots are being used to perform dangerous tasks. (Who or what is *it*?)
Clearer	**The** *New York Times'* **article** stated that robots are being used to perform dangerous tasks.

This, that, and *which* should refer to a specific antecedent.

Vague	My girlfriend said that the seminar was boring. I was glad she told me <u>this</u>. (What is *this*?)
Clearer	My girlfriend said that the seminar was boring. I was glad she told me **this information**.

HINT: Avoid Repeating the Subject

When you clearly mention a subject, do not repeat the subject in pronoun form.

Technology ~~it~~ is advancing at a fast pace.

Practice 3

The next paragraphs contain vague pronouns or repeated subjects. Correct the eight errors in this selection. You may need to rewrite some sentences.

               Experts
EXAMPLE: ~~They~~ say that many items are invented accidently.

1.   When Frank Epperson was eleven years old, he accidentally left a fruit drink with a stick in it outside. The temperature plummeted overnight. This caused the liquid to freeze, and the Popsicle was created. They say that Epperson introduced the "Epsicle ice pop" at a fireman's ball in 1922. The firemen, they were thrilled with the "stick of frozen juice." Epperson's children later convinced their father to name the ice pop "Popsicle."

2. People started talking about the product. This caused reporters to interview Frank Epperson. Frank was told by his friend Jack Steele that he was going to become famous. Jack he advised Frank to take out a patent. Three years later, in 1925, it stated that the Joe Lowe Company bought Frank's patent, and the Popsicle became even more popular. Children, as well as adults, like to eat Popsicles. This has led to the creation of other similar products, such as the Fudgsicle and the Creamsicle.

Pronoun Shifts

31.4 Avoid unnecessary pronoun shifts.

If your essays contain unnecessary shifts in person or number, you may confuse readers. They will not know exactly who or how many you are referring to. Carefully edit your writing to ensure that all pronouns are consistent.

Making Pronouns Consistent in Number

If the antecedent is singular, then the pronoun must be singular. If the antecedent is plural, then the pronoun must be plural.

singular   his or her

The **director** is showing ~~their~~ 3D films to a major distributor.

plural   their

Many companies market new apps for ~~its~~ cell phones.

Making Pronouns Consistent in Person

Person is the writer's perspective. For some writing assignments, you might use the first person (*I, we*). For other assignments, especially most college essays, you will likely use the third person (*he, she, it, they*).

Shifting the point of view for no reason confuses readers. If you begin writing from one point of view, do not shift unnecessarily to another point of view.

When **parents** buy **their** sons or daughters a new video game, **they** should be careful. **They** should read about the video game. ^{They} ~~You~~ should avoid buying violent video games.

Practice 4

Correct five pronoun shift errors.

EXAMPLE: French fries are very popular, and ~~it~~ ^{they} can come with a variety of seasonings.

The history of French fries is complicated. Some say that in the eighteenth century, a young Belgian man was hungry, but they couldn't fish because the river was frozen. Traditionally, Belgians fried small fish in oil, and we would cut the fish into strips to fry. The man decided that you could try to cut potatoes into thin strips and fry them the same way as the fish. However, others say that French fries were invented in France. Antoine-Augustine Parmentier realized that when one offered fried potatoes in his restaurant, customers would rave about them. Some say that Parmentier is responsible for the invention of French fries. Most people love French fries, but we should not eat them too often.

Pronoun Case

31.5 Use the three main pronoun cases correctly.

Pronouns are formed according to the role they play in a sentence. A pronoun can be the subject of the sentence or the object of the sentence. It can also show possession. This chart shows the three main pronoun cases: subjective, objective, and possessive.

Pronouns

	Subjective	Objective	Possessive	
			Possessive Adjective	Possessive Pronoun
Singular				
1st person	I	me	my	mine
2nd person	you	you	your	yours
3rd person	he, she, it, who, whoever	him, her, it, whom, whomever	his, her, its, whose	his, hers
Plural				
1st person	we	us	our	ours
2nd person	you	you	your	yours
3rd person	they	them	their	theirs

Subjective Case and Objective Case

When a pronoun is the subject of the sentence, use the subjective form of the pronoun. When a pronoun is the object in the sentence, use the objective form of the pronoun.

subject   subject   object
He left the umbrella at work, and **I** asked **him** to bring it home.

Possessive Case

A possessive pronoun shows ownership.

- **Possessive adjectives** come before the noun that they modify.

  She finished **her** research on electric cars, but we did not finish **our** research.

- **Possessive pronouns** replace the possessive adjective and the noun that follows it. In the next sentence, the possessive pronoun *ours* replaces both the possessive adjective *our* and the noun *research*.

        possessive adjective   possessive pronoun
  She finished **her** research on electric cars, but we did not finish **ours**.

Problems with Possessive Pronouns

Some possessive adjectives sound like certain contractions. When using the possessive adjectives *their*, *your*, and *its*, be careful that you do not confuse them with *they're* (they + are), *you're* (you + are), and *it's* (it + is).

> **GRAMMAR LINK**
> For more information about apostrophes, see Chapter 36.

                        hers   theirs
The book on gadgets is ~~her's~~. The robotics magazine is ~~their's~~.

HINT: Choosing *His* or *Her*

To choose the correct possessive adjective, think about the possessor (not the object that is possessed).

If something belongs to a female, use *her* + noun.

Malina and **her** husband are inventors.

If something belongs to a male, use *his* + noun.

Cliff used **his** new camera to make videos.

Practice 5

Underline the correct possessive pronouns or possessive adjectives in parentheses.

EXAMPLE: Hedy Lamarr received praise for (<u>her</u> / hers) invention.

1. Many people have become famous for (their / there / they're) inventions. For example, Alfred Nobel invented dynamite, and (its / it's / their) usefulness made Nobel rich. Women have also invented products, but (their / there / theirs) are often not as well known.

2. Hedy Lamarr was famous during (her / hers) lifetime. She was known as an actress, not as an inventor. However, she and (her / his) friend George Antheil developed a secret communications system during World War II. (Their / They're / Theirs) invention altered radio waves and created an unbreakable coding system. The code prevented the enemy from understanding classified messages.

3. For (our / ours) film studies class, we made a documentary about Hedy Lamarr. All of the students submitted (their / they're / there) films to a contest. (Our / Ours) won first prize. In class, students watched (our / ours) documentary, and we watched (their / theirs).

Pronouns in Comparisons with *Than* or *As*

Avoid making errors in pronoun case when the pronoun follows *than* or *as*. If the pronoun is a subject, use the subjective case, and if the pronoun is an object, use the objective case.

If you use the incorrect case, your sentence may have a meaning that you do not intend it to have. Review the next examples. When the sentence ends with the subjective pronoun, you may find it helpful to add a verb after the pronoun.

objective case
I like new technology as much as **him**.

(I like new technology <u>as much as I like him</u>.)

subjective case
I like new technology as much as **he** (does).

(I like new technology <u>as much as he likes new technology</u>.)

HINT: Complete the Thought

To test which pronoun case to use, complete the thought.

> Eva understands him more than **I** [understand him].
> (Do I want to say that Eva understands him more than I understand him?)

> Eva understands him more than [she understands] **me**.
> (Or, do I want to say that Eva understands him more than she understands me?)

Pronouns in Prepositional Phrases

In a prepositional phrase, the noun or pronoun that follows the preposition is the object of the preposition. Therefore, always use the objective case of the pronoun after a preposition.

> To **him**, a cutback in funding is not a big deal. <u>Between</u> **you** and **me**, I think he's misinformed.

Pronouns with *And* or *Or*

Use the correct case when nouns and pronouns are joined by *and* or *or*. If the pronouns are the subject, use the subjective case. If the pronouns are the object, use the objective case.

>   She and I
> ~~Her and me~~ had to read about Alexander Graham Bell, and then the instructor
>   her and me
> asked ~~she and I~~ to summarize the information.
>   I
> Frances or ~~me~~ could give a seminar on a new invention. The students asked
>   me
> Frances or ~~I~~ to show how the invention worked.

HINT: Finding the Correct Case

To determine that your case is correct, try saying the sentence with either the subjective case or the objective case.

Sentence	The professor asked her and (**I or me**) to research the topic.
Possible answers	The professor asked **I** to research the topic. (This would not make sense.)
	The professor asked **me** to research the topic. (This would make sense.)
Correct answer	The professor asked **her** and **me** to research the topic.

Practice 6

Correct any errors with pronoun case. If the pronouns in a sentence are correct, write **C** beside it.

EXAMPLE: Zach and ~~me~~ laughed at all the weird apps.

1. My friend Zach and me use our smartphones to look up new apps.

2. Both him and me compete to find the most ridiculous apps.

3. Zach is better at finding weird apps than me.

4. One app that Zach shared with me was really weird. It featured homicidal doughnuts that kidnap a player's family.

5. Between you and I, I love that app!

6. Our friend, Sarah, showed us another app in which we could simulate living the life of a goat.

7. She found that app as funny as us.

8. Us smartphone addicts spend too much money on apps sometimes, but they are good for a laugh.

Relative Pronouns

31.6 Use relative pronouns correctly.

Relative pronouns can join two short sentences. Relative pronouns include *who, whom, whoever, whomever, which, that,* and *whose.*

GRAMMAR LINK
For more information about relative pronouns, see Chapter 22.

Choosing *Who* or *Whom*

To determine whether to use *who* or *whom*, replace *who* or *whom* with another pronoun. If the replacement is a subjective pronoun such as *he* or *she*, use **who**. If the replacement is an objective pronoun such as *her* or *him*, use **whom**.

I know a man **who** studies systems design.
(He studies systems design.)

The man to **whom** you gave your résumé is my boss.
(You gave your résumé to him.)

Practice 7

Underline the correct relative pronoun in the parentheses.

EXAMPLE: My friends, (<u>who</u> / whom) are environmentalists, told me about a new type of plastic.

1. Mark Herreman, (who / whom) I met at a party, is the CEO of Newlight Technologies.

2. Herreman, (who / whom) knows a friend of mine, helped create AirCarbon plastic with the research team at the company.

3. The researchers, (who / whom) I also know, developed a technology to capture carbon emissions from landfills.

4. Normally, oil is needed to produce plastic. However, the researchers at Newlight, (who / whom) are among the world's best scientific minds, have discovered a way to combine oxygen with carbon from landfills to create plastic.

5. Barbara Grady is a reporter (who / whom) writes about environmental technology.

6. Herreman, (who / whom) Grady interviewed for greenbiz.com, is confident that AirCarbon technology will become increasingly popular.

Final Review

Correct the fifteen pronoun errors in the next paragraphs.

EXAMPLE: Anne and ~~his~~ her friends went to an exhibition on robots.

1.   Inventors and they're inventions make fascinating stories. Matt Richtel, whom is a journalist for the *New York Times*, suggests that some well-known inventions had earlier versions. For instance, in February 1878, Thomas Edison patented a sound device. However, they say that an unknown French inventor had made a sound recording seventeen years earlier.

2. Nobody knows why their ideas are remembered better than somebody else's ideas. For example, consider the cases of Alexander Graham Bell and Elisha Gray. Both filed his telephone device patents on February 14, 1876. Although Elisha Gray is known, Alexander Graham Bell is more famous than him. Moreover, my friend Louis and me discovered that Antonio Meucci had created a sound machine some years earlier. Most people don't know that.

3. Sometimes, many innovators contribute to new technologies. The two most famous innovators, Bill Gates and Steve Jobs, made his fortunes in the computer industry. But does either Microsoft or Apple deserve their reputation as one of the first developers of personal computers? People don't know about Dennis Allison. However, if they had read about the history of computers, you would have recognized his name. Between you and I, Dennis Allison deserves some credit as a computer innovator.

4. My cousin Sarah, who I admire, likes to invent gadgets. You should show her you're inventions, and she will show you her's.

The Writer's Room

Write about one of the following topics. Proofread your text to ensure there are no pronoun errors.

1. Explain how to make a website or how to choose a cell phone. What are the steps you would take?
2. What is currently the world's most useful invention? Argue that a particular invention is the most useful. To find out about interesting inventions, do an Internet search.

32 Adjectives and Adverbs

SECTION THEME: Inventions and Discoveries

In this chapter, you read about ancient inventions and discoveries.

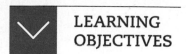

LEARNING OBJECTIVES

32.1 Practice using adjectives.

32.2 Practice using adverbs.

32.3 Distinguish comparative and superlative forms.

Adjectives

32.1 Practice using adjectives.

Adjectives describe nouns (people, places, or things) and pronouns (words that replace nouns). They add information explaining how many, what kind, or which one. They also describe how things look, smell, feel, taste, and sound. In the following examples, the adjectives are boldfaced, and the nouns are underlined.

The **enthusiastic** <u>students</u> wanted to make a **short** <u>documentary</u> on **ancient mechanical** <u>devices</u>.

> ## HINT: Placement of Adjectives
>
> You can place adjectives either before a noun or after a linking verb such as *be*, *look*, *appear*, *smell*, or *become*.
>
> **Before the noun**   The **nervous** inventor gave a **suitable** speech.
> **After the linking verb** The engineer was **disappointed**, and he was **angry**.

Problems with Adjectives

You can recognize many adjectives by their endings. Be particularly careful when you use the following adjective forms.

ADJECTIVES ENDING IN *-FUL* OR *-LESS*

Some adjectives end in *-ful* or *-less*. Remember that *ful* ends in one *l* and *less* ends in double *s*.

> The **cheerful** inventor developed many **useless** products.

ADJECTIVES ENDING IN *-ED* AND *-ING*

Some adjectives look like verbs because they end in *-ing* or *-ed*. When the adjective ends in *-ed*, it describes the person's or animal's expression or feeling. When the adjective ends in *-ing*, it describes the quality of the person or thing.

> The **frustrated** but **prepared** historian confronted the politician, and his **challenging** and **convincing** arguments got her attention.

> ## HINT: Keep Adjectives in the Singular Form
>
> Always make an adjective singular, even if the noun following the adjective is plural.
>
>   year
> Lucia was a forty-five-~~years~~-old woman when she took out a
>   dollar
> five-thousand-~~dollars~~ bank loan and opened her own antique store.

Adverbs

32.2 Practice using adverbs.

Adverbs add information to adjectives, verbs, or other adverbs. They give more specific information about how, when, where, and to what extent an action or event occurred. Some adverbs look exactly like adjectives, such as *early*, *late*, *soon*, *often*, and *hard*. However, most adverbs end in *-ly*.

verb   adverb
Archaeologists studied the ancient documents **carefully**.

adverb adverb
They released the results **quite** quickly.

adverb   adjective
The **very** eloquent speaker was Dr. Ying.

Forms of Adverbs

Adverbs often end in *-ly*. In fact, you can change many adjectives into adverbs by adding *-ly* endings.

- If you add *-ly* to a word that ends in *l*, then your new word will have a double *l*.

professional + ly

  The journalist covered the story **professionally**.

- If you add *-ly* to a word that ends in *e*, keep the *e*. (Exceptions are *true–truly* and *due–duly*.)

close + ly

  The two journalists worked together **closely**.

HINT: Placement of Frequency Adverbs

Frequency adverbs are words that indicate how often someone performs an action or when an event occurs. Common frequency adverbs are *always, ever, never, often, sometimes,* and *usually*. They can appear at the beginnings of sentences, or they can appear in the following locations.

- Place frequency adverbs before regular verbs in the simple present and simple past tenses.

  Politicians **sometimes** forget the importance of ancient structures.

- Place frequency adverbs after all forms of the verb *be*.

  She is **often** an advisor for the historical society.

- Place frequency adverbs after an initial helping verb.

  They have **never** donated to a museum.

Practice 1

Correct eight errors with adjectives or adverbs.

EXAMPLE: The ancient Greeks created many ~~wonderfull~~ ^{wonderful} artifacts.

1. People think usually that computers are a modern invention. In 1900, some Greek sponge divers discovered an interested shipwreck. Among the plentifull artifacts, the divers stumbled across a piece of stone with brass in it. They showed the relic to Valerios Stais, a Greek archaeologist. The exciting archaeologist identified the piece as the Antikythera mechanism.

2. Recently, experts successfuly X-rayed the treasure; it contains thirty gears. The two-thousand-years-old instrument is the first mechanical analog computer. Greek astronomers used frequently the instrument to calculate the movement of stars and planets. Today the Antikythera mechanism is housed in the National Archaeological Museum in Athens. Scientists continue to examine this astounded discovery.

Problems with Adverbs

Many times, people use an adjective instead of an adverb after a verb. Ensure that you always modify your verbs using an adverb.

The students read about the scrolls ~~real quick~~ ^{really quickly}. They examined the script ^{slowly} ~~slow~~.

Practice 2

Correct nine mistakes with adjectives and adverbs.

EXAMPLE: These days, I am ~~real~~ ^{really} tired.

1. In Laos, tourists can see an amazed site. Hundreds of stone containers are scattered throughout an isolating area called the Plain of Jars. The jars, which are made of rock, are fascinated. Believing the jars are real old, archaeologists speculate the vessels were created in the Iron Age, around 2,500 years ago. The jars are between 3 feet and 6 feet tall and are hollow inside.

2. No one knows what the purpose of these jars was, how they were made, or how they came to be placed in such a remote area. Some experts have offered interested theories. The jars might have been used as cremation vessels, to collect rainwater, or to store grain.

3. When tourists visit the Plain of Jars, they have to be very carefull. The U.S. military bombed the area between 1964 and 1973, and many unexploded bombs remain hidden and are dangerous close to walking paths. Tourists must walk cautious in the area and stay on the marked footpaths. The Laos government is convincing that the Plain of Jars should become a world heritage site.

Good and *Well* / *Bad* and *Badly*

Good is an adjective, and *well* is an adverb. However, as an exception, you can use *well* to describe a person's health (for example, *I do not feel **well***).

Adjective	The archaeologist gave a **good** account of the events.
Adverb	Archimedes slept **well** after he talked to his mentor.

Bad is an adjective, and *badly* is an adverb.

Adjective	The antique clock was in **bad** condition.
Adverb	The historian described the event **badly**.

HINT: Linking Verbs + Adjectives or Adverbs

The following verbs change their meaning when used with an adverb.

look good (appearance)	look well (healthy)
feel good (state of mind)	feel well (healthy / not sick)

Blair wants to **look good** for his interview. He bought a new shirt.

Nina has a high fever. She does not **look well**.

Practice 3

Underline the correct adjectives or adverbs.

EXAMPLE: There are many (<u>good</u> / well) books on Egyptian pyramids.

1.   The Aztecs, Mayans, and Egyptians all built pyramids very (good / well). The pyramids of Egypt are the most famous. There are about 101 pyramids known in Egypt, but only some remain in (good / well) condition. The step pyramid was built more than four thousand years ago. It is in a (bad / badly) state, but archaeologists are repairing it. The Great Pyramid at Giza is the largest pyramid. It contains over two million limestone blocks of (good / well) quality.

2.   Researchers are trying to gain a (good / well) understanding of construction practices in ancient Egypt. The pharaohs prepared for the afterlife really (good / well). They believed that if they planned (bad / badly), then they would not reach heaven. They hired laborers who were in (good / well) shape to build the pyramids. Even if the laborers did not feel (good / well), they still had to work. Most laborers wanted to work on the pyramids. The laborers thought that (bad / badly) actions in their present life would be cancelled if they served the pharaoh. Then, they could also have a (good / well) afterlife. The pharaohs also used slaves for construction work. Generally, Egyptian citizens treated their slaves (bad / badly) and provided their slaves with (bad / badly) working conditions. But when slaves worked on the pyramids, they did not live (bad / badly). All workers had to eat (good / well) because they had to work hard. (Good / Well) workers also received a tax break, as well as housing and clothes.

Comparative and Superlative Forms

32.3 **Distinguish comparative and superlative forms.**

Use the **comparative form** to compare two items. Use the **superlative form** to compare three or more items. You can write comparative and superlative forms by remembering a few simple guidelines.

Using *-er* and *-est* Endings

Add *-er* and *-est* endings to one-syllable adjectives and adverbs. Double the last letter when the adjective ends in *one vowel + one consonant*.

short	short**er** than	the short**est**
hot	hot**ter** than	the hot**test**

When a two-syllable adjective ends in *-y*, change the *-y* to *-i* and add *-er* or *-est*.

happy	happ**ier** than	the happ**iest**

Using *More* and *The Most*

Generally, add *more* and *the most* to adjectives and adverbs of two or more syllables.

beautiful	**more** beautiful than	the **most** beautiful

Using Irregular Comparative and Superlative Forms

Some adjectives and adverbs have unique comparative and superlative forms. Study this list to remember some of the most common ones.

good / well	better than	the best
bad / badly	worse than	the worst
some / much / many	more than	the most
little (a small amount)	less than	the least
few	fewer than	the fewest
far	farther / further	the farthest / the furthest

> **GRAMMAR LINK**
> Farther indicates a physical distance. Further means "additional." For more commonly confused words, see Chapter 34.

Practice 4

Fill in the blanks with the correct comparative and superlative forms of the words in parentheses.

EXAMPLE: Ferdinand Magellan was one of the (good) _____best_____ navigators in recorded history.

1.   Ferdinand Magellan is one of the (famous) _____

explorers of the sixteenth century. Magellan was the son of Portuguese

royalty, and he rose quickly through the ranks of Portugal's colony in

India. From a young age, Magellan was (good) _____

than any of his peers at sea navigation and commanding ships. He served

with distinction as a soldier, although his last military campaign was

(dangerous) _____ than the others; he was badly

wounded and walked with a limp the rest of his life.

2.   Magellan's greatest achievement was finding a route to the New

World that was (short) _____ than any previous

route that had been discovered. Leading a fleet of ships leaving

from Spain in 1519, Magellan led the (long) _____

expedition in history to that point. Unfortunately, Magellan was killed

in one of the (bad) _____ battles he had ever faced.

Even though a tribal conflict in the Philippines ended with Magellan's

death, his fleet pressed on and became the first to travel all the way

around the globe.

Problems with Comparative and Superlative Forms

USING *MORE* AND *-ER*

In the comparative form, never use *more* and *-er* to modify the same word. In the superlative form, never use *most* and *-est* to modify the same word.

The photographs of the old radios were ~~more~~ better than the ones of the toasters, but the photos of the gramophones were the ~~most~~ best in the exhibition.

USING *FEWER* AND *LESS*

In the comparative form, use *fewer* before count nouns (*fewer people*, *fewer houses*) and use *less* before noncount nouns (*less information*, *less evidence*).

> Researchers have **less** <u>time</u> than they used to. They hire **fewer** <u>students</u> than before.

GRAMMAR LINK
For a list of common noncount nouns, refer to page 400 in Chapter 30.

HINT: Using *the* in the Comparative Form

Although you would usually use *the* in superlative forms, you can use it in some two-part comparatives. In these expressions, the second part is the result of the first part.

    action   result

<u>The more</u> you read about ancient Egypt, <u>the better</u> you will understand the culture.

Practice 5

Correct the nine adjective and adverb errors in the next paragraphs.

                                                        more

EXAMPLE: The more the public sees the Dead Sea Scrolls, the ~~most~~ interested they become in the origins of the scrolls.

1.   The Dead Sea Scrolls consist of about one thousand biblical and nonbiblical texts. They are one of the most largest collections of ancient texts in Israel. In the late 1950s, the scientific community became real excited when they heard about the scrolls.

2.   In 1947, a Bedouin boy's goats wandered into a cave near the Dead Sea. The more he tried to coax his goats out of the cave, the farthest they retreated into the cave. The boy threw rocks into the cave to get the goats out. He accidently hit some pottery jars, and they broke, exposing the scrolls. The boy never had seen such documents, so he showed them to an archaeologist. The expert went back to the cave really quick and was relieved to see that most of the jars had remained intact. The boy had broken less jars than the expert had first believed.

3.   At the beginning of their investigation, scientists damaged some of the scrolls bad. They did not know how fragile the documents were, and the scrolls became damaged by smoke from the scientists' cigarettes. The experts discovered that the worse problem was that the manuscripts faded when exposed to air. Soon, they realized their mistakes and ever since have been making digital copies of the scrolls. The more the experts analyze the scrolls, the more better they understand their significance.

Final Review

Correct fifteen errors in adjectives and adverbs.

EXAMPLE: The experts studied the ~~interested~~ ^{interesting} artifact.

1.   Researchers always have wanted to study the cultural history of North American tribes. Most native groups have left no written records. Scientists believe that the more they study human remains, the more better they understand indigenous history. They want to examine skeletons in burial grounds real carefully. However, distressing native groups feel that the excavation of burial sites is demeaning to their ancestors. The Dickson Mounds Museum in Illinois is one of the most best examples of this issue.

2.   In 1927, Don Dickson, an Illinois farmer, saw a small hill on his land. The more closely he examined it, the most interested he became. He discovered that the hill was a tribal burial ground. He dug up the area quite quick and saw clear that the site contained beautifull ancient

artifacts and human skeletons. The farmer built a museum over the site and opened it for the general public.

3.   The museum contained thousand-years-old bones. Scientists came often to analyze the skeletons and to continue hunting for remains. However, archaeologists actually excavated less sites than they wanted. In the 1970s, many native groups protested such excavations. They argued passionate that their ancestors could not rest in peace if their bones were on display. By the 1990s, the government passed a law requiring any federally funded institution to give back its collection to Native American tribes that claimed ownership over burial grounds. The concerning Dickson Mounds Museum officials responded good. In 1992, the museum officials reburied the skeletons because they wanted to respect native groups.

READING LINK
For more readings

"Tips for Breaking Free of Compulsive Smartphone Use" p. 134
"Marketing New Inventions" p. 543
"Paradox of New Technologies" p. 550
"Can We Talk" p. 547
"How Companies Deceive Us" p. 524

The Writer's Room

Write about one of the following topics. Proofread your text to ensure that there are no adjective and adverb mistakes.

1. Compare two inventions from the past. Do some research on the Internet for ideas.

2. How important is history as a school subject? Should history be a compulsory subject at school?

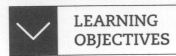

LEARNING OBJECTIVES

33.1 Use specific and detailed vocabulary.

33.2 Avoid wordiness and redundancy.

33.3 Avoid clichés.

33.4 Use standard English.

In this chapter, you read about plants.

Using Specific and Detailed Vocabulary

33.1 Use specific and detailed vocabulary.

Effective writing evokes an emotional response from the reader. Great writers not only use correct grammatical structures, but they also infuse their writing with precise and vivid details that make their work come alive.

When you proofread your work, revise words that are too vague. **Vague words** lack precision and detail. For example, the words *nice* and *bad* are vague. Readers cannot get a clear picture from them.

Compare the following sets of sentences.

Vague	The tree was big.
Precise	The 250-foot-tall redwood seemed to touch the cloudless sky.

Vague	The gardener planted flowers.
Precise	The gardener, Mr. Oliver, planted azaleas, hyacinths, and irises.

Creating Vivid Language

When you choose the precise word, you convey your meaning exactly. Moreover, you can make your writing clearer and more impressive by using specific and detailed vocabulary. To create vivid language, do the following:

- **Modify your nouns.** If your noun is vague, make it more specific by adding one or more adjectives. You could also rename the noun with a more specific term.

Vague	the child	
Vivid	the ecstatic girl	the agile ten-year-old ballerina

- **Modify your verbs.** Use more vivid, precise verbs. You could also use adverbs.

Vague	talk	
More vivid	bicker	debate passionately

- **Include more details.** Add information to make the sentence more detailed and complete.

Vague	Some plants are good for the health.
Precise	Garlic has antibiotic properties that can fight bacteria and viruses.

> **WRITING LINK**
> You can find more information about appealing to the five senses in Chapter 8, "Description."

Practice 1

Underline vague words in the following sentences. Then replace them with more precise and detailed vocabulary.

EXAMPLE: Our town is <u>pretty</u>.

Our town has many Victorian buildings, a Gothic church, and a

small lake surrounded by wildflowers.

1. The government buildings in our town are surrounded by trees.

   _____

   _____

2. Every spring, people come to admire the tree blossoms.

   _____

   _____

3. Nice flowers grow beside the lake.

   _____

   _____

4. Town residents can do many activities in the park.

   _____

   _____

5. The park in the town center is pretty.

   _____

   _____

Avoiding Wordiness and Redundancy

33.2 Avoid wordiness and redundancy.

Sometimes students fill their writing assignments with extra words to meet the length requirement. However, good ideas can get lost in work that is too wordy. Also, if the explanations are unnecessarily long, readers will become bored.

To improve your writing style, use only as many words or phrases as you need to fully explain your ideas.

The farm was big ~~in size~~.

(*Big* is a measure of size, so you do not need to say "in size.")

Correcting Wordiness

You can cut the number of words needed to express an idea by substituting a wordy phrase with a single word. You could also remove the wordy phrase completely.

                                      because

I don't like gardening ~~due to the fact that~~ I spend most of the time just pulling out weeds.

Some Common Wordy Expressions and Substitutions

Wordy	Substitution	Wordy	Substitution
at this point in time	now, currently	gave the appearance of being	looked like
at that point in time	then, at that time	in close proximity	close or in proximity
big / small in size	big / small	in order to	to
a difficult dilemma	a dilemma	in spite of the fact	in spite of
due to the fact	because	in the final analysis	finally, lastly
equally as good as	as good as	past history	past or history
exactly the same	the same	period of time	period
exceptions to the rule	exceptions	still remain	remain
final completion	end	a true fact	a fact
for the purpose of	for	the fact of the matter is	in fact

Practice 2

Edit the following sentences by crossing out all unnecessary words or phrases. If necessary, find more concise substitutes for wordy expressions.

EXAMPLE: The Bodhi tree has grown to be big ~~in size~~.

1. Some trees around the world have become famous due to the fact that they are associated with myths and legends.

2. A Bodhi tree is located in close proximity to the village of Bodh Gaya, India.

3. Legend states that Siddhartha Gautama, the Buddha, overcame a difficult dilemma and attained spiritual enlightenment near the tree.

4. After he attained enlightenment, the Buddha spent many days in exactly the same spot to illuminate his disciples.

5. Many pilgrims visited the Buddha under the tree in order to hear his teachings.

6. The original Bodhi tree has died, but at this point in time, another tree is sprouting from the ancestor tree.

7. The Bodhi tree still remains an important destination for pilgrims who want to pay homage to the Buddha.

Avoiding Clichés

33.3 Avoid clichés.

Clichés are overused expressions. Avoid boring your readers with clichés, and use more direct and vivid language instead.

cliché	direct words
<u>In this neck of the woods</u>, she is considered an expert on orchids.	In this area

Other Common Clichés	
a drop in the bucket	crystal clear
add insult to injury	easier said than done
as luck would have it	go with the flow
at a loss for words	hyped and lighten up
axe to grind	in the nick of time
bend over backwards	keep your eyes peeled
better late than never	time and time again
between a rock and a hard place	tried and true
break the ice	under the weather
calm, cool, and collected	

HINT: Modifying Clichés

To modify a cliché, change it into a direct term. You might also try playing with language to come up with a more interesting description.

Cliché	She was as happy as a lark.
Direct language	She was thrilled.
Interesting description	She was as happy as a teenager whose parents had gone away for the weekend.

Practice 3

Cross out the clichéd expression in each sentence. If necessary, replace it with fresh or direct language.

EXAMPLE: I was ~~blown away~~ ^{greatly impressed} by how old the trees were.

1. I kept my eyes peeled online for the recently revealed photos of the Ancient Yuda Forest in China.

2.   This forest might have been lost forever, but as luck would have it, archeologists discovered the forest buried under a layer of volcanic ash.

3.   After the forest was discovered, scientists estimated that it is over three hundred million years old. When I read an article about this discovery, I was at a loss for words.

4.   The forest contained fossils of many extinct plant species. The amazing variety of flora in the forest became crystal clear to researchers after uncovering the amazing archeological find.

5.   Researchers have time and time again discovered amazing things buried under volcanic ash. The ash helps to preserve what is buried underneath, as was also the case with the lost city of Pompeii in Italy.

6.   I am going to spend a month in Italy next year. I'm super hyped to visit Pompei.

Using Standard English

33.4 Use standard English.

Most of your instructors will want you to write using **standard English**. The word "standard" does not imply better. Standard English is the common language generally used and expected in schools, businesses, and government institutions in North America. **Slang** is nonstandard language. It is used in informal situations to communicate common cultural knowledge. In any academic or professional context, do not use slang.

Slang	Me an' some bros wanted to make some dough, so we worked on a farm picking apples. We made a bit of coin, and our grub was included. It was real cool. On the weekends, we mostly chilled.
Standard English	My friends and I wanted to make some money, so we worked on a farm picking apples. We were paid well, and our food was included. We had a memorable time. On the weekends, we mostly relaxed.

HINT: Reasons to Avoid Slang

Slang changes depending on generational, regional, cultural, and historical influences. For example, one group might say "upset" whereas others might say "freaked out" or "having a fit." You should avoid using slang expressions in your writing because they can change very quickly.

Practice 4

Substitute the underlined slang expressions with the best possible choice of standard English.

                                                                body odor
EXAMPLE: Since ancient times people have eaten garlic even if it causes B.O.

1. Recently, there has been a lot of <u>hype</u> about the medicinal properties of garlic.

2. In the past, when people <u>were under the weather</u>, they believed the magical properties of garlic would help them heal.

3. In Greek mythology, Circe <u>had the hots for</u> Ulysses, who ate garlic to protect himself from her advances.

4. Spanish bullfighters wore garlic necklaces so they would have the <u>guts</u> to fight bulls.

5. Ancient Egyptian <u>chicks</u> would put garlic in their belly buttons to find out if they were <u>knocked up</u>.

6. In Eastern Europe, people wore garlic <u>24/7</u> to ward off evil spirits.

7. Today, scientists believe that garlic is <u>awesome</u> because it may help fight cancer.

Final Review

Edit the following paragraphs for twenty errors in wordiness, slang, clichés, and vague language to make the text more effective.

1.   At this point in time, many people are freaking out about

genetically modified foods. Genetic modification (GM) is a technology

that lets scientists fool around with the genetic composition of plants.

Historically, people have always tried to change the characteristics of

plants for the purpose of making them more disease-resistant. That

process has traditionally been done through hybridization, a tried and

true method. That is, two parent plants from the same genus are bred

to create an improved hybrid plant. One true fact is that hybrid wheat

is hardier than traditional wheat.

2.   Today, in North America, hundreds of foods are genetically

modified. In the final analysis, there is great controversy about

genetically modified foods. Proponents of this technology say

time and time again that food will contain higher levels of nutrition,

be resistant to disease, and produce higher yields. In spite of the

fact of such arguments, opponents are all fired up about genetically

modified foods because they say that there is not enough knowledge

about how such foods will affect human health. They believe the foods

might be a death trap. For example, will humans who are allergic to

peanuts have a reaction if they eat tomatoes that have been genetically

modified with a peanut gene? Furthermore, opponents believe that

the loss of diversity in crops and plants really bites. Another worry is

that food production will go into the hands of super-sized agricultural companies who will control the growth and distribution of food. Moreover, the bigwigs in this debate stress out about the ethics of mixing genes from species to species.

3.   The genetically modified food industry is growing rapidly in size. But it is important to have a rational, open debate about this issue. Presently, consumers are faced with a difficult dilemma. Most people are in a fog and unknowingly buy genetically modified foods because such foods lack complete labeling. For example, most cooking oil comes from genetically modified grains. The public should be in the know about this technology. Consumers need to be clued in so that they can make the right choices.

The Writer's Room

Write about one of the following topics. Proofread your text to ensure that you have used detailed vocabulary and avoided wordiness, clichés, and slang.

1. Examine the photo below. What are some terms that come to mind? Some ideas might be *family farm*, *organic food*, *eco-farming*, *locally grown*, *farm fresh*, *fair trade*, and so on.
2. Why are fast foods and other unhealthy foods so popular? Think of some reasons.

34 Spelling and Commonly Confused Words

SECTION THEME: Our Natural World

In this chapter, you read about insects.

LEARNING OBJECTIVES

34.1 Learn and apply spelling rules.

34.2 Review 120 commonly misspelled words.

34.3 Distinguish look-alike and sound-alike words.

Spelling Rules

34.1 Learn and apply spelling rules.

It is important to spell correctly because spelling mistakes can detract from important ideas in your work. Here are some strategies for improving your spelling skills.

How to Become a Better Speller

- **Look up words** using the most current dictionary because it will contain new or updated words. For tips on dictionary usage, see page 510 in Chapter 40.

- **Keep a record of words that you commonly misspell**. For example, write the words and definitions in a spelling log, which could be in a journal or binder.

- **Use memory cards or flash cards** to help you memorize the spelling of difficult words. With a friend or a classmate, take turns asking each other to spell difficult words.

- **Write out the spelling of difficult words at least ten times** to help you remember how to spell them. After you have written these words, try writing them in a complete sentence.

Six Common Spelling Rules

Memorize the following common rules of spelling. If you follow these rules, your spelling will become more accurate. Also try to remember the exceptions to these rules.

1. **Writing *ie* or *ei***

   Write *i* before *e*, except after *c* or when *ei* is pronounced as *ay*, as in *neighbor* and *weigh*.

i **before** *e*	brief	field	priest
ei **after** *c*	receipt	deceit	receive
ei **pronounced as** *ay*	weigh	beige	vein

   Here are some exceptions:

ancient	either	neither	foreigner	leisure	height
science	species	society	seize	their	weird

2. **Adding *-s* or *-es***

   Add *-s* to form plural nouns and to create present tense verbs that are third-person singular. However, add *-es* to words in the following situations.

   - When words end in *-s*, *-sh*, *-ss*, *-ch*, or *-x*, add *-es*.

noun	box–boxes	**verb**	miss–misses

   - When words end in consonant *-y*, change the *-y* to *-i* and add *-es*.

noun	baby–babies	**verb**	marry–marries

   - When words end in *-o*, add *-es*. Exceptions are *pianos*, *radios*, *logos*, *stereos*, *autos*, *typos*, and *casinos*.

noun	tomato–tomatoes	**verb**	go–goes

   - When words end in *-f* or *-fe*, change the *-f* to a *-v* and add *-es*. Exceptions are *beliefs* and *roofs*.

life–lives	wolf–wolves	shelf–shelves

3. **Adding Prefixes and Suffixes**

   A **prefix** is added to the beginning of a word, and it changes the word's meaning. For example, *con-*, *dis-*, *pre-*, *un-*, and *il-* are prefixes. When you add a prefix to a word, keep the last letter of the prefix and the first letter of the main word.

im + mature = immature   mis + spell = misspell

A **suffix** is added to the ending of a word, and it changes the word's tense or meaning. For example, -*ly*, -*ment*, -*ed*, and -*ing* are suffixes. When you add the suffix -*ly* to words that end in -*l*, keep the -*l* of the root word. The new word will have two -*l*s.

casual + ly = casually   factual + ly = factually

4. Adding Suffixes to Words Ending in -*e*

If the suffix begins with a vowel, drop the -*e* on the main word. Some common suffixes beginning with vowels are -*ed, -er, -est, -ing, -able, -ent*, and -*ist*.

bake–baking   create–created

Some exceptions are words that end in -*ge*, which keep the -*e* and add the suffix.

outrage–outrageous   manage–manageable

If the suffix begins with a consonant, keep the -*e*. Some common suffixes beginning with consonants are -*ly, -ment, -less*, and -*ful*. Some exceptions are *acknowledgment, argument*, and *truly*.

sure–surely   aware–awareness

5. Adding Suffixes to Words Ending in -*y*

If the word has a consonant before the final -*y*, change the -*y* to an -*i* before adding the suffix. Some exceptions are *ladybug, dryness*, and *shyness*.

pretty–prettiest   happy–happiness

If the word has a vowel before the final -*y*, if it is a proper name, or if the suffix is -*ing*, do not change the *y* to an *i*. Some exceptions are *daily, laid*, and *said*.

employ–employed   apply–applying   Levinsky–Levinskys

6. Doubling the Final Consonant

Double the final consonant of one-syllable words ending in a consonant–vowel–consonant pattern.

ship–shipping   swim–swimmer   hop–hopped

Double the final consonant of words ending in a stressed consonant–vowel–consonant pattern. If the final syllable is not stressed, then do not double the last letter.

refer–referred   occur–occurred   happen–happened

120 Commonly Misspelled Words

34.2 Review 120 commonly misspelled words.

The next list contains some of the most commonly misspelled words in English.

absence	curriculum	loneliness	reference
absorption	definite	maintenance	responsible
accommodate	definitely	mathematics	rhythm
acquaintance	desperate	medicine	schedule
address	developed	millennium	scientific
aggressive	dilemma	minuscule	separate
already	disappoint	mischievous	sincerely
aluminum	embarrass	mortgage	spaghetti
analyze	encouragement	necessary	strength
appointment	environment	ninety	success
approximate	especially	noticeable	surprise
argument	exaggerate	occasion	technique
athlete	exercise	occurrence	thorough
bargain	extraordinarily	opposite	tomato
beginning	familiar	outrageous	tomatoes
behavior	February	parallel	tomorrow
believable	finally	performance	truly
business	foreign	perseverance	Tuesday
calendar	government	personality	until
campaign	grammar	physically	usually
careful	harassment	possess	vacuum
ceiling	height	precious	Wednesday
cemetery	immediately	prejudice	weird
clientele	independent	privilege	woman
committee	jewelry	probably	women
comparison	judgment	professor	wreckage
competent	laboratory	psychology	writer
conscience	ledge	questionnaire	writing
conscientious	leisure	receive	written
convenient	license	recommend	zealous

Practice 1

Edit the next paragraphs for twenty misspelled words.

EXAMPLE: ~~Profesor~~ **Professor** Wright studies ants.

1. Most people usualy become anxious when ants invade their homes. They think that ants are aggresive and creepy. But anybody familar with ants knows that they definitly have their positive points.

2. Ants evolved around 130 million years ago. Scientists have identified over twelve thousand speceis of ants. Ants are social creatures. They are hard working and show a lot of perseverence. Most types of ants use complicated technics to build their colonies.

3. Ant societies have a queen as their leader. The queen ant is responsable for laying thousands of eggs, which will guarantee the survival of the colony. The female worker ants are very compitant. They search for food, build the nest, take care of the queen and her eggs, and guard the colony from predators. In comparason to her workers, the queen does miniscule amounts of work. Male ants are necesary for only one important duty: They mate with the queen.

4. Ants are extraordinaryly important insects. Scientists study them in labratories because ant behavor can sometimes parralel human conduct. For example, scientists beleive that unlike most other insects, ants learn from each other. Ants are also important for the enviroment. For instance, ants eat rotting plants and animals, and some animals and fungi eat ants. In addition, ants control pests, aerate soil, and spread the seeds of certain trees. Moreover, in some cultures, people happyly eat ants the way other groups eat tomatos.

Look-Alike and Sound-Alike Words

34.3 Distinguish look-alike and sound-alike words.

Sometimes two English words can sound the same but have different spellings and meanings. These words are called **homonyms**. Here are a few commonly confused words and their basic meanings. (For more specific definitions for these and other words, consult a dictionary.)

Some Commonly Confused Words		
accept	to receive; to admit	We must accept the vital role that insects play in our culture.
except	excluding; other than	I like all insects except ants.
allowed	permitted	We were not allowed to view the exhibit.
aloud	spoken audibly	We could not speak aloud, so we whispered.
affect	to influence	Pesticides affect the environment.
effect	the result of something	Scientists are examining the effects of pesticides on our health.
been	past participle of the verb *to be*	He has been to the Imax film about caterpillars.
being	present progressive form (the *-ing* form) of the verb *to be*	She was being kind when she donated to the butterfly museum.
by	preposition meaning *next to, on,* or *before*	A bee flew by the flowers. By evening, the crickets were making a lot of noise.
buy	to purchase	Will you buy me that scarab necklace?
complement	an addition; to complete	The film about the monarch butterfly was a nice complement to the exhibit.
compliment	nice comment about someone	The film was informative, and the director received many compliments.
conscience	a personal sense of right or wrong	After spraying pesticides, the gardener had a guilty conscience.
conscious	aware; awake	He made us conscious of the important role insects play in our society.

Practice 2

Underline the correct word in the parentheses.

EXAMPLE: Many people (by / <u>buy</u>) clothes made out of silk.

1. Silk has (been / being) produced (by / buy) the Chinese for at least four thousand years. The silkworm is actually a caterpillar that eats nothing (accept / except) mulberry leaves, grows quickly, and then encircles itself into a cocoon of raw silk. The cocoon contains a single thread around 300 to 900 yards in length, so it's not surprising that it takes about 2,000 cocoons to make one pound of silk. (Been / Being) very (conscious / conscience) of the long and intense silk-making process, most people (accept / except) the high cost of the material.

2.   The Chinese valued silk and carefully guarded the secret of its making. In ancient China, only the emperor and his family were (allowed / aloud) to wear silk garments. Sometimes, members of royalty wore the fabric as a (complement / compliment) to their regular clothes. Of course, less fortunate people admired the emperor's beautiful clothes and always (complimented / complemented) him.

3.   By the fifth century, the secret of silk-making had been revealed to Korea, Japan, and India. How did the secret get out? Legend says that a princess with no (conscious / conscience) smuggled silkworm larvae to Korea by hiding them in her hair. The emperor was outraged (by / buy) the actions of the princess, and there was great debate about her treachery. The scandal had a negative (affect / effect) on her health.

More Commonly Confused Words		
everyday	ordinary or common	Swatting mosquitoes is an everyday ritual of camping.
every day	each day	Every day, I check my roses for aphids.
imminent	soon to happen	The journalist reported that the arrival of locusts in parts of Africa was imminent.
eminent	distinguished; superior	Professor Maurice Kanyogo is an eminent entomologist.
imply	to suggest	The entomologist implied that he had received a large grant.
infer	to conclude	His students inferred that they would have summer jobs because of the grant.
its	possessive case of the pronoun *it*	The worker bee went into its hive.
it's	contraction for *it is*	It's well known that the queen bee is the largest in the colony.
knew	past tense of *to know*	I knew that I should study for my test on worms.
new	recent or unused	But my new book on honey making was more interesting.
know	to have knowledge of	The beekeepers know that there has been a decline in bees in recent years.
no	a negative	There were no books on beekeeping in the library.

lose	to misplace or forfeit something	Do not <u>lose</u> the mosquito repellent.
loose	too baggy; not fixed	You should wear <u>loose</u> clothes when camping.
loss	a decrease in an amount; a serious blow	Farmers would experience a <u>loss</u> if there were no bees to pollinate crops.
peace	calmness; an end to violence	The <u>peace</u> in the woods was wonderful.
piece	a part of something else; one item in a group of items	The two <u>pieces</u> of amber had insects in them.
principal	director of a school; main	The <u>principal</u> of our school is an expert on beetles. They are his <u>principal</u> hobby.
principle	rule or standard	Julius Corrant wrote a book about environmental <u>principles</u>.
quiet	silent	The crickets remained <u>quiet</u> this evening.
quite	very	They usually make <u>quite</u> a noise.
quit	stop	I would like them to <u>quit</u> making so much noise.

Practice 3

Identify and correct ten word choice errors.

$$\overset{\text{peace}}{}$$

EXAMPLE: I need some ~~piece~~ and quiet.

1.   Professor Zoe Truger, an imminent entomologist, specializes in butterfly behavior. I am reading her book. Its very interesting. On it's cover, there is a beautiful photograph of a butterfly. Everyday, during the summer, thousands of monarch butterflies are found in southern Canada, their summer home. As autumn arrives, these butterflies know that migration to warmer climates is eminent.

2.   The principle of Jake's school took the students on a nature walk to look for earthworms. The students were very quite when the guide told them there are 2,700 species of earthworms.

3.   Did you no that beekeeping is one of the world's oldest professions? Beekeepers wear lose clothing and protective gear. Some beekeepers must quiet their profession because they are allergic to bee stings.

More Commonly-Confused Words		
taught	past tense of *to teach*	I taught a class on pollination.
thought	past tense of *to think*	I thought the students enjoyed it.
than	word used to compare items	There are more mosquitoes at the lake than in the city.
then	at a particular time; after a specific time	He found the termite nest. Then he called the exterminators.
that	word used to introduce a clause	They told him that they would come immediately.
their	possessive form of *they*	They wore scarab amulets to show their respect for the god Khepera.
there	a place or location; an introductory phrase in sentences stating that something does or does not exist	The ant colony is over there. There is a beehive in the tree.
they're	contraction of *they are*	The ants work hard. They're very industrious.
to	part of an infinitive; indicates direction or movement	I want to hunt for bugs. I will go to the hiking path and look under some rocks.
too	very or also	My friend is too scared of bugs. My brother is, too.
two	the number after *one*	There were two types of butterflies in the garden today.
where	question word indicating location	Where did you buy the book on ladybugs?
were	past tense of *be*	There were hundreds of ladybugs on the bush.
we're	contraction of *we are*	We're wondering why we have this infestation.
who's	contraction of *who is*	Isabelle, who's a horticulturist, also keeps a butterfly garden.
whose	pronoun showing ownership	Whose garden is that?
write	to draw symbols that represent words	I will write an essay about the common earthworm.
right	the opposite of the direction left; correct	In the right corner of the garden, there is the compost bin with many worms in it.
		You are right when you say that earthworms are necessary for composting.

Practice 4

Identify and correct fifteen word choice errors.

EXAMPLE: ~~Their~~ **There** are many different types of bees.

1.　　In 2007, their were reports than the honeybee population was
mysteriously disappearing. According too scientists at Pennsylvania
State University, a large percentage of honeybee colonies where dying.
The demise of the honeybee population was worrisome because bees

pollinate crops. People who's livelihoods depended on the agricultural industry worried about losing income. Records showed that, in 2007, honeybee populations declined at a greater rate that at any time in the past. Entomologists traveled to different countries were they observed bee colonies. They taught parasites or a virus might be responsible for the deaths.

2.   Presently, scientists are seeing some confusing statistics. There finding that declines in honeybee populations vary in different countries. Annie May Tricot, whose a specialist in bees, is studying this problem. She has thought to courses on honeybee behavior. Her research shows that honeybee populations in China and Argentina are increasing. Tricot will right an article about this phenomenon. Scientists hope that the situation will write itself in the near future. Were looking forward to hearing what Tricot has to say in her lecture on bees tonight.

Final Review

Correct the twenty spelling errors and mistakes with commonly confused words in the essay.

ceiling
EXAMPLE: Spiderwebs are often found on the ~~cieling~~.

1.   Most of us think spiders look wierd and scary. When we find them in our homes, we are often surprized and frightened. Indeed, some spiders can be dangerous, although, in general, their bites have an affect that is not life threatening. Most spiders are basically harmless, and their webs often trap other insects that might harrass us in our sleep.

2.   In fact, spiders are definitly more complex than previously thought. A recent scientifique study suggests that they might have individual personalities. One way to test the personalities of spiders is to put them in front of a mirror to see how they react to there own

reflection. Spiders who are more agressive will charge toward the reflection, while shy spiders will retreat. Spiders are clearly conscience of their surroundings, and, like humans, their personality can be influenced by toxins in the enviroment.

3.   Insecticides often harm ecosystems. A study at McGill University in Montreal found that spiders often loose their original personality after being exposed to pesticides. According to proffessor and evolutionary ecologist Pierre-Olivier Montiglio, the results of the study are troubling. The study shows that some spiders experience difficulty catching prey after being exposed to pesticides. We also now no that spiders may be less adventurous after long-term exposure to toxins. This means that spiders that have been exposed to pesticides may not have sound jugement when hunting or choosing a place to live. If these findings are accurate, than pesticides might have catastrophic effects on spiders in the future.

4.   Were there are pesticides, negative impacts on the surrounding ecosystem often follow. Not only can these poisons negatively affect insects and animals, they can also be harmfull to human health. Its important to remember that spiders are important for our agricultural systems, as well. Spiders eat many of the insects that can destroy certain crops, so there often welcomed by farmers. Any conscienscious agricultural firms should reconsider the decision to use pesticides.

The Writer's Room

Write about one of the following topics. Proofread your text to ensure there are no spelling and commonly confused word errors.

1. Discuss types of insects that are particularly annoying, repulsive, or frightening.

2. Are laws banning the use of pesticides on lawns a good idea? Explain your ideas.

READING LINK
Readings on the natural world:

"With an Open Mouth" p. 123
"Swamps and Pesticides" p.184
"Nature Returns to the Cities" p. 536

35 Commas

SECTION THEME: Human Development

In this chapter, you read about life stages.

What Is a Comma?

35.1 Practice using commas correctly.

A **comma (,)** is a punctuation mark that helps identify distinct ideas. There are many ways to use a comma. In this chapter, you learn some helpful rules about comma usage.

Notice how comma placement changes the meanings of the following sentences.

The baby hits, her mother cries, and then they hug each other.

The baby hits her mother, cries, and then they hug each other.

Commas in a Series

35.2 Use a comma in a series.

Use a comma to separate items in a series of three or more items. Remember to put a comma before the final *and* or *or*.

Unit 1	,	unit 2	,	and	unit 3
			,	or	

Canada, the United States, and Mexico have psychology conferences.

The experiment required patience, perseverance, and energy.

Some teens may work part time, volunteer in the community, and maintain high grades at school.

HINT: Comma Before *and*

There is a trend, especially in the media, to omit the comma before the final *and* in a series. However, in academic writing, it is preferable to include the comma because it clarifies your meaning and makes the items more distinct.

Practice 1

Underline series of items. Then add eighteen missing commas.

EXAMPLE: Some psychological studies are simple͵obvious͵and <u>extremely</u>
<u>important</u>.

1.   Renowned psychoanalyst Sigmund Freud worked in Austria France

and the United Kingdom. His work covered subjects such as the

unconscious mind psychosexual development and the interpretation

of dreams. Opinions vary wildly on his work, and his theories have

been described as visionary radical unscientific and even dangerous.

However, Freud was clearly a very skilled writer whose work is still

widely read today.

2.   Freud claimed that the human psyche is composed of the id the ego and the super-ego. According to Freud, our wants needs and impulses come from the id. The ego helps people organize their thoughts separate the real from the unreal and use the faculty of reason. What is often referred to as "common sense" comes from the ego. The super-ego is the last part of the human psyche to develop. Family members friends teachers and other role models can influence the development of our conscience. Our super-ego strives for perfection controls our sense of right and wrong and punishes us with feelings of guilt.

Commas After Introductory Words and Phrases

35.3 Use commas after introductory words and phrases.

Place a comma after an **introductory word** or **phrase**. Introductory words include interjections (*well*), adverbs (*usually*), or transitional words (*therefore*). Introductory phrases can be transitional expressions (*of course*), prepositional phrases (*in the winter*), or modifiers (*born in Egypt*).

Introductory word(s)	,	sentence.
Introductory word	<u>Yes</u>, the last stage of life is very important.	
Introductory phrase	<u>After the experiment</u>, the children returned home. <u>Feeling bored</u>, he volunteered at a nearby clinic.	

Practice 2

Underline each introductory word or phrase. Then add twelve missing commas.

EXAMPLE: <u>Before leaving home</u>, adolescents assert their independence.

1.   In *Childhood and Society* Erik Erikson explained his views about the stages of life. According to Erikson there are eight life stages. In his opinion each stage is characterized by a developmental crisis.

2.   In the infancy stage babies must learn to trust others. Wanting others to fulfill their needs babies expect life to be pleasant. Neglected babies may end up mistrusting the world.

3.   During adolescence a young man or woman may have an identity crisis. Confronted with physical and emotional changes teenagers must develop a sense of self. According to Erikson some adolescents are unable to solve their identity crisis. Lacking self-awareness they cannot commit themselves to certain goals and values.

4.   In Erikson's view each crisis must be solved before a person develops in the next life stage. For example a person may become an adult chronologically. However that person may not be an adult emotionally.

Commas Around Interrupting Words and Phrases

35.4 Use commas around interrupting words and phrases.

Interrupting words or phrases appear in the middle of sentences, and while they interrupt the sentence's flow, they do not affect its overall meaning. Some interrupters are *as a matter of fact*, *as you know*, and *for example*. Prepositional phrases can also interrupt sentences.

Sentence	, interrupter,	sentence.

The doctor, for example, has never studied child psychology.

Adolescence, as you know, is a difficult life stage.

The child, feeling nervous, started to laugh.

HINT: Using Commas with Appositives

An appositive gives further information about a noun or pronoun. It can appear at the beginning, in the middle, or at the end of the sentence. Set off an appositive with commas.

beginning
A large hospital, the Mayo Clinic has some of the world's best researchers.

middle
Gail Sheehy, a journalist, has written about life passages.

end
My office is next to Sims Wholesale, a local grocery store.

Practice 3

The next sentences contain introductory words and phrases, interrupters, and series of items. Add the missing commas. If the sentence is correct, write C in the space provided.

EXAMPLE: Last year, I met several people from Kenya and Tanzania. _____

1. Indigenous to parts of Kenya and Tanzania the Maasai people have many interesting and important initiation rituals. _____

2. From the ages of twelve to fifteen boys are initiated into the "warrior class" of the tribe. _____

3. In the days before the ceremony the boys must shave their heads discard their belongings, and spend time alone in nature. _____

4. In the forest, they cannot carry spears sticks, or knives. _____

5. The initiates, after undergoing a circumcision must walk to other settlements in the region. _____

6. Other communities welcome the initiates, provide them with food, and give them shelter. _____

7. After the initiation, each young man is greeted as an adult a valuable member of the community. _____

8. The Masaii, semi-nomadic people are trying to preserve their cultural traditions. _____

9. In many countries around the world there are rite-of-passage ceremonies for adolescents. _____

Commas in Compound Sentences

35.5 Use commas in compound sentences.

In compound sentences, place a comma before the coordinating conjunction (*for, and, nor, but, or, yet, so*).

| Sentence | , coordinating conjunction | sentence. |

Adulthood has three stages, **and** each stage has its particular challenge.

Carolina lives with her mother, **but** her sister lives on her own.

She goes to school, **yet** she also works forty hours a week.

HINT: Commas and Coordinators

To ensure that a sentence is compound, cover the conjunction with your finger and read the two parts of the sentence. If one part of the sentence is incomplete, then no comma is necessary. If each part of the sentence contains a complete idea, then you need to add a comma.

No comma	Ben still lives with his parents **but** is very self-sufficient.
Comma	Ben still lives with his parents, **but** he is very self-sufficient.

Practice 4

Edit the next paragraphs, and add twelve missing commas.

EXAMPLE: She is not an adult , yet she is not a child.

1. Adulthood is another stage in life but the exact age of adulthood
    is unclear. Some cultures celebrate adulthood with high school
    graduation ceremonies and others celebrate with marriage. Some
    people define adulthood as the moment a person has full-time work
    and is self sufficient yet many people only become independent in
    their thirties.

2. Are you an adult? Researchers asked this question to people in
    their thirties and the results were surprising. Most did not feel fully
    adult until their late twenties or early thirties. Compared with previous
    generations people today move into markers of adulthood slowly. They
    marry later and they have children later.

3. Additionally, various cultures treat early adulthood differently. Adela
    Pelaez has a culturally mixed background. Her mother's lineage is
    British and her father's lineage is Spanish. At age nineteen she was

encouraged to find an apartment. Today, twenty-one-year-old Adela pays her own bills and she does her own cooking. Alexis Khoury is thirty-one but she still lives with her parents. They are Greek immigrants and they want their daughter to stay home until she marries. Alexis will respect her parents' wishes and she will not leave home until she finds a life partner.

Commas in Complex Sentences

35.6 Use commas in complex sentences.

A **complex sentence** contains one or more dependent clauses (or incomplete ideas). When you add a **subordinating conjunction**—a word such as *because, although*, or *unless*—to a clause, you make the clause dependent.

GRAMMAR LINK
For a list of subordinating conjunctions, see Chapter 21, page 318.

        dependent clause   independent clause
After Jason graduated from college, he moved out of the family home.

Using Commas After Dependent Clauses

If a sentence begins with a dependent clause, place a comma after the clause. Remember that a dependent clause has a subject and a verb, but it cannot stand alone. When the subordinating conjunction comes in the middle of the sentence, it is generally not necessary to use a comma.

Dependent clause	,	main clause.

Comma   When I find a better job, I will move into an apartment.

Main clause	dependent clause.

No comma   I will move into an apartment when I find a better job.

Practice 5

Edit the following sentences by adding or deleting commas.

EXAMPLE: Although thirty-year-old Samuel Chong lives at home, he is not ashamed.

1. When he examined the 2001 census Mark Noble noticed a clear trend.

2. Although most people in their twenties lived on their own about 40 percent of young adults still lived with their parents.

3. In 1981, the results were different, because only 25 percent of young adults lived at home.

4. After examining the statistics Noble determined several causes for the shift.

5. Because the marriage rate is declining fewer people buy their own homes.

6. When the cost of education increases people cannot afford to study and pay rent.

7. Other young adults stay with their parents, because rental rates are so high.

8. Because these conditions are not changing many young adults will probably continue to live with their parents.

Using Commas to Set Off Nonrestrictive Clauses

GRAMMAR LINK
For more information about choosing which or that, see Chapter 22, "Sentence Variety."

Clauses beginning with *who, that,* and *which* can be restrictive or nonrestrictive. A **restrictive clause** contains essential information about the subject. Do not place commas around restrictive clauses. In the following example, the underlined clause is necessary to understand the meaning of the sentence.

No commas   The local company that creates computer graphics has no job openings.

A **nonrestrictive clause** gives nonessential or additional information about the noun but does not restrict or define the noun. Place commas around nonrestrictive clauses. In the following sentence, the underlined clause contains extra information, but if you removed that clause, the sentence would still have a clear meaning.

Commas   Her book, which is in bookstores, is about successful entrepreneurs.

HINT: *Which, That,* and *Who*

Which   Use commas to set off clauses that begin with *which.*

The brain, **which is a complex organ**, develops rapidly.

That   Do not use commas to set off clauses that begin with *that.*

The house **that I grew up in** was demolished last year.

Who   If the *who* clause contains nonessential information, put commas around it. If the *who* clause is essential to the meaning of the sentence, then it does not require commas.

Essential   Many people **who have brain injuries** undergo subtle personality changes.

Not essential   Dr. Jay Giedd, **who lives in Maryland**, made an important discovery.

Practice 6

Edit the following essay by adding twelve missing commas. Also remove two unnecessary commas.

EXAMPLE: If people want to have longer lives ˏthey can exercise, eat well ˏ
    and avoid risky behavior.

1.   In 350 BC, Aristotle wrote that humans have a maximum life span and nothing can be done to prolong that span. Until recently, scientists agreed with Aristotle. However a group of researchers believes that human life expectancy will increase significantly in the future.

2.   Dr. James Vaupel a researcher at Duke University, believes that our life spans can be extended. He gives a concrete example. In 1840 the average Swedish woman lived to age forty-five. Today, Japanese women, who live to an average age of eighty-five have the world's longest life expectancy. This huge increase in life expectancy was partly due to the decrease in infant mortality. Surgery, vaccines and antibiotics have helped to lower childhood death rates. Also, because they have access to new medical interventions people over age 65 are living longer. Still, only about 2 percent of the population lives to one hundred years of age.

3.   According to Dr. Vaupel, today's babies will have much longer life expectancies than their parents had and half of all newborns could live to one hundred years of age. Certainly, cures for cancer, and heart disease could help increase life expectancy. Because so many women delay childbirth the period of human fertility may lengthen which could have an eventual impact on life expectancy. Also, some research labs are experimenting with ways of increasing the life spans of cells. For example scientists have isolated a part of the chromosome that shrinks with age. If scientists find a way to slow down cell aging the results could significantly increase life expectancies of all humans.

4.   A very long life expectancy, would force humans to rethink life stages. When would childhood end? Would you want to live to 150 years of age or more?

> **GRAMMAR LINK**
> For information about comma usage in business letters, see Chapter 19, "The Résumé and Letter of Application."

FINAL REVIEW

This essay has twenty punctuation errors. Add eighteen missing commas. Also, remove two unnecessary commas.

EXAMPLE: The money, which was in the cash box˅disappeared.

1.   Dan Ariely, a professor of psychology at Duke University has written about honesty in his book *The (Honest) Truth about Dishonesty*. Although, people like to believe that they are honest they fool themselves. Furthermore people from all classes and in all societies may be dishonest sometimes.

2. In April 2011 college student Dan Weiss was hired by the Kennedy Center for the Performing Arts in Washington, DC. His job, which was part time was to take the stock inventory at the center's gift shop. Meanwhile about three hundred well-intentioned volunteers worked at the shop. The shop which relied on the volunteers sold about $400,000 of merchandise annually. Each year about $150,000 disappeared. The gift shop which had no cash registers, just had a cash box that volunteers put the money into.

3. Weiss, who worked alone was determined to find the thief. Undoubtedly the thief was one of the volunteers. He suspected a young man who brought the cash box to the bank each night. Weiss set up a sting operation. He put some marked bills into the box and he and a detective waited in a bush outside the bank. When the young volunteer left the bank they searched him. He had $60 of marked bills in his pocket so he was fired. Nevertheless, the thefts continued.

4. Weiss, who was undeterred discovered that hundreds of the volunteers were pilfering objects or money. He decided to put a cash register, and an itemized logbook into the gift shop. Before then, money disappeared every day but no money disappeared after the cash register was installed.

5. We can learn the following lesson from this story: On the one hand all types of people can be dishonest. On the other hand, people's bad behavior can be modified when temptation is removed.

The Writer's Room

Write about one of the following topics. After you finish writing, make sure that you have used commas correctly.

1. What problems could occur if the human life expectancy gets a lot longer? Think about the effects of an increased life expectancy.

2. Which life stage is the most interesting? Give supporting examples to back up your views.

36 Apostrophes

SECTION THEME: Human Development

In this chapter, you read about artistic ability and creativity.

LEARNING OBJECTIVES

36.1 Explain the purpose of an apostrophe.

36.2 Form contractions with apostrophes.

36.3 Use apostrophes to show ownership.

36.4 Use apostrophes in expressions of time.

What Is an Apostrophe?

36.1 Explain the purpose of an apostrophe.

An **apostrophe** is a punctuation mark showing a contraction or ownership.

Emma **Chong's** art gallery is very successful, and **it's** still growing.

Apostrophes in Contractions

36.2 Form contractions with apostrophes.

To form a **contraction**, join two words into one and add an apostrophe to replace the omitted letter(s). The following are examples of common contractions.

1. Join a verb with *not*. The apostrophe replaces the letter "o" in *not*.

is + not = isn't	has + not = hasn't
are + not = aren't	have + not = haven't
could + not = couldn't	should + not = shouldn't
did + not = didn't	was + not = wasn't
do + not = don't	were + not = weren't
does + not = doesn't	would + not = wouldn't

Exception: will + not = <u>won't</u>, can + not = <u>can't</u>

2. **Join a subject and a verb.** Sometimes you must remove several letters to form the contraction.

I + will = I'll	she + will = she'll
I + would = I'd	Tina + is = Tina's
he + is = he's	they + are = they're
he + will = he'll	we + will = we'll
Joe + is = Joe's	who + is = who's
she + has = she's	who + would = who'd

Note: Do not contract a subject with *was*, *were*, or *did*.

HINT: Common Apostrophe Errors

Do not use apostrophes before the final *-s* of a verb or a plural noun.

           wants   galleries
Mr. Garcia ~~want's~~ to open several ~~gallerie's~~.

In contractions with *not*, remember that the apostrophe replaces the missing *o*.

      doesn't
He ~~does'nt~~ understand the problem.

Practice 1

Edit the next sentences for twelve apostrophe errors. You may need to add, move, or remove apostrophes.

                     isn't
EXAMPLE: Making a great work of art ~~isnt~~ a simple process.

1.   Whos a great artist? Why do some people have amazing artistic abilities whereas others do'nt? Neurologists look inside the brain to answer questions about creativity. Theyve said that the left portion of the brains responsible for logical processing and verbal skills. The right sides responsible for artistic, abstract thinking. In the past, neurologists did'nt believe that the left side of the brain had an impact on creative impulses, but recent brain scan's have shown that both sides of the brain are used in creative thinking.

2.   Whats the source of creativity? Maybe its never going to be understood. What everybody know's for certain is that artistic talent isnt evenly distributed. Some people are'nt as talented as others.

HINT: Contractions with Two Meanings

Sometimes one contraction can have two different meanings.

I'd = I had *or* I would   **He's** = he is or he has

When you read, you should be able to figure out the meaning of the contraction by looking at the words in context.

Joe's working on a painting.   **Joe's** been working on it for a month.
(Joe is)   (Joe has)

Practice 2

Look at each underlined contraction, and then write out the complete words.

EXAMPLE: They <u>weren't</u> ready to start a business.   **were not**

1. <u>Banksy's</u> a very good graffiti artist.   _____

2. <u>He's</u> been a graffiti artist since 2002.   _____

3. <u>He's</u> an extremely creative man.   _____

4. I wish <u>I'd</u> gone to art school.   _____

5. <u>I'd</u> like to be an artist, too.   _____

Apostrophes to Show Ownership

36.3 Use apostrophes to show ownership.

You can also use apostrophes to show ownership. Review the following rules.

Possessive Form of Singular Nouns

Add -'s to the end of a singular noun to indicate ownership. If the singular noun ends in s, you must still add -'s.

Lautrec's artwork was very revolutionary.

Morris's wife is a professional dancer.

Possessive Form of Plural Nouns

When a plural noun ends in -*s*, add only an apostrophe to indicate ownership. Add -'*s* to irregular plural nouns.

Many **galleries'** websites contain images from their exhibits.

The **men's** and **women's** paintings are in separate rooms.

Possessive Form of Compound Nouns

When two people have joint ownership, add the apostrophe to the second name. When two people have separate ownership, add apostrophes to both names.

Joint ownership   Marian and **Jake's** gallery is successful.
Separate ownership   **Marian's** and **Jake's** studios are in different buildings.

Practice 3

Write the possessive forms of the following phrases.

EXAMPLE: the sister of the doctor <u>the doctor's sister</u>

1. the brush of the artist   _____

2. the brushes of the artists   _____

3. the rooms of the children   _____

4. the entrances of the galleries   _____

5. the photo of Ross and Anna   _____

6. the photo of Ross and the
   photo of Anna   _____

HINT: Possessive Pronouns Do Not Have Apostrophes

Some contractions sound like possessive pronouns. For example, *you're* sounds like *your*, and *it's* sounds like *its*. Remember that the possessive pronouns *yours*, *hers*, *its*, and *ours* never have apostrophes.

                        its
The conference is on i̶t̶'s̶ last day.
                  yours   hers
The document is y̶o̶u̶r̶'s̶ and not h̶e̶r̶'s̶.

Practice 4

Underline and correct twelve errors. You may need to add, remove, or move apostrophes.

EXAMPLE: The <u>magazines</u> cover featured a work of art by influential
              magazine's
           street artist JR.

1.   Many artist's works reflect an interesting perspective about society. JR, a French street artist, tags his images using only his initials and keeps his true identity a secret. What makes his work unique is it's combination of photography and graffiti and its focus on social issues. Normal people are typically featured in JR's art, and theyre the main inspiration for much of his work.

2.   JR has done many provocative art pieces. One of his most famous installation's was done in a Rio de Janeiro slum. He covered several tenement buildings facades with giant eyes. The local womens eyes seemed to look down on the city. Initially, peoples' reactions were mixed, as the street art forced locals to notice the slums. JR is a global artist, and hes also well known for a controversial installation called Face 2 Face. On the wall's of several cities in Israel and Palestine, he plastered images of Israeli and Palestinian faces looking at each other. Today, his artworks are appreciated because theyre truly poignant and thought-provoking. Though JRs work typically appears on streets, his pieces are also in many art galleries collections.

Apostrophes in Expressions of Time

36.4 Use apostrophes in expressions of time.

If an expression of time (*year, week, month, day*) appears to possess something, use the possessive form of that word.

Alice Ray gave two **weeks'** notice before she left the dance company.

When you write out a year in numerals, an apostrophe can replace the missing numbers.

The graduates of the class of '**99** hoped to find good jobs.

However, if you are writing the numeral of a decade or century, do not put an apostrophe before the final -*s*.

In the **1900s**, many innovations in art occurred.

Practice 5

Underline and correct ten errors. You may need to add or remove apostrophes.

EXAMPLE: Jackson Pollock <u>wasnt</u> a conventional artist.
wasn't

1. In 1992, truck driver Teri Horton shopped for the weeks groceries, and then she passed by a thrift shop. She bought a painting for $5. She had planned to give it to a friend as a gag gift, but the large painting wouldnt fit through the door of her friends mobile home. A few month's after that, Horton put the artwork in her garage sale.

2. Three hour's later, a local art teacher saw the painting and said, "Maybe its Jackson Pollocks work!" Horton spent the rest of the 1990's trying to prove that shed bought an original Pollock. Today, art expert's opinions are still divided.

Final Review

Underline and correct eighteen apostrophe errors. You may need to add, remove, or move apostrophes.

EXAMPLE: What is an <u>artists</u> motivation to create?
artist's

1. The street artist Banksy grew up in Bristol, England. When he was fourteen year's old, he began to paint graffiti on walls. He noticed that many of his friend's favorite graffiti spots were being watched by police officers. Banksy was worried; he didnt want to be arrested. One day, while he

was hiding from a policewoman, he noticed the stenciled letters on the officers cruiser. Banksy realized that he could paint more quickly if he used stencils. "I wasnt very good at free-hand drawing," he said in an interview. "I was too slow."

2. In the early 2000's, many of Banksy's stencils began to have political content. For example, he painted several murals on the wall in Israels' West Bank. In one image, there appear's to be a hole in the wall with a sandy beach on the other side. Under the hole are two smiling children, and the childrens' buckets are full of sand. Banksy has also snuck his art into some of the worlds most prestigious galleries'. In 2003, he used tape to post a painting on the wall of Londons Tate gallery. Its amazing that the security guards didnt see him do it.

3. The artists reputation has increased because his images have captured the publics' imagination. In fact, in 2013, someone went to the trouble to remove a London stores brick wall, which had a Banksy mural on it. An auction house sold the work for $1.1 million. Although he now has international fame, Banksy doesnt want people to discover his true identity.

The Writer's Room

Write about one of the following topics. After you finish writing, make sure that you have used apostrophes correctly.

1. What are some jobs that require creativity? List examples of such jobs, and describe how they are creative.

2. Define a term or expression that relates to this photo. Some ideas might be *creativity, graffiti, social commentary, vandalism,* or *beauty.*

37 Quotation Marks, Capitalization, and Titles

SECTION THEME: Human Development

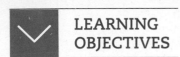

LEARNING OBJECTIVES

37.1 Use quotation marks correctly.

37.2 Use quotations in research essays.

37.3 Learn capitalization rules.

37.4 Style titles correctly.

In this chapter, you read about musicians and creativity.

Quotation Marks (" ")

37.1 Use quotation marks correctly.

Use **quotation marks** to set off the exact words of a speaker or writer. When you include the exact words of more than one person in a text, then you must make a new paragraph each time the speaker changes. If the quotation is a complete sentence, punctuate it in the following ways.

- Capitalize the first word of the quotation.
- Place quotation marks around the complete quotation.
- Place the end punctuation inside the closing quotation marks.
- Generally, attach the name of the speaker or writer to the quotation in some way.

  Oscar Wilde declared, "All art is useless."

Review the following rules.

1. **Introductory Phrase**

   When the quotation is introduced by a phrase, place a comma after the introductory phrase.

   > Merryn Edgar said, "The best art is truthful."

2. **Interrupting Phrase**

   When the quotation is interrupted, place a comma before and after the interrupting phrase.

   > "In the end," says dancer Alice Cook, "everyone has special talents."

3. **End Phrase**

   When you place a phrase at the end of a quotation, end the quotation with a comma instead of a period.

   > "Great art makes viewers react emotionally," said curator Frank Marshall.

   If your quotation ends with other punctuation, put it inside the quotation mark.

   > "Who is the greatest painter?" the student asked.

   > "That question cannot be answered!" the curator replied.

4. **Introductory Sentence**

   When you introduce a quotation with a complete sentence, place a colon (:) after the introductory sentence.

   > George Simons explains his philosophy about dance: "Dance is the most expressive of the arts."

5. **Inside Quotations**

   If one quotation is inside another quotation, then use single quotation marks (' ') around the inside quotation.

   > To her mother, Veronica Corelli explained, "I am not sure if I will succeed, but you've always said, 'Your work should be your passion.' "

HINT: Integrated Quotations

If the quotation is not a complete sentence, and you simply integrate it into your sentence, do not capitalize the first word of the quotation.

> Composer Ludwig van Beethoven called music "the mediator between the spiritual and the sensual life."

Practice 1

In each sentence, the quotation is set off in a color. Add quotation marks and periods, commas, or colons. Also, capitalize the first word of the quotation, if necessary.

EXAMPLE: Producer Kelsey Martin asks' "Where are the great singers?"

1. Kelsey Martin says   right now, an average voice can sound perfect with new technologies.

2. Auto-tune was originally created to fix pitch and tone problems in singers' voices according to Anna Pulley.

3. The auto-tune effect corrected my low notes proclaimed rapper J. Lowes.

4. I know auto-tune really well said Lowes and it has helped me create a better record

5. Writer Kaleb Brock says that technology can transform a pitchy voice into a perfect voice

6. It makes singers sound too perfect says music lover Andrea Berezan and perfect singing is boring

7. Guitarist Pierre Roi shows his contempt for auto-tune when singers use auto-tune, their voices sound fake

8. Too many pop stars also lip-synch in concert declares Jay Segal.

9. Neil McCormack mentions an incident at a live show I saw Madonna drop her microphone, and her singing was still audible

10. Music fan Chelsea Oberman says When I pay $80 to see a live concert, and the singer lip-synchs, I sometimes shout   use your voice

Practice 2

Correct ten punctuation errors in the next dialogue.

EXAMPLE: She told me, "Your future is in your hands".

Maya confronted her son, "Your drums are too loud"!

Jonell looked at his mother and replied: "I need to practice for my band."

"How will you make a living as a drummer" she asked?

He replied, "I do not need to earn a lot of money to be happy."

"You're being very naive." Maya responded.

Jonell said, "I'm just following your advice. You always say, "Find work that you love.""

"Perhaps you have to take some chances" his mother responded, "and learn from your own mistakes."

Jonell stated firmly, "my decision will not be a mistake!"

Using Quotations in Research Essays

37.2 Use quotations in research essays.

Use quotations to reveal the opinions of an expert or to highlight ideas that are particularly memorable and important. When quoting sources, remember to limit how many you use in a single paper and to vary your quotations by using both direct and indirect quotations.

Direct and Indirect Quotations

A **direct quotation** contains the exact words of the speaker or writer, and it is set off with quotation marks.

Bruno Fonseca writes, "Mexican painters have been recognized for their talents."

An **indirect quotation** keeps the author's meaning but is not set off by quotation marks. Note that an indirect quotation is also called a paraphrase.

Bruno Fonseca writes that Mexico has produced talented painters.

Integrating Quotations

SHORT QUOTATIONS

Introduce short quotations with a phrase or sentence. (Short quotations should not stand alone.) Read the following original selection, and then view how the quotation has been introduced using three common methods. The selection, written by Michael J. Strada, appeared on page 60 of his book *Through the Global Lens*.

Original Selection

Maps turned out to be very helpful to London officials a century ago, when they were used to track the spread of a cholera epidemic to the city's water system. Since maps aim to simulate reality, the drawing of maps may seem simple and straightforward. The process, however, is anything but simple.

Phrase Introduction

In *Through the Global Lens*, Michael J. Strada writes, "Since maps aim to simulate reality, the drawing of maps may seem simple and straightforward" (60).

Sentence Introduction

In his book, *Through the Global Lens*, Michael J. Strada suggests that drawing maps can be complicated: "Since maps aim to simulate reality, the drawing of maps may seem simple and straightforward" (60).

Integrated Quotation

In *Through the Global Lens*, Michael J. Strada reveals that drawing a map "is anything but simple" (60).

HINT: Words That Introduce Quotations

Here are some common words that can introduce quotations.

admits	concludes	mentions	speculates
claims	explains	observes	suggests
comments	maintains	reports	warns

The doctor **states**, "_____."

"_____," **observes** Dr. Hannah.

Dr. Hannah **speculates** that _____.

LONG QUOTATIONS

If you use a quotation in MLA style that has four or more lines (or in APA style, more than forty words), insert the quotation in your research paper in the following way.

- Introduce the quotation with a sentence ending with a colon.
- Indent the entire quotation from the left margin of your document.
- Use double spacing.
- Do not use quotation marks.
- Cite the author and page number in parentheses after the punctuation mark in the last sentence of the quotation (or in APA style, cite the author, year of publication, and page number).

Review the next example from a student essay about art history that uses MLA style. The quotation is from page 132 of Germaine Greer's *The Obstacle Race*. The explanatory sentence introduces the quotation and is part of an essay.

Much great art has been lost owing to a variety of factors:

> Panels decay as wood decays. Canvas rots, tears, and sags. The stretchers spring and warp. As color dries out, it loses its flexibility and begins to separate from its unstable ground; dry color flakes off shrinking or swelling wood and drooping canvas. (Greer 132)

HINT: Using Long Quotations

If your research paper is short (two or three pages), avoid using many long quotations. Long quotations will only overwhelm your own ideas. Instead, try summarizing a long passage or using shorter quotations.

Using Ellipses (. . .)

If you want to quote key ideas from an author, but do not want to quote the entire paragraph, you can use **ellipses**. Ensure that your new sentence, with the ellipses, is grammatically correct. These three periods show that you have omitted unnecessary information from a quotation. Leave a space before and after each period. If the omitted section goes to the end of the sentence or includes one or more complete sentences, insert a final period before the ellipses (. . . .). The original selection appeared on page 173 of the book *Crossroads* by Elizabeth F. Barkley.

Original Selection
The guitarist slides the steel bar across the strings, which are tuned to a single cord, and the steel bar changes the pitch of the chord by its location on the strings. The sliding of the bar gives the guitar a distinctive wavering timbre.

Quotation with Omissions
In *Crossroads*, Elizabeth F. Barkley writes, "The guitarist slides the steel bar across the strings. . . . The sliding of the bar gives the guitar a distinctive wavering timbre" (173).

Practice 3

Read the quotation, and then answer the questions. The selection, written by Richard Paul Janaro, appeared on page 200 of *The Art of Being Human*.

Original Selection

Blues music is almost always about the empty aftermath of a once burning passion. The songs are written from either a male or a female point of view. Men sing of the faithlessness of women, and women return the compliment about men.

1. Write a direct quotation. Remember to introduce the title and author.

   _____

   _____

   _____

2. Write a direct quotation with an omission. Remember to introduce the title and author.

   _____

   _____

   _____

Capitalization

37.3 Learn capitalization rules.

Remember to capitalize the following:

- **The pronoun *I* and the first word of every sentence**

   My brothers and I share an apartment.

- **Days of the week, months, and holidays**

Thursday	June 22	Labor Day

   Do not capitalize the seasons: summer, fall, winter, spring.

- **Titles of specific institutions, departments, companies, and schools**

Microsoft	Department of Finance	Elmwood High School

   Do not capitalize general references.

the company	the department	the school

- **Names of specific places such as buildings, streets, parks, cities, states, and bodies of water**

Eiffel Tower	Times Square	Los Angeles, California
Sunset Boulevard	Florida	Lake Erie

Do not capitalize general references.

the street   the state   the lake

- **Names of specific planets but not the sun or the moon**

    Earth   Mars   Venus

- **Specific languages, nationalities, tribes, races, and religions**

    Greek   Mohawk   Buddhist   a French restaurant

- **Titles of specific individuals**

    General Franklin   President Obama   Doctor Blain

    Professor Sayf   Prime Minister Trudeau   Mrs. Robinson

If you are referring to the profession in general, or if the title follows the name, do not use capital letters.

    my doctor   the professors   Ted Cruz, a senator

- **Specific course and program titles**

    Physics 201   Marketing 101   Advanced Algebra

If you refer to a course without mentioning the course title, then it is unnecessary to use capitals. Also, do not capitalize the names of programs.

    He is in his math class.   I am in the music program.

Do not capitalize academic degrees when spelled out. Only capitalize the abbreviated form.

    Mike has a master of arts in literature, but his sister did not complete her **MA**.

    I have a bachelor of science degree, and Melissa has a **PhD**.

- **The major words in titles of newspapers, magazines, and literary or artistic works**

    Miami Herald   *Great Expectations*   *House of Cards*

- **Historical events, eras, and movements**

    World War II   Post-Impressionism   Baby Boomers

HINT: Capitalizing Computer Terms

Always capitalize the following computer terms.

    Google   World Wide Web   Microsoft Office

Practice 4

Add fifteen missing capital letters to the following paragraphs.

EXAMPLE: The musician was born on ~~m~~^March 21.

1.   The New York academy of Sciences has examined how people respond to music. The study, done in april 2005, examines whether musical training can make people smarter. The researchers found that listening to a song such as "in my life" can enhance brain functions.

2.   Gordon Shaw, who passed away in 2005, earned his bachelor of science degree and later completed a doctorate in physics at cornell university. He was the co-founder of the Music intelligence neuronal development institute. He also wrote the book *Keeping Mozart in mind*. Shaw determined that music can enhance math abilities. I wish I had known that when I took math 401 at Greendale high school. Maybe I will study music in college.

Titles

37.4 Style titles correctly.

Place the title of a short work in quotation marks. Italicize the titles of longer documents, or underline such titles when the document is handwritten.

Short Works		Long Works	
short story	"The Lottery"	novel	*Catch-22*
chapter	"Early Accomplishments"	book	*The Art of Emily Carr*
newspaper article	"The City's Hottest Ticket"	newspaper	*The New York Times*
magazine article	"New Artists"	magazine	*Rolling Stone*
Web article	"Music Artists Lose Out"	website	*CNET News*
essay	"Hip-Hop Nation"	textbook	*Common Culture*
TV episode	"The Search Party"	TV series/ film title	*Lost/Rush*
song	"Mouths to Feed"	CD	*Release Therapy*
poem	"Howl"	anthology	*Collected Poems of Beat Writers*

Capitalizing Titles

When you write a title, capitalize the first letter of the first word and all the major words.

To Kill a Mockingbird   "Stairway to Heaven"

Do not capitalize the word ".com" in a Web address. Also, do not capitalize the following words, unless they are the first word in the title.

articles	a, an, the
coordinators	for, and, nor, but, or, yet, so
prepositions	at, by, in, of, to, up (and so on)

HINT: Your Own Essay Titles

In essays that you write for your courses, do not underline your title or put quotation marks around it. Simply capitalize the first word and the main words.

Why Music Is Important

Practice 5

Add ten capital letters to the next selection, and add quotation marks or underlines to ten titles. Add quotation marks to the titles of short works. For long works, underline titles to show that they should be in italics.

EXAMPLE: The magazine ~~b~~usiness ~~w~~eek featured successful singers.

1.   Rolling stone, a music magazine, published an article called The 500

    Greatest songs of All Time. The first item on the list is the Bob Dylan

    song Like a Rolling Stone. According to the magazine, the greatest

    album is Sergeant Pepper's Lonely Hearts Club band.

2.   I heard my favorite song in a movie. The song Mad World was

    first recorded by the british band Tears for Fears. Released in august

    1982 on the album The hurting, the song was moderately successful.

    Then, for the 2001 movie Donnie Darko, the song was redone

    in a slower tempo with piano music. The version by Gary Jules

    mesmerized filmgoers and helped give the movie a cult following.

In fact, last friday, when the movie played at a theater on arrow street in Cambridge, Massachusetts, the film sold out. The song has appeared as background music in television shows such as Third Watch and Without a trace. Then, nearly thirty years after the song was first released, Adam Lambert sang it during an episode of American Idol. Once again, the song became a great hit.

Final Review

Identify and correct twenty-five errors.

- Correct fourteen errors with capitalization.
- Set off six titles by adding quotation marks or by underlining titles that should be in italics.
- Correct five other punctuation errors.

EXAMPLE: The researcher said ʼ"Artificial intelligence will change music forever."

1.   Artificial intelligence impacts different scientific fields. But until recently, people assumed that artistic tasks, like creating music, could not be done by machines. On the website GizMag, the article Computer Composers Changing How Music is made discusses computer-generated music. University of California Santa cruz music professor David Cope says, "It seemed even early in my teenage years perfectly logical to do creative things with algorithms". While in High School, Cope dreamed of a future where an algorithm could do his homework or paint a picture.

2.   David Cope was born in san Francisco on saturday, may 17, 1941. Cope originally considered developing music through algorithms in 1981. After releasing an album called Concert for Piano and orchestra

in 1980, he developed writer's block. To overcome this problem, Cope wrote an algorithm to help him complete songs more quickly and efficiently. He describes the benefit he gained from this method, "with algorithms we can experiment to produce a piece in fifteen minutes, and we can know immediately if it's going to work or not." According to Cope, these programs can free up a great deal of time for songwriters, which opens "An arena of creativity that could not have been imagined even fifty years ago".

3.   In the article When Robots write Songs, which appeared in The Atlantic magazine in august 2014, a team of American and french computer scientists describe how their songwriting algorithm works. Thousands of hours of music are entered into the program, and the information is synthesized to compose original music. Such artificial intelligence programs can write music in the style of rock legends or even in the style of famous classical composers like Bach or Mozart. Francois Pachet, the head of Sony's Computer science Lab in Paris, claims that his team is "quite close now to programming computers to generate nice melodies in the style of pop composers such as LeGrand or McCartney."

4.   Even famous musicians can be fooled by the more modern music algorithms. "It's truly impressive." says legendary jazz guitarist Pat Metheny about Pachet's jazz-bot. When Metheny played a computer-generated jazz song for his bandmate, his saxophone player "immediately started guessing" who composed the track.

5.   Some people are scared of the idea of artificially generated music because of what it says about humanity. Ray Kurzweil, author of The Age of Spiritual Machines, wonders who the artist is if a song is composed by an algorithm. However, David Cope disagrees. In an interview, Cope said: "We could do amazing things if we'd just give up a little bit of our ego and attempt to not pit ourselves against our own creations—our own computers—but embrace the two of us together and, in one way or another, continue to grow."

The Writer's Room

Write about one of the following topics. Include some direct quotations. Proofread to ensure that your punctuation and capitalization are correct.

1. List some characteristics of your generation. What political events, social issues, music, and fashion bind your generation?

2. List three categories of art. Describe some details about each category.

3. Examine the photograph. What do you think the people are talking about? Write a brief dialogue from their conversation.

38 Numbers and Additional Punctuation

SECTION THEME: Human Development

In this chapter, you read about photography and photographers.

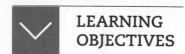

LEARNING OBJECTIVES

38.1 Review the rules for using numbers in academic writing.

38.2 Learn about additional forms of punctuation.

Numbers

38.1 Review the rules for using numbers in academic writing.

There are two basic styles for number usage. Business and technical documents use one style, and academic writing uses another. **In business and technical fields**, use numerals instead of words in charts, statistics, graphs, financial documents, and advertising. The numbers one to ten are written as words only when they appear in sentences.

However, **in academic writing**, numbers are spelled out more often. Review the rules for using numbers in academic writing.

- Spell out numbers that can be expressed in one or two words.

  We spent **eighteen** days in Mexico City.

  There were **forty-seven** people waiting for another flight.

  The airline had room for **four hundred**.

  That day, **thousands** of people cleared customs.

- Use numerals with numbers of more than two words.

  The manager booked rooms for **358** guests.

- Spell out fractions.

  Only **one-third** of the residents have their own homes.

- When the sentence begins with a number, spell out the number. If the number has more than two words, do not place it at the beginning of the sentence.

  Three hundred people were invited to the gallery.
  There were **158** guests.

- Use a numeral before million or billion, but spell out *million* or *billion*. (It is easier to read *20 million* than *20,000,000*.)

  The company hopes to sell about **14 million** units.

- Use numerals when writing addresses, dates, times, degrees, pages, measurements, or divisions of a book. Also use numerals with prices and percentages. Always write out *percent*. For prices, you can write *dollars* or use the $ symbol.

  A yearly subscription costs **$29**, which is about **15** percent less than the cover price.

HINT: Several Numbers in a Sentence

When writing two consecutive numbers, write out the shorter number.

  Each digital camera used **one 2GB** memory card.

Be consistent when writing a series of numbers. If some numbers require numerals, then use numerals for all of the numbers.

  The gallery guests consumed **300** appetizers, **8** pounds of cheese, and **120** glasses of wine.

Practice 1

Correct any errors with numbers in the next sentences.

nine

Example: She was just ~~9~~ ^{nine} years old when she picked up a camera.

1. Nature photographer Jillian Wolf has four digital cameras, 3 printers, and one hundred and sixteen pieces of photography paper.

2. She has worked professionally as a photographer for 5 years.

3. Last year, Wolf published her own photography book, and each book sold for ninety-five dollars.

4. She self-published 50 132-page books.

5. She rented a gallery space and exhibited 25 of her nature photos.

6. 65 people came to see her photos.

Additional Punctuation

38.2 Learn about additional forms of punctuation.

Semicolon (;)

Use a semicolon

- between two complete and related ideas.

    The photograph was stunning; Sherman was very pleased.

- between items in a series of ideas, if the items have internal punctuation (like commas) or if the items are longer phrases.

    Sherman's works were exhibited in Birmingham, Alabama; Fort Worth, Texas; Toronto, Ontario; and London, England.

Colon (:)

Use a colon

- after a complete sentence that introduces a quotation.

    Photographer Henri Cartier-Bresson stated his view: "Photographers are dealing with things that are continually vanishing."

- to introduce a series or a list after a complete sentence.

    The new museum includes the work of some great photographers: Ansel Adams, Cindy Sherman, Edward Weston, Alfred Stieglitz, Dorothea Lange, and Annie Leibovitz.

- to introduce an explanation or example.

    The tiny sculpture is outrageously expensive: $2.5 million.

- after the expression "the following."

    Please do the following: read, review, and respond.

> **GRAMMAR LINK**
> For practice using semicolons, see Chapters 21 and 24.

- to separate the hour and minutes in expressions of time.

    The exhibit will open at 12:30 P.M.

Hyphen (-)

Use a hyphen

- with some compound nouns. (Note that *compound* means "more than one part.") The following nouns always require a hyphen.

    sister-in-law   mother-in-law   show-off

- when you write the complete words for compound numbers between twenty-one and ninety-nine.

    twenty-five   ninety-two   seventy-seven

- after some prefixes such as *self-*, *mid-*, or *ex-*.

    self-assured   mid-December   ex-husband

- when you use a compound adjective before a noun. The compound adjective must express a single thought. There is no hyphen if the compound adjective appears after the noun.

    | one-way street | well-known actor | thirty-year-old woman |
    | The street is one way. | The actor was well known. | The woman is thirty years old. |

HINT: Nonhyphenated Compound Adjectives

Some compound adjectives never take a hyphen, even when they appear before a noun. Here are some common examples.

World Wide Web   high school senior   real estate agent

DASH (—)

You can use dashes to indicate long pauses or to dramatically emphasize words. Use dashes sparingly.

Ansel Adams waited until the sun was setting to capture the image—the perfect moment.

The gallery owner—hiding his excitement—offered to buy the rare photo.

Parentheses ( )

You can use parentheses to set off incidental information such as a date or abbreviation. Use parentheses sparingly.

> Lange's photo of the migrant mother, which was taken during the height of the Depression era (1936), has become an enduring image.

> The United Press Photographer's Association (UPPA) was founded in 1946.

HINT: Using Abbreviations

An **abbreviation** is the shortened form of a word. Avoid using abbreviations in academic writing except for titles and time references.

> Dr. = Doctor   Mr. = Mister   P.M. = post meridiem (after noon)

An **acronym** is formed with the first letters of a group of words. Many companies and organizations use acronyms. In an academic paper, give the complete name of the organization the first time you mention it and write the acronym in parentheses immediately after the full name. Use the acronym in the rest of the essay.

> The North Atlantic Treaty Organization (NATO) signed the agreement in 1949. Today, NATO's headquarters are in Belgium.

Practice 2

Add any missing colons, hyphens, dashes, or parentheses.

Example: He took a famous photo of an eighteen-year-old woman.
                                                      ^   ^

1. American photographer Steve McCurry was born in Philadelphia, Pennsylvania, and he is best known for a striking photograph "Afghan Girl."

2. In 1985, McCurry made his way into a dangerous area along the border of Afghanistan and Pakistan during the Soviet-Afghan War 1979–1989 .

3. At a refugee camp in Pakistan, McCurry, then a thirty five year old man, took a photo of a girl with green eyes and a red scarf.

4. The well known photo first appeared on the cover of *National Geographic* magazine.

5. During a nearly twenty year period after the famous cover was published, investigators tried to find the woman who appeared in the photo.

6. Finally, in 2002, *National Geographic* researchers found what they were looking for in a remote part of Afghanistan a woman named Sharbat Gula.

7. Gula was identified as the "Afghan Girl" using iris scanning technology.

8. McCurry has also worked in the following war torn regions Iraq, the former Yugoslavia, and Cambodia.

9. McCurry has won four consecutive World Press Photo WPP Photo of the Year awards.

10. In an interview, McCurry described his artistic process "If you wait, people will forget your camera, and the soul will drift up into view."

FINAL REVIEW

Identify and correct any errors in numbers, colons, hyphens, dashes, or parentheses.

Example: Richard Avedon took large-format photos.

1. Richard Avedon 1923–2004 was a great fashion photographer.

2. Before he joined the Merchant Marines, his father in law gave him a camera a gift that changed his life.

3. At the beginning of his career, he took photos with his ten year old Rolleiflex camera.

4. He became a staff photographer for *Vogue* he also worked for *Harper's Bazaar*.

5. Many of his photos featured three items a chair, a white backdrop, and a face.

6. One of his greatest photos a masterpiece of shadow and light showed Audrey Hepburn's face.

7. He took 100s of photos of Hepburn, his favorite model.

8. His photographs have been exhibited at New York's Museum of Modern Art MOMA.

9. He published the best selling book *Portraits*, and he co authored another book, *The Sixties*.

10. His book has twenty-nine fashion shots, 125 portraits, and twelve war images.

11. One of his photos—an iconic image of Marilyn Monroe has been reproduced in 1000s of books and magazines.

12. Avedon compared photography to music "The way I see is comparable to the way musicians hear."

READING LINK

More readings on human development and creativity:
"We're Watching What We Eat" p. 83
"Tips for Breaking Free of Compulsive Smartphone Use" p. 134
"Nudge" p. 572
"How Cults Become Religions" p. 576
"The Untranslatable Word 'Macho'" p. 579
"Chance and Circumstance" p. 583
"The Happiness Factor" p. 587
"The Veldt" p. 590

The Writer's Room

Write about one of the following topics. Proofread for errors in numbers or punctuation.

1. Describe a personal photograph that you cherish. When was the photo taken? What is in the photo? Why is it so compelling?

2. Compare two art forms. For example, you could compare a photograph and a painting or two pieces of music.

39 Editing Practice

LEARNING OBJECTIVE

39.1 Practice revising and editing essays and different types of writing.

To conquer Mount Everest, climbers meet the physical and mental challenges through practice and training. To write good essays, students perfect their skills by revising and editing.

Why Bother Editing?

39.1 Practice revising and editing essays and different types of writing.

After you finish writing the first draft of an essay, always make time to edit it. Editing for errors in grammar, punctuation, sentence structure, and capitalization can make the difference between a failing paper and a passing one or between a good essay and a great one. Editing is not always easy; it takes time and attention to detail. However, it gets easier the more you do it. Also, the more you edit your essays (and your peers' essays, too), the better your writing will be!

Practice 1

Correct fifteen errors in this essay. An editing symbol appears above each error. To understand the meaning of each symbol, refer to the revising and editing symbols on the inside back cover of this book.

1.   Films such as *Into the wild* and television shows such as *Survivor*
^{cap}

^{agr}
is very popular. But watching shows about survival is not the same as

surviving alone in the outdoors. If you enjoy hiking in the wild, you

^{sp}
should definitly learn basic outdoor survival techniques.

2.   First, plan your trip in advance. Buy a detailed map of the area,

^{pl}
and find out informations about the weather. Also, take a survival

kit with you. Packing essential items is more important than

^{//}
to buy expensive equipment. For example, a butane lighter and a

^{frag}
tarp are necessary. Especially if you are hiking in the outback. Most

importantly, tell someone where you are going and when you are

returning before you set off on an outdoor trip. This information

^{shift}
will prove vital if something unexpected happened.

3.   Second, if you get lost try to remain calm. Panic can cause you to
^p

^{ad}
make the wrong choices. The most best way to stop the panic is to sit

^{ad}   ^{ro}
down and breathe deep. You should probably stay where you are you

have informed someone of your plans.

4.   Next, build a shelter. Persons have died from extreme
^{pl}

temperatures. For example, Mike and Janice were hiking in the Grand

Tetons when it started to rain. They were stranded on the side of a

^m
mountain wearing wet clothes. Fortunately, they knew how to build a

shelter and had packed extra clothes.

5.   By following these basic rules, you will increase you're chances of [sp above "you're"]

survival in an emergency. Outdoor hiking is a lot of fun, but we should [shift above "we should"]

always remember Lord Baden-Powell's motto for young scouts: Be

prepared.

Practice 2

Correct twenty errors in this essay. An editing symbol appears above each error. To understand the meaning of each symbol, refer to the revising and editing symbols on the inside back cover of this book.

1.   Since 1900, many products been defective. In his book *Business ethics*, [vt above "been"; cap above "ethics"]

Richard T. De George discusses a famous product defect case. In the

early 1970's, American automakers was losing market share to smaller [p above "1970's"; agr above "was"]

Japanese imports. Lee Iacocca, the CEO of Ford Motor Company [p superscript after "Company"]

wanted to produce a car that was inexpensive, lightweight, and had an

attractive look. Engineers developped the Ford Pinto. [// above "attractive"; sp above "developped"]

2.   Because Ford wanted the product on the market real quickly, the [ad above "real"]

car was not test for rear-end impacts. After the Pintos been produced, [vt above "test"; vt above "been"]

they were put in collision tests, they failed the tests. When the Pinto [ro above "they"]

was hitted from behind, a bolt on the bumper will sometimes puncture [sp above "hitted"; wc above "will"]

the fuel tank. And cause an explosion. [frag above "And"]

3. Ford conducted a study and determined that a^wc inexpensive

baffle could be placed between the bumper and the gas tank. After

conducting a cost–benefit analysis, a^m decision was made. It was less

expensive to fight lawsuits than inserting^// the baffle.

4. In 1976, Pintos had thirteen explosions from rear-end impacts.

Comparable cars had less^ad problems. When it be^vt too late, the company

realized that the lawsuits and the bad publicity were worst^ad for the

company than the cost of the repairs would have been. After seven

years and many deaths, the Pintos were recalled.

Practice 3: Edit a Formal Letter

Correct fifteen errors in this formal business letter.

Rachel and Rob Connors

7955 Howard street north

Richmond, CA 94805

July 7, 2018

Customer Service

Home Sharing services

1572 Central avenue

Renata, CA 92567

Subject: Inaccurate advertising

Attention: Director of sales

GRAMMAR LINK
Learn more about
business letter
formatting in
Chapter 19.

We used your service to rent a room in a house on july 2 2018. On thursday, I check the rating of the people who were renting the room. The site gave them a perfect five-star rating. However, I think that this rating is fake and I believe that this situation may be a widespread practice on your site. When we arrived, the room was not ready for guests. It was filthy, and when I politely asked the owners about it, they were rude. They also had a noisy party the night we slept there! Its a shame that we have to do this, but we'd like to lodge formal complaint with your company. We would also like to be reimbursed for the full amount paid for the night's stay.

Thank you for you're cooperation in this matter. We look forward to receive your response.

Yours Sincerely,

Rachel and Rob Connors

Practice 4: Edit a Workplace Memo

Correct ten errors in the following excerpt from a memo.

To: Career development faculty members

From: Maddison Healey

Re: Internships

I'm gonna take this opportunity to remind you that their are financial resources for hiring two new interns for the Career development Program. If anyone wishes to participate in this collaboration, please let Danielle or I know. The current deadline for applying to the internship program is the beginning of april. The internship program, provides valuable mentoring to college students. Treating interns with respect, it is very important. If you hire an intern, you are responsible for training them. For those who are interested, please let me know as quick us possible.

Practice 5: Edit a Short Article

Correct twenty errors in the next selection.

1. Pluto's status has been hotly debated in academic circles for years. In 2006, the International Astronomical union (IAU) declared that Pluto would no longer be considered a planet. According to scientists, a planet must orbit the sun, it must be having a spherical shape, and it must have a clear orbit. Pluto's orbit sometimes overlaps with Neptune's, and thats how Pluto lost its status as a planet. According to famous astrophysicist Neil de Grasse Tyson, calling Pluto a planet would be "an insult to the other planets". However, much other prominent scientists disagrees. For example, the lead scientist for the New Horizons satellite mission says that the IAU "embarrassed itself" by designating Pluto a "dwarf planet." According to this scientist, under the rules espoused by the IAU, even Earth would occasionaly not be considered a planet.

2. We are learning more about the "dwarf planet" than ever before, on July 21, 2015, data from the New Horizons mission showed evidence of an ancient lake, as well signs of ice and liquid on the surface of Pluto. Scientists assume that the liquid and ices are composed of nitrogen. This new data is very excited for researchers at NASA. For example, we now know the exact tilt of Pluto. Its atmospheric pressure also varies great over time. The ten-years-old New Horizons satellite constantly sends new informations about the cosmos, and we will soon learn even more about tiny Pluto.

3.   Astronomers still disagree on how to properly classify Pluto. Some say that it should never have been classified as a planet. Planetary scientists state that while Pluto may not be a nineth planet, it is still more similar to a planet than other asteroids in the solar system. We may eventualy learn more details about Pluto that will make it an oficial planet once more.

4.   A surprising number of people feel passionately about Pluto's status. As a planet. Its unclear why are people so preoccupied with this matter. Maybe people are gonna get used to Pluto as a "dwarf" planet rather than a "real" planet. Only time will tell!

Part V
Reading Selections and Strategies

In Chapter 40, you will learn strategies that can help you improve your reading skills. You will review the reading process, practice previewing, and apply active reading techniques to determine main and supporting ideas. You will also determine word meanings by using context clues, looking at word parts, and using dictionaries effectively. Finally, you will use critical thinking strategies such as inferencing.

In Chapter 41, essays are organized according to the same themes used in the grammar chapters. You will read essays that present a wide range of view points about topics related to conflict, urban development, our natural world, inventions and discoveries, travel and survival, and human development. The writers of these essays achieve their purpose using one or more of these writing patterns: Illustration, Narration, Description, Process, Definition, Classification, Comparison and Contrast, Cause and Effect, and Argument. You will also read a short story by the acclaimed author Ray Bradbury.

40 Reading Strategies

LEARNING OBJECTIVES

40.1 Review the reading process.

40.2 Preview titles, headings, and visual cues to determine a text's subject, audience, and purpose.

40.3 Apply active reading techniques to determine main idea and support.

40.4 Apply vocabulary development skills to figure out word meanings.

40.5 Use clues in the text to infer meaning.

40.6 Interpret information in visuals, including photos and charts.

Art students study techniques when they learn to paint or sculpt. In the same way, you can improve your reading skills by learning different reading strategies.

An Overview of the Reading Process

40.1 Review the reading process.

In college, you will read different types of texts and view many images and videos that may be part of print or online textbooks. You will also write responses or essays to clarify what you have read or offer your own opinions. As a reader and a writer, you engage in similar activities to understand written passages and produce your own texts. For example, when reading an article, you intuitively try to figure out what the writer aims to say and the details used to support that main idea. As a writer, you try to express a clear point of view and give relevant facts, examples, and anecdotes to support your main idea.

Becoming a Proficient Reader

To improve your reading skills, actively engage with what you read. The reading process involves the following steps:

- **Exploring:** Preview the text to get a basic idea of what subject it is about.

- **Understanding vocabulary:** Use strategies to comprehend and remember new vocabulary words.

- **Analyzing the text:** To demonstrate your understanding of the main and supporting ideas, you can try mapping (similar to clustering, explained in Chapter 1) as well as summarizing and paraphrasing (see Chapter 16). Also, think critically about the text and formulate opinions about it.

Previewing

40.2 **Preview titles, headings, and visual cues to determine a text's subject, audience, and purpose.**

Previewing is like window shopping; it gives you a chance to see what the writer is offering. One way to preview is to **skim** a text. Read it quickly and get the gist or general overview. You can also **scan**, or look for particular information, such as **key words**. You can use skimming and scanning to look quickly for visual clues so that you can determine the selection's key points. Preview the following:

- Titles or subheadings (if any)
- Table of contents
- The first and last sentences of the introduction
- The first sentence of each paragraph
- The concluding sentences in the full selection
- Key words (which may be in bold)
- Any photos, graphs, or charts
- The index, which is at the back of the book

Consider the Topic, Audience, and Purpose

Another previewing strategy is to determine the main point of view of an article. You look for the **subject** of the text, the **purpose** of the author, and the **audience** the author is writing for.

TOPIC

In reading material, the subject or **topic** is what the text is about. Often, the title hints at the subject of a text. For example, a newspaper article titled "Excess Drinking on College Campuses" is likely about student alcohol abuse.

AUDIENCE

Writers write for an intended **audience**. For example, you are the intended audience for your course textbooks. Other types of texts (novels, blogs, journal articles) target different audiences. In those situations, ask yourself who the intended audience might be. For instance, an editorial about local by-laws in a town newspaper is probably intended for the town's citizens, while a complex article on open-heart surgery may be aimed at medical students who have specific knowledge of the subject. If you are asked to read a challenging article, don't panic. Follow the reading process, and you'll be surprised how much information you can grasp.

PURPOSE

An author writes for a specific reason. The **purpose** of most texts is to inform, to persuade, or to entertain. Sometimes a writer may have more than one purpose. For example, in an opinion article about improving housing opportunities, the purposes could be to inform and to persuade.

Practice 1

Preview this textbook and answer the following questions.

1. What is the title of this textbook? _____

_____

2. On what pages is the Table of Contents? _____
3. How many parts does this textbook have? _____
4. What is the title of Chapter 3? _____
5. How many major subtitles does Chapter 5 have? _____
6. Refer to the index of this textbook. On what page is "Rehabilitation" by Jack McKelvey? _____
7. Who is the audience for this textbook? _____
8. What is the purpose of this textbook? _____

_____

Activate Your Prior Knowledge

After you have determined the topic, audience, and purpose of the text, activate your prior knowledge. What do you already know about the subject? Make a connection between the text and your own experiences and the world at large. For example, you've been asked to read an article titled "Parents Mistrust

Vaccinations." You may not know a lot about vaccinations, but you probably know a little. Maybe you've had to decide whether to be vaccinated or have your children vaccinated. Or you might have seen some online headlines about the topic. Here are tips to tap into your prior knowledge about a subject.

- **Brainstorming:** Make a list of the information you already know about the subject. You may also write down what your opinions are on it. In this way, you can have a point of reference for further research.
- **Mapping:** Write down the most important word or concept about the topic. Then, think of other ideas that relate to that word and connect them. Keep adding words or even images that link to each other.

Reading Actively

40.3 Apply active reading techniques to determine main idea and support.

Find the Main Idea

After previewing, engage in active reading. Search for the **main idea**, which is the central point that the writer is trying to make. In an essay, a college writer usually places the main idea somewhere in the first few paragraphs in the form of a **thesis statement**. However, some professional writers build up to the main idea and state it only in the middle or at the end of the essay. Additionally, some professional writers do not state the main idea directly.

HINT: Missing Statement of Main Idea

If a reading does not contain a clear thesis statement, you can determine the main idea by asking yourself *who, what, when, where, why,* and *how* questions. Then, using the answers to those questions, write a statement that sums up the main point of the reading.

Find the Supporting Ideas

Different writers use different types of supporting ideas. They may give steps for a process, use examples to illustrate a point, give reasons for an argument, and so on. Try to identify the author's supporting ideas.

Highlight and Make Annotations

After you read a long text, you may forget some of the author's ideas. To help you remember and quickly find the important points, you can highlight key ideas and make annotations. An **annotation** is a comment, question, or reaction that you write in the margin of a page. Each time you read a passage, follow the next steps.

- Look in the introductory and concluding paragraphs. Underline sentences that sum up the main idea. Using your own words, rewrite the main idea in the margin.

- Underline or highlight supporting ideas. You might even number the arguments or ideas to help you visualize how the writer organized ideas.

- Circle words that you do not understand.

- Write questions in the margin if you have trouble figuring out what the author is trying to say.

- Write notes beside passages that you find unique or that relate to your own experiences.

- Jot down any ideas that might make interesting writing topics.

Here is an annotated passage from "The Rules of Survival" by Laurence Gonzales on page 553 of this textbook.

main point ⟶

Ralston from movie *127 Hours*? ⟶

I would have panicked ⟶

steps to control fear ⟶

look up word ⟶

In the initial crisis, survivors are not ruled by fear; instead, they make use of it. Their fear often feels like (and turns into) anger, which motivates them and makes them feel sharper. Aron Ralston, the hiker who had to cut off his hand to free himself from a stone that had trapped him in a slot canyon in Utah, initially panicked and began slamming himself over and over against the boulder that had caught his hand. But very quickly he stopped himself, did some deep breathing, and began thinking about his options. He eventually spent five days progressing through the stages necessary to convince him of what decisive action he had to take to save his own life.

HINT: Use the SQ3R Method

Another reading strategy you can use to understand a text is SQ3R, which stands for survey, question, read, recite, and review.

- **Survey** (look over) the text. Observe how the writer organized it. Look for titles, key words, subtitles, and so on.

- **Question** while you survey. Brainstorm a list of questions about the text. For instance, you can turn titles and headings into questions. You can also ask yourself what you know about the topic.

- **Read** the text and look for answers to your questions.

- **Recite** what you have read. Look away from the text and orally answer the questions you asked. Only look at the text if you can't find an answer.

- **Review** what you have read. Check the main and subheadings again and recall your questions.

Understanding Difficult Words

40.4 Apply vocabulary development skills to figure out word meanings.

When you read a document and come across a new word, what do you generally do? If you skip over difficult words, you might end up with a very fuzzy idea about what you read. Constantly using a dictionary or glossary slows down your reading and may make you feel frustrated.

An effective way to determine a word's meaning is to look for hints in the surrounding words and sentences. **Context clues** are hints in the text that help define a word.

For example, can you define *crestfallen*?   Yes ___   No ___

Can you define *implore*?   Yes __   No ___

Now read the words in context, and you should be able to guess what they mean.

When the judge read the sentence, Trevor slumped in his seat, **crestfallen**. His mother rose up, and in a strong voice, she **implored** the judge to have mercy on her son.

Now write your own definitions of the words.

1. crestfallen: _____

2. implored: _____

HINT: Cognates

Cognates are English words that may look and sound like words in another language. For example, the English word *graduation* is similar to the Spanish word *graduacion*, but it is spelled differently.

If English is not your first language, and you see an English word that looks similar to a word in your language, check how the word is being used in context. It may or may not mean the same in English that it means in your language. For example, in English, *deception* means "to deliberately mislead someone." In Spanish, *decepcion* means "disappointment." Both English and German have the word *fast*, but in German it means "almost." If you are not sure of a word's meaning, you can always consult a dictionary.

Use Context Clues

An effective way to determine a word's meaning is to look for **context clues**—hints in the surrounding words and sentences. Look for the following types of context clues.

DEFINITION OR RESTATEMENT

Writers, and especially textbook authors, often provide complete definitions of difficult words to ensure that readers will understand.

A **pediatrician** is a medical practitioner who works with children.

SYNONYM

Sometimes, instead of defining a word, writers simply use a **synonym**—a word or phrase that is close in meaning—to help readers understand the term.

The doctor tried to **mitigate**—or decrease—the suffering of her patient.
(*Decrease* is a synonym for *mitigate*.)

ANTONYM

An **antonym** is a word that has the opposite meaning of another word. By understanding the contrasting word, you can guess the difficult word's meaning.

The child, initially happy and hopeful about her father's visit, became **despondent** when he did not appear.
(*Happy* and *hopeful* are the opposite of *despondent*, which means "without hope.")

EXAMPLE

Writers sometimes include examples that make a word's meaning clear.

When Mrs. Carey returned home from the hospital, her son was **solicitous**, bringing her food, washing her feet, and keeping her company when she felt lonely.
(The examples help you understand that *solicitous* means "showing concern and attention.")

LOGICAL DEDUCTION

Often, you can **infer**—or guess—a word's meaning simply by using your reasoning skills. Maybe the tone or atmosphere helps you guess. The surrounding sentences can also help you determine the word's meaning. In the following sentence, you can guess the meaning of euphoric simply by imagining how you would feel in Marcia's place.

When Marcia's name was called, she felt **euphoric**. After years of hard work, she was finally receiving her law degree!
(You can deduce that *euphoric* means "extremely happy.")

Practice 2

Guess the meanings of difficult words by using context clues. Choose the word that best defines the word in bold.

1. The factory burst into flames, and the fire caused considerable damage to an apartment building that is **adjacent** to it.

    a. open
    b. distant
    c. old
    d. nearby

2. The manager faced a **conundrum**. If she fired the grumpy graphic designer, the project would not be finished in time. If she kept him employed, the team would continue to feel stressed out by his negative attitude.

    a. prize
    b. happiness
    c. problem
    d. creation

3. The era in which you grow up bonds you with the millions of others who were born during the same period. Your needs and preferences change as you grow older—often **in concert** with those of others your own age.

    a. a show
    b. at the same time as
    c. at different times than
    d. because

4. Please stop **dithering**. Your dilly-dallying is driving us crazy. Either you will come with us or you will stay home. Make up your mind.

    a. acting compulsively
    b. being indecisive
    c. laughing
    d. refusing

Practice 3

Guess the meanings of the words in bold. First, look for context clues in the sentence. Then, use your own words to define each word.

1. After her managers praised Kendra's job performance, she wisely decided to **broach** the subject of her salary increase.

    broach: _____

2. Stop being so **morose**! Yes, you have a cold, but the world is not ending.

    morose: _____

3. In many ways, *Breaking Bad* was a ground-breaking series, and Vince Gilligan was a powerful **trailblazer**. He broke from television history, and he insisted on casting a drug dealer as a sympathetic character.

    _____

4. *Breaking Bad* included scenes of **gratuitous** violence. For instance, the scene of a man's bloody, sliced-off head **perched** on the back of a tortoise upset many viewers.

    gratuitous: _____   perched: _____

5. Thousands of people **thronged** into the packed stadium. Sweat streamed down our bodies, thus the extreme heat contributed to a **rank** experience.

thronged: _____   rank: _____

Practice 4

The following selections appear in college textbooks. Define the words in bold using context clues.

A. Hostility comes from the Latin word *hostis*, which means "enemy." For the hostile, enemies seem to **abound**. They are everywhere at the office, on the freeway, and in the home. Hostile personality types walk around in a state of **wrath**. They get equally angry about cold soup and racial injustice.

—Karren, Keith J. et al. *Mind Body Health*. 4th ed., Pearson, 2010, p. 97.

1. abound

    a. occur in great numbers   c. jump or leap

    b. live in another place   d. be confined by ropes or straps

2. wrath

    a. sadness   c. rage

    b. suspicion   d. peacefulness

B. Cleckley described the psychopath, also called a sociopath, as a "moral idiot" whose central defining characteristic is the inability to **empathize** with others. Hence, it becomes possible for a psychopath to **inflict** pain and engage in cruelty without appreciation for the victim's suffering.

—Schmalleger, Frank. *Criminal Justice*. 13th ed., Pearson, 2015, p. 85.

3. empathize

    a. refuse   c. offer

    b. realize   d. care about

4. inflict

    a. impose or dish out   c. cheat

    b. throw   d. help

C. By 1930, twenty Hollywood studios were **churning** out features and shorts for a weekly audience of 40 million people. The demand for movies was so **incessant** that most theaters which weren't downtown movie palaces changed their features at least two, sometimes three times a week.

—Giannetti, Louis, and Scott Eyman. *Flashback: A Brief History of Film*. 5th ed., Pearson, 2006, p. 46.

5. churning

    a. twirling   c. quickly producing

    b. agitating   d. removing

6. incessant

    a. nonstop   c. rare

    b. occasional   d. friendly

Understand Word Parts

Another effective way to understand a difficult word is to look at its structure. Often, there are clues within a word that can help you determine the meaning. All words have a **root**, but some longer and more complex words may have a **prefix** before the root word or a **suffix** after it. Words have the following parts. Become familiar with the following terms.

Base Words and Root Words

The root is the basic part of a word that conveys its core meaning. For example, *compilation* contains the root word *compile*. Most root words are also **base words**; that is, they can stand alone. *Interest*, *help*, and *play* are root and base words.

Some words have more than one root. A **compound word** has two.

    root   root

market + place = marketplace

SOME SPECIAL ROOTS

Some roots are the starting points for larger words. For instance, *bio* means "life," but it can't stand alone as a word. It needs to be combined with a suffix such as *-logy* to create the word *biology*. Review some common roots that generally do not stand alone.

Root	Meaning	Example	Definition
aqua/hydro	water	hydroplane	water plane
aud / audit	sound	audible	able to be heard
bio	life	biography	story of a life
cred	believe	credible	believable
man	hand	manual	done by hand
mater	mother	maternal	motherly
pater	father	patricide	killing of a father
socio	society	sociology	study of society

Prefixes

A **prefix** appears at the beginning of a word, and it modifies the word's meaning. For example, *un-* means "not," *anti-* means "against," and *pre-* means "before."

prefix root

anti + war = antiwar

SOME COMMON PREFIXES

Prefix	Meaning	Example	Definition
ante-/pre-	before	prejudge	judge before
bi-	two	bicycle	two wheels
inter-	between	interstate	between two states
mega-	large	megaproject	large project
micro- / mini-	small	minibus	small bus
multi- / poly-	many	multipurpose	many purposes
post-	after	postpartum	after birth
re-	again	review	view again
retro-	back	retrospective	look back
semi-	half	semicircle	half a circle
sub-	under	subterranean	underground
tri-	three	triangle	three angles

Suffixes

A **suffix** is added to the ending of a word, and it can change a word's meaning and part of speech. For example, when you add the suffix *-ful* to the verb *play*, you end up with the adjective *playful*. Words can have more than one suffix. For instance, *helpfully* is made of the root word *help* and two suffixes: *ful + ly*.

root verb   suffix noun

discuss + ion = discussion

SOME COMMON SUFFIXES

Suffix	Meaning	Example	Definition
-al	process of	refusal	process of refusing
-able	able to be	preventable	able to be prevented
-aholic / -oholic	with an obsession	workaholic	obsessed with work
-arian	a person who	vegetarian	a person who eats vegetables
-arium / -orium	a place for	auditorium	a place for listening
-dom	quality / realm	kingdom	realm or place of the king
-er / -or	one who	teacher	one who teaches
-ful	full of	peaceful	full of peace
-less	without	hopeless	without hope
-ness / -ship	state of being	sadness	state of being sad

MEDICAL-RELATED ROOTS, PREFIXES, AND SUFFIXES

Prefix		Root		Suffix	
alter-	other	adeno	gland	-ant	connected with
an-	without, lacking	carcin	cancer	-cide	killing
ante-	before	cardi	heart	-ical	related to or consisting of
anti-	against	cede	word	-ician	specialist
hyper-	over	commun	share	-ism	practice of
hypo-	under	derma	skin	-ist	one that adheres to a doctrine; specialist
mono-	one	hepato	liver	-itis	inflammation
omni-	all	neuro	nervous system	-logue	speech
poly-	many	onco/oma	tumor	-ology	study of
pre-	before	osteo	bone	-ous	quality or state
proto-	first	psych	mind	-path	practitioner; disease
sub-	under	rhino	nose	-phile	love of
trans	across	scient	knowing; skillful	-ular	relating to

Practice 5

Break down each term into its parts to define it.

EXAMPLE: psychology <u>*study of the mind*</u>

1. dermatology _____

2. osteopath _____

3. antecedent _____

4. cardiologist _____

5. patricide _____

6. communist _____

7. rhinitis _____

8. carcinoma _____

9. omniscient _____

10. hepatitis _____

Practice 6

Read the following passages. Define the words in bold. Look for context clues and look at the word parts. Then, without using a dictionary, write the meaning of each word in bold.

A. Advertisers know that the **pathway** to the emotional brain is quicker than the route to the logical brain, so they appeal to our **subconscious**. They want us to respond without thinking, and they hope to imprint brands on people's identities.

1. pathway _____

2. subconscious _____

B. The new 25 percent tax on alcohol is **retroactive**. The reasons for the tax are **socioeconomic**. Excessive consumption of alcohol causes almost 80,000 deaths annually, and it inflates costs for medical and policing services. Opponents of the tax point out that small increases have occurred **biannually**, and that the new increase is **unequitable** because responsible drinkers must also pay the tax.

1. retroactive _____

2. socioeconomic _____

3. biannually _____

4. unequitable _____

Use a Dictionary and Thesaurus

DICTIONARY

If you do not understand the meaning of an unfamiliar word after using context clues, look up the word in a dictionary. You might check an online dictionary, a smartphone app, or a word processor's built-in dictionary. Review the following tips:

- **Look at the front matter if using a print dictionary.** The preface contains explanations about the various symbols and abbreviations.

- **Read all of the definitions listed for the word.** Look for the meaning that best fits the context of the sentence you are reading.

- **Look up root words, if necessary.** If the difficult word has a prefix such as *un-* or *anti-*, you may have to look up the root word.

THESAURUS

To avoid repeating the same word over and over in a text, writers may use **synonyms** (different words that have a similar meaning). If you are unsure about a word's meaning, you can consult a **thesaurus**, which provides synonyms as well as **antonyms** (words with an opposite meaning).

When using a thesaurus, be careful because some synonyms have similar but not exact meanings. For example, the synonyms for the word *nice* have particular nuances, or shades of meaning.

> **nice**, adj: affable, compassionate, docile, gracious, helpful, pliable, sweet-tempered, sympathetic, tender, well-mannered

ONLINE AND ELECTRONIC RESOURCES

Here are some digital options for looking up words:

- Online sites—including *Merriam-Webster*, *Oxford*, *Dictionary.reference.com*, and the *Longman Dictionary of Contemporary English*—offer word origins, spellings, meanings, pronunciations, and more.

- Smartphone apps offer word meanings, synonyms, antonyms, and even language translations.

- Word processing programs have built-in dictionary and thesaurus functionality. For example, in MS Word, you can right-click on words, and a menu appears that includes a definition, synonym, and translation.

Review some features of an online dictionary.

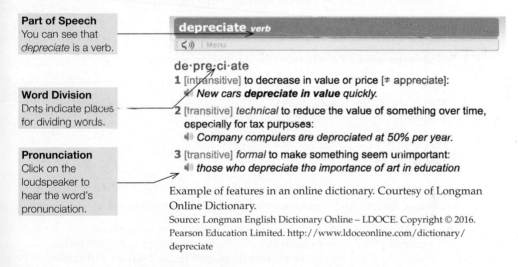

Part of Speech
You can see that *depreciate* is a verb.

depreciate *verb*

◁)) | Menu

de·pre·ci·ate

1 [intransitive] to decrease in value or price [≠ appreciate]:
◀ *New cars* **depreciate in value** *quickly.*

Word Division
Dots indicate places for dividing words.

2 [transitive] *technical* to reduce the value of something over time, especially for tax purposes:
◀) *Company computers are depreciated at 50% per year.*

Pronunciation
Click on the loudspeaker to hear the word's pronunciation.

3 [transitive] *formal* to make something seem unimportant:
◀) *those who depreciate the importance of art in education*

Example of features in an online dictionary. Courtesy of Longman Online Dictionary.
Source: Longman English Dictionary Online – LDOCE. Copyright © 2016. Pearson Education Limited. http://www.ldoceonline.com/dictionary/depreciate

Making Inferences

40.5 Use clues in the text to infer meaning.

Sometimes writers do not state points of view obviously. That is, in a paragraph, you may not find the topic sentence because the author has not stated it concretely. He or she may have suggested the point of view. You, the reader, must use critical thinking skills, like inferring, to figure it out. When you **infer**, you "read between the lines" and use clues in the text to understand its meaning. To infer, follow the next steps:

- Read the paragraph carefully and search for details.
- Verify any meanings of words you don't know.
- Ask *who*, *what*, *where*, *when*, *why*, and *how* questions.
- Jot down the facts and other important ideas. Make a list of any details, opinions, or information the author gives.
- Think about causes and effects.
- Activate your prior knowledge of the topic. What information do you already know or what opinion do you already have?

Example

The band cost about $4,500 for the night. The hall rented for $1,500, and we figured we got a good deal. We had to decorate it ourselves. There were flowers on every table ($35 for each bouquet); rented china and silverware ($950); and tablecloths, tables, and chairs ($900). The catered food worked out to be $65 per person, multiplied by 300. This is not counting the dresses, the tuxedos, the photographer, or the rented limos. Sure, it was a special night. It is too bad our guests of honor split up three months later.

1. What is the subject of the paragraph? _____

2. What is the writer's relationship to the guests of honor? _____
   _____

3. What is the writer's main point? _____

Practice 7

Read the next paragraphs and answer the questions. Read between the lines and make inferences, or guesses, based on the information in the text.

A.   What is wrong with this picture? Every year, mass shootings occur in public places such as schools, movie theaters, or post offices. Such tragic events dominate headlines and ignite endless and futile debates. And, of course, there are the everyday shootings: children mishandling the family firearm, alcohol-fueled street fighters killing their opponents, or jealous lovers executing their partners. Americans have more guns, on average, than any other citizens in the world. In an article for *The Guardian*, journalist Henry Porter pointed out that more Americans have been killed by privately owned guns since 1968 than have been killed in all U.S. wars.

—Adele Berridge, student

1. What is the subject of this text?

   _____

2. What points can you infer that the writer is making?

   _____

   _____

   _____

B.   The Vietnam conflict was the first war to be completely televised. At the beginning of the conflict, televised news reports showed images of Americans winning the war. But by the mid-sixties, Americans began to see images of death and destruction. In 1968, Walter Cronkite, a well-respected anchor on *CBS Evening News*, made a personal editorial at the end of the news program. He stated that the government should negotiate with the communists in North Vietnam, the Viet Cong. By the end of the 1960s, news programs depicted mainly violent images, such as photos of soldiers arriving in body bags and children fleeing napalm attacks. Support for the war plummeted.

1. How did the news media portray the Vietnam War at the beginning of the conflict?

   _____

2. What images did the television news show of the Vietnam War in the mid-sixties?

   _____

   _____

3. What kinds of images was the television news showing of the Vietnam War in the late 1960s?

   _____

4. What can you infer about the attitude of the media toward the Vietnam War in the 1960s?

   _____

   _____

Find Connotations and Denotations

A **denotation** is the literal meaning for a word that may be found in the dictionary. For example, the dictionary definition of *mother* is "a female parent." A **connotation** is the implied or associated meaning. It can be a cultural value judgment. For instance, the word *mother* may trigger feelings of comfort, security, anger, or resentment in a listener, depending on that person's experience with mothers. Authors can influence readers by carefully choosing words that have specific connotations. For example, review the next two descriptions. Which one has a more negative connotation?

Terry left his family.   Andrew abandoned his family.

Practice 8

Try the following activities alone or with a partner.

1. Go online and ask the search engine to find "connotation words" or "denotation examples." Record at least three examples in your writing journal and explain why these words or phrases show bias.

2. Go online and find an article that has biased language. You can look for an article about politics or about controversial topics such as gun control, pesticide usage, and so on. Print out the article and highlight words that have strong connotations.

Analyzing Visuals

40.6 Interpret information in visuals, including photos and charts.

Our culture is dominated by visual images. Many texts use visuals to express ideas that words can't describe as effectively or to emphasize a point. For example, in newspapers, you will find cartoons that express views about political events. Sometimes, there may be a **caption** accompanying an image to clarify a cartoonist's thoughts about an event.

Many textbooks contain **illustrations**, **graphs**, **charts**, or **statistics**. These are used to present data. For example, a textbook on the environment may include charts that show how certain areas of the world are becoming deforested over a specific time period. Three common types of such images are **pie charts**, **bar charts**, and **line graphs**.

Analyzing an image is very similar to analyzing a text. Think about the topic, audience, and purpose of the image. Ask yourself the following questions:

- What kind of image is this?
- Who is the audience? Is the image aimed at one particular group of people or many different groups of people (different races, religions, classes, ages, and so on)? Will different groups of people react to the image in different ways? Will it evoke an emotional reaction?
- What is the purpose of the image? Is it trying to inform, to entertain, or to persuade?
- What is the title of the image? What is the most important feature?
- Does the image lead to a better understanding of the text? What information does the image contain? Is there a direct link between the image and specific information in the text? Does it support the information in the text?
- What is it comparing? Does the data show a pattern? How is it relevant to the topic of the text?

Types of Visuals

Types	Purpose	Example
Symbols	To inform Some symbols help associate a quality to a brand, a movement, or a belief, while others represent a command. Two examples: The Nike Swoosh immediately makes the viewer think about sports equipment. The stop sign is a universally known traffic symbol that obliges drivers to stop.	
Photographs	To inform; to entertain; to persuade Photographs show rather than tell us how items appear. They can also be used as a form of entertainment or express a point of view. For example, a photo of someone holding a ballot might persuade people to get out and vote.	
Pie charts	To inform; to persuade Pie charts help compare a part to a whole. They do not show changes to data over a period of time.	
Line graphs	To inform Line graphs show changes over a short or long period of time.	
Bar graphs	To inform Bar graphs compare things between groups.	
Diagrams	To inform Diagrams show how things are designed, or they can show a cause-and-effect relationship or a process.	

Practice 9

Analyze the following charts and answer the questions.

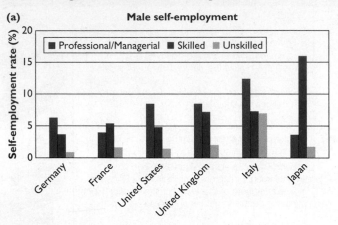

(a) **Male self-employment**

(b) **Female self-employment**

1. What type of images are these? _____

2. What information do the charts offer? _____
   _____

3. Chart A contains data for
   a. males   b. females

4. How many countries are used to collect data? _____

5. Which country has the highest number of skilled self-employed males?
   _____

6. Which country has the highest number of unskilled self-employed
   females? _____

7. What is the purpose of this image? _____

8. Who is the audience for this image? _____

Practice 10

Look at the next image and answer the questions.

1. What type of image is this?
   a. pie chart   b. diagram   c. photo
2. What is the topic of this image? _____
3. Who is the audience for this image? _____
4. What is the image comparing? _____
5. What is the purpose of this image?

   _____

6. In your opinion, does the photo provoke a strong reaction? Explain your answer.

   _____

   _____

   _____

In the next chapter, you practice the reading strategies you've learned in this chapter (and throughout *The Writer's World*) by reading professional essays, articles, and other texts. The questions about each selection help reinforce strategies such as previewing, focusing on vocabulary, and looking for bias and hidden meaning.

41 Reading Selections

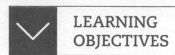

LEARNING OBJECTIVES

41.1 Practice combined reading skills by analyzing different texts.

Aspiring actors study ordinary people, psychological profiles, and the work of other actors to fully develop the characters they play. In the same way, by observing how different writers create their work, you can learn how to use those techniques in your own writing.

The Link Between Reading and Writing

The ability to understand another writer's ideas and express your own ideas in written form is very useful in your personal, academic, and professional life.

After you finish reading a selection, you could try these strategies to make sure that you have understood it.

Summarize the reading. When you summarize, you use your own words to write a condensed version of the reading. You leave out all information except for the main points. You can find a detailed explanation about summaries in Chapter 16.

Outline the reading. An outline is a visual plan of the reading that looks like an essay plan. First, you write the main idea of the essay, and then write down the most important idea from each paragraph. You could make further indentations, and under each idea, include a detail or example.

Analyze the reading. When you read, look critically at the writer's arguments and evaluate them, point by point. Also analyze how the writer builds the argument and ask yourself questions such as *Do I agree? Are the author's arguments*

518

convincing? Then, when you write your analysis, you can break down the author's explanations and either refute or agree with them, using your own experiences and examples to support your view.

Write a response. Your instructor may ask you to write about your reaction to a reading. These are some questions you might ask yourself before you respond in writing.

- What is the writer's main point?
- What is the writer's purpose? Is the writer trying to entertain, persuade, or inform?
- Who is the audience? Is the writer directing his or her message at someone like me?
- Do I agree or disagree with the writer's main point?
- Are there any aspects of the topic to which I can relate? What are they?

After you answer the questions, you will have more ideas to use in your written response.

Reading Selections

41.1 Practice combined reading skills by analyzing different texts.

Conflict

Urban Development and Our Natural World

Inventions and Discoveries

Travel and Survival

Human Development

Theme: Conflict

Reading 1
My Bully, My Best Friend

Yannick LeJacq

Yannick LeJacq is a freelance writer and photographer living in New York City. His work has appeared in *Kill Screen*, the *Wall Street Journal*, *The Atlantic*, and other publications. In the following essay, he relates a personal experience about bullying.

1   The first time someone called me a "faggot," I didn't hear it at all. That's because my head was being slammed against a locker, the syllables crashing together like cymbals in my ear. In the locker room after lacrosse, Fred, tall, clear-skinned, and golden, would snap at my ankles with his stick. I lived the next months in fear. Before the start of high school, I asked my brother if he could teach me how to punch somebody. But I didn't have to learn. Fred left our school. I heard his dad was seen screaming in the office about what a screw-up his son was, a detail I relished with a grim smile. Mostly, I was relieved Fred was gone, and I could stop jumping every time I heard a locker slam.

2   Life was good. It got even better when I met John during soccer practice. He was quirky; he wore the same pair of purple sweatpants to school every day, and he joked about how much he masturbated. We became best friends.

3   I was happy to have someone to sit with at lunch, but eventually John started to do something I didn't understand—he would constantly tell me I was gay. He wrote it on my textbook in biology, where we sat together, and he would whisper it while pointing at me. At that point, I was fourteen and barely knew what sex was beyond the definitions I'd gleaned from health class and pornography. But I knew that "gay" meant more than having sex with men. "Gay" was a word that boys tossed around like

a hot potato, everyone hurling the insult in the vain hope it wouldn't stick to them. It was a word to be feared, but still buoyant enough not to always be taken seriously. I figured John was using it playfully, among friends, the way he would also call me "Jew."

4   A few weeks later, John invited me to join an online conference using our school's in-house email system for a movie he wanted to make. The film was about one of our heavier friends, Drew, escaping from fat camp. Fat. Gay. Jew. The words were piling up, but I didn't care. I had finally wedged my foot in the door. We went over to John's house to mess around with a camera one Saturday, but all we ended up filming was Drew chasing a line of bagels rolling down the street while chanting "donut, donut, donut!" Instead, the conference became a place to jab at each other while sitting on school computers. Eventually, John started making more of his gay jokes.

5   At first I was flattered. This was still a form of attention. And, frankly, I craved attention. But things got weird around spring break. John wrote stories about me taking little boys and animals into the woods to have sex with them and other stories about me being molested by priests and loving it.

6   Finally, I asked him to stop. The insults meant nothing, I told him in an email, but I would bow out of the group. Still, I stayed up late at night at the family computer, reading and re-reading more elaborately crafted insults and waiting for the page to refresh. "Since Yannick isn't reading any more" he posted, "I can now say, 'Yannick is GAY GAY GAY GAY GAY GAY GAY GAY.'" It went on like that for a while. The other boys just laughed.

7   One morning, I checked my email in the school library and saw a note from our IT adviser. He had discovered the online conference. The news spread quietly through the administration, which did its best to stop any further damage. A faculty member reminded kids during Monday announcements to be mindful of the correspondence we keep on the school's email. John was identified as the ringleader and quietly whisked away for probation. I was rushed in to meet with the head of the upper school, my old lacrosse coach. He asked me that bland, unanswerable question, "Are you OK?" Tears were in his eyes as he apologized for what the school had let happen to me.

8   There's a weird tension once authorities become involved in teenage arguments. It was a relief that someone finally made it stop. But it was equally bizarre to hear our conversations reinterpreted by adults who were trying to determine the arbitrary moment when a cruel jest slid into unacceptable hatred.

9   The night the news broke at school, John's mother called me. She was livid with him, she said, and didn't understand why someone would do something like this. She couldn't say she was sorry enough. I stammered out the same response I would learn to tell everybody: "It's okay, I'm fine."

Then she put John on the phone. It was the first time we'd spoken since an army of adults swarmed around us. It was the last time we would really speak for almost three years.

10   "Yannick?" John's voice was frail, as if he had barely finished crying. I thought about his parents standing above him as he sat on the couch in his living room, face buried in his palms, trying to explain things he couldn't and didn't want to. It was the same position I had been in earlier that day, the same position I would be in many times in the coming weeks. "I'm really sorry."

11   "It's okay," I said. "I'm fine."

12   "I really don't know why I did that. I don't know what I was thinking. Still friends?" he asked me.

13   "Still friends."

14   We both knew the words were hollow. I switched seats in biology, and we avoided each other. My mother called John a monster. My brother fumed about how the school needed to expel him. Everyone wanted me to be angry, but all I wanted was to have my friend back.

15   Hating Fred was much simpler. The violence of getting my head kicked into a locker is so obvious, and I could redirect it. At night, I would stare at the knife rack in my kitchen and wonder what it would be like to make one of us bleed. But John hadn't hurt me in a way I understood. So I did my best to disappear. I spent days down in the photo lab, bringing my lunch there to avoid the cafeteria. I took as many classes as I could. I pretended to search through my locker until the hallway was empty so I could walk to class alone. I tied and retied my shoes. Then the next fall, I dropped out of soccer. The coach didn't ask why.

16   John went to the varsity team and became class president. Every time he did something remotely public, someone would whisk me into an office and ask how I felt. "It's okay," I would say. "I'm fine." For a long time, I didn't hate the people in high school so much as I loathed the school itself.

17   We can gaze aghast at the horror of bullies every time a new tragedy surfaces, but asking where this violence truly comes from is much more difficult. Years later, after my school recorded its first case of cyber-bullying, the same administrator who cried in front of me in his office did his best to stop the school's Gay Straight Alliance from hosting a queer prom. Lower-school parents, he explained, had seen posters in the high school hallways and didn't want their children to be affected.

Yannick LeJacq, "My Bully, My Best Friend," Salon.com, May 26, 2012. This article first appears in Salon.com, at http://www.Salon.com. An online version remains in the Salon archives. Reprinted with permission.

Comprehension and Critical Thinking

1. In paragraph 3, what does *gleaned* mean?
   - a. joyful feeling
   - b. discovered
   - c. engaged in
   - d. forgotten

2. How did Yannick react when he was first called "gay" by John? See paragraph 3.

   _____

3. In paragraph 4, the writer says, "I had finally wedged my foot in the door." What is he referring to in that statement?

   _____

4. How did Yannick's relationship with John evolve? List the main events of what happened from the time they first met.

   _____

   _____

   _____

   _____

   _____

   _____

   _____

   _____

5. How did Yannick respond when school authorities and then parents got involved in the conflict?

   _____

6. In paragraph 14, Yannick says, "We both knew the words were hollow." What words is he referring to? Also, what does he mean by *hollow?*

   _____

   _____

7. The writer compares his hatred of John with his hatred of Fred. What are the similarities or differences?

   _____

   _____

   _____

8. After adults learn about the name-calling, Yannick repeatedly tells them that he is "okay." But how does his experience with being called "gay" actually affect Yannick?

   _____

   _____

   _____

9. Find examples in paragraph 1 of imagery that appeals to the following senses. (For a detailed explanation of imagery, see pages 107-108 in Chapter 8.)

Sight: _____

_____

Sound: _____

_____

Touch: _____

_____

10. What point is the writer making in the concluding paragraph?

_____

_____

_____

_____

_____

Writing Topics

Write about one of the following topics. Remember to explore, develop, and revise and edit your work.

1. Write about a time when you felt like an outsider. What happened to make you feel that way?

2. Narrate your encounter with someone who is different from others. What did that person show you or teach you? Describe a specific incident and explain what happened.

3. What can school administrators do to reduce bullying in schools? Suggest some clear actions that schools should take.

Reading 2
How Companies Deceive Us

Megan Griffith-Greene

Megan Griffith-Greene is a Toronto-based writer and producer. In the next essay, she discusses some ways that companies boost their online reputations.

1   Are you trying a new sushi spot or booking into a hotel? Do you check online before you check it out? Millions of consumers look at online

references to "followers," "likes," and "shares" to try to determine if a business is popular and legitimate before deciding to spend their money there. But how much can you trust a company's online reputation? The Canadian Broadcasting Corporation (CBC) television show *Marketplace* investigated how companies artificially inflate their online credibility through paid testimonials and fake reviews. *Marketplace* set up a fake food business, and then tried to buy a good online reputation. What they discovered was shocking. It's easy and inexpensive to deceive consumers online.

2   Companies artificially inflate their online credibility through paid testimonials and fake reviews. "I think it's really amazing how easy it is to purchase deception now on the Internet," says Jeff Hancock, a professor who researches online language and behavior at Cornell University. "You can get fake likes, fake comments, fake reviews, fake everything." So why do most people fall for companies' fake reviews and false reputation? "We believe other people," says Hancock.

3   For some companies hoping to look good online, there are lots of ways they can try to boost their business. Here are four ways that companies can fake it online.

Fake reviews

4   Research published in 2011 by the Harvard Business School found that a one-star increase on the popular review site Yelp meant a 5 to 9 percent increase in revenue for independent restaurants. "If you're an owner of property that gets reviewed—and there is hardly anything that isn't reviewed now—there is real pressure to have good online reviews because if you don't, your business is going to be hurt," says Hancock. Additionally, a 2012 study from IT research analysts Gartner found that 10 to 15 percent of reviews on social media are fake.

5   Last year, the State of New York cracked down on fake reviews in a sting operation dubbed Operation Clean Turf. It fined nineteen businesses a total of USD $350,000. "Consumers rely on reviews from their peers to make daily purchasing decisions on anything from food and clothing to recreation and sightseeing," wrote New York attorney general Eric Schneiderman in a news release. He described the practice as false advertising.

6   Some Internet marketing and online reputation management companies bolster a business's online image with fake testimonials on a variety of popular review websites for a price. Other websites connect businesses with freelancers who post fake reviews. CBC's *Marketplace*,

in an investigative report, paid as little as $5 for testimonials about their invented business.

7   Review sites like Yelp and Google say they do what they can to delete fake reviews. In a statement to *Marketplace*, Google said that the company takes down thousands of suspicious reviews every month, but "there is a small subset of bad apples out there. We take verification very seriously." The Google representative pointed out that there is a link next to each review "allowing users to help flag suspicious reviews."

Fake YouTube views

8   With more than 100 hours of video uploaded to YouTube every minute, it can be hard for companies to compete for video views. But *Marketplace* found it was easy—and inexpensive—to buy them. The show bought 10,000 video views from a company for its video promoting its fake business. How much were the views? They cost a mere $30.

9   In December 2012, YouTube stripped almost two billion fake views from music videos that were produced by major labels including Universal, Sony/BMG, and RCA. In February 2015, Google, which owns YouTube, announced that it was increasing efforts to audit video views and remove fake views from the site. Software engineer Philipp Pfeiffenberger wrote in a blog post: "When some bad actors try to game the system by artificially inflating view counts, they're not just misleading fans about the popularity of a video, they're undermining one of YouTube's most important and unique qualities."

Fake Twitter followers

10   Last year, Italian security researchers Andrea Stroppa and Carlo De Micheli researched fake Twitter followers. They estimated that 4 percent— or 20 million—Twitter accounts were fake. According to the researchers, fake Twitter accounts have become a multimillion-dollar business. Research by Internet security analysts at Barracuda Labs found that as of the end of 2013, there were fifty-two sellers on eBay selling fake Twitter followers. How much does a fake follower go for? Not a lot: the cost was an average of $11 per 1,000 followers.

11   Twitter's rules prohibit buying and selling fake followers. "When you purchase followers, retweets and favorites, you are often purchasing bot (fake) or hacked accounts," the site reads. "Any account caught participating in this behavior will be in violation of the Twitter rules and may be suspended."

Fake Facebook likes

12   Facebook is another platform popular for posers. The company estimates that as many as 1.2 percent of accounts are fake. With 1.2 billion active monthly users, that number represents as many as 14 million fake accounts. Like many other sites, Facebook says it tries to crack down on fakers. "Fraudulent activity is bad for everyone—including page owners, advertisers, Facebook, and people on our platform," wrote Facebook site integrity engineer Matt Jones in a blog post. "We adapt our defences constantly to stay ahead of spammers' techniques, and one area we've focused on for several years is fake 'likes.' "

13   Although some "likes" and "reviews" are not genuine, Hancock says that many are honest and useful. "Most businesses really want to provide a genuine service; most businesses are real," he says. If a business is desperate and buys fake reviews, it won't last, in Hancock's opinion. If a business is caught cheating, it can damage its reputation. "If I had one piece of advice, not for the consumers but for business owners, don't do it," says Hancock. "It's too easy to get caught. One of the main things with deception on the Internet is it leaves a record."

Comprehension and Critical Thinking

1. Find a word in paragraph 6 that means "increase." _____

2. What type of introduction style is used in this essay?

   a. anecdote   b. general background   c. definition

3. Which statement best sums up the main idea of the essay?

   a. There are four easy and inexpensive ways to deceive consumers online.
   b. Don't trust online reviews because many are fake.
   c. The Internet is full of false information and people should be careful.
   d. How do companies manipulate us?

4. This essay includes expert opinions and statistics. Underline four statistics.

5. Using your own words, briefly sum up the four manipulation methods that companies use.

   1. _____

       _____

   2. _____

       _____

   3. _____

       _____

   4. _____

       _____

6. In the *Marketplace* investigation, how much does it cost to buy the following items?

   Fake reviews: _____

   Fake YouTube views: _____

   Fake Twitter followers: _____

7. How are governments and websites fighting back against the fake reviews, view counts, likes, and followers? Provide four examples from the text.

   _____

   _____

   _____

   _____

8. This essay has no conclusion. Write a conclusion of five or six sentences on a separate piece of paper.

9. This essay classifies online manipulation, but it also suggests an argument. What is the essay's message? Make an inference or guess.

   _____

   _____

Writing Topics

Write about one of the following topics. Remember to explore, develop, and revise and edit your work.

1. What are the some types of consumers? Write an essay classifying consumers into three or four types.

2. What are the main types of online reviewers? Classify reviewers into three or four types. For example, you could discuss the easily pleased reviewer, the cranky reviewer, and the critical but fair reviewer.

Reading 3
The Price of Public Shaming in the Internet Age

Todd Leopold

Todd Leopold is a writer and producer for CNN. Read about the shocking effects of public shaming.

1   Do you believe in forgiveness and second chances? Of course you do. Everybody makes mistakes. To err is human, to forgive divine. Right?

2   Well, it is not true in the age of social media. Take the case of Victor Paul Alvarez. In January, the Boston reporter wrote a brief news story

containing a bad joke about politician **John Boehner**. The wrath of
social media fell on his head. Despite an apology, he was fired. Three
months later, he's still looking for full-time work. And Justine Sacco is
the public relations executive who tweeted, "Going to Africa. Hope I
don't get **AIDS**. Just kidding. I'm white!" Thanks to public shaming,
she lost her job and was left wandering in the wilderness. Or there is
the case of the woman who posed mockingly at Arlington National
Cemetery. [She mimed a scream and held up her middle finger.] Such
stupid acts are perhaps worthy of some kind of punishment. But is this
justice? These days, public shaming has devastating consequences for
individuals.

John Boehner:
Republican speaker of
the house from 2011
to 2015

**AIDS (autoimmune
deficiency disorder):**
disease of the immune
system

3   Jon Ronson, author of *So You've Been Publicly Shamed*, looks at the
"piling-on" phenomenon. In centuries past, villagers would cast out
the dishonored. Colonial Americans had the stockade. For most, the
punishment was finite, and the person's sins eventually forgiven. These
days, it's not enough for someone who screwed up to be rebuked. Even an
apology and remorse are rarely enough. On social media—with its global
reach and lack of irony—that person must be destroyed.

4   Father James Martin, the editor-at-large of *America* magazine,
observes that what starts out as disapproval ends up "as a complete
shaming of the person." The biblical admonition of "an eye for an eye,"
after all, was a way to describe proportionate justice, not go overboard.
The new shaming is much more relentless. "There's a real cruelty that
comes with this mob mentality," he said. "I sometimes compare it to
bullies in a schoolyard all ganging up on a person who, for one second,
said the wrong thing."

5   If someone says something offensive, others are certainly allowed to
respond. If the person is a public figure who says something "outrageously
sexist or racist or homophobic, then perhaps it would be appropriate that
that person resign his or her position," Ronson said in a phone interview.
But, he added, the idea "that the person should have to pay for it the rest
of his or her life is unjust."

6   On August 1, 2012, Adam Mark Smith posted a video of himself
haranguing a Chick-fil-A employee at a drive-through. An executive
for the chicken restaurant chain had made intolerant statements about
gay marriage. Smith didn't like the stance and believed he could "make
a difference," he told CNN. The video, which showed Smith berating
the drive-through cashier, was cringe-worthy. She was, after all, just an

employee. Smith posted the video, but by the next morning, he regretted his rudeness. He posted an apology and attempted to apologize—in person—to the drive-through worker. (She didn't want to talk.) By the time he got to work that day, the situation was out of his control.

7   The video went viral, and Smith—the Chief Financial Officer (CFO) of a Tucson, Arizona-based medical device manufacturer—lost his well-paying job. That was bad enough, but things were going to get worse. Over the next 72 hours, his email was filled with vitriolic threats. His personal information was released, including the address for his children's school. Letters were nailed to his front door.

8   He says he flipped back and forth between anger and wondering whether he deserved his fate. "There was a tremendous amount of shame I felt. There were truths: I was rude," he said. "And then there were elements of 'no, I don't (deserve this). This is not right.' So I was on both sides depending on the minute." What is more discouraging is how that episode has dogged him. On the advice of an attorney, he kept the incident private after taking a new job in Portland, Oregon, but was asked to resign when the news got out. Since then, he's been up-front with prospective employers and even received job offers, but before long, they pull back. "I went into depression," he said. At one point, he considered suicide, saying at least that way his family could be provided for.

9   In his book, Ronson investigates ways of combating the lingering impact of public shaming, since the Internet is seemingly forever. Fame and fortune help, as can be inferred by the number of celebrities still active after disastrous posts. On the other hand, if you're a nobody, the terrible event can be debilitating.

10   Alvarez, the Boston reporter, says his poor joke is still following him around. However, he's not worried about his legacy. "If anything, I'm very proud of how I handled the fallout, and someone who wants to hire me and decides not to because they didn't take the time to look at how I handled basically the worst week of my life isn't someone I'd want to work for," he said. "It's easy to be your best when nothing bad has happened to you."

11   There have been positive uses for Internet shaming, says Ronson. He praises Twitter hashtags, such as #blacklivesmatter, #whyIstayed, and #Yesallwomen, for highlighting social issues that were once hidden. There is less homophobia, for example, because of such campaigns. Nevertheless, he wishes there was more willingness to pause before firing,

to put ourselves in another's shoes. Ronson knows it's a tough sell because
outrage and demonization can be more satisfying than compassion, but
he hopes that the trend is changing. "I think people will have to change
because there's clearly something wrong," he said.

Comprehension and Critical Thinking

1. In paragraph 6, what does *haranguing* mean?

   a. ordering food   b. addressing a crowd   c. verbally attacking

2. In paragraph 8, what does *dogged* mean?

   a. followed   b. acted like a canine   c. physically hurt

3. What is the main idea of the essay? Underline the thesis statement.
Remember that it may not be in the first paragraph.

4. What is online shaming? Define it based on information in the text.

_____

_____

5. In paragraphs 2 and 3, the writer compares shaming in the past and
present. What are the similarities or differences?

_____

_____

6. What are some of the effects of public shaming? List at least four negative
consequences.

_____

_____

7. The writer supports his main idea with several examples. Briefly explain
who the following people are. Also sum up what happened to each person.

Victor Paul Alvarez: _____

_____

_____

Justine Sacco: _____

_____

_____

Adam Mark Smith: _____

_____

_____

8. Why did Adam Mark Smith become the subject of such intense online rage? Make an inference—or guess—based on information in the text.

_____

_____

_____

9. What are some positive effects of Internet shaming?

_____

_____

Writing Topics

Write about one of the following topics. Remember to explore, develop, and revise and edit your work.

1. Write an argument essay about online shaming. For instance, you could argue that schools should have compulsory courses on online etiquette. Or you could suggest that penalties for online shaming should be more severe.

2. What should people do if they become the victim of online bullying? List some steps people could take.

Theme: Urban Development and Our Natural World

Reading 4
Living Environments

Avi Friedman

Avi Friedman is a professor at the McGill School of Architecture. In the following article, which appeared in the _Montreal Gazette_, Friedman reflects on designing an appropriate house for the individual needs of families.

1   When invited to design a home, I first like to know what kind of dwellers my clients are. In our first meeting, I ask them to take me on a guided tour of their current residence and describe how each room is used—when and by whom. Walking through hallways, scanning the interior of rooms, peeping into closets, looking at kitchen cupboards, and pausing at family photos have helped me devise several common categories of occupants.

2   The "neat" household regards the house as a gallery. The home is spotless. The placement of every item, be it hanging artwork, a memento on a shelf, or furniture, is highly choreographed. The color scheme is coordinated and the lighting superb. It feels as if one has walked into an *Architectural Digest* magazine spread. Recent trends, professional touches, and carefully selected pieces are the marks of the place.

3   The "utilitarian" family is very **pragmatic**. They are minimalists, believing that they get only what they need. Environmental concerns play an important role in buying goods. The place, often painted in light tones, is sparsely decorated with very few well-selected items. Souvenirs from a recent trip are displayed, and some photos or paintings are on the wall. They will resist excess consumption and will squeeze as much use as they can from each piece.

pragmatic: practical

4   The home of the "collector" family is stuffed to the brim. It is hard to find additional space for furniture or a wall area to hang a painting. Books, magazines, and weekend papers are everywhere. Newspaper cutouts and personal notes are crammed under magnets on the fridge door. The collector family seems to pay less attention to how things appear and more to comfort. Stress reduction is a motto. Being an excessively clean "show house" is not a concern. Placing dirty breakfast dishes in the sink and the morning paper in the rack before leaving home is not a priority as long as things are moving along.

5   Of course, these are only a few household types, but at the end of a house tour, I have a pretty good idea about my clients. More than the notes that I take during a meeting, these real-life images tell me all about my client's home life and desired domestic environment. When I began practicing, I quickly realized house design is about people more than architecture. As hard as I might try, I will never be able to tailor a new personality to someone by placing them in a trendy style, one that does not reflect who they really are. I can attempt to illustrate options other than their current life habits and decorating choices. But in the end, when they move into their new place, they will bring along their old habits.

6   My experience has taught me some homeowners have been trying hard to emulate lifestyles and decors that are really not theirs. The endless decorating shows on television and the many magazines that crowd supermarket racks provide a tempting opportunity to become someone else. Some homeowners are under constant pressure, it feels, to undergo

extreme makeovers and borrow rather than mature into their natural selves. They search for a readymade packaged interior style rather than discovering their own.

7   I am often at a loss when clients ask me what style I subscribe to, or solicit advice on the style they are to adopt. I reply that styles are trendy and comfort is permanent, and that they should see beyond the first day of occupancy into everyday living. Sipping a freshly brewed coffee on the back porch on a summer Sunday and letting the morning paper litter the floor while watching a squirrel on the tree across the yard is a treasured moment. It will never be able to fit into a well-defined architectural style. Home design needs to create the backdrop for such opportunities. It is these types of moments that make us enjoy life.

8   If someone wants to read, why not have a wall of books? Does someone love listening to music? Then a music room or corner should be created, even if it is not trendy. Does someone want to interact with the children? He or she might add a hobby space, even if it is outdated and cannot be found in most magazines.

9   Referring to technological advances, the renowned French architect Le Corbusier once described the home as a "machine for living." It is partially true. Home is the site where mundane and utilitarian activities take place. It is also where special moments, uniquely ours, are created and treasured.

Comprehension and Critical Thinking

1. Find a four-word expression in paragraph 4 that means "completely filled."

_____

2. Find a word in paragraph 6 that means "to copy."

_____

3. Underline the thesis statement.

4. Underline the topic sentences in paragraphs 2–7.

5. Paragraph 8 is missing a topic sentence. Which sentence best expresses the main idea of that paragraph?

    a. People can create a music room in their homes.
    b. Everybody should think about his or her likes and dislikes.
    c. People should create spaces in their homes to accommodate their personal interests.
    d. Hobby rooms and bookshelves can help make a home feel unique.

6. How does Friedman assess the needs of families when designing a house?

_____

_____

_____

7. What are the three categories of households that Friedman describes in this article?

_____   _____   _____

8. In your own words, describe the characteristics for each type of household.

_____

_____

_____

_____

9. a. What influences families when they choose a design for their homes?

_____

b. Does Friedman think that such influences are positive or negative? Explain your answer.

_____

_____

_____

10. According to Friedman, what is the most important factor that home design should take into consideration?

_____

_____

Writing Topics

Write about one of the following topics. Remember to explore, develop, and revise and edit your work.

1. Use a different classification method to describe types of living environments.

2. Friedman writes, "Home is the site where mundane and utilitarian activities take place. It is also where special moments, uniquely ours, are created and treasured." Write about different categories of special or memorable moments.

Reading 5
Nature Returns to the Cities

John Roach

An urban raccoon

John Roach is a writer for *National Geographic,* and he has written many articles about nature. In the next essay, he describes animal life in our concrete jungles.

1   The concrete jungle isn't just for people anymore. Thirty years of good environmental stewardship combined with wildlife's innate ability to adapt has given rise to a resurgence of nature in America's urban centers. In New York City, raccoons have walked through the front door and into the kitchen to raid the refrigerator. In southern California, mountain lions have been seen cooling off under garden sprinklers and breaking into homes near Disneyland. In Chicago, beavers gnaw and fell trees and snarl traffic. In her book *Wild Nights: Nature Returns to the City*, Anne Matthews describes such incidents as she explores the resurgence of wildlife in New York and other cities. "Thirty years of environmental protection and absence of hunting [in cities] have allowed animal populations to soar," she notes.

2   The implications of the wildlife resurgence in cities vary. People may marvel at the presence of a falcon nest on the twenty-seventh floor of New York Hospital. On the other hand, some people were literally sickened to death in the fall of 2000 by the West Nile virus, which had been carried to the city by migrating birds and transmitted to mosquitoes, which passed it on to humans.

3   Overcrowded cities and urban sprawl have put more people and wild animals in proximity than at any other time in American history, says Matthews. Encounters between these two groups are beginning to exceed what scientists call the cultural carrying capacity, defined in *Wild Nights* as "the moment humans stop saying 'Aww' and start calling 911." This change in the nature of the relationship between people and wildlife, says Matthews, is forcing people to reconsider their ethical and practical role as top predator.

4   Nature's return to U.S. cities has resulted in part from passage of the Clean Air Act in 1970 and the Clean Water Act in 1972. These laws of environmental protection that helped make air safer to breathe and water safer to drink also made cities more hospitable to wildlife, according to

Matthews. After being cleaned up, New York Harbor is now home to booming populations of blue crabs and fiddler crabs, which in turn attract thousands of long-legged wading birds such as herons and egrets. With the air now cleaner, owls have flocked in growing numbers to the suburbs in search of easy prey: pets such as schnauzers, chihuahuas, and cats. In parts of the South and Midwest, forests that were logged in the nineteenth century have grown back over the last hundred years, allowing animal populations to recover. Car collisions with moose are now common along Interstate 95, the main East Coast traffic corridor. Crocodiles, who were all but erased by development pressure in Florida, are now breeding at four times their normal rate in the cooling canals of Florida's nuclear power plants.

5   Some creatures, such as rats, never really left the city. Today, an estimated 28 million rats—which are nonnative, like much of the city's human population—inhabit New York. The greater New York area is home to eight million people, which means there are more than three rats to every person. Matthews explains how it happened. "Rats are smart," she writes. "Although a fast-forward version of natural selection has made rats in many big cities immune to nearly all conventional poisons, they still may press one pack member into service as a taster; if the test rat dies, the others resolutely avoid the bait."

6   Matthews says the strong adaptive ability of nonnative species has begun to change the definition of wilderness. Rats were introduced into U.S. cities in the 1700s after arriving as stowaways on merchant ships. Zebra mussels, which have caused major problems in the Great Lakes by clogging intake pipes, were imported in the ballast water of international ships. "The most important thing is to realize that a city is wilder than we tend to imagine, and the land we think of as untouched or wild really isn't," says Matthews. "There has been so much human interference and reshaping that we really don't know what a pristine planet is." Matthews thinks people should not try to undo the effects of this increased interference with wildlife but to improve their understanding of it and continue to make room for nature in their lives.

7   Matthews says it's crucial that people consider what kind of world they want their grandchildren to inherit and act to ensure that such a world will exist. One immediate concern is what the impacts of global warming will be in fifty years. Citing the results of computer models

showing future conditions if no action is taken to mitigate global warming, Matthews says much of New York will be under water, as sea levels rise three feet. New Orleans, Louisiana, already eight feet below sea level, might become the next Atlantis. What can we do? "What you can do is as small as don't use air conditioning as much, don't use your gas-guzzling [sport utility vehicle], walk more," says Matthews. "On the macro level, urge your congressperson to do something about environmental issues."

Comprehension and Critical Thinking

1. In paragraph 1, circle a word that means "reappearance."
2. Define *prey*. Look in paragraph 4 for context clues.

   _____

3. Underline the thesis statement.
4. What are at least two reasons the writer gives for animals returning to urban environments?

   _____

   _____

   _____

   _____

5. What are at least three effects of wildlife in cities?

   _____

   _____

   _____

   _____

6. In paragraph 4, what is the writer implying?
   a. The Clean Air and Clean Water Acts did not help the environment.
   b. The Clean Air and Clean Water Acts were quite effective in helping to improve the quality of the air and water.
   c. Logging practices are much more detrimental to the environment today than they were in the past.
   d. Many dangerous predators such as crocodiles now roam the cities.
7. What is Matthews's opinion about abundant wildlife in the city?

   _____

   _____

8. What is Matthews's definition of wilderness in paragraph 6?

   _____

   _____

9. Although this is mainly a cause and effect essay, there are also elements of process. Which paragraph gives the readers clear steps to take to help the environment? ____

10. What incorrect assumption or belief do many people today have about the relationship between wildlife and cities?

_____

_____

_____

Writing Topics

Write about one of the following topics. Remember to explore, develop, and revise and edit your work.

1. Describe your own experiences with wildlife in your home, yard, or neighborhood. What causes or caused the bird, animal, or insect to settle in your area? How does it or how did it affect you and your neighbors?

2. Do you have a pet in your home? Why or why not? Describe the causes or effects (or both) of your decision about having pets.

Reading 6
Slum Tourism

Eric Weiner

Eric Weiner is the author of *The Geography of Bliss: One Grump's Search for the Happiest Places in the World*. In his essay, Weiner analyzes slum tourism.

1   Michael Cronin's job as a college admissions officer took him to India two or three times a year, so he had already seen the usual sites—temples, monuments, and markets—when one day he happened across a flier advertising slum tours. "It just resonated with me immediately," said Mr. Cronin, who was staying at the posh Taj Hotel in Mumbai where, he noted, a bottle of champagne cost the equivalent of two years' salary for many Indians. "But I didn't know what to expect," he said.

2   Soon, Mr. Cronin, forty-one years old, found himself skirting open sewers and ducking to avoid exposed electrical wires as he toured the sprawling Dharavi slum, home to more than a million. He joined a cricket game and saw small-scale industry, from embroidery to tannery, which

Slum in São Paulo, Brazil

quietly thrives in the slum. "Nothing is considered garbage there," he said. "Everything is used again." Mr. Cronin was briefly shaken when a man, "obviously drunk," rifled through his pockets, but the two-and-a-half-hour tour changed his image of India. "Everybody in the slum wants to work, and everybody wants to make themselves better," he said.

3   Slum tourism, or "poorism," as some call it, is catching on. From the shantytowns of Rio de Janeiro to the townships of Johannesburg to the garbage dumps of Mexico, tourists are forsaking, at least for a while, beaches and museums for crowded, dirty—and in many ways surprising—slums. When a British man named Chris Way founded Reality Tours and Travel in Mumbai two years ago, he could barely **muster** enough customers for one tour a day. Now, he's running two or three a day and recently expanded to rural areas.

muster: gather together

4   Slum tourism isn't for everyone. Critics charge that ogling the poorest of the poor isn't tourism at all. It's voyeurism. The tours are exploitative, these critics say, and have no place on an ethical traveler's itinerary. "Would you want people stopping outside of your front door every day, or maybe twice a day, snapping a few pictures of you and making some observations about your lifestyle?" asked David Fennell, a professor of tourism and environment at Brock University in Ontario. Slum tourism, he says, is just another example of tourism finding a new niche to exploit. The real purpose, he believes, is to make Westerners feel better about their station in life. "It affirms in my mind how lucky I am—or how unlucky they are," he states.

5   Not so fast, proponents of slum tourism say. Ignoring poverty won't make it go away. "Tourism is one of the few ways that you or I are ever going to understand what poverty means," says Harold Goodwin, director of the International Center for Responsible Tourism in Leeds, England. "To just kind of turn a blind eye and pretend that poverty doesn't exist seems to me a very denial of our humanity." The crucial question, Mr. Goodwin and other experts say, is not whether slum tours should exist but how they are conducted. Do they limit the excursions to small groups, interacting respectfully with residents? Or do they travel in buses, snapping photos from the windows as if on safari?

6   Many tour organizers are sensitive to charges of exploitation. Some encourage—and in at least one case require—participants to play an active role in helping residents. A church group in Mazatlan, Mexico, runs tours

of the local garbage dump where scavengers earn a living picking through trash, some of it from nearby luxury resorts. The group doesn't charge anything but asks participants to help make sandwiches and fill bottles with filtered water. The tours have proven so popular that during high season the church group has to turn people away. "We see ourselves as a bridge to connect the tourists to the real world," said Fred Collom, the minister who runs the tours.

7   By most accounts, slum tourism began in Brazil sixteen years ago, when a young man named Marcelo Armstrong took a few tourists into Rocinha, Rio de Janeiro's largest favela, or shantytown. His company, Favela Tour, grew and spawned half a dozen imitators. Today, on any given day in Rio, dozens of tourists hop in minivans, then motorcycles, and venture into places even Brazil's police dare not tread. Organizers insist the tours are safe, though they routinely check security conditions. Luiz Fantozzi, founder of the Rio-based Be a Local Tours, says that about once a year he cancels a tour for security reasons.

8   The tours may be safe, but they can be tense. Rajika Bhasin, a lawyer from New York, recalls how, at one point during a favela tour, the guide told everyone to stop taking pictures. A young man approached the group, smiling and holding a cocked gun. Ms. Bhasin said she didn't exactly feel threatened, "just very aware of my surroundings, and aware of the fact that I was on this guy's turf." Still, she said, the experience, which included visiting galleries featuring the work of local artists, was positive. "Honestly, I would say it was a life-changing experience," Ms. Bhasin said. Saying she understood the objections, she **parried,** "It has everything to do with who you are and why you're going."

parried: replied

9   Chuck Geyer, of Reston, Virginia, arrived for a tour in Mumbai armed with hand sanitizer and the expectation of human misery incarnate. He left with a changed mind. Instead of being solicited by beggars, Mr. Geyer found himself the recipient of gifts: fruit and dye to smear on his hands and face as people celebrated the Hindu festival of Holi. "I was shocked at how friendly and gracious these people were," Mr. Geyer said.

10   Proponents of slum tourism say that's the point: to change the reputation of the slums one tourist at a time. Tour organizers say they provide employment for local guides and a chance to sell souvenirs. Chris Way has vowed to put 80 percent of his profits back into the Dharavi slum. The catch, though, is that Mr. Way's company has yet to earn a profit on the tours, for which he charges 300 rupees (around $7.50). After receiving

concedes:
acknowledges

besieged:
overtaken

flak from the Indian press ("a fair criticism," Mr. Way **concedes**), he used his own money to open a community center in the slum. It offers English classes, and Mr. Way himself mentors a chess club. Many of those running favela tours in Brazil also channel a portion of their profits into the slums. Luiz Fantozzi contributes to a school and day-care center.

11 But slum tourism isn't just about charity, its proponents say; it also fosters an entrepreneurial spirit. "At first, the tourists were **besieged** by beggars, but not anymore," said Kevin Outterson, a law professor from Boston who has taken several favela tours. Mr. Fantozzi has taught people, Mr. Outterson said, "that you're not going to get anything from my people begging, but if you make something, people are going to buy it."

12 Even critics of slum tourism concede it allows a few dollars to trickle into the shantytowns but say that's no substitute for development programs. Mr. Fennell, the professor of tourism in Ontario, wonders whether the relatively minuscule tourist revenue can make a difference. "If you're so concerned about helping these people, then write a check," he said.

Comprehension and Critical Thinking

1. In paragraph 3, what is the meaning of *forsaking?* Read the word in context before making your guess.

   _____

2. In paragraph 4, find a word that means "staring."

   _____

3. In your own words, define slum tourism.

   _____

   _____

4. How did slum tourism develop?

   _____

   _____

5. What are some criticisms of slum tourism?

   _____

   _____

6. What arguments support slum tourism?

_____

_____

_____

7. List two examples of how people's outlook was changed when they toured slums.

_____

_____

_____

8. How should tourists behave when they tour slums?

_____

_____

_____

9. According to the article, what is the best way to help slum dwellers?

_____

_____

Writing Topics

Write about one of the following topics. Remember to explore, develop, and revise and edit your work.

1. What is the opposite of a slum? Come up with a new term for a wealthy neighborhood, and define it. Use examples to support your definition.

2. Compare two very different places that you have visited. You can compare two neighborhoods, two towns, or a rural area with an urban area.

3. Is touring a slum _tourism_ or _voyeurism?_ Argue your point of view by using examples from your own city, state, or country.

Theme: Inventions and Discoveries

Reading 7
Marketing New Inventions

Robert Rodriguez

Robert Rodriguez is a journalist for McClatchy Newspapers. In the next essay, he lists some problems that can occur when someone tries to market a new invention.

The Hula-Hoop

1   When a Fresno mother-and-daughter duo's idea for a hide-and-seek doll made it onto the shelves of one of the nation's largest toy stores, they felt as if they had won the lottery. Shelly Conte and her mother, Cindy Reichman, were riding high. Their patented Hide-N-Seek Hayley doll was being sold at Toys R Us stores nationwide, becoming a top seller during the 2005 holiday season. "I remember someone telling us that we were going to be millionaires," said Ms. Conte. "And I was thinking about it, no doubt." But the pair's dreams of fame and fortune began to unravel about a year later when a major player in the industry put a new spin on its popular Care Bear by introducing a hide-and-seek version. It soon edged out Hide-N-Seek Hayley, whose sales began to plummet. Business experts say that in a fiercely competitive market for new products, copycats and timing all play a part in whether a new product stays on a store's shelves or is relegated to the bargain bin. To survive, an entrepreneur must be market savvy, develop brand loyalty, and "sleep with one eye open."

2   "This can be a very tough business, and knockoff products are commonplace," said Tim Walsh, a Florida-based toy inventor and author of *Timeless Toys,* a book that looks at classic toys and the people who created them. "The problem is that success often prompts others to want in on what you are doing." Mr. Walsh said a classic example is the Hula-Hoop. The name was trademarked in 1958 by Wham-O, but it didn't stop others from cashing in on the plastic hoop's popularity. Mr. Walsh estimated over the years Wham-O has kept only a quarter of the market.

3   Inventors say they never rest easy: The possibility of a much larger competitor taking them out is always a chief concern. "I know I could wake up one day, and it could all be gone," said Kathleen Whitehurst, who is co-inventor of DaysAgo, a digital day-counter that attaches to food containers and measures freshness of refrigerated products. "It is a cruel world out there, and that's why you have to cover all your bases." Part of Ms. Whitehurst's strategy was to get her product distributed in foreign markets, where copycats often spring up. The DaysAgo counter is sold in the United States, Canada, Sweden, Norway, Iceland, Australia, and Japan. "You basically have to get out there first and establish yourself as the recognizable brand," she says. "But you are never safe. You just have to keep pedaling as fast as you can." Jennifer Barney, a

Fresno mom who created Barney Butter, an almond spread, credits her survival to maintaining strong relationships with the grocery stores that carry her product. She holds product demonstrations in as many of the stores as she can. It is exhausting because her butter is sold in six states and 106 stores.

4   Rookie inventors Reichman and Conte said their tumble from Toys R Us taught them many hard lessons; the most sobering is that patents don't always protect inventors from copycats. Shocked and frustrated by their abrupt sales slide, the team terminated their contract last year with Hayley's manufacturer, the Kid-riffic toy company in St. Louis, which they fault for a lack of promotion. "We are almost in the exact same position we were eight years ago, when we started this idea," Ms. Reichman said. "We should not be in this position. This was a once-in-a-lifetime chance for us, and look at what's happened." They considered suing Play Along, the Florida-based Care Bear makers, but backed off after a lawyer specializing in such cases advised that they didn't have a strong enough case. Their patent attorney, Richard Ryan, says Play Along was careful not to copy the name "Hayley" or the specific technology used by the doll to play hide and seek.

5   Mike Summers, director of technology development and commercialization at California State University, said bringing an idea to the marketplace can be daunting for inventors who lack the experience and knowledge. An inventor himself, Summers developed a lifesaving device that inflates when hurled into water. Rather than compete head-to-head with much larger companies that also produce lifesaving devices, he approached the No. 2 player in the market. After some negotiation, that company agreed to buy his idea. "Sometimes the collaborative route is the easier route to take," Summers said. The "enemy" could end up being a best friend.

Comprehension and Critical Thinking

1. In paragraph 4, what does *sobering* mean?
  a. discouraging   c. falling
  b. abstaining from alcohol   d. reliable

2. Find a word in paragraph 5 that means "thrown." _____

3. Underline the thesis statement.

4. What is the essay illustrating?

   a. the reasons to invent a new product
   b. great marketing success stories
   c. examples of successes and failures of new products
   d. the value of patenting a product

5. In paragraph 3, what is the meaning of the expression "You just have to keep pedaling as fast as you can"?

_____

_____

6. Explain what happened to each of the following products.

Hide-N-Seek Hayley: _____

_____

Hula-Hoop: _____

_____

DaysAgo Counter: _____

_____

Barney Butter: _____

_____

7. According to the essay, which product is most widely distributed?

   a. Hide-N-Seek Hayley   b. DaysAgo counter   c. Barney Butter

8. What are the main problems that can occur when you try to market a new product?

_____

_____

_____

9. What are possible problems with patents, according to paragraph 4?

_____

_____

10. What did Mike Summers do with his inflatable lifesaving device?

_____

Writing Topics

Write about one of the following topics. Remember to explore, develop, and revise and edit your work.

1. List some of your greatest successes or your worst mistakes. Provide specific details about each event.

2. What are some of the most useful or useless inventions that have been developed? Think about products that you love or hate.

Reading 8
Can We Talk?

Josh Freed

Josh Freed is an award-winning columnist for the *Montreal Gazette*. Freed has published many books, including *Fear of Frying and Other Fax of Life*. In this essay, Freed ponders technology and privacy.

1   We keep hearing that technology is destroying our privacy by spreading our personal information on the Web—from our credit card passwords to our naked beach photos on Facebook. But technology is also creating more privacy than we've ever had and probably more than we need.

2   Phoning friends has become a more isolating experience. For much of my life, I called my friends at home and never knew who'd pick up the phone. I might end up talking to their spouse or their kids or their cleaning person. I would have interesting, unexpected chats. But during the last couple of years, I barely remember my friends' home numbers. I just call their cell phones, which they answer immediately. As a result, I never have random chats with whoever else answers because no one else does. Even when I do call friends' homes, I get an answering machine because family members see my name flashing and know it's not for them, so they don't answer. It's all more efficient, but it has practically wiped out my chance personal conversations and shrunk my sense of community.

3   In our new technology-tailored world, it's rarer and rarer to have an unexpected conversation with people we don't know well. In recent years, bank machines have ended our chats with tellers, while the phone operator has long vanished, replaced by PRESS 1 machines. It is the same when we phone offices. In the past, I used to speak with personal secretaries whom I would gradually get to know. But now a voice machine answers instead. An hour later, the person returns my call and leaves a message, and later I call and leave one for that person. By the time we're through messaging, we have said what we have needed to say and don't end up speaking with one another.

4   When we travel, it is increasingly difficult to have a good yak with a stranger because technology gets in the way. On

airplanes, no one talks to his or her seatmate anymore. We're all too busy watching our little television screens. Everyone is wearing earphones, so our seatmates won't hear us even if we shout, "The plane is on fire!" Cabbies used to be great chatterers; they were armchair experts on everything from traffic jams to politics in their native lands. But now they always yak on their cell phones, using hands-free headsets, while I yak on mine. Ask them a question, and they'll say, "I am very sorry, sir, but I am talking to my mother in Cairo here." Taxis are even more isolating in New York where most now have passenger TVs, so I end up watching my own screen in back while the driver chats privately up front. I don't even talk at the end of the ride. I just slide my credit card along the bottom of the TV screen and then leave—with barely a word spoken between us. We may as well have robot-taxis, which would probably be chattier. "Welcome to Robo-Cab. Please state your destination."

5   The future looks even more private and isolating. Most teens don't even talk to their own friends on the phone anymore—they text. They don't hang out in streets or parks together—they gather online where they only chat with those they choose. We adults aren't much better. We don't call office colleagues anymore to chat about work decisions. We email them to avoid conversation because less time is lost in random chatter.

6   Something else is lost as we live more insular and isolated lives. We walk in crowds of people, all talking on cell phones, while ignoring those around us; we listen to iPods, isolated in our own soundtracks; we stare at iPhones and iPads, lost in our own world and literally screening out those beside us. The irony is that we are eliminating the idea of "long distance" phone calls, as rates to faraway countries fall drastically. But we are putting long distance into the relationships in our own lives.

7   For now, home landlines and accidental conversations still exist, but cell phone companies are advertising unlimited talk and text monthly plans. Eventually the idea of a shared family phone will be history. We will all get our own cell phones at two years old and live in our own private cells.

Comprehension and Critical Thinking

1. In paragraph 3, what does "technology-tailored world" mean?

_____

2. Look in paragraphs 2 and 4, and underline three slang words. Suggest standard alternatives for those words.

   _____

3. Highlight the thesis statement.

4. List some examples of technology the author gives that prevent us from communicating with strangers.

   _____

   _____

5. According to the author, what is the difference between how people used phones in the past and how they use phones in the present?

   _____

   _____

   _____

   _____

6. According to the author, how has travel become an isolating experience? Give two examples.

   _____

   _____

   _____

7. In paragraph 6, the author states, "But we are putting long distance into the relationships in our own lives." What does he mean by that statement?

   _____

   _____

   _____

   _____

8. How does the author think our future communication with others will change?

   _____

9. What is the author's attitude toward his subject?

   _____

10. Irony conveys the opposite meaning of what is stated or intended. What is ironic about the way technology affects our lives?

    _____

    _____

    _____

Writing Topics

Write about one of the following topics. Remember to explore, develop, and revise and edit your work.

1. List some ways in which technology has changed the world.

2. How has technology made your life better or worse? Provide specific examples.

Reading 9
The Paradox of New Technologies

Dorothy Nixon

Dorothy Nixon, a freelance writer, has written ads for radio and television and articles for many well-known publications. She is also the author of *Furies Cross the Mersey* and several other historical novels set in the 1910 era. Her novels are available on Amazon's Kindle.

1   These days, Americans use their smart phones not only to "reach out and touch someone" and for fun and games, but also to access vital information about healthcare and government services, to find out about educational opportunities, to do their personal banking, and so much more. For the most part, Americans describe these smart phones as indispensable. Sure, smart phones can be a bit of a distraction at times, and also a bit of a leash—for instance, if dad and mom keep texting asking where you are—but the instant-gratification makes these glorious gadgets worthwhile. The truth is, for every new technology, we seem to gain something but, at the same time, we lose something.

2   In 1910, AT&T, the American telephone company, ran a compelling advertisement in blue-ink in one of the women's magazines. The ad showed a sketch of a middle-aged mother, her greying hair piled on top of her head in a bun, sitting over a an upright, table-top candlestick telephone. "The comfort the telephone affords to the women in the homes of America cannot be measured. The mother of children can find out where they are at any particular hour of the day—*and how they are*—even though their visits carry them to the country village or the city hundreds of miles away." So ran the copy.

Candlestick phone

3   The early 1900s was a period of rapid social change; droves of young people in North America left the farm or the small town to find work or love. At that time, most Americans relied on the postal service or snail mail for news about their loved ones. In 1904, only 3 percent of homes had

telephones. By 1910 that figure had already risen to 25 percent. Sometimes, a mom just couldn't wait for a letter to arrive giving news of her children, or she felt an urgent need to hear the child's voice. At least, AT&T's marketers wanted mothers to feel such urgency.

4   Fast forward to today, and the smart phone, the great, great grandchild of that clunky candlestick telephone, is cherished by families all over the world. People now can feel more connected than ever. But consider the following event from 2015. Seven people in their twenties, from parts of Europe and North America, went to New Zealand for a big adventure. They met at a hostel and did a two-day trek to a remote area of the South Island. These young people were all equipped with smart phones, of course, but for about three hours, they found themselves out of range of any cell tower. They were not in the least worried, but the minute they got back into range, all of their phones started beeping, trilling, and singing with text messages from back home: "Where have you been? I am scared. Why don't you answer?" Back in 1910, if a grown child trekked off to far-off New Zealand, there was good chance the parents wouldn't hear from him for months, even years. These days, anyone, almost anywhere on the planet, is just one quick text message away. That is, unless he has ventured somewhere with no cell phone coverage. Then, it can mean high anxiety for dad and mom back home.

5   So, what really have we gained here with this amazing new technology? It is certainly not peace of mind. Mitch Kapoor, the founder of the Lotus Corporation, has said, "We are living in an era of anxiety produced by computer and communications technology." Judging from the New Zealand story, he is bang on. If a son has a mobile phone and doesn't answer it right away, this can send waves of anxiety over the ether to his dad and mom. If someone's wife is late getting home and driving in a storm, and the husband can't reach her on the cellphone, he might wonder if she has had a serious road accident. Just, maybe, it was less worrying back in 1910 when people were not able to contact a loved one at any given moment in time.

6   Cell technology is terrific for efficiently getting around, especially in the car. There is no more crossing paths all evening long with friends you planned to meet at X location at Y hour. (Yes, kids, that actually happened in the old days.) There are no more tearful fights between co-pilot and driver as the passenger pores, dazed, over a sprawled out paper map while the driver shouts in exasperation, "Give me advance warning. I can't change lanes at the last minute!" Right? Well, no. People still argue in cars

even when the voice from the dashboard GPS is the one giving directions. Computer programs, at times, can be more clueless than humans. My GPS has told me, among other things, to do a U-Turn on a divided highway and to turn left into a construction hole. There's also evidence, at least in my house, that smartphone technology is making us less proficient in the use of any navigation and map-reading skills we might have had in the first place.

7   Sure, that small rectangular screen in our app-addicted twenty-first century hands serves up immeasurable wonders, but does smartphone technology (or any new technology for that matter) actually make us feel safer and more secure and less anxious about our lives and about our loved ones? That question is best left to the individual user, I suspect, or, maybe, it's a matter for philosophers. No computer program, however sophisticated, will ever be able to figure that one out.

Comprehension and Critical Thinking

1. Find two words in paragraph 1 that mean "necessary."

   _____   _____

2. Highlight the thesis statement.

3. Underline the topic sentence in paragraph 2.

4. Which sentence best expresses the main idea of paragraph 3?
   a. In the early 1900s, young people left their homes to find work.
   b. Every family bought a telephone for their homes in the early 1900s.
   c. In the early 1900s, anxious parents began to realize the value of a telephone for keeping in touch with their children.

5. In which paragraph does the author use the following types of support?
   • an extended example: _____
   • an expert opinion: _____
   • acknowledge opposing viewpoints: _____

6. This argument essay also uses elements of comparison and contrast. What is being compared?

   _____

7. What message have companies used to market the phone since it was first invented?

   _____

   _____

8. What is the meaning of the title of the essay?

   _____

   _____

Writing Topics

1. Write an argument essay about the impact of technology on our lives. For example, you could argue that we are becoming addicted to certain devices.

2. Which apps do you find most useful for your smartphone? Explain your answer.

Theme: Travel and Survival

Reading 10
The Rules of Survival

Laurence Gonzales

Laurence Gonzales won the National Magazine Award in 2001 and 2002. His work has appeared in such publications as *Harper's*, *National Geographic Adventure*, and *Smithsonian Air and Space*, just to name a few. The next excerpt is from his latest book, *Deep Survival*.

1   As a journalist, I've been writing about accidents for more than thirty years. In the last fifteen or so years, I've concentrated on accidents in outdoor recreation in an effort to understand who lives, who dies, and why. To my surprise, I found an eerie uniformity in the way people survive seemingly impossible circumstances. Decades and sometimes centuries apart, separated by culture, geography, race, language, and tradition, the most successful survivors—those who practice what I call "deep survival"—go through the same patterns of thought and behavior, the same transformation and spiritual discovery, in the course of keeping themselves alive. It doesn't seem to matter whether they are surviving being lost in the wilderness or battling cancer; the strategies remain the same.

2   Survival should be thought of as a journey or vision quest of the sort that Native Americans have had as a rite of passage for thousands of years. Once people pass the precipitating event—for instance, they are cast away at sea or told they have cancer—they are enrolled in one of the oldest schools in history. Here are a few things I've learned about survival.

Stay Calm

3   In the initial crisis, survivors are not ruled by fear; instead, they make use of it. Their fear often feels like (and turns into) anger, which motivates

them and makes them feel sharper. Aron Ralston, the hiker who had to cut off his hand to free himself from a stone that had trapped him in a slot canyon in Utah, initially panicked and began slamming himself over and over against the boulder that had caught his hand. But very quickly he stopped himself, did some deep breathing, and began thinking about his options. He eventually spent five days progressing through the stages necessary to convince him of what decisive action he had to take to save his own life.

Think, Analyze, and Plan

4   Survivors quickly organize, set up routines, and institute discipline. When Lance Armstrong was diagnosed with cancer, he organized his fight against it the way he would organize his training for a race. He read everything he could about it, put himself on a training schedule, and put together a team from among friends, family, and doctors to support his efforts. Such conscious, organized effort in the face of grave danger requires a split between reason and emotion in which reason gives direction and emotion provides the power source. Survivors often report experiencing reason as an audible "voice."

5   Steve Callahan, a sailor and boat designer, was rammed by a whale, and his boat sunk while he was on a solo voyage in 1982. Adrift in the Atlantic for seventy-six days on a five-and-a-half-foot raft, he experienced his survival voyage as taking place under the command of a "captain" who gave him his orders and kept him on his water ration, even as his own mutinous (emotional) spirit complained. His captain routinely lectured "the crew." Thus under strict control, he was able to push away thoughts that his situation was hopeless and take the necessary first steps of the survival journey: to think clearly, analyze his situation, and formulate a plan.

Celebrate Every Victory

6   Survivors take great joy from even their smallest successes. This attitude helps keep motivation high and prevents a lethal plunge into hopelessness. It also provides relief from the unspeakable strain of a life-threatening situation.

7   Lauren Elder was the only survivor of a light plane crash in the High Sierra. Stranded on a 12,000 foot peak, one arm broken, she could see the San Joaquin Valley in California below, but a vast wilderness and sheer

and icy cliffs separated her from safety. Wearing a wrap-around skirt and blouse but no underwear, with two-inch heeled boots, she crawled "on all fours, doing a kind of sideways spiderwalk," as she put it later, "balancing myself on the ice crust, punching through it with my hands and feet." She had thirty-six hours of climbing ahead of her—a seemingly impossible task. But Elder allowed herself to think only as far as the next big rock. Once she had completed her descent of the first pitch, Elder said that she looked up at the impossibly steep slope and thought, "Look what I've done! Exhilarated, I gave a whoop that echoed down the silent pass." Even with a broken arm, joy was Elder's constant companion. A good survivor always tells herself, "Count your blessings—you're alive."

Enjoy the Survival Journey

8   It may seem counterintuitive, but even in the worst circumstances, survivors find something to enjoy, some way to play and laugh. Survival can be tedious, and waiting itself is an art. Elder found herself laughing out loud when she started to worry that someone might see up her skirt as she climbed. Even as Callahan's boat was sinking, he stopped to laugh at himself as he clutched a knife in his teeth like a pirate while trying to get into his life raft. And Viktor Frankl ordered some of his companions in **Auschwitz** who were threatening to give up hope to force themselves to think of one funny thing each day. Singing, playing mind games, reciting poetry, and doing mathematical problems can make waiting tolerable, while heightening perception and quieting fear.

Auschwitz: a Nazi concentration camp

Never Give Up

9   Yes, you might die. In fact, you will die—we all do. But perhaps it doesn't have to be today. Don't let it worry you. Forget about rescue. Everything you need is inside you already. Dougal Robertson, a sailor who was cast away at sea for thirty-eight days after his boat sank, advised thinking of survival this way: "Rescue will come as a welcome interruption of . . . the survival voyage." One survival psychologist calls that "resignation without giving up. It is survival by surrender."

10   Survivors are not easily discouraged by setbacks. They accept that the environment is constantly changing and know that they must adapt. When they fall, they pick themselves up and start the entire process over again, breaking it down into manageable bits. When *Apollo 13's* oxygen tank exploded, apparently dooming the crew, Commander Jim Lovell chose to keep on transmitting whatever data he could back to mission control, even

as they burned up on re-entry. Elder and Callahan were equally determined and knew this final truth: If you're still alive, there is always one more thing that you can do.

Comprehension and Critical Thinking

1. What is the meaning of *precipitating* in paragraph 2?

   a. ending   b. unexpected   c. initiating or triggering

2. In paragraph 7, what is the meaning of *pitch?*

   a. throw   b. slope   c. tone

3. How does the author introduce the text?

   a. general background   c. anecdote
   b. historical background   d. contrasting position

4. In this process essay, the author describes the experiences of several survivors. Briefly explain what challenge the following people faced.

   Aron Ralston: _____

   _____

   Lance Armstrong: _____

   _____

   Lauren Elder: _____

   _____

   Viktor Frankl: _____

   _____

   Dougal Robertson: _____

   _____

5. a. What do most of the stories of survival have in common? What kinds of threats were they surviving?

   _____

   _____

   b. How is Frankl's journey different from those of the others mentioned in the essay?

   _____

   _____

6. This process essay also uses narration and cause and effect. What are some of the effects of positive thinking while in a dangerous situation?

   _____

   _____

7. What is the author's specific purpose?

_____

_____

8. Who was probably the target audience for this essay?

   a. an academic or intellectual audience

   b. children

   c. a general audience

Give some reasons for your choice.

_____

_____

9. What lessons does this essay have for the reader?

_____

_____

_____

10. Using your own words, explain why it is important to enjoy the survival journey.

_____

_____

Writing Topics

Write about one of the following topics. Remember to explore, develop, and revise and edit your work.

1. Describe a difficult physical ordeal that you or someone you know went through. What happened? What steps were taken to get through the ordeal?

2. Explain the steps people should take when they have an emotional crisis. For example, how can they survive a breakup, a public humiliation, or the loss of a friend?

Reading 11
Into Thin Air

Jon Krakauer

Jon Krakauer is a mountaineer and writer. In his memoir, _Into Thin Air,_ Krakauer recounts the tragic tale of the 1996 Mount Everest climbing expedition in which he participated. During this expedition, many people who were Krakauer's climbing companions died when a sudden ferocious storm engulfed them. The next reading is an excerpt from Krakauer's best-selling book.

1   The literature of Everest is rife with accounts of hallucinatory experiences attributable to hypoxia and fatigue. In 1933, the noted English climber Frank Smythe observed "two curious looking objects floating in the sky" directly above him at 27,000 feet: "[One] possessed what appeared to be squat underdeveloped wings, and the other a protuberance suggestive of a beak. They hovered motionless but seemed slowly to pulsate." In 1980, during his solo ascent, Reinhold Messner imagined that an invisible companion was climbing beside him. Gradually, I became aware that my mind had gone haywire in a similar fashion, and I observed my own slide from reality with a blend of fascination and horror.

2   I was so far beyond ordinary exhaustion that I experienced a queer detachment from my body, as if I were observing my descent from a few feet overhead. I imagined that I was dressed in a green cardigan and wingtips. And although the gale was generating a windchill in excess of seventy below zero Fahrenheit, I felt strangely and disturbingly warm.

Climber on Mount Everest

3   At 6:30, as the last of the daylight seeped from the sky, I'd descended to within 200 vertical feet of Camp Four. Only one obstacle now stood between me and safety: a bulging incline of hard, glassy ice that I would have to descend without a rope. Snow pellets borne by 70-knot gusts stung my face; any exposed flesh was instantly frozen. The tents, no more than 650 horizontal feet away, were only intermittently visible through the whiteout. There was no margin for error. Worried about making a critical blunder, I sat down to **marshal** my energy before descending further.

marshal: gather

4   Once I was off my feet, inertia took hold. It was so much easier to remain at rest than to summon the initiative to tackle the dangerous ice slope. I just sat there as the storm roared around me, letting my mind drift, doing nothing for perhaps forty-five minutes.

5   I'd tightened the drawstrings on my hood until only a tiny opening remained around my eyes, and I was removing the useless, frozen oxygen mask from beneath my chin when Andy Harris suddenly appeared out of the gloom beside me. Shining my headlamp in his direction, I reflexively recoiled when I saw the appalling condition of his face. His cheeks were coated with an armor of frost, one eye was frozen shut, and he was slurring his words badly. He looked in serious trouble. "Which way to the tents?" Andy blurted, frantic to reach shelter.

6   I pointed in the direction of Camp Four, and then warned him about the ice just below us. "It is steeper than it looks!" I yelled, straining to

make myself heard over the tempest. "Maybe I should go down first and get a rope from camp—" As I was in midsentence, Andy abruptly turned away and moved over the lip of the ice slope, leaving me sitting there dumbfounded.

7   Scooting on his butt, he started down the steepest part of the incline. "Andy," I shouted after him, "it's crazy to try it like that! You're going to blow it for sure!" He yelled something back, but his words were carried off by the screaming wind. A second later he lost his purchase, flipped ass over teakettle, and was suddenly rocketing headfirst down the ice.

8   Two hundred feet below, I could just make out Andy's motionless form slumped at the foot of the incline. I was sure he'd broken at least a leg, or maybe his neck. But then, incredibly, he stood up, waved that he was okay, and started lurching toward Camp Four, which at the moment was in plain sight, 500 feet beyond.

9   My backpack held little more than three empty oxygen canisters and a pint of frozen lemonade; it probably weighed no more than sixteen or eighteen pounds. But I was tired and worried about getting down the incline without breaking a leg, so I tossed the pack over the edge and hoped it would come to rest where I could retrieve it. Then I stood up and started down the ice, which was as smooth and hard as the surface of a bowling ball.

10   Fifteen minutes of dicey, fatiguing **crampon** work brought me safely to the bottom of the incline where I easily located my pack, and another ten minutes after that I was in camp myself. I lunged into my tent with my crampons still on, zipped the door tight, and sprawled across the frost-covered floor too tired to even sit upright. For the first time I had a sense of how wasted I was: I was more exhausted than I'd ever been in my life. But I was safe.

crampon: steel spikes attached to the soles of mountain-climbing boots to create a better grip on ice and prevent slipping

Comprehension and Critical Thinking

1. In paragraph 1, *protuberance* means

  a. a bulge   b. a disturbance   c. a bird

2. In paragraph 3, what is the meaning of *blunder*?

_____

3. What type of narration is used in this essay?

  a. first person   b. third person

4. What can you infer or guess about Krakauer's personality?

_____

_____

5. In your own words, sum up the story in a couple of sentences. Answer who, what, when, where, why, and how questions.

_____

_____

_____

6. Describe the author's physical and mental state at the beginning of the essay.

_____

_____

7. What were some obstacles that the narrator faced during his descent to Camp Four?

_____

_____

_____

8. This excerpt contains examples of imagery (description using the senses). Give examples of imagery that appeal to touch, sight, and hearing.

touch: _____

_____

sight: _____

_____

hearing: _____

_____

9. Which organizational method does the author use in this essay?

a. time order   b. space order   c. emphatic order

10. The author uses dialogue in this essay. What is the purpose of the dialogue?

_____

_____

Writing Topics

Write about one of the following topics. Remember to explore, develop, and revise and edit your work.

1. Have you or someone you know participated in a risky activity? What happened? Include descriptive details that appeal to the senses.

2. In Krakauer's story, he describes his reactions during a challenging moment from his past. Think about a time when you felt extremely excited, ashamed, or moved. Where were you and what were you doing? Describe what happened, and include descriptive details.

Reading 12
Buried Alive

Ainsley Doty

In this text from *Maclean's* magazine, Ainsley Doty describes a harrowing natural event.

1   In early 2003, a group of backcountry skiers ventured into British Columbia's Glacier National Park and encountered one of the deadliest avalanches in Canadian history. Seven school kids lost their lives. Journalists tried to make sense of an incomprehensible tragedy, but those who made their way off the mountain refused to speak publicly about what had happened. Twenty-eight-year-old Will Johnson, one of the kids who walked away that day, has broken the silence.

2   It was around 6 a.m. on January 31 when fifteen-year-old Johnson loaded his gear into the back of a white charter bus along with sixteen other high-school students. The air buzzed with anticipation for the adventure ahead, a four-day backcountry skiing expedition to Rogers Pass. The high school had facilitated dozens of trips to the area without incident. Teacher Andrew Nicholson, better known as Mr. Nick, had overseen several of them himself. Mr. Nick had a spotless record. If he found any reason to doubt the safety of Rogers Pass, the group would ski elsewhere—no questions asked.

3   The group unloaded the bus and skied to a cabin. Along the trails, Mr. Nick guided the students through avalanche-assessment exercises. They dug pits and tested the snowpack and excavated caves for shelter. They buried their beacons and practiced using transceivers to pick up the signal; the deeper the snow, the weaker the pulse. Around 5:30 P.M., they arrived at a picturesque three-room log cabin where the students hauled firewood, made dinner, and then settled for the night.

4   The temperature hovered around zero degrees when the group got its start at 9:30 the following morning. It was a perfect day to challenge the rugged terrain. They would reach their destination in under three hours.

It was hard work and, at about the halfway point, they stopped to refuel. While they munched on sandwiches and trail mix, a pair of seasoned skiers came through the trees and offered a quick greeting before pressing on.

5   At 11:45 A.M., the group paused at the edge of the forest and prepared to cross a major slide path. Across the valley, the summit of Mount Cheops was hidden behind low clouds. As their training had taught them, the students minimized risk by partnering off and staggering their starts, creating 50-foot gaps between each pair of skiers. With two adults bringing up the rear, the students followed Mr. Nick out onto the slide path.

6   There wasn't a breath of wind; the air was cool and silent except for the murmur of skis atop virgin snow. "It was warm enough that I didn't have my hat on. My jacket was wide open. I think I was maybe third or fourth back from the front," Johnson recalls. "Then someone yelled."

7   That Saturday was a day off for Abby Watkins and Rich Marshall, certified backcountry guides. When they passed the large group of teenagers, Marshall noted that the students were equipped with appropriate gear, including carbon probes, collapsible shovels, and transceivers. They shared a few words with Mr. Nick and continued on their way. An hour later, they stopped to sip tea from a thermos and to take in the scenery. They spotted the school group emerging from the trees into a clearing 300 feet below them, a procession of shadows floating across a snow-white sheet. The vignette was shattered by a sound they recognized instantly.

8   There was no earthly tremble, but only a loud crack, followed by a massive avalanche crashing down from the peaks of Mount Cheops. The school group was directly in its path. Marshall tried to warn them, shouting, "Avalanche!" repeatedly. The snow barreled down the mountain and back up the far side of the valley toward the unsuspecting group of students.

9   Johnson doesn't remember hearing the crack, but he stopped in his tracks and tried to locate the source of the shouts. Instinctively, he looked uphill, but found the landscape undisturbed. He turned downhill to face the valley and Mount Cheops. Clouds initially hid the slide from view, but Johnson watched as an avalanche burst through the coverage and thundered down Mount Cheops. At first, it felt like the slide was far away, and his initial response was fascination. "It was surreal," he says. "But then I saw that our leader had his backpack off, his skis off; he was

ditching everything. I remember starting to get one ski off. Then there was this wall of powder."

10   The avalanche was massive. On Parks Canada's five-point size scale, it ranked a 3.5, large enough to topple a building. Five thousand tons of snow slammed into the valley bottom before surging up its opposite side. Travelling at 95 miles/hour, the avalanche swallowed everything— and everyone—in its path.

11   "The next thing I remember was being in the snow. . . . At first, the snow was so fluid, but it settled into concrete. I couldn't move anything. I couldn't wiggle my fingers. Which way is up? Which way is down? I couldn't do anything. I couldn't see anything. It was completely dark." Disoriented and panicking, Johnson realized he'd just been buried alive. Snow was packed so tightly around him that it prevented his chest from expanding: "Every time I breathed [through my nose], my ribs hit a snow wall. My mouth was packed with snow. It was terrifying." Johnson clung to the hope that he would be found. He had no way of knowing that every member of his group was trapped beneath the snow.

12   Johnson's body temperature plummeted as blood rushed to his core to protect his vital organs, but he doesn't remember feeling cold. Hypothermia was the least of his worries. He was running out of air: "I tried to count out breaths. Eight seconds in, eight seconds out. I knew that eventually I was going to pass out. I've thought a lot about that. If they hadn't gotten to me, the last thing I would have remembered was counting my breaths." He's not sure how long it took to lose consciousness.

13   After watching the group below them disappear, Watkins and Marshall braced for the inevitable impact, but it never got there. The guides were alive and the only people who knew that the school group was in trouble. The threat of a second slide was palpable, but valuable seconds were ticking by. After half an hour, the survival rate of an avalanche victim drops to 50 percent. If a person is buried without an air pocket, it's the same as being underwater.

14   Carefully, Watkins and Marshall skied down and spotted a glove sticking out above the snow. The hand belonged to Mr. Nick. Once his face and upper body were cleared, they left him to dig himself out, and they moved on to search for other beacon signals. Finding the leader first was a stroke of luck. Mr. Nick carried the group's only satellite phone and immediately called for help, and then he joined the guides in the desperate search for his students.

15   Johnson blacked out beneath the snow. It wasn't painful; he was conscious one minute and gone the next. Just as suddenly, he thundered back into the waking world. He was standing on top of the snow, struggling to zip up his jacket, with no idea how he had gotten there. The memories of that moment come back to him in fragments: "I couldn't move my hands. I was freezing. Shivering. I couldn't really think." Numb and disoriented, Johnson stared down into the yard-deep hole they'd pulled him from. "I was incredibly lucky where I ended up," he says. "There was another burial site that they found first, but [that person] was three-and-a-half yards deep. They marked it and moved on. I was the next site."

16   When he overcame the shock, Johnson climbed to where another site was being excavated, arriving as an unconscious body was pulled from the snow. The rescuers had to move on quickly, so Johnson and another classmate were tasked with performing CPR. Johnson's purpose became singular: "We just focused on compressions and breaths."

17   In under an hour, seven helicopters, forty-eight rescuers, and three rescue dogs were on the hill. Johnson continued to perform CPR until paramedics came. "They told us to move on, which I think was the first moment that I realized people had died," Johnson recalls. Dazed, with the dead body of a friend at his feet, he surveyed the destruction. Staring out across the slide, Johnson spotted vertical probes, all marking burial sites. As Johnson realized the truth, the weight of it was crushing: "Anyone who's not up is not coming up." When he reached safety, he learned that seven students were gone.

18   As details of the disaster emerged, the news was met with anger, devastation, and a never-ending list of questions. Why were minors led into what was being called a highly dangerous situation? With all the technology available, why had no one predicted the avalanche? A lot of criticism was directed at the school, but it also received countless letters of support. A lengthy investigation concluded that the deaths were the result of a horrible accident.

19   Safely back at home, Johnson struggled to dig himself out. He knew he should feel grateful that he was among the survivors, but he couldn't come to terms with the outcome. Despite the support of friends, family, and even strangers, there were parts of Johnson that would never be the same. He battled with depression. Mostly, he drank to forget, but he also drank to fall asleep. There were nights when, lying on his back, eyes probing the

darkness, he felt the rise and fall of his chest and counted his breaths. It took him back under the snow, where he drew what could have been his last breath. Even today, falling asleep feels a lot like dying.

20   Nearly a decade passed before he finally asked for help. He checked himself into a treatment program and took four months off work to "move to B.C., grow a beard, do yoga, and just deal with it." It's a process that will likely never be finished, but Johnson knows he's made progress. He continues to take avalanche-safety courses and returns to the backcountry each year for a ski trip with friends. Telling his story is an important step forward. He still wrestles with big questions: "Why me? What am I supposed to do now?" He doesn't blame anyone for what happened: "Can you blame a mountain? No. A mountain is just a mountain. Snow is just snow."

Comprehension and Critical Thinking

1. In paragraph 5, what does *staggering* mean?
   a. swaying   b. walking unsteadily   c. spreading out
2. What type of narration is this essay?
   a. first person   b. third person
3. In your own words, summarize what happened in this story.

   _____

   _____

   _____

4. What preparations did the group make to deal with emergency situations?

   _____

   _____

5. Describe how Johnson felt physically after the snow hit him.

   _____

   _____

6. How did he feel psychologically?

   _____

   _____

   _____

7. How did some members of the group get rescued?

   _____

   _____

8. This essay contains examples of imagery—description using the senses. Give examples of imagery that appeals to the following senses.

sight: _____

_____

hearing: _____

_____

touch: _____

_____

9. How did this experience affect Johnson? _____

_____

_____

10. Has Johnson overcome his traumatic experience? _____

_____

_____

Writing Topics

Write about one of the following topics. Remember to explore, develop, and revise and edit your work.

1. Describe an intensely emotional event. Use imagery that appeals to the senses.

2. Describe a sport or an outdoor activity you enjoy and tell a story about a memorable moment that occurred while you were doing that activity.

Reading 13
460 Days

Amanda Lindhout

Amanda Lindhout is a journalist. In August 2003, while working on a story, she and a friend were taken hostage in southern Somalia. The following excerpt is taken from her book *A House in the Sky: A Memoir*.

1   When I describe what happened to me on August 23, 2008, I say that I was taken—on an empty stretch of road outside Mogadishu, the capital of Somalia, out of the back seat of a four-wheel-drive Mitsubishi by a dozen or so men whose faces were swaddled in checkered scarves. Each one of them carried an AK-47.

2   The truth of it dawned slowly on me, as the men seemed to rise up out of the sand, circling the car with their guns hefted, as they shouted a

few words at our driver, as someone tugged open a door. We—me, my traveling companion Nigel Brennan, and the three Somali men helping us with our work—were headed that day to a sprawling settlement just outside the city to do some reporting. We were waved out from our air-conditioned vehicle into the sweltering equatorial heat. I remember in that instant a narrow-shouldered woman dressed in a flowing hijab hurrying past on foot. She pointedly looked away, as if a couple of white Westerners getting pulled from a car and being forced to lie spread-eagle in the ditch at the side of the road were an everyday occurrence or, in any event, something she had no power to stop.

3   I was twenty-seven years old. I had spent most of the last seven years traveling the world, often by myself, as a backpacker, financing extended low-budget trips with stints working as a waitress in a couple of fancy cocktail lounges back home. Each trip bolstered my confidence, convincing me that even while strife and terror hogged the international headlines, there was always something more hopeful and humane to be found on the ground.

4   Before going to Somalia, I spent the last year trying to transition to more serious work, learning photography and teaching myself how to produce a television report. I did a six-month stint in Kabul, followed by seven months in Baghdad. As a freelancer, I filed stories for a couple of English-language cable networks, taking whatever work I could get. I was getting by, but just barely.

5   My plan was to spend a week in Somalia, which had no shortage of potential stories to cover. Knowing it was risky, I took what felt like the necessary precautions—hiring a local fixer to arrange our logistics and paying for a pair of armed government guards to escort us around Mogadishu. For me, going to Somalia felt like a steppingstone, though I recognized it was a dangerous one.

6   I know now that kidnappings for ransom happen more frequently than most of us would think. They happen in Mexico, Nigeria, and Iraq. They happen in India, Pakistan, Algeria, China, Colombia, and plenty of other places. Sometimes the motivation is political or personal, but most often it's about money. Hostage taking is a business, a speculative one, fueled by people like me—the wandering targets, the fish out of water, the comparatively rich moving against a backdrop of poor. The stories pop up in the news and then often disappear: An American traveler is grabbed in Benin. A Dutch consultant is held for ransom in Johannesburg. A British tourist is dragged from a bus in Turkey.

7   The first call to my family from Somalia came on August 24, a day after we were taken. A rumbly voice surfaced on my father's voice mail, the man named Adam saying, "Hello, we have your daughter." He said he would call again to talk about money and then hung up.

8   In early October—roughly six weeks after we were taken—they moved us into a concrete building. We sometimes heard gunfire between warring militias outside our windows and sometimes a mother singing nearby to her child, her voice low and sweet. The sound of it filled me with longing. Our room was large and unfurnished. Nigel and I lived like a two-person family, doing what we could to fight off depression and to distract ourselves from the gnawing hunger. I poured the tea, and Nigel washed our clothes. Our captors had given us basic supplies—two tubes of toothpaste, some Q-tips, nail clippers, a packet of acetaminophen tablets as large as horse pills. I received a cloak-like dress and headscarf, both made from red polyester. Nigel was given a couple of collared shirts. Between us, we had two tin plates and a single spoon. With what little food we were given, we made menus, eating our meals on a table-size square of brown linoleum. Some days we ate the buns followed by the tuna; other days it was tuna followed by the buns.

9   On January 14, a Wednesday, I stepped into the hallway, headed toward the shower, and noticed a new stillness in the house. The shoes belonging to our Somali colleagues, Abdi, Mahad, and Marwali—had disappeared, all three pairs. A while later, I was able to ask Abddullah where they went. He didn't hesitate. Seemingly pleased with himself, he lifted a finger and made an emphatic throat-slitting gesture. If our captors had killed their fellow Somalis, Muslim brothers all three, it didn't bode well for me and Nigel.

10   Was there some way out? There had to be. Nigel told me he had been studying the window in the bathroom we shared and thought we could climb through it. I, too, had looked at that window plenty of times, seeing no option there. About eight feet off the bathroom floor, recessed far back in the thick wall, up near the ceiling, there was a ledge maybe two feet deep, almost like an alcove. But what was at the end of it hardly counted as a window. It was rather a screen made of decorative bricks with a few gaps, serving as ventilation holes for the bathroom. The bricks were cemented together. And then, as if that weren't enough, laid horizontally in front of the bricks was a series of five metal bars anchored into the window frame.

11   "Are you crazy?" I said to Nigel. "It's impossible. How would we get out?"

12   "You should crawl up there," he said. "I've been looking at the bricks. The mortar is crumbling. We could dig it out."

13   Standing at our windows, we began to work on a plan. What time of day would we go? Who would we seek out, and what would we say? The considerations were enormous.

14   On the start of the third day, Nigel announced that he had carved out the final brick. He then had to contend with the metal bars, but the first one was already loose, and he said it would take only one more to create enough space to pass through. After dawn broke, Nigel and I stood at our sills deciding that we had to leave immediately. We knew from the calls of the muezzin that there was a mosque somewhere close by. It seemed like the one good option, a place to find a crowd. We waited for the midday prayer, for the heat to arrive, and the boys to start nodding off. I knocked for the bathroom, and Nigel met me there, holding my backpack.

15   Early that morning, he had pulled out a third window bar. I waited while he quickly unstacked the bricks. I didn't hesitate. I got one leg out the window and then the second. I slid a few inches on my stomach to lessen the distance to the ground, holding on to one of the remaining window bars for support, and then I let myself drop.

16   Things were bad. I knew it the instant I touched the soil. Nothing appeared the way I had imagined it. To the left was a sideways-leaning fence made of patchwork pieces of colored tin and old, flattened oilcans. To the right was a row of shanties, built from more tin and pieces of loose burlap. There wasn't a bit of vegetation in sight, beyond a few brambly thorn bushes. More alarming was the emaciated child, a boy of maybe seven, standing only a few feet away from me, naked but for a pair of shorts, swaybacked and wide-eyed and looking as if he might scream.

17   The boy took off at a sprint—heading, I was sure, toward the first adult he could find.

18   It was as if a starting gun had been shot, as if a seismic disturbance had unsettled the air, rippling over the rooftops to the patio where our captors lay in repose. Everything became instinctual then. Nigel and I didn't even look at each other. We just started, madly, to run. Every strategy we plotted at our windowsills flew out of heads. Every bit of reason lifted away as we dashed down the alleyway.

19   The mosque was tall and wide, painted green and white with a crescent moon on top and a short set of wooden steps leading to a wooden platform and an entrance. The platform was heaped with shoes, signaling that the place was full of people. Moving up the stairs behind Nigel, I felt the first trickle of relief so unfamiliar that I almost couldn't identify it.

20   Just then, a lone person came skidding around the street corner. It was Hassam, one of the younger guards. His expression was one of disbelief and selfish terror. I saw Abdullah run up, just behind him. I bolted forward into the mosque, forgetting to remove my shoes. A crowd magnetized around us, men with puzzled faces, some showing alarm. And then Abdullah was upon me, having blasted through the door with Jamal right behind, both of them holding guns.

21   My fear organized itself into speed. I ducked through a doorway leading out into the air. With Abdullah two paces behind me, I leapt over the three stairs that descended from the side door of the mosque, landing in heavy sand, shedding my flip-flops as I ran. A gunshot ripped overhead, hollowing out the air. I looked back to see Abdullah, who had stopped running long enough to fire at me. My mind circled back toward the mosque. Nigel was inside. Inside was safer than outside. Keeping my shoulders low, I did a high-speed 20-yard end run around Abdullah, throwing myself back up the stairs and into the mosque.

22   But before anyone could respond, the dynamic in the room changed suddenly. Two of the leaders of the kidnappers had marched into the mosque, looking disheveled and furious, with the captain next to them, waving a pistol. One of them—a man called Ahmed—located me and pointed a finger. "You!" he shouted. "You have made a big problem!" The air in the mosque had grown stuffy and uncertain, filled with noise. Then came a loud, concussive crack, a gun going off somewhere inside the room.

23   The sound of it broke the spell, the holding pattern. I saw Abdullah pushing through the crowd in my direction, his head lowered like a bull's. I screamed as he dove at me. He caught my feet with his hands and began dragging me in the direction of the side door. I clawed at the ground as he pulled. I don't remember any of the onlookers trying to stop him.

24   I was being pushed to my feet and toward a truck. I saw two other men hauling Nigel through the door of the mosque and in our direction.

The sight of him brought a wash of solace and a hammer blow of anxiety. It had been all of 45 minutes since we'd slipped through the window. We'd made it out but not truly out. We'd crossed the river only halfway. Things would get worse from here. Everything that followed would be aftermath, punishment.

Comprehension and Critical Thinking

1. Why was Amanda Lindhout in Somalia?

_____

2. Why was she kidnapped? _____

3. In paragraph 6, she writes, "the hostage taking is a business." Why does she call hostage taking a business?

_____

_____

4. What were their living conditions like? _____

_____

_____

5. How did the writer and her companion cope with the emotional distress of being kidnapped?

_____

6. What pushed the writer and her companion to attempt to escape?

_____

_____

7. How did they escape? _____

_____

8. Why did they plan to run to the mosque after they had escaped? You will have to infer or guess. _____

_____

9. Why did no one at the mosque help the writer to get free from the kidnappers? You may have to infer or guess.

_____

_____

_____

10. Does the writer acknowledge any personal responsibility for her predicament? Reread paragraphs 5 and 6 and make a guess.

_____

_____

_____

Writing Topics

Write about one of the following topics. Remember to explore, develop, and revise and edit your work.

1. Have you ever gone on a road trip? Write about your experience. Who were you with, where did you go, and what happened?

2. Have you or someone you know ever been in a dangerous situation? You could think about a time when you traveled to a different city or country. Or you could think of a situation closer to home. Write about what happened and how you felt.

3. What strategies should tourists take to keep themselves safe when they travel to foreign countries?

Theme: Human Development

Reading 14
Nudge

Terry O'Reilly

Terry O'Reilly is a broadcast producer and the host of a radio series about advertising. In this next essay, O'Reilly discusses the persuasive power of whispers.

1   Schools, marketers, and even governments are now using small nudges to gently steer people toward making more positive decisions in their lives. Those nudges included sending people a handwritten note when they are behind on their taxes because a handwritten note gets their attention. Nudges—small and almost invisible—are a controversial and highly effective method of influence.

2   Back in 1974, George Foreman was the undisputed boss of the heavyweight boxing division. George was a menacing, dangerous, 6 foot 3, 220 pound machine that struck terror in the hearts of men who fought for a living.

3   Before that, in 1971, undefeated Muhammad Ali lost to heavyweight champion Joe Frazier. In 1973, Muhammad Ali lost to Ken Norton. Norton broke Ali's jaw in a 12-round slugfest.

4   Now, to put all this in some context: When George Foreman met champion Joe Frazier—the man who beat Ali—Foreman knocked him down *six times* before the referee stopped the fight. When he met the man who broke Ali's jaw, Foreman knocked Norton down three times

before the ref stopped the fight. So when "The Rumble in the Jungle" was announced, it was to be an epic battle for the ages—George Foreman versus Muhammad Ali. The fight was held in Zaire, Africa. When the night of the fight finally arrived, the boxing world was on edge. Most felt Ali would take a savage beating. Even the atmosphere in Ali's dressing room was quiet as a funeral, provoking Ali to ask everyone there why they were all so quiet. But the reason was clear; they feared for Ali's life.

5   When the first round began, Ali traded punches with Foreman, but soon Foreman began pounding on Ali's body with those huge arms. Ali started to cover up to protect himself. Three minutes later, the bell rang to end the first round.

6   Then the most remarkable thing happened. Ali went to his corner, but he didn't sit down. He just stared across the ring at Foreman. You could see his mind racing. He had felt the punishing power of Foreman's punches, the power that had crushed Frazier and Norton. Ali realized he couldn't go toe-to-toe with Foreman. He had to win another way. And in *that moment*, Ali changed his entire fight plan.

7   When the second round started, Ali just leaned against the ropes and let Foreman do all the punching. He let Foreman pound his body, round after round. But people at the ringside started to notice Ali was whispering in Foreman's ear. What nobody knew was that Ali was asking Foreman why he was doing most of his punching with his right hand. He taunted Foreman, saying he must not have much of a left.

8   After rounds of whispering to Foreman, Foreman changed hands. He began punching Ali with his left. It was genius, because Ali's left side was starting to go numb from Foreman's right punches. By nudging Foreman to change sides, Ali bought the time to get the feeling back in his left arm again. Meanwhile, Foreman was getting exhausted punching Ali. Then, in the 8th round, Ali saw an opportunity and did the impossible. He knocked out the mighty George Foreman.

9   Ali didn't beat Foreman with his fists; he beat him with his mind. Those whispers in Foreman's ear convinced him to make a small change, and that small change helped give the heavyweight title to Muhammad Ali.

10   The term "nudge" was first put forth in the fascinating book, *Nudge*, by behavioral science professors Richard Thaler and Cass Sunstein. The art of the nudge has been adopted by schools, charities, marketers, and even governments. For example, in Britain, the government tried to encourage

subsidies:
sums of money
provided by the
government

homeowners to insulate their attics to save energy costs. As part of that campaign, the government put forth compelling economic arguments to persuade the public. On top of that, generous **subsidies** were offered. Yet, nothing seemed to work. Members of the public appeared to have no interest in insulating their attics and saving money, which puzzled the government. But when government officials dug further, they stumbled upon the reason for the resistance. Apparently, UK homeowners simply didn't want to clear the junk out of their attics.

11   In the UK, attics are storage spaces, and just the thought of having to clear out their attics was enough for people to forgo the energy savings of insulating. Once the government had isolated that reason, they got to work on an interesting solution. They teamed up with a local home improvement company and offered an attic-cleaning service. With that, the amount of people who insulated soared. The attic cleaning offer was the "nudge" to get people to do the bigger thing—which was to insulate.

12   The airport in Amsterdam, Holland, wanted to solve a persistent problem in the men's washrooms. So they etched the image of a housefly into the urinals near the drain. Overspray was reduced by 80 percent. The housefly was a nudge—because men just love to aim at things.

13   Many retailers have added a digital tipping feature to their tablet and mobile apps. Calculating a tip is frustrating for many people. Research has shown that if you can lessen the amount of mental effort required to work out a tip, the greater the chance of people leaving one. So customers have three digital options: 15 percent, 18 percent, or the nice fat 20 percent tip. The presence of those three nudges has resulted in more people leaving more—and bigger—tips.

14   In *Nudge*, Thaler and Sunstein tell the story of a school in Texas that wanted to increase the number of students that went on to college. At that time, two-thirds of high schoolers did not go on to higher education. But the school officials didn't have any outside funding to help with the problem, so they decided to nudge from within. First, the teachers talked to the students in terms they would understand. They didn't try to sell the high-mindedness of college education. Instead, the brilliant nudge they employed was simple and powerful. In order to graduate from the high school, students had to complete a college application. It was a stipulation of graduation. To gain acceptance to the community college, students simply needed a high school diploma and proof that they took a standardized test. Filling out the application was almost a guarantee of

acceptance. So teachers helped them with the test, and made sure *everyone* filled out a college application.

15   In the end, that application nudge produced remarkable results: From 2004 to 2005, the percentage of high school students who went on to college rose from 11 percent to 45 percent. Just the act of filling out an application convinced more students to pursue a college education: a small nudge that would affect the entire course of their lives.

16   There is a lot to be said for the power of a nudge. It can make people choose healthier foods, it can help them save money, and just the right nudge can even influence someone to pursue a college education. And when nudges scale up, they have the potential to save governments billions of dollars.

Comprehension and Critical Thinking

1. Use your own words to describe the term *nudge* as it is used in this essay.

_____

_____

2. Underline the thesis statement.

3. What type of introduction does this essay use?
   a. general background
   b. anecdote
   c. historical information

4. In a few sentences, sum up what happened in the George Forman–Mohammed Ali fight. See paragraphs 2–9.

_____

_____

_____

_____

_____

_____

5. The British tried to convince people to insulate their attics. Why did generous subsidies not work?

_____

6. Why was the British government's nudge so successful?

_____

_____

_____

7. A school in Texas nudged students to go to college. What was the nudge and why was it successful?

_____

_____

8. What do the examples of nudges have in common? In other words, what common technique do the nudgers use?

_____

_____

Writing Topics

Write about one of the following topics. Remember to explore, develop, and revise and edit your work.

1. Who or what has influenced you to change a behavior or habit? Describe the causes and effects of your new behavior.

2. What are some techniques people can use to influence others? Think of three techniques, and provide specific examples for each technique.

Reading 15
How Cults Become Religions

John D. Carl

John D. Carl is a college professor and textbook author. In the following adapted essay, he discusses how religious institutions evolve.

1   Sociologist Emile Durkheim believed that religion binds the community together through ritual and tradition. Although most societies have some sort of dominant religion, there are many different religions, each of which comes with its own set of beliefs and customs. But how does a set of beliefs become an accepted religion? Religions go through a series of stages as they become an integrated part of society.

2   Sociologically, all religions begin as cults. Cults are new religious movements led by charismatic leaders with few followers. The teachings and practices of cults are often at odds with the dominant culture and religion, so society is likely to reject the cult. For example, since the Chinese revolution, the Chinese government has cracked down on any faith-based group that it considers to be nonconformist, according to

Jonathan Kaiman, journalist for the *Guardian*. The Chinese authorities consider a cult such as Falun Gong to be subversive and have tried to obliterate it. In 1999, the Chinese authorities initiated a crackdown on Falun Gong members. According to human rights groups, thousands of practitioners have been imprisoned.

3   A cult demands intense commitment and involvement of its members, and it relies on finding new adherents by using outside recruitment. Most cults fail because they cannot attract enough followers to sustain themselves. However, once a cult has enough members to support itself, it becomes a sect. Sects still go against society's norms, but members have greater social standing and are usually better integrated into society than cult members are. As a result, sect members are less likely to be persecuted by the dominant society. For instance, in the United States, the Church of Scientology and the Unification Church are more or less integrated into society. As time passes and the sect grows, the members tend to become respectable members of society. For example, the Church of Scientology boasts Tom Cruise and John Travolta as followers.

4   Eventually, sects can evolve into a church. The term church does not specifically refer to a building or a denomination of a religion; instead, it is a large, highly organized group of believers. Churches are bureaucratized institutions and may include national and international offices, and leaders must undergo special training to perform established rituals. A good example is the Catholic Church, where priests go to special colleges to get ordained. The Catholic Church maintains a strict hierarchy in the offices of the Church. According to the Pew Research Center, about 25 percent of the population of the United States is Catholic. There are just under two hundred **dioceses** overseen by bishops, and each diocese has individual parishes, which are run by priests.

diocese: a religious district supervised by a bishop

5   If a church becomes highly integrated into the dominant culture, it may join with the state. A state religion, or theocracy, is formed when government and religion work together to shape society. Citizenship automatically makes one a member, so most citizens belong to the dominant religion. For example, Iran has a theocratic government and goes so far as to place religious leaders at the pinnacle of executive government decision-making. The Grand Ayatollah holds the highest political office and is the moral authority in Iran. Vatican City is another example of a theocracy because the community is ruled by an established religious organization, and the Pope is the head of state.

6 As societies modernize, religions begin going through secularization, which is the overall decline in the importance and power of religion in people's lives. Institutional religion weakens as societies become more scientifically advanced. Sociologists generally argue that as a civilization becomes more complex, people become less tied to the "old ways" and are more inclined to pursue other avenues. This phenomenon seems to indicate that secularization is inevitable. According to the Web site *PollingReport.com*, there has been a decline in the number of people in the United States who say that religion is very important in their lives, while the number of people who say it is fairly important has risen. The number of people who say that religion is not very important in their lives has doubled since 1965.

7 Durkheim argues that religious beliefs and society are intrinsically connected. Cults begin by endorsing practices outside of the dominant religion, but eventually some cults integrate into society. Religions in general function to provide cultural norms and values that bind followers together. Because human beings desire knowledge about the meaning of life and the purpose of death, they have developed complex belief systems, which have developed into various great religions.

Comprehension and Critical Thinking

1. In paragraph 2, what does the word *nonconformist* mean?

_____

_____

2. Find a word in paragraph 2 that means "rebellious." _____

3. Underline the thesis statement of this essay.

4. What type of process does the author use to explain the development of religions?

 a. complete a process   b. understand a process

5. According to paragraph 2, why do societies have a negative attitude toward cults? You may have to infer or guess.

_____

_____

6. What are some similarities and differences between a cult and a sect?

 Similarities: _____

_____

Differences: _____

_____

7. According to paragraph 4, what are three characteristics of a church?

_____

_____

8. In which paragraphs does the author use the following supporting details?

Informed opinion: _____

Statistics: _____

Examples: _____

9. According to the text, what causes the decline of religions? _____

_____

_____

Writing Topics

Write about one of the following topics. Remember to explore, develop, and revise and edit your work.

1. Do you follow a cult, sect, or church, or are you indifferent to religion? Explain the process you went through to develop your current beliefs.

2. Should religious beliefs, such as intelligent design and others, be taught in public schools? Why or why not? Provide examples to back up your argument.

3. According to the author, religion can interfere with politics. Should religious beliefs influence political decisions? Include examples in your own country where religious beliefs may have had an impact on government policy.

Reading 16
The Untranslatable Word "Macho"

Rose del Castillo Guilbault

Rose del Castillo Guilbault is a journalist and the editorial director of the ABC affiliate station KGO-TV in San Francisco, California. In this essay, Castillo Guilbault compares how two cultures define the term *macho*.

1   What is *macho?* That depends on which side of the border you come from. Although it's not unusual for words and expressions to lose their subtlety in translation, the negative connotations of *macho* in this country are troublesome to Hispanics.

2   Take the newspaper descriptions of alleged mass murderer Ramon Salcido. That an insensitive, insanely jealous, hard-drinking, violent Latin male is referred to as macho makes Hispanics cringe. "Es muy macho" the women in my family nod approvingly, describing a man they respect. But in the United States, when women say, "He's so macho," it's with disdain.

3   The Hispanic *macho* is manly, responsible, hardworking, a man in charge, and a patriarch. He is a man who expresses strength through silence, or what the Yiddish language would call a *mensch.*

4   The American *macho* is a chauvinist, a brute, uncouth, selfish, loud, abrasive, capable of inflicting pain, and sexually promiscuous. Quintessential *macho* models in this country are Sylvester Stallone, Arnold Schwarzenegger, and Charles Bronson. In their movies, they exude toughness, independence, and masculinity. But a closer look reveals their machismo is really violence masquerading as courage, sullenness disguised as silence, and irresponsibility camouflaged as independence.

5   If the Hispanic ideal of *macho* were translated to American screen roles, they might be Jimmy Stewart, Sean Connery, and Laurence Olivier. In Spanish, macho ennobles Latin males. In English, it devalues them. This pattern seems consistent with the conflicts ethnic minority males experience in this country. Typically, the cultural traits other societies value don't translate as desirable characteristics in America.

recalcitrant:
unmanageable

6   I watched my own father struggle with these cultural ambiguities. He worked on a farm for twenty years. He laid down miles of irrigation pipe, carefully plowed long, neat rows in fields, hacked away at **recalcitrant** weeds, and drove tractors through whirlpools of dust. He stoically worked twenty-hour days during harvest season, accepting the long hours as part of agricultural work. When the boss complained or upbraided him for minor mistakes, he kept quiet, even when it was obvious the boss had erred.

7   He handled the most menial tasks with pride. At home he was a good provider, helped out my mother's family in Mexico without complaint, and was indulgent with me. Arguments between my mother and him generally had to do with money or with his stubborn reluctance to share his troubles. He tried to work them out in his own silence. He didn't want to trouble my mother—a course that backfired because the imagined is always worse than the reality.

8   Americans regarded my father as decidedly un-macho. His character was interpreted as nonassertive, his loyalty as a lack of ambition, and his quietness as ignorance. I once overheard the boss's son blame him for plowing crooked rows in a field. My father merely smiled at the lie, knowing the boy had done it, but didn't refute it, confident his good work was well known. But the boss instead ridiculed him for being "stupid" and letting a kid get away with a lie. Seeing my embarrassment, my father dismissed the incident, saying, "They're the dumb ones. Imagine, me fighting with a kid." I tried not to look at him with American eyes because sometimes the reflection hurt.

9   Listening to my aunts' clucks of approval, my vision focused on the qualities America overlooked. "He's such a hard worker. So serious, so responsible." My aunts would secretly compliment my mother. The unspoken comparison was that he was not like some of their husbands, who drank and womanized. My uncles represented the darker side of macho.

10   In a patriarchal society, few challenge their roles. If men drink, it's because it's the manly thing to do. If they gamble, it's because it's how men relax. And if they fool around, well, it's because a man simply can't hold back so much man! My aunts didn't exactly meekly sit back, but they put up with these transgressions because Mexican society dictated this was their lot in life.

11   In the United States, I believe it was the feminist movement of the early seventies that changed macho's meaning. Perhaps my generation of Latin women was in part responsible. I recall Chicanas complaining about the chauvinistic nature of Latin men and the notion they wanted their women barefoot, pregnant, and in the kitchen. The generalization that Latin men embodied chauvinistic traits led to this interesting twist of semantics. Suddenly a word that represented something positive in one culture became a negative prototype in another.

12   The problem with the use of macho today is that it's become an accepted stereotype of the Latin male. And like all stereotypes, it distorts truth. The impact of language in our society is undeniable. And the misuse of macho hints at a deeper cultural misunderstanding that extends beyond mere word definitions.

Comprehension and Critical Thinking

1. Find a word in paragraph 2 that means "contempt." _____

2. Underline the thesis statement.

3. What is the writer comparing and contrasting in this essay?

   _____

   _____

4. What connotations does the word *macho* have in Latin culture?

   _____

   _____

5. What connotations does the word *macho* have in American culture?

   _____

   _____

6. According to the writer, why do men like Jimmy Stewart, Sean Connery, and Laurence Olivier better exemplify the word *macho* than men like Sylvester Stallone or Charles Bronson?

   _____

   _____

   _____

7. In paragraph 8, the writer mentions that she tried not to look at her father "with American eyes." In her opinion, how did Americans view her father?

   _____

8. According to the writer, does the word *macho* in Latin cultures only have a positive connotation? Explain your answer.

   _____

   _____

   _____

9. How did the meaning of the word *macho* evolve in Latin communities in North America?

   _____

   _____

   _____

10. Although the predominant pattern in this essay is comparison and contrast, the writer also uses definition and narration. How do they help develop her central argument?

    _____

    _____

Writing Topics

Write about one of the following topics. Remember to explore, develop, and revise and edit your work.

1. What are some stereotypes of your nationality, religion, or gender? Compare the stereotypes with the reality.

2. Compare and contrast two people in your life who have very different personalities.

Reading 17
Chance and Circumstance

David Leonhardt

David Leonhardt is a columnist for the *New York Times*. His columns focus on economics and society. In the following essay, he examines the theories of Malcolm Gladwell and ponders on the definition and the causes of success.

1   In 1984, a young man named Malcolm graduated from the University of Toronto and moved to the United States to try his hand at journalism. Thanks to his uncommonly clear writing style and keen eye for a story, he quickly landed a job at the *Washington Post*. After less than a decade at the *Post*, he moved up to the pinnacle of literary journalism, the *New Yorker*. There, he wrote articles full of big ideas about the hidden patterns of ordinary life, which then became grist for two No. 1 best-selling books. In the vast world of nonfiction writing, he is as close to a singular talent as exists today.

2   Or at least that's one version of the story of Malcolm Gladwell. Here is another: In 1984, a young man named Malcolm graduated from the University of Toronto and moved to the United States to try his hand at journalism. No one could know it then, but he arrived with nearly the perfect background for his time. His mother was a psychotherapist, and his father a mathematician. Their professions pointed young Malcolm toward the behavioral sciences, whose popularity would explode in the 1990s. His mother also just happened to be a writer on the side. So unlike most children of mathematicians and therapists, he came to learn, as he would later recall, "that there is beauty in saying something clearly and simply." As a journalist, he plumbed the behavioral research for optimistic

lessons about the human condition, and he found an eager audience during the heady, proudly geeky '90s. His first book, *The Tipping Point*, was published in March 2000, just days before the **NASDAQ** peaked.

NASDAQ: an electronic stock market started in 1971

3   These two stories about Gladwell are both true, and yet they are also very different. The first personalizes his success. It is the classically American version of his career, in that it gives individual characteristics—talent, hard work, **Horatio Alger**-like pluck—the starring role. The second version does not necessarily deny these characteristics, but it does sublimate them. The protagonist is not a singularly talented person who took advantage of opportunities. He is instead a talented person who took advantage of singular opportunities.

Horatio Alger: American author (1832–1899) who wrote children's adventure novels

4   Gladwell's book *Outliers* is a passionate argument for taking the second version of the story more seriously than we now do. "It is not the brightest who succeed," Gladwell writes, "nor is success simply the sum of the decisions and efforts we make on our own behalf. It is, rather, a gift. Outliers are those who have been given opportunities—and who have had the strength and presence of mind to seize them."

5   He starts with a tale of individual greatness, about the Beatles, the titans of Silicon Valley, or the enormously successful generation of New York Jews born in the early twentieth century. Then he adds details that undercut that tale. So Bill Gates is introduced as a young computer programmer from Seattle whose brilliance and ambition outshine the brilliance and ambition of the thousands of other young programmers. But then Gladwell takes us back to Seattle, and we discover that Gates's high school happened to have a computer club when almost no other high schools did. He then lucked into the opportunity to use the computers at the University of Washington, for hours on end. By the time he turned twenty, he had spent well more than ten thousand hours as a programmer.

6   At the end of this revisionist tale, Gladwell asks Gates himself how many other teenagers in the world had as much experience as he had by the early 1970s. "If there were fifty in the world, I'd be stunned," Gates says. "I had a better exposure to software development at a young age than I think anyone did in that period of time, and all because of an incredibly lucky series of events." Gates's talent and drive were surely unusual. But Gladwell suggests that his opportunities may have been even more so.

7 Gladwell explores the **anomaly** of hockey players' birthdays. In many of the best leagues in the world, amateur or professional, roughly 40 percent of the players were born in January, February, or March, while only 10 percent were born in October, November, or December. It's a profoundly strange pattern, with a simple explanation. The cutoff birth date for many youth hockey leagues is January 1. So the children born in the first three months of the year are just a little older, bigger, and stronger than their peers. These older children are then funneled into all-star teams that offer the best, most intense training. By the time they become teenagers, their random initial advantage has turned into a real one.

anomaly: peculiarity or strange quality

8 At the championship game of the top Canadian junior league, Gladwell interviews the father of one player born on January 4. More than half of the players on his team—the Medicine Hat Tigers—were born in January, February, or March. But when Gladwell asks the father to explain his son's success, the calendar has nothing to do with it. He instead mentions passion, talent, and hard work—before adding, as an aside, that the boy was always big for his age. Just imagine, Gladwell writes, if Canada created another youth hockey league for children born in the second half of the year. It would one day find itself with twice as many great hockey players.

Young hockey players

9 *Outliers* is almost a political manifesto. "We look at the young Bill Gates and marvel that our world allowed that thirteen-year-old to become a fabulously successful entrepreneur," he writes at the end. "But that's the wrong lesson. Our world only allowed one thirteen-year-old unlimited access to a time-sharing terminal in 1968. If a million teenagers had been given the same opportunity, how many more Microsofts would we have today?"

10 After a decade—and, really, a generation—in which this country has done fairly little to build up the institutions that can foster success, Gladwell is urging us to rethink. Once again, his timing may prove to be pretty good.

Comprehension and Critical Thinking

1. Find a word in paragraph 1 that means "height or peak." _____
2. Find a word in paragraph 2 that means "examined deeply." _____

3. What is the introductory style of the essay?

    a. definition   b. contrasting position   c. anecdote

4. Underline a sentence in the essay that defines *outliers*.

5. According to Gladwell, why is Bill Gates an outlier?

_____

_____

_____

6. According to Gladwell, why is it luckier for hockey players to be born in the first three months of the year?

_____

_____

_____

7. How is Gladwell's perception of successful individuals different from how the general public views successful individuals?

_____

_____

_____

8. In paragraph 9, the writer says that Gladwell's book is "almost a political manifesto." Explain.

_____

_____

_____

9. What is the writer's opinion of Gladwell's thesis?

_____

_____

Writing Topics

Write about one of the following topics. Remember to explore, develop, and revise and edit your work.

1. What is *blind ambition?* Define the term, and use examples to support your ideas.

2. Describe someone you consider "successful." What contributed to that person's success? How has success affected that person? Write about the causes or effects of the person's success.

3. Nowadays, more boys than girls drop out of school. Colleges and universities now have more female than male graduates in many of their programs. Explain what can be done to convince young men to stay in school and pursue higher education.

Reading 18
The Happiness Factor

David Brooks

David Brooks writes for the *New York Times*, *The Weekly Standard*, *Newsweek*, and the *Atlantic Monthly*. He is also a commentator on *The NewsHour with Jim Lehrer*. In the following essay, Brooks makes an interesting comparison.

1   Two things happened to Sandra Bullock in 2010. First, she won an Academy Award for best actress. Then came the news reports claiming that her husband was an adulterous jerk. So the philosophic question of the day is: Would you take that as a deal? Would you exchange a tremendous professional triumph for a severe personal blow? On the one hand, an Academy Award is nothing to sneeze at. Bullock has earned the admiration of her peers in a way very few experience. She'll make more money for years to come. She may even live longer. Research by Donald A. Redelmeier and Sheldon M. Singh has found that, on average, Oscar winners live nearly four years longer than nominees that don't win.

2   Nonetheless, if you had to take more than three seconds to think about this question, you are absolutely crazy. Marital happiness is far more important than anything else in determining personal well-being. If you have a successful marriage, it doesn't matter how many professional setbacks you endure, you will be reasonably happy. If you have an unsuccessful marriage, it doesn't matter how many career triumphs you record, you will remain significantly unfulfilled.

3   This isn't just sermonizing. This is the age of research, so there's data to back this up. Over the past few decades, teams of researchers have been studying happiness. Their work, which seemed flimsy at first, has developed an impressive rigor, and one of the key findings is that, just as the old sages predicted, worldly success has shallow roots while interpersonal bonds permeate through and through.

4   For example, the relationship between happiness and income is complicated, and after a point, tenuous. It is true that poor nations become happier as they become middle-class nations. But once the basic necessities have been achieved, future income is lightly connected to well-being. Growing countries are slightly less happy than countries with slower growth rates, according to Carol Graham of the Brookings Institution and Eduardo Lora. The United States is much richer than it was fifty years

ago, but this has produced no measurable increase in overall happiness. On the other hand, it has become a much more unequal country, but this inequality doesn't seem to have reduced national happiness.

5   On a personal scale, winning the lottery doesn't seem to produce lasting gains in well-being. People aren't happiest during the years when they are winning the most promotions. Instead, people are happy in their twenties, dip in middle age and then, on average, hit peak happiness just after retirement at age sixty-five. People get slightly happier as they climb the income scale, but this depends on how they experience growth. Does wealth inflame unrealistic expectations? Does it destabilize settled relationships? Or does it flow from a virtuous cycle in which an interesting job produces hard work that in turn leads to more interesting opportunities?

Does money buy happiness?

6   If the relationship between money and well-being is complicated, the correspondence between personal relationships and happiness is not. The daily activities most associated with happiness are sex, socializing after work, and having dinner with others. The daily activity most injurious to happiness is commuting. According to one study, joining a group that meets even just once a month produces the same happiness gain as doubling your income. According to another, being married produces a psychic gain equivalent to more than $100,000 a year.

7   If you want to find a good place to live, just ask people if they trust their neighbors. Levels of social trust vary enormously, but countries with high social trust have happier people, better health, more efficient government, more economic growth, and less fear of crime (regardless of whether actual crime rates are increasing or decreasing). The overall impression from this research is that economic and professional success exist on the surface of life, and that they emerge out of interpersonal relationships, which are much deeper and more important.

8   The second impression is that most of us pay attention to the wrong things. Most people vastly overestimate the extent to which more money would improve their lives. Most schools and colleges spend too much time preparing students for careers and not enough preparing them to make social decisions. Most governments release a ton of data on economic trends but not enough on trust and other social conditions. In short, modern societies have developed vast institutions oriented around the things that are easy to count, not around the things that matter most. They have an affinity for material concerns and a primordial fear of moral and social ones.

9   This may be changing. There is a rash of compelling books—including *The Hidden Wealth of Nations* by David Halpern and *The Politics of Happiness* by Derek Bok—that argue that public institutions should pay attention to well-being and not just material growth narrowly conceived. Governments keep initiating policies they think will produce prosperity, only to get sacked, time and again, from their spiritual blind side.

Comprehension and Critical Thinking

1. In paragraph 4 what is the meaning of *tenuous*?
   a. unconvincing or questionable
   b. strong and convincing
   c. complete

2. In your own words, what is the writer's main point?

_____

_____

_____

3. According to the essay, what factors are associated with increased levels of happiness?

_____

_____

4. In which paragraphs does the writer use expert opinion?

_____

5. In paragraph 5, the writer states that people are happy in their twenties and after retirement, but not in their middle age. Why are people probably less happy in middle age? Make two or three guesses.

_____

_____

_____

_____

6. In paragraph 7, the writer mentions social trust but doesn't clearly define it. Infer or guess what social trust is.

_____

_____

7. In paragraph 8, the writer criticizes colleges because they don't prepare students to make social decisions. Think of ways that colleges could teach students to make moral and social decisions.

_____

_____

_____

Writing Topics

Write about one of the following topics. Remember to explore, develop, and revise and edit your work.

1. Compare two jobs you've had. What elements in the jobs provided you with the most pleasure?

2. Define personal happiness, and give examples to support your definition.

3. Define social trust. Break the topic down into categories, and list examples for each category. For instance, you could write about trust in the government, trust in the police, and trust in one's neighbors.

Reading 19
The Veldt

Ray Bradbury

Ray Bradbury (1920–2012) was a prolific writer of mystery, fantasy, and science fiction. His best-known novels are *The Martian Chronicles* and *Fahrenheit 451*. "The Veldt" was published in 1951 and appeared in his collection of short stories in *The Illustrated Man*.

1   "George, I wish you'd look at the nursery."

2   "What's wrong with it?"

3   "I don't know."

4   "Well, then."

5   "I just want you to look at it, is all, or call a psychologist in to look at it."

6   "What would a psychologist want with a nursery?"

7   "You know very well what he'd want." His wife paused in the middle of the kitchen and watched the stove busy humming to itself, making supper for four.

8   "It's just that the nursery is different now than it was."

9   "All right, let's have a look."

10   They walked down the hall of their soundproofed, Happylife Home, which had cost them thirty thousand dollars installed, this house which clothed and fed and rocked them to sleep and played and sang and was good to them. Their approach sensitized a switch somewhere, and the nursery light flicked on when they came within ten feet of it. Similarly, behind them, in the halls, lights went on and off as they left them behind, with a soft automaticity.

11   "Well," said George Hadley.

12   They stood on the thatched floor of the nursery. It was forty feet across by forty feet long and thirty feet high—it had cost half again as much as the rest of the house. "But nothing's too good for our children," George had said.

13   The nursery was silent. It was empty as a jungle glade at hot high noon. The walls were blank and two dimensional. Now, as George and Lydia Hadley stood in the center of the room, the walls began to purr and recede into crystalline distance, it seemed, and presently an African veldt appeared, in three dimensions; on all sides, in colors reproduced to the final pebble and bit of straw. The ceiling above them became a deep sky with a hot yellow sun.

14   George Hadley felt the perspiration start on his brow.

15   "Let's get out of the sun," he said. "This is a little too real. But I don't see anything wrong."

16   "Wait a moment, you'll see," said his wife.

17   Now the hidden odorophonics were beginning to blow a wind of odor at the two people in the middle of the baked veldtland. The hot straw smell of lion grass, the cool green smell of the hidden water hole, the great rusty smell of animals, the smell of dust like a red paprika in the hot air. And now the sounds: the thump of distant antelope feet on grassy sod, the papery rustling of vultures. A shadow passed through the sky. The shadow flickered on George Hadley's upturned, sweating face.

18   "Filthy creatures," he heard his wife say.

19   "The vultures."

20   "You see, there are the lions, far over, that way. Now they're on their way to the water hole. They've just been eating," said Lydia. "I don't know what."

21   "Some animal." George Hadley put his hand up to shield off the burning light from his squinted eyes. "A zebra or a baby giraffe, maybe."

22   "Are you sure?" His wife sounded peculiarly tense.

23   "No, it's a little late to be sure," he said, amused. "Nothing over there I can see but cleaned bone, and the vultures dropping for what's left."

24   "Did you hear that scream?" she asked.

25   "No."

26   "About a minute ago?"

27   "Sorry, no."

28   The lions were coming. And again George Hadley was filled with admiration for the mechanical genius who had conceived this room. A miracle of efficiency selling for an absurdly low price. Every home should have one. Oh, occasionally they frightened you with their clinical accuracy, they startled you, gave you a twinge, but most of the time what fun for everyone, not only your own son and daughter, but for yourself when you felt like a quick jaunt to a foreign land, a quick change of scenery. Well, here it was!

29   And here were the lions now, fifteen feet away, so real, so feverishly and startlingly real that you could feel the prickling fur on your hand, and your mouth was stuffed with the dusty upholstery smell of their heated pelts, and the yellow of them was in your eyes like the yellow of an exquisite French tapestry, the yellows of lions and summer grass, and the sound of the matted lion lungs exhaling on the silent noontide, and the smell of meat from the panting, dripping mouths.

30   The lions stood looking at George and Lydia Hadley with terrible green-yellow eyes.

31   "Watch out!" screamed Lydia.

32   The lions came running at them.

33   Lydia bolted and ran. Instinctively, George sprang after her. Outside, in the hall, with the door slammed, he was laughing and she was crying, and they both stood appalled at the other's reaction.

34   "George!"

35   "Lydia! Oh, my dear poor sweet Lydia!"

36   "They almost got us!"

37   "Walls, Lydia, remember; crystal walls, that's all they are. Oh, they look real, I must admit—Africa in your parlor—but it's all dimensional superreactionary, supersensitive color film and mental tape film behind glass screens. It's all odorophonics and sonics, Lydia. Here's my handkerchief."

38   "I'm afraid." She came to him and put her body against him and cried steadily. "Did you see? Did you feel? It's too real."

39   "Now, Lydia . . ."

40   "You've got to tell Wendy and Peter not to read any more on Africa."

41   "Of course—of course." He patted her.

42   "Promise?"

43   "Sure."

44   "And lock the nursery for a few days until I get my nerves settled."

45   "You know how difficult Peter is about that. When I punished him a month ago by locking the nursery for even a few hours—the tantrum he threw! And Wendy too. They live for the nursery."

46   "It's got to be locked; that's all there is to it."

47   "All right." Reluctantly he locked the huge door. "You've been working too hard. You need a rest."

48   "I don't know—I don't know," she said, blowing her nose, sitting down in a chair that immediately began to rock and comfort her. "Maybe I don't have enough to do. Maybe I have time to think too much. Why don't we shut the whole house off for a few days and take a vacation?"

49   "You mean you want to fry my eggs for me?"

50   "Yes." She nodded.

51   "And darn my socks?"

52   "Yes." A frantic, watery-eyed nodding.

53   "And sweep the house?"

54   "Yes, yes—oh, yes!"

55   "But I thought that's why we bought this house, so we wouldn't have to do anything?"

56   "That's just it. I feel like I don't belong here. The house is wife and mother now and nursemaid. Can I compete with an African veldt? Can I give a bath and scrub the children as efficiently or quickly as the automatic scrub bath can? I cannot. And it isn't just me. It's you. You've been awfully nervous lately."

57   "I suppose I have been smoking too much."

58   "You look as if you didn't know what to do with yourself in this house, either. You smoke a little more every morning and drink a little more every afternoon and need a little more sedative every night. You're beginning to feel unnecessary too."

59   "Am I?" He paused and tried to feel into himself to see what was really there.

60   "Oh, George!" She looked beyond him, at the nursery door. "Those lions can't get out of there, can they?"

61   He looked at the door and saw it tremble as if something had jumped against it from the other side.

62   "Of course not," he said.

63   At dinner they ate alone, for Wendy and Peter were at a special plastic carnival across town and had televised home to say they'd be late, to go ahead eating. So George Hadley, bemused, sat watching the dining-room table produce warm dishes of food from its mechanical interior.

64   "We forgot the ketchup," he said.

65   "Sorry," said a small voice within the table, and ketchup appeared.

66   As for the nursery, thought George Hadley, it won't hurt for the children to be locked out of it awhile. Too much of anything isn't good for anyone. And it was clearly indicated that the children had been spending a little too much time on Africa. That sun. He could feel it on his neck, still, like a hot paw. And the lions. And the smell of blood. Remarkable how the nursery caught the telepathic emanations of the children's minds and created life to fill their every desire. The children thought lions, and there were lions. The children thought zebras, and there were zebras. Sun—sun. Giraffes—giraffes. Death and death.

67   That last. He chewed tastelessly on the meat that the table had cut for him. Death thoughts. They were awfully young, Wendy and Peter, for death thoughts. Or, no, you were never too young, really. Long before you knew what death was you were wishing it on someone else. When you were two years old you were shooting people with cap pistols.

68   But this—the long, hot African veldt—the awful death in the jaws of a lion. And repeated again and again.

69   "Where are you going?"

70   He didn't answer Lydia. Preoccupied, he let the lights glow softly on ahead of him, extinguished behind him as he padded to the nursery door. He listened against it. Far away, a lion roared.

71   He unlocked the door and opened it. Just before he stepped inside, he heard a faraway scream. And then another roar from the lions, which subsided quickly.

72   He stepped into Africa. How many times in the last year had he opened this door and found Wonderland, Alice, the Mock Turtle, or Aladdin and his Magical Lamp, or Jack Pumpkinhead of Oz, or Dr. Doolittle, or the cow jumping over a very real-appearing moon—all the delightful contraptions of a make-believe world. How often had he seen Pegasus flying in the sky ceiling, or seen fountains of red fireworks, or heard angel voices singing. But now, this yellow hot Africa, this bake oven with murder in the heat. Perhaps Lydia was right. Perhaps they needed a

little vacation from the fantasy, which was growing a bit too real for ten-year-old children. It was all right to exercise one's mind with gymnastic fantasies, but when the lively child mind settled on one pattern . . . ? It seemed that, at a distance, for the past month, he had heard lions roaring, and smelled their strong odor seeping as far away as his study door. But, being busy, he had paid it no attention.

73   George Hadley stood on the African grassland alone. The lions looked up from their feeding, watching him. The only flaw to the illusion was the open door through which he could see his wife, far down the dark hall, like a framed picture, eating her dinner abstractedly.

74   "Go away," he said to the lions.

75   They did not go.

76   He knew the principle of the room exactly. You sent out your thoughts. Whatever you thought would appear.

77   "Let's have Aladdin and his lamp," he snapped.

78   The veldtland remained; the lions remained.

79   "Come on, room! I demand Aladdin!" he said.

80   Nothing happened. The lions mumbled in their baked pelts.

81   "Aladdin!"

82   He went back to dinner. "The fool room's out of order," he said. "It won't respond."

83   "Or."

84   "Or what?"

85   "Or it can't respond," said Lydia, "because the children have thought about Africa and lions and killing so many days that the room's in a rut."

86   "Could be."

87   "Or Peter's set it to remain that way."

88   "Set it?"

89   "He may have got into the machinery and fixed something."

90   "Peter doesn't know machinery."

91   "He's a wise one for ten. That I.Q. of his—"

92   "Nevertheless."

93   "Hello, Mom. Hello, Dad."

94   The Hadleys turned. Wendy and Peter were coming in the front door, cheeks like peppermint candy, eyes like bright blue agate marbles, a smell of ozone on their jumpers from their trip in the helicopter.

95 "You're just in time for supper," said both parents.

96 "We're full of strawberry ice cream and hot dogs," said the children, holding hands. "But we'll sit and watch."

97 "Yes, come tell us about the nursery," said George Hadley.

98 The brother and sister blinked at him and then at each other. "Nursery?"

99 "All about Africa and everything," said the father with false joviality.

100 "I don't understand," said Peter.

101 "Your mother and I were just traveling through Africa with rod and reel; Tom Swift and his Electric Lion," said George Hadley.

102 "There's no Africa in the nursery," said Peter simply.

103 "Oh, come now, Peter. We know better."

104 "I don't remember any Africa," said Peter to Wendy. "Do you?"

105 "No."

106 "Run see and come tell."

107 She obeyed.

108 "Wendy, come back here!" said George Hadley, but she was gone. The house lights followed her like a flock of fireflies. Too late, he realized he had forgotten to lock the nursery door after his last inspection.

109 "Wendy'll look and come tell us," said Peter.

110 "She doesn't have to tell me. I've seen it."

111 "I'm sure you're mistaken, Father."

112 "I'm not, Peter. Come along now."

113 But Wendy was back. "It's not Africa," she said breathlessly.

114 "We'll see about this," said George Hadley, and they all walked down the hall together and opened the nursery door.

115 There was a green, lovely forest, a lovely river, a purple mountain, high voices singing, and Rima, lovely and mysterious, lurking in the trees with colorful flights of butterflies, like animated bouquets, lingering on her long hair. The African veldtland was gone. The lions were gone. Only Rima was here now, singing a song so beautiful that it brought tears to your eyes.

116 George Hadley looked in at the changed scene. "Go to bed," he said to the children.

117 They opened their mouths.

118 "You heard me," he said.

119 They went off to the air closet, where a wind sucked them like brown leaves up the flue to their slumber rooms.

120   George Hadley walked through the singing glade and picked up something that lay in the corner near where the lions had been. He walked slowly back to his wife.

121   "What is that?" she asked.

122   He showed it to her. The smell of hot grass was on it and the smell of a lion. There were drops of saliva on it, it had been chewed, and there were blood smears on both sides.

123   He closed the nursery door and locked it, tight.

124   In the middle of the night he was still awake, and he knew his wife was awake. "Do you think Wendy changed it?" she said at last, in the dark room.

125   "Of course."

126   "Made it from a veldt into a forest and put Rima there instead of lions?"

127   "Yes."

128   "Why?"

129   "I don't know. But it's staying locked until I find out."

130   "How did your wallet get there?"

131   "I don't know anything," he said, "except that I'm beginning to be sorry we bought that room for the children. If children are neurotic at all, a room like that—"

132   "It's supposed to help them work off their neuroses in a healthful way."

133   "I'm starting to wonder." He stared at the ceiling.

134   "We've given the children everything they ever wanted. Is this our reward—secrecy, disobedience?"

135   "Who was it said, 'Children are carpets, they should be stepped on occasionally'? We've never lifted a hand. They're insufferable—let's admit it. They come and go when they like; they treat us as if we were offspring. They're spoiled, and we're spoiled."

136   "They've been acting funny ever since you forbade them to take the rocket to New York a few months ago."

137   "They're not old enough to do that alone, I explained."

138   "Nevertheless, I've noticed they've been decidedly cool toward us since."

139   "I think I'll have David McClean come tomorrow morning to have a look at Africa."

140   "But it's not Africa now, it's Green Mansions country and Rima."

141   "I have a feeling it'll be Africa again before then."

142   A moment later they heard the screams.

143   Two screams. Two people screaming from downstairs. And then a roar of lions.

144   "Wendy and Peter aren't in their rooms," said his wife.

145   He lay in his bed with his beating heart. "No," he said. "They've broken into the nursery."

146   "Those screams—they sound familiar."

147   "Do they?"

148   "Yes, awfully."

149   And although their beds tried very hard, the two adults couldn't be rocked to sleep for another hour. A smell of cats was in the night air.

150   "Father?" said Peter.

151   "Yes."

152   Peter looked at his shoes. He never looked at his father anymore, nor at his mother. "You aren't going to lock up the nursery for good, are you?"

153   "That all depends."

154   "On what?" snapped Peter.

155   "On you and your sister. If you intersperse this Africa with a little variety—oh, Sweden perhaps, or Denmark or China—"

156   "I thought we were free to play as we wished."

157   "You are, within reasonable bounds."

158   "What's wrong with Africa, Father?"

159   "Oh, so now you admit you have been conjuring up Africa, do you?"

160   "I wouldn't want the nursery locked up," said Peter coldly. "Ever."

161   "Matter of fact, we're thinking of turning the whole house off for about a month. Live sort of a carefree one-for-all existence."

162   "That sounds dreadful! Would I have to tie my own shoes instead of letting the shoe tier do it? And brush my own teeth and comb my hair and give myself a bath?"

163   "It would be fun for a change, don't you think?"

164   "No, it would be horrid. I didn't like it when you took out the picture painter last month."

165   "That's because I wanted you to learn to paint all by yourself, son."

166   "I don't want to do anything but look and listen and smell; what else is there to do?"

167   "All right, go play in Africa."

168   "Will you shut off the house sometime soon?"

169   "We're considering it."

170   "I don't think you'd better consider it any more, Father."

171   "I won't have any threats from my son!"

172   "Very well." And Peter strolled off to the nursery.

173   "Am I on time?" said David McClean.

174   "Breakfast?" asked George Hadley.

175   "Thanks, had some. What's the trouble?"

176   "David, you're a psychologist."

177   "I should hope so."

178   "Well, then, have a look at our nursery. You saw it a year ago when you dropped by; did you notice anything peculiar about it then?"

179   "Can't say I did; the usual violences, a tendency toward a slight paranoia here or there, usual in children because they feel persecuted by parents constantly, but, oh, really nothing."

180   They walked down the hall. "I locked the nursery up," explained the father, "and the children broke back into it during the night. I let them stay so they could form the patterns for you to see."

181   There was a terrible screaming from the nursery.

182   "There it is," said George Hadley. "See what you make of it."

183   They walked in on the children without rapping.

184   The screams had faded. The lions were feeding.

185   "Run outside a moment, children," said George Hadley. "No, don't change the mental combination. Leave the walls as they are. Get!"

186   With the children gone, the two men stood studying the lions clustered at a distance, eating with great relish whatever it was they had caught.

187   "I wish I knew what it was," said George Hadley. "Sometimes I can almost see. Do you think if I brought high-powered binoculars here and—"

188   David McClean laughed dryly. "Hardly." He turned to study all four walls. "How long has this been going on?"

189   "A little over a month."

190   "It certainly doesn't feel good."

191   "I want facts, not feelings."

192   "My dear George, a psychologist never saw a fact in his life. He only hears about feelings, vague things. This doesn't feel good, I tell you. Trust

my hunches and my instincts. I have a nose for something bad. This is very bad. My advice to you is to have the whole damn room torn down, and your children brought to me every day during the next year for treatment."

193   "Is it that bad?"

194   "I'm afraid so. One of the original uses of these nurseries was so that we could study the patterns left on the walls by the child's mind, study at our leisure, and help the child. In this case, however, the room has become a channel toward—destructive thoughts, instead of a release away from them."

195   "Didn't you sense this before?"

196   "I sensed only that you had spoiled your children more than most. And now you're letting them down in some way. What way?"

197   "I wouldn't let them go to New York."

198   "What else?"

199   "I've taken a few machines from the house and threatened them, a month ago, with closing up the nursery unless they did their homework. I did close it for a few days to show I meant business."

200   "Ah, ha!"

201   "Does that mean anything?"

202   "Everything. Where before they had a Santa Claus, now they have a Scrooge. Children prefer Santas. You've let this room and this house replace you and your wife in your children's affections. This room is their mother and father, far more important in their lives than their real parents. And now you come along and want to shut it off. No wonder there's hatred here. You can feel it coming out of the sky. Feel that sun. George, you'll have to change your life. Like too many others, you've built it around creature comforts. Why, you'd starve tomorrow if something went wrong in your kitchen. You wouldn't know how to tap an egg. Nevertheless, turn everything off. Start anew. It'll take time. But we'll make good children out of bad in a year, wait and see."

203   "But won't the shock be too much for the children, shutting the room up abruptly, for good?"

204   "I don't want them going any deeper into this, that's all."

205   The lions were finished with their red feast.

206   The lions were standing on the edge of the clearing watching the two men.

207   "Now I'm feeling persecuted," said McClean. "Let's get out of here. I never have cared for these damned rooms. Make me nervous."

208   "The lions look real, don't they?" said George Hadley. "I don't suppose there's any way—"

209   "What?"

210   "—that they could become real?"

211   "Not that I know."

212   "Some flaw in the machinery, a tampering or something?"

213   "No."

214   They went to the door.

215   "I don't imagine the room will like being turned off," said the father.

216   "Nothing ever likes to die—even a room."

217   "I wonder if it hates me for wanting to switch it off?"

218   "Paranoia is thick around here today," said David McClean. "You can follow it like a spoor. Hello." He bent and picked up a bloody scarf. "This yours?"

219   "No." George Hadley's face was rigid. "It belongs to Lydia."

220   They went to the fuse box together and threw the switch that killed the nursery.

221   The two children were in hysterics. They screamed and pranced and threw things. They yelled and sobbed and swore and jumped at the furniture.

222   "You can't do that to the nursery, you can't!"

223   "Now, children."

224   The children flung themselves onto a couch, weeping.

225   "George," said Lydia Hadley, "turn on the nursery, just for a few moments. You can't be so abrupt."

226   "No."

227   "You can't be so cruel."

228   "Lydia, it's off, and it stays off. And the whole damn house dies as of here and now. The more I see of the mess we've put ourselves in, the more it sickens me. We've been contemplating our mechanical, electronic navels for too long. My God, how we need a breath of honest air!"

229   And he marched about the house turning off the voice clocks, the stoves, the heaters, the shoe shiners, the shoe lacers, the body scrubbers and swabbers and massagers, and every other machine he could put his hand to.

230   The house was full of dead bodies, it seemed. It felt like a mechanical cemetery. So silent. None of the humming hidden energy of machines waiting to function at the tap of a button.

231   "Don't let them do it!" wailed Peter at the ceiling as if he was talking to the house, the nursery. "Don't let Father kill everything." He turned to his father. "Oh, I hate you!"

232   "Insults won't get you anywhere."

233   "I wish you were dead!"

234   "We were, for a long while. Now we're going to really start living. Instead of being handled and massaged, we're going to live."

235   Wendy was still crying and Peter joined her again. "Just a moment, just one moment, just another moment of nursery," they wailed.

236   "Oh, George," said the wife, "it can't hurt."

237   "All right—all right, if they'll only just shut up. One minute, mind you, and then off forever."

238   "Daddy, Daddy, Daddy!" sang the children, smiling with wet faces.

239   "And then we're going on a vacation. David McClean is coming back in half an hour to help us move out and get to the airport. I'm going to dress. You turn the nursery on for a minute, Lydia, just a minute, mind you."

240   And the three of them went babbling off while he let himself be vacuumed upstairs through the air flue and set about dressing himself. A minute later Lydia appeared.

241   "I'll be glad when we get away," she sighed.

242   "Did you leave them in the nursery?"

243   "I wanted to dress too. Oh, that horrid Africa. What can they see in it?"

244   "Well, in five minutes we'll be on our way to Iowa. Lord, how did we ever get in this house? What prompted us to buy a nightmare?"

245   "Pride, money, foolishness."

246   "I think we'd better get downstairs before those kids get engrossed with those damned beasts again."

247   Just then they heard the children calling, "Daddy, Mommy, come quick—quick!"

248   They went downstairs in the air flue and ran down the hall. The children were nowhere in sight. "Wendy? Peter!"

249   They ran into the nursery. The veldtland was empty save for the lions waiting, looking at them. "Peter, Wendy?"

250   The door slammed.

251   "Wendy, Peter!"

252   George Hadley and his wife whirled and ran back to the door.

253   "Open the door!" cried George Hadley, trying the knob. "Why, they've locked it from the outside! Peter!" He beat at the door.

254   "Open up!"

255   He heard Peter's voice outside, against the door.

256   "Don't let them switch off the nursery and the house," he was saying.

257   Mr. and Mrs. George Hadley beat at the door. "Now, don't be ridiculous, children. It's time to go. Mr. McClean'll be here in a minute and . . ."

258   And then they heard the sounds.

259   The lions on three sides of them, in the yellow veldt grass, padding through the dry straw, rumbling and roaring in their throats.

260   The lions.

261   Mr. Hadley looked at his wife and they turned and looked back at the beasts edging slowly forward, crouching, tails stiff.

262   Mr. and Mrs. Hadley screamed.

263   And suddenly they realized why those other screams had sounded familiar.

264   "Well, here I am," said David McClean in the nursery doorway.

265   "Oh, hello." He stared at the two children seated in the center of the open glade eating a little picnic lunch. Beyond them was the water hole and the yellow veldtland; above was the hot sun. He began to perspire. "Where are your father and mother?"

266   The children looked up and smiled. "Oh, they'll be here directly."

267   "Good, we must get going." At a distance Mr. McClean saw the lions fighting and clawing and then quieting down to feed in silence under the shady trees.

268   He squinted at the lions with his hand up to his eyes.

269   Now the lions were done feeding. They moved to the water hole to drink.

270   A shadow flickered over Mr. McClean's hot face. Many shadows flickered. The vultures were dropping down the blazing sky.

271   "A cup of tea?" asked Wendy in the silence.

Comprehension and Critical Thinking

1. What are some functions that the Happylife Home can perform? List at least four.

   _____

   _____

2. What kind of a relationship do the Hadley parents have with their children?

   _____

   _____

3. What is the original purpose of the nursery?

   _____

   _____

4. Why are George and Lydia worried about the nursery?

   _____

   _____

5. What have the children turned the nursery into?

   _____

   _____

6. Provide some examples from the story of imagery that appeal to the following senses. (See pages 107-108 in Chapter 8 for more information about imagery.)

   Sight: _____

   _____

   Sound: _____

   _____

   Smell: _____

   _____

   Touch: _____

   _____

7. Why do the children become extremely upset with their parents?

   _____

   _____

8. What does the Happylife Home and nursery represent to the children?

   _____

   _____

9. What happens to the parents at the end of the story?

_____

_____

10. Although the story is fictional, it presents some universal truths. What is one of the story's messages?

_____

_____

_____

Writing Topics

Write about one of the following topics. Remember to explore, develop, and revise and edit your work.

1. Ray Bradbury wrote this story long before there were personal computers or 3D television screens. Argue that our current world has some similarities to Bradbury's predictions. Support your argument with specific examples from the story.

2. Respond to the story. For information about writing a response essay, see Chapter 18.

3. Narrative writing can be fictional or nonfictional. A work of fiction is created in the writer's imagination. A work of nonfiction presents factual events. Which type of narration do you prefer: fiction or nonfiction? Provide supporting evidence from "The Veldt" and from a narrative essay in this book such as "My Bully, My Best Friend" (page 520), "Buried Alive" (page 561), "Into Thin Air" (page 557), or "460 Days" (page 566).

Appendix 1 Irregular Verbs

Irregular Verb List

Base Form	Simple Past	Past Participle	Base Form	Simple Past	Past Participle
arise	arose	arisen	fall	fell	fallen
be	was, were	been	feed	fed	fed
bear	bore	borne/born	feel	felt	felt
beat	beat	beat/beaten	fight	fought	fought
become	became	become	find	found	found
begin	began	begun	flee	fled	fled
bend	bent	bent	fly	flew	flown
bet	bet	bet	forbid	forbade	forbidden
bind	bound	bound	forget	forgot	forgotten
bite	bit	bitten	forgive	forgave	forgiven
bleed	bled	bled	forsake	forsook	forsaken
blow	blew	blown	freeze	froze	frozen
break	broke	broken	get	got	got, gotten
breed	bred	bred	give	gave	given
bring	brought	brought	go	went	gone
build	built	built	grind	ground	ground
burst	burst	burst	grow	grew	grown
buy	bought	bought	hang	hung	hung
catch	caught	caught	have	had	had
choose	chose	chosen	hear	heard	heard
cling	clung	clung	hide	hid	hidden
come	came	come	hit	hit	hit
cost	cost	cost	hold	held	held
creep	crept	crept	hurt	hurt	hurt
cut	cut	cut	keep	kept	kept
deal	dealt	dealt	kneel	knelt	knelt
dig	dug	dug	know	knew	known
do	did	done	lay	laid	laid
draw	drew	drawn	lead	led	led
drink	drank	drunk	leave	left	left
drive	drove	driven	lend	lent	lent
eat	ate	eaten	let	let	let

Base Form	Simple Past	Past Participle	Base Form	Simple Past	Past Participle
lie[1]	lay	lain	speak	spoke	spoken
light	lit	lit	speed	sped	sped
lose	lost	lost	spend	spent	spent
make	made	made	spin	spun	spun
mean	meant	meant	split	split	split
meet	met	met	spread	spread	spread
mistake	mistook	mistaken	spring	sprang	sprung
pay	paid	paid	stand	stood	stood
put	put	put	steal	stole	stolen
prove	proved	proved / proven	stick	stuck	stuck
			sting	stung	stung
quit	quit	quit	stink	stank	stunk
read	read	read	strike	struck	struck
rid	rid	rid	swear	swore	sworn
ride	rode	ridden	sweep	swept	swept
ring	rang	rung	swell	swelled	swollen
rise	rose	risen	swim	swam	swum
run	ran	run	swing	swung	swung
say	said	said	take	took	taken
see	saw	seen	teach	taught	taught
sell	sold	sold	tear	tore	torn
send	sent	sent	tell	told	told
set	set	set	think	thought	thought
shake	shook	shaken	throw	threw	thrown
shine	shone	shone	thrust	thrust	thrust
shoot	shot	shot	understand	understood	understood
show	showed	shown	upset	upset	upset
shrink	shrank	shrunk	wake	woke	woken
shut	shut	shut	wear	wore	worn
sing	sang	sung	weep	wept	wept
sink	sank	sunk	win	won	won
sit	sat	sat	wind	wound	wound
sleep	slept	slept	withdraw	withdrew	withdrawn
slide	slid	slid	write	wrote	written
slit	slit	slit			

[1] *Lie* can mean "to rest in a flat position." When *lie* means "tell a false statement," then it is a regular verb: *lie, lied, lied*.

Appendix 2   Using APA Style

In Chapter 17, you learned about researching, evaluating, and integrating sources in academic papers and documenting your sources using the Modern Language Association's (MLA) style. The American Psychological Association (APA) documentation style is another style that is commonly used in scientific or technical fields such as social sciences, economics, and nursing. Before you write a research essay for any course, ask your instructor which documentation style he or she prefers.

HINT: APA Website

For general information about some basic style questions, you can view the APA Style website (*www.apastyle.org*). On the home page, you will find the organization's blog as well as links to specific style questions and answers. Before writing a paper in APA style, check the site for any updates. Style guidelines, particularly those for electronic sources, can change as technology develops.

APA: Including In-Text Citations

In-text citations appear in the body of a research essay. You use them to indicate that you have borrowed ideas or quoted from outside sources (published authors, web pages, interviews, data, and so on). Here are two basic options for inserting parenthetical citations in an APA-style research essay.

1. **Enclose the author(s), the publication year, and the page number(s) in parentheses.** Include the last name(s) of the source's author(s). For more than one author, separate the authors' names using & (the ampersand sign). Follow with the publication year. If you are making a direct quotation, then include the page number or the page range where the material appears, using *p.* or *pp.* Separate the names, date, and page references with commas, and place the final period after the closing parenthesis. Note that for indirect quotations—paraphrases and summaries—the page number is encouraged but not required.

   Sometimes rioters lose control and "take out their anger and frustration on any individual" (Locher, 2002, p. 92).

   A dozen men are responsible for the development of the movie camera (Giannetti & Eyman, 2006, p. 4).

2. **Introduce the source directly in the text.** When you include a short quotation within a sentence, place the publication year in parentheses immediately after you mention the author's name. Present the quotation, and then write the page number in parentheses immediately after it.

> Sociologist David A. Locher (2002) explains, "Violent mobs often take out their anger and frustration on any individual" (p. 92).

> As Giannetti and Eyman (2006) explained, a dozen men are responsible for the development of the movie camera (p. 4).

APA: Making a References List

Similar to the MLA Works Cited list, the APA References list gives details about each source you have used, and it appears at the end of your paper. Follow these basic guidelines to prepare References using the APA format.

1. Write "References" at the top of the page and center it. Do not italicize it, bold it, underline it, or put quotation marks around it.
2. List each source alphabetically, using the last names of the authors.
3. Indent the second line and all subsequent lines of each reference one-half inch from the left margin.
4. Double-space the list.

HINT: Writing the Author, Date, Title, and Place Using APA Style

Author
On the References page, write the complete last name and use the first and middle initials (if provided). Do not write complete first names.

Date of Publication
Put the date of publication in parentheses immediately after the name. If you do not have the author's name, then put the date immediately after the title. If no date is available, write (n.d.).

Title
Capitalize the first word of the title, the first word of the subtitle, and the first word after a colon or a dash in Reference lists. Do not add quotation marks or any other special marks around the titles of short works. Italicize titles of longer works such as books, newspapers, or magazines.

Place of Publication
Mention the name of the city and the postal abbreviation of the state or province. Here is an example of a complete entry for a References list in APA style.

Miller, B. (2017). *Cultural anthropology in a globalizing world* (4th ed.).
Hoboken, NJ: Pearson.

Books

Carefully review the punctuation of the following example.

> Last name, Initial(s). (date). *Title of the book*. City, State of
> Publication: Publisher.

ONE AUTHOR

Reverse the name of the author. Put the complete last name and the first initial.

Franzen, J. (2015). *Purity*. New York, NY: Random House.

TWO OR MORE AUTHORS

Reverse the name of each author.

McCurdy, D. W., Shandy, D., & Spradley, J. (2016). *Conformity and
conflict: Readings in cultural anthropology* (15th ed.). Boston,
MA: Pearson.

BOOK WITH AN EDITOR INSTEAD OF AN AUTHOR

Put the editor's name followed by (Ed.).

Koppleman, S. (Ed.). (1984). *Old maids: Short stories by nineteenth-
century US women writers*. Boston, MA: Pandora Press.

TWO OR MORE BOOKS BY THE SAME AUTHOR

Include the author's name in all references. Arrange the works by year of
publication, putting the earliest work first.

Donoghue, E. (2010). *Room*. Toronto, ON, Canada: HarperCollins.

Donoghue, E. (2014). *Frog music*. Toronto, ON, Canada:
HarperCollins.

A WORK IN AN ANTHOLOGY

Munroe, A. (2003). Boys and girls. In R. S. Gwynn & W. Campbell
(Eds.), *Literature* (pp. 313–326). Toronto, ON: Pearson Longman.

ENCYCLOPEDIA AND DICTIONARY

Democracy. (2005). In *Columbia encyclopedia* (6th ed.). New York,
NY: Columbia University Press.

Legitimate. (2014). In *Merriam-Webster's collegiate dictionary* (11th
ed.) Springfield, MA: Britannica.

Newspapers, Magazines, and Journals

When citing newspapers or magazines, write as much of the following information as is available.

> Last name, Initials. (Year, Month and day). Title of article. *Title of the Magazine or Newspaper, Volume number*, Pages.

ARTICLE IN A MAGAZINE

Goodell, J. (2016, March 10). The rise of intelligent machines. *Rolling Stone, 1256*, 44–51.

ARTICLE IN A NEWSPAPER

Gillis, J. (2016, February 21). In Zika epidemic, a warning on climate change. *New York Times*, pp. 6–7.

ARTICLE IN A JOURNAL

> Last name, Initials. (Year, Month). Title of article. *Title of Journal. Volume* (Issue), Pages.

Seligman, M. (1998). The American way of blame. *APA Monitor, 29 (7)*, 97.

Electronic Sources

If the source was published on the Internet, include as much of the following information as you can find. Keep in mind that some sites do not contain complete source information.

> Last name, Initials. (date of most recent update). Title of article. *Title of Site or Online Publication*. Retrieved from http://site_address.html

E-BOOK

For references, mention the book's digital object identifier (DOI) or the uniform resource locator (URL) of the site where you downloaded the e-book. A DOI is a special identification number that will lead you directly to the document on the Internet. If you cannot find the DOI, then go to crossref.org and do a DOI search.

Leav, L. (2015). *Memories* [Kindle DX version]. Retrieved from www.amazon.com.

ARTICLE ON A PERSONAL WEBSITE

Krystek, L. (2006). Crop circles from outer space? *Museum of unnatural mystery*. Retrieved from www.unmuseum.org.

ARTICLE IN AN ONLINE JOURNAL

If the article includes a DOI, include it instead of the URL. After the name of the journal, put a comma followed by the journal number (all in italics.)

Naremore, J. (2008). Films of the year, 2007. *Film Quarterly, 61*(4), 48–61. doi:10.1525/fq.2008.61.4.48

GOVERNMENT SITE (OR OTHER SITES WITHOUT AUTHOR INFORMATION)

If the author is not mentioned on the site, begin with the title followed by the date, and include as much information as you can find. Generally, you do not need to include date of retrieval unless your source is highly changeable such as Wikipedia.

Dangerous jobs. (1997). *US Department of Labor*. Retrieved May 28, 2006, from http://stats.bls.gov/iif/oshwc/cfar0020.pdf

Other Types of Sources

INTERVIEW THAT YOU CONDUCTED

In APA style, do not include a personal interview in your References list. In the actual text, just include the parenthetical notation along with the exact date of the communication. For example: (personal communication, June 15, 2017).

FILM OR VIDEO

Curtiz, M. (Director). (2003). *Casablanca* [DVD]. United States: Warner Bros. (Original movie released 1942)

SOUND RECORDING

Nirvana. (1994). About a girl. On *Unplugged in New York* [CD]. New York, NY: Geffen.

Practice 1

Imagine that you are using the following sources in a research paper. Arrange the sources for a References page using APA style.

- You use a definition of "stress" from the site Dictionary.com. You retrieved the definition from http://www.dictionary.com. There is no publication date.

- You quote from the 12th edition of the textbook *Society: The Basics* by John J. Macionis. The book was published by Pearson in Boston, MA, in 2017.

- You quote from the article "Is Stress Contagious?" by Beth Levine from the magazine titled *O, The Oprah Magazine*. The article is on page 81 in the June 2014 issue.

- You use statistics from the article "Sleeping Disorder Statistics." It is on the website Statistic Brain in the year 2016. There is no author. You retrieved the article from http://www.statisticbrain.com.

- You quote from a Kindle book called *Resilience*. The authors are Steven M. Southwick and Dennis S. Charney. The publication year is 2013. The website where you retrieved the book is www.amazon.com.

- You quote from the article "Post Traumatic Stress Disorder" by Rachel Yehuda, Ph.D. It was in the *New England Journal of Medicine*, published in 2002, volume 346. You used pages 108 to 114. The DOI is 10.1056/NEJMra012941.

References

_____

_____

_____

_____

_____

_____

_____

_____

_____

_____

Credits

TEXT

Page 7: From Under the Tuscan Sun by Frances Mayes (Broadway Books: New York, 1997, p. 62); **p. 7:** From Sociology (11th ed.) by John J. Macionis (Pearson: Upper Saddle River, 2007, p. 95); **p. 40:** From Flashback: A Brief History of Film, 3rd Ed. by Louis Giannetti, Scott Eyman, Published by Pearson Education, © 1996; **p. 41:** From Concise Guide to Jazz, 6th Ed. by Mark C. Gridley. Published by Pearson Education, © 2009; **p. 48:** From "Let's Stop Being Stupid About IQ" by Dorothy Nixon. Copyright © Dorothy Nixon; **p. 48:** From Enviornment by Jay Withgott and Matthew Laposta; **p. 62:** From Sociology by John J. Macionis. Published by Pearson Education © 2012; **p. 74:** "Enough is Enough" by Molly Yesho; **p. 81:** Courtesy of Julian Krajewski. Used with permission; **p. 83:** Kratina, Al, "Watching What We Eat," March 30, 2011. Material republished with the express permission of: Vancouver Sun, a division of Postmedia Network, Inc; **p. 89:** McKelvey, Jack. "Rehabilitation"; **p. 98:** "A Memorable Trip" by Van Nguyen; **p. 107:** Sharman Apt Russell, "Beauty on the Wing" Science & Spirit, Jan/Feb 2004, Vol. 15, Issue 1, p. 58; **p. 108:** R.W. Apple Jr., "Making Texas Cows Proud" New York Times, May 31, 2006; **p. 108:** "Park of Personal Pleasure" by Laura Wilson; **p. 117:** "Tornado" by Kelsey Spell; **p. 119:** Reprinted from The Spell of the Tiger copyright 2008 by Sy Montgomery, with permission by Chelsea Green Publishing (www.chelseagreen.com); **p. 125:** Neal, Leander. "What's Cooking in my Kitchen."; **p. 132:** "Preparations for Traveling to a Different Country" by Mary Chandler Izard; **p. 134:** Smith, Melinda, Lawrence Robinson, and Jeanne Segal, "Tips for Breaking Free of Compulsive Smartphone Use," April 2016. Courtesy of Helpguide.org. Copyright © 2016. Used with permission; **p. 141:** "Have Some Manners" by Jessica Bailey; **p. 153:** Courtesy of Kara Bruce. Used with permission; **p. 155:** Hopper, Tristin, "Voluntourism," National Post, April 19, 2013. Material republished with the express permission of: National Post, a division of Postmedia Network Inc; **p. 159:** "Discrimination in the 21st Century" by Victoria Johnson; **p. 169:** Courtesy of Diego Pelaez. Used with permission; **p. 172:** BRITZ, MARJIE T., COMPUTER FORENSICS AND CYBER CRIME: AN INTRODUCTION, 3rd Ed., (c) 2013 pp. 149-150. Reprinted and Electronically reproduced by permission of Pearson Education, Inc., New York, NY; **p. 180:** "Swamps and Pesticides" by Corey Kaminska; **p. 191:** Kuszewski, Andrea, "Heroes Versus Sociopaths." Excerpt from "Addicted to Being Good? The Psychopathology of Heroism," September 28, 2009. Reprinted from Science 2.0. Copyright © 2009. Used by permission.; **p. 197:** "College Students and the Challenge of Credit Card Debt" by Katie Earnest; **p. 205:** Courtesy of Emily Dubois. Used with permission; **p. 208:** Mapes, Diane, "Walking Disaster? Why Some People Are Accident Prone." NBC News. May 5, 2009. Copyright © 2009. NBCUniversal Archives. Used by permission; **p. 215:** "Graffiti as Art" by Jordan Foster. Used by permission; **p. 224:** Vallières, Chloé, "Age Matters." Used with permission; **p. 227:** Wilson, Audra, "Cheerleaders and No Pay," October 5, 2015. Material republished with the express permission of: National Post, a division of Postmedia Network, Inc; **p. 238:** Courtesy of John Marshall. Used with permission; **p. 244:** Stephanie Goddard, "Top Ten Ways to Beat Stress at Work" Work-Stress-Solutions.com. Used with permission; **p. 245:** From Virginia Postrel, "The Case for Debt," Atlantic, Nov. 2008; **p. 245:** From Consumer Behavior by Michael R. Solomon. Copyright © 2013 Pearson Education; **p. 246:** MACIONIS, JOHN J., SOCIOLOGY, 14th Ed., (c) 2012, p. 481. Reprinted and Electronically reproduced by permission of Pearson Education, Inc., New York, NY; **p. 259:** Screenshot from "Science Daily". Copyright © 1995–2010. Used by permission of Science Daily; **p. 264:** From Consumer Behavior by Michael R. Solomon. Copyright © 2013 by Pearson Education; **p. 267:** From "Psychology" by Saundra K Ciccarelli. Copyright © 2006 by Pearson Education; **p. 267:** From Think: Social Problems 2 Ed. by John D. Carl. Copyright © 2012 by Pearson Education, Inc., Upper Saddle River, New Jersey; **p. 276:** "Women in Direct Combat: A Scrutiny of Physical Impediments to Combat Effectiveness" by John Carey Nuez; **p. 285:** Courtesy of Murray Marshall. Used with permission; **p. 287:** "Lessons from 'For Whom the Bell Tolls'" by Diego Pelaez. Used by permission of the author; **p. 502:** From Laurence Gonzales, The Rules of Survival, Deep Survival: Who Lives, Who Dies, and Why; **p. 516:** MANZA, JEFF; ARUM, RICHARD, SOCIOLOGY PROJECT, THE: INTRODUCING THE SOCIOLOGICAL IMAGINATION, 1st Ed., (c) 2013. Reprinted and Electronically reproduced by permission of Pearson Education, Inc., New York, NY; **p. 524:** Megan Griffith-Greene, Fake Online Reviews: Four Ways Companies Can Deceive You. CBC News. November 6, 2014. Used with permission; **p. 532:** Courtesy of Avi Friedman. Used with permission; **p. 536:** John Roach/National Geographic Creative. All rights reserved; **p. 543:** "Marketing New Inventions" by Robert Rodriguez, from Robert Rodriguez, Marketing New Invention can be Tough Sell, McClatchy Newspapers. Used with permission; **p. 547:** Courtesy of Josh Freed. Used with permission; **p. 550:** Nixon, Dorothy, "The Paradox of New Technologies." Dorothy Nixon is the author of THRESHOLD GIRL and FURIES CROSS THE MERSEY. Used with permission; **p. 553:** From DEEP SURVIVAL: WHO LIVES, WHO DIES, AND WHY by Laurence Gonzales. Copyright (c) 2003 by Laurence Gonzales. Used by permission of W.W. Norton & Company, Inc; **p. 557:** Excerpt(s) from INTO THIN AIR: A PERSONAL ACCOUNT OF THE MOUNT EVEREST DISASTER by Jon Krakauer, copyright (c) 1997 by Jon Krakauer. Used by permission of Villard Books, an imprint of Random House, a division of Penguin Random House LLC. All rights reserved; **p. 561:** "Buried alive: An avalanche survivor breaks his silence, by Ainsley Doty, in Macleans, March 29, 2015. Originally published in Maclean's(TM) magazine on March 29, 2015. Used with permission of Rogers Media Inc. All rights reserved; **p. 566:** Lindhout, Amanda with Sara Corbett, "460 Days" from THE BEST AMERICAN TRAVEL WRITING, 2014, which is a brief version of what appeared in The New York Times Magazine, August 28, 2013, titled "12 Minutes of Freedom in 460 Days of Captivity." Used by Permission. All rights reserved; **p. 572:** Terry O'Reilly, The Persuasive Power of Whispers. Under the Influence. CBC Radio-Canada. March 20,

2015. Used with permission; **p. 576:** CARL, JOHN D., THINK SOCIOLOGY, 2nd Ed., (c) 2011. Reprinted and Electronically reproduced by permission of Pearson Education, Inc., Upper Saddle River, New Jersey; **p. 579:** Roso Castillo Guilbault is author of "Farmworker's Daughter" and "The Latina's Guide to Success in the Workplace." She is a former journalist and TV executive; **p. 590:** Bradbury, Ray, "The Veldt," Reprinted by permission of Don Congdon Associates, Inc. Copyrighyt © 1950 by the Curtis Publishing Company, renewed 1977 by Ray Bradbury.

PHOTOS

Pages 3, 1: NinaMalyna/Fotolia; **p. 8:** Vivian Seefeld/Fotolia; **p. 11:** Lynne Gaetz; **p. 13:** Vuk Vukmirovic/Fotolia; **pp. 014, 1:** malinkaphoto/Fotolia; **p. 21:** yod77/Fotolia; **p. 27:** evok20/Fotolia; **p. 31:** Banana Republic/Fotolia; **p. 38:** oocoskun/Fotolia; **pp. 53, 1:** Andris T/Fotolia; **p. 54:** Leonid Tit/Fotolia; **p. 54:** JJ'Studio/Fotolia; **p. 56:** PHB.cz/Fotolia; **p. 57:** rnl/Fotolia; **p. 59:** veneratio/Fotolia; **p. 63:** innershadows/Fotolia; **pp. 72, 71:** georgejmclittle/Fotolia; **p. 74:** trekandphoto/Fotolia; **p. 86:** The Ad Council, the Humane Society of the United States, and Maddie's Fund; **p. 86:** Paul Gilmartin/The Mental Illness Happy Hour; **p. 86:** Fox Searchlight Pictures/Everett Collection; **pp. 87, 71:** Razihusin/Fotolia; **p. 88 (l):** Galaxy Photo/Fotolia; **p. 88 (m):** Andrei Rybachuk/Fotolia; **p. 88 (r):** Pikselstock/Fotolia; **p. 104:** AF archive/Alamy Stock Photo; **pp. 105, 71:** Dattatreya Phadke; **p. 106 (l):** lynea/Shutterstock; **p. 106 (m):** Mary Evans Picture Library/Alamy Stock Photo; **p. 106 (r):** NikArt/Fotolia; **p. 122:** Universal Pictures/Everett Collection; **pp. 123, 71:** Olena Turovtseva/Fotolia; **p. 124 (l):** Albertocc311/Fotolia; **p. 124 (m):** Africa Studio/Fotolia; **p. 124 (r):** Monkey Business/Fotolia; **p. 137:** AF archive/Alamy Stock Photo; **p. 137:** Photos 12/Archives du 7e Art/Touchstone Pictures/Alamy Stock Photo; **pp. 138, 71:** Michaeljung/Fotolia; **p. 139:** iko/Fotolia; **p. 155:** Warner Bros/Everett Collection; **p. 155:** Twentieth Century Fox Film Corporation/Everett Collection; **pp. 156, 71:** Vladislav Kochelaevs/Fotolia; **p. 157 (l):** StepStock/Fotolia; **p. 157 (r):** Africa Studio/Fotolia; **p. 157 (m):** Darren Kemper/Corbis/Getty Images; **p. 164:** Shutterstock; **p. 176:** Josh Bearman/This American Life; **p. 176:** Everett Collection; **p. 177:** Diego cervo/Fotolia; **p. 178 (l):** ZUMA Press, Inc/Alamy Stock Photo; **p. 178 (lm):** ArenaCreative/Fotolia; **p. 178 (rm):** Imabase/Fotolia; **p. 178 (r):** Yanlev/Fotolia; **p. 194:** Sony Pictures Classics/Everett Collection; **p. 194:** AF archive / Alamy Stock Photo; **p. 194:** American Broadcasting Companies, Inc; **pp. 195, 71:** Tadeas/Fotolia; **p. 196 (l):** Fotopak/Fotolia; **p. 196 (m):** Barneyboogles/Fotolia; **p. 196 (r):** mocker_bat/Fotolia; **p. 211:** Centers for Disease Control and Prevention (CDC); **p. 211:** Archives du 7e Art/Sony Pictures Television/Photos 12/Alamy Stock Photo; **p. 211: PLACEHOLDER: Paramount Pictures/Everett Collection; pp. 212, 71:** Rido/Fotolia; **p. 213 (l):** goodluz/Fotolia; **p. 213 (m):** taka/Fotolia; **p. 213 (r):** Nadiyka/Fotolia; **p. 230:** AF archive/Alamy Stock Photo; **p. 230:** Moviestore collection Ltd/Alamy Stock Photo; **p. 230:** National Institutes of Health; **pp. 232, 231:** papa/Fotolia; **p. 233:** DragonImages/Fotolia; **p. 240:** Picture-Factory/Fotolia; **pp. 241, 231:** Monet/Fotolia; **p. 242:** vvoe/Fotolia; **pp. 248, 231:** corbis_infinite/Fotolia; **p. 250:** WavebreakmediaMicro/Fotolia; **p. 251:** alexmat46/Fotolia; **p. 257:** Copyright © 2014 Harper's Magazine. All Rights Reserved. Reproduced from the January issue by special permission; **p. 257:** Dan Hallman/UpperCut Images/Getty Images; **p. 257:** Copyright © 2014 Harper's Magazine. All Rights Reserved. Reproduced from the January issue by special permission; **p. 258:** Philadelphia Inquirer, June 10, 2016 Cover. Copyright © 2016. Used by permission of The YGS Group; **p. 258:** Philadelphia Inquirer, A15 Business section page, June 10, 2016. Copyright © 2016. Used by permission of The YGS Group; **p. 259:** Stock Foundry Images/Alamy Stock Photo; **pp. 283, 231:** visivasnc/Fotolia; **p. 286:** Scanrail/Fotolia; **pp. 290, 231:** nicoletaionescu/Fotolia; **pp. 299, 297:** LaCozza/Fotolia; **p. 300:** Polina Ponomareva/Fotolia; **p. 301:** Edie Layland/Fotolia; **pp. 306, 297:** Junial Enterprises/Fotolia; **p. 307:** frenta/Fotolia; **p. 313:** Anyka/Fotolia; **p. 315:** sakhorn38/Fotolia; **pp. 317, 297:** wong yu liang/Fotolia; **p. 318:** abxyz/Shutterstock; **p. 320:** joyt/Fotolia; **p. 321:** ia_64/Fotolia; **p. 326:** koszivu/Fotolia; **pp. 327, 297:** Alexmar/Fotolia; **p. 330:** Konstantin L/Fotolia; **p. 335 (t):** de_nise/Fotolia; **p. 335 (b):** trekandphoto/Fotolia; **pp. 336, 297:** pipop_b/Fotolia; **p. 337:** Gary Blakeley/Fotolia; **p. 339:** Haider Y. Abdulla/Fotolia; **p. 342:** Captain/Fotolia; **p. 343:** 2bears/Fotolia; **p. 344:** voddol/Fotolia; **pp. 345, 297:** Jenifoto/Fotolia; **p. 347:** aigarsr/Fotolia; **pp. 351, 300:** overcrew/Fotolia; **p. 353:** lucazzitto/Fotolia; **p. 355:** axz65/Fotolia; **p. 357:** Deyan Georgiev/Fotolia; **pp. 358, 300:** samott/Fotolia; **p. 361:** Sergey Chayko/Fotolia; **p. 363:** zsuriel/Fotolia; **p. 366:** Friday/Fotolia; **p. 368:** tororo reaction/Fotolia; **p. 369:** mitgirl/Fotolia; **pp. 370, 300:** jessivanova/Fotolia; **p. 372:** fotola70/Fotolia; **p. 374:** Subbotina Anna/Fotolia; **p. 381:** AZP Worldwide/Fotolia; **p. 384:** noskaphoto/Fotolia; **p. 385 (t):** moomusician/Fotolia; **p. 385 (b):** andreaobzerova/Fotolia; **pp. 386, 300:** soft_light/Fotolia; **p. 387:** Photocreo Bednarek/Fotolia; **p. 389:** cfired/Fotolia; **p. 392:** bussiclick/Fotolia; **p. 396:** Luis Echeverri Urrea/Fotolia; **p. 398 (l):** vetal1983/Fotolia; **p. 398 (m):** Greg Epperson/Fotolia; **p. 398 (r):** Lynne Gaetz; **pp. 399, 300:** Vladimirfloyd/Fotolia; **p. 407:** Jim/Fotolia; **pp. 408, 300:** kopitinphoto/Fotolia; **p. 412:** graja/Fotolia; **p. 414:** gosphotodesign/Fotolia; **pp. 421, 300:** Catmando/Fotolia; **p. 424:** seree tan/Fotolia; **p. 426:** Pius Lee/Fotolia; **p. 428:** Juulijs/Fotolia; **p. 430:** ymgerman/Fotolia; **pp. 432, 300:** Unclesam/Fotolia; **p. 434:** PixAchi/Fotolia; **p. 437:** arkanto/Fotolia; **p. 440:** steverts/Fotolia; **pp. 441, 300:** constantincornel/Fotolia; **p. 445:** fabiosa_93/Fotolia; **p. 449:** luciap/Fotolia; **p. 451:** Andrea Izzotti/Fotolia; **pp. 452, 300:** Andy Dean/Fotolia; **p. 456:** RobertHarding/Fotolia; **p. 460:** iceteaimages/Fotolia; **p. 462:** inpefessa/Fotolia; **pp. 463, 300:** Giuliano Maciocci/Fotolia; **p. 467:** Vanderlei Almeida/AFP/Getty Images; **p. 468:** Vaughn Youtz/ZUMA Press/Alamy Stock Photo; **p. 469:** Patrik Stedrak/Fotolia; **pp. 470, 300:** pixbox77/Fotolia; **p. 472:** Caryblade/Fotolia; **p. 476:** wickerwood/Fotolia; **p. 478:** learchitecto/Fotolia; **p. 482 (t):** Inok/Fotolia; **p. 482 (b):** CJM Grafx/Fotolia; **pp. 483, 300:** Vaclavkrizek/Fotolia; **pp. 490, 300:** Galyna Andrushko/Fotolia; **p. 498:** Ohsuriya/Fotolia; **p. 515 a:** Teracreonte/Fotolia; **p. 515 b :** Lisa F. Young/Fotolia; **p. 515 c:** Robu_s/Fotolia; **p. 515 d:** Zaniman/Fotolia; **p. 515 e:** krash20/Fotolia; **p. 515 f:** Athanasia Nomikou/Fotolia; **p. 516:** Pearson Education; **p. 517:** Adam121/Fotolia; **p. 518:** Andrey Kiselev/Fotolia; **p. 529:** Creativa Images/Fotolia; **p. 533:** Banus/Fotolia; **p. 536:** Karin Jähne/Fotolia; **p. 539:** Cifotart/Fotolia; **p. 544:** Edbockstock/Fotolia; **p. 547:** Bst2012/Fotolia; **p. 550:** everettovrk/Fotolia; **p. 558:** THPStock/Fotolia; **p. 561:** anzebizjan/Fotolia; **p. 585:** iofoto/Fotolia; **p. 588:** Tijana/Fotolia.

Index

Revising Checklist for an Essay

Does the introduction
- ❑ contain a clearly identifiable thesis statement?
- ❑ build up to the thesis statement?

Does the thesis statement
- ❑ convey the essay's controlling idea?
- ❑ make a valid and supportable point?
- ❑ appear as the last sentence in the introduction?
- ❑ make a direct point and not contain expressions such as *I think that* or *I will explain*?

Do the body paragraphs
- ❑ have **adequate support**? Does each body paragraph have a topic sentence that clearly supports the thesis statement? Are there enough details to support each paragraph's topic sentence?
- ❑ have **coherence**? Are ideas presented in an effective and logical manner? Do transitional words and phrases help the ideas flow smoothly?
- ❑ have **unity**? Is the essay unified around one central topic? Does each body paragraph focus on one topic?
- ❑ have **style**? Are sentences varied in length? Is the language creative and precise?

Does the conclusion
- ❑ bring the essay to a satisfactory end?
- ❑ briefly summarize the ideas that the writer discusses in the essay?
- ❑ avoid introducing new or contradictory ideas?
- ❑ possibly end with a quotation, suggestion, or prediction?